The Cambridge Companion to Proust aims to provide a broad account of the major features of Marcel Proust's great work *A la recherche du temps perdu* (1913–27). The specially commissioned essays, by acknowledged experts on Proust, address a wide range of issues relating to his work. Progressing from background and biographical material, the chapters investigate such essential areas as the composition of the novel, its social dimension, the language in which it is couched, its intellectual parameters, its humour, its analytical profundity and its wide appeal and influence. Particular emphasis is placed on illustrating the discussion of issues by frequent recourse to textual quotation (in both French and English) and close analysis. This is the only contributory volume of its kind on Proust currently available. Together with its supportive material, a detailed chronology and bibliography, it will be of interest to scholars and students alike.

THE CAMBRIDGE
COMPANION TO
PROUST

CAMBRIDGE COMPANIONS TO LITERATURE

CAMBRIDGE COMPANIONS TO CULTURE

An extract from the manuscript pages describing the death of the fictional novelist Bergotte, as he contemplates Vermeer's *View of Delft*. (Bibliothèque Nationale de France, NAF 16702, p. 58r; cliché Bibliothèque Nationale de France.)

THE CAMBRIDGE
COMPANION TO
PROUST

EDITED BY
RICHARD BALES
Queen's University, Belfast

CAMBRIDGE
UNIVERSITY PRESS

PUBLISHED BY THE PRESS SYNDICATE OF THE UNIVERSITY OF CAMBRIDGE
The Pitt Building, Trumpington Street, Cambridge, United Kingdom

CAMBRIDGE UNIVERSITY PRESS
The Edinburgh Building, Cambridge CB2 2RU, UK
40 West 20th Street, New York, NY 10011–4211, USA
10 Stamford Road, Oakleigh, VIC 3166, Australia
Ruiz de Alarcón 13, 28014 Madrid, Spain
Dock House, The Waterfront, Cape Town 8001, South Africa

http://www.cambridge.org

© Cambridge University Press 2001

First published 2001

Printed in the United Kingdom at the University Press, Cambridge

Typeface Adobe Sabon 10/13pt   *System* QuarkXpress® [SE]

A *catalogue record for this book is available from the British Library*

ISBN 0 521 66019 X hardback
ISBN 0 521 66961 8 paperback

CONTENTS

CONTENTS

NOTES ON CONTRIBUTORS

RICHARD BALES is Professor of Modern French Literature at Queen's University, Belfast. He is the author of three books and many articles on Proust. His other publications include a book on nineteenth-century authors (*Persuasion in the French Personal Novel*, 1996) and an edition of plays by the Belgian symbolist Georges Rodenbach (1999).

MALCOLM BOWIE is Marshal Foch Professor of French Literature in the University of Oxford, and a Fellow of All Souls College. He is the author of *Henri Michaux: a Study of his Literary Works* (1973), *Mallarmé and the Art of Being Difficult* (1978), *Freud, Proust and Lacan: Theory as Fiction* (1987), *Lacan* (1991), *Psychoanalysis and the Future of Theory* (1993), and *Proust among the Stars* (1998).

WILLIAM C. CARTER, Professor of French at the University of Alabama at Birmingham, is the author of *The Proustian Quest* (1992) and co-producer of the documentary film *Marcel Proust: a Writer's Life* (1993). His *Marcel Proust: a Life* (2000) is the first biography in English to take into account the letters, memoirs and manuscripts available since Painter's biography. He is on the editorial board of the *Bulletin Marcel Proust* and is a permanent correspondent of the *Centre de recherches proustiennes* (Sorbonne nouvelle).

DAVID R. ELLISON is Professor of French and Comparative Literature at the University of Miami. He is the author of *The Reading of Proust* (1984), *Understanding Albert Camus* (1990), and *Of Words and the World: Referential Anxiety in Contemporary French Fiction* (1993). His current project is a book on the topic *From the Sublime to the Uncanny: Ethics and Aesthetics of European Modernism*.

ALISON FINCH is Professor of French at the University of Oxford and a Fellow of Merton College. She is the author of *Proust's Additions* (1977), *Stendhal: La Chartreuse de Parme* (1984), *Concordance de Stendhal* (1991), *Women's Writing in Nineteenth-Century France* (2000), and a number of essays on post-1800 French literature.

CYNTHIA GAMBLE is Research Fellow, Ruskin Programme, University of Lancaster. She is the author of numerous articles and papers on Proust, with a particular focus on the relationship between Proust and Ruskin. In collaboration with others, she is preparing an edition of *La Bible d'Amiens*, and is co-curating a major exhibition on Proust and Ruskin for the Musée de Picardie, Amiens.

HOLLIE MARKLAND HARDER is a Lecturer at Brandeis University. She has published articles on Proust and Zola, and is currently writing on the figure of the 'amazone' in Balzac, Sand and Fromentin. She is also working on a book-length study of *A la recherche du temps perdu*, focusing on the role of Françoise in the evolution of the Protagonist's sense of time and art.

EDWARD J. HUGHES is Reader in Modern French Literature at Royal Holloway, University of London. He is the author of *Marcel Proust: a Study in the Quality of Awareness* (1983) and *Albert Camus: La Peste/Le Premier Homme* (1995). He is co-editor (with Peter Dunwoodie) of *Constructing Memories: Camus, Algeria and 'Le Premier Homme'* (1998), and has just completed a book entitled *Writing Cultural Marginality in Modern French Literature: from Loti to Genet* (2001).

JACK JORDAN is Associate Professor of French at Mississippi State University. He is the author of articles on Proust and on Francophone literature of the French Antilles. He has also published a book entitled *Marcel Proust's 'A la recherche du temps perdu': a Search for Certainty* (1993).

JOSHUA LANDY is Assistant Professor of French at Stanford University. He is co-editor (with Claude Bremond and Thomas Pavel) of *Thematics: New Approaches* (1995), and is currently completing a study on images of subjectivity in the first-person novel.

DIANE R. LEONARD is Associate Professor of Comparative Literature at the University of North Carolina at Chapel Hill. She has written numerous articles on Proust and Ruskin, and is completing a book-length study on Proust's re-inscription of Ruskin's texts in *A la recherche du temps perdu*.

BRIAN ROGERS, a former Fellow of Trinity College, Cambridge, and a member of the Institut des Textes et Manuscrits Modernes, Paris, is the author of *Proust's Narrative Techniques* (1965; revised edition forthcoming), and *Le Dessous des cartes: Proust et Barbey d'Aurevilly* (2000). He is one of the major contributors to the recent Pléiade edition of *A la recherche du temps perdu*, and has also published studies of Barbey d'Aurevilly and Charles Nodier.

MARION SCHMID is Lecturer in French at the University of Edinburgh. She has written widely on textual criticism, with particular reference to Flaubert and Proust. Her publications include *Processes of Literary Creation: Flaubert and Proust* (1998), as well as articles on Proust addressing such topics as his alleged anti-semitism, his representation of the First World War and his reception of Baudelaire. She is currently working on the role of self-censorship in the making of *A la recherche du temps perdu*.

ROGER SHATTUCK has published *The Banquet Years* (1958), *Proust's Binoculars* (1963), *Marcel Proust* (1974), *Forbidden Knowledge: from Prometheus to Pornography* (1996), *Candor and Perversion: Literature, Education, and the Arts* (1999), and *Proust's Way: a Field Guide to 'In Search of Lost Time'* (2000). He recently retired from Boston University and lives in Lincoln, Vermont.

Truly great authors can never have enough books written about them, and no one can now deny that Proust has long since joined that select band. This seemed impossible back in the 1920s when *A la recherche du temps perdu* was being revealed in its entirety: in spite of his winning the *Prix Goncourt* in 1919, Proust's reputation in those years was largely that of a disorganised, if brilliant, amateur. As the years have rolled by, however, his achievement looks ever more masterly, to the extent that a single work of art has come to dominate the entire French literary scene of the twentieth century. And not just the French scene: across the world, Proust's novel is pointed to as representing the *ne plus ultra* of aesthetic profundity, laying forth all manner of analytical, compositional and expressive techniques. Of course, *A la recherche du temps perdu* did not emerge with sudden maturity: on the contrary, years of apprenticeship preceded it, and painstaking effort was put into its elaboration – the famous manuscripts are graphic and eloquent proof of this. If, in our *Companion*, we devote the greater amount of space to the *magnum opus*, this is simply because there is so much to say about it – and even then, we can only hope to scratch the surface of what will always remain, in Walter Benjamin's memorable formulation in *Illuminations*, 'this great special case of literature' in which 'everything transcends the norm'.

Richard Bales

ACKNOWLEDGEMENTS

I am exceptionally grateful for the unfailing courtesy and helpfulness of the contributors to this volume. Special thanks are due to Cynthia Gamble and Hollie Harder for going beyond the call of duty, and to Eddie Hughes for his customary wisdom. Vintage books were kind enough to provide copies of the British edition of Proust's novel. Queen's University, Belfast allowed me a semester's study leave, which came at exactly the right moment. Denise McColl expertly deciphered my handwriting and put it on disk. As ever, Tim Unwin has been a great inspiration and help. At Cambridge University Press, Linda Bree and Rachel De Wachter have shown almost heroic patience and faith in the project: my greatest thanks go to them.

Belfast

PRELIMINARY NOTES

Titles

A la recherche du temps perdu is now translated as *In Search of Lost Time*, a close rendition. It formerly appeared as *Remembrance of Things Past*, a quotation from Shakespeare's *Sonnet 30*. The novel consists of seven separately named parts, as follows:

Du côté de chez Swann (*Swann's Way*). Subdivided into:
  'Combray'
  'Un amour de Swann' ('Swann in Love')
  'Noms de pays: le nom' ('Place-names: the Name').
A l'ombre des jeunes filles en fleurs (*Within a Budding Grove*). Subdivided into:
  'Autour de Mme Swann' ('Madame Swann at Home')
  'Noms de pays: le pays' ('Place-names: the Place').
Le Côté de Guermantes (*The Guermantes Way*).
Sodome et Gomorrhe (*Sodom and Gomorrah*).
La Prisonnière (*The Captive*).
Albertine disparue or *La Fugitive** (*The Fugitive*).
Le Temps retrouvé (*Time Regained*).

In the running text, the novel is designated in different ways: some writers prefer the full French title, others an abbreviated one, still others an English version such as *The Search*. Everyone has his or her favourite.

Editions

Marcel Proust, *A la recherche du temps perdu*. 4 vols. Paris: Gallimard (Pléiade), 1987–9.

*See Chapter 3 for an explanation regarding these alternative titles.

In Search of Lost Time. 6 vols. London: Vintage, 1992 [1996].
In Search of Lost Time. 6 vols. New York: The Modern Library, 1993 [1999].

The Pléiade edition has been chosen because it is broadly recognised as the most scholarly and authoritative, and has established itself as the benchmark text. The English translation (originally by C.K. Scott-Moncrieff, updated by Terence Kilmartin, then by D.J. Enright) takes account of the corrections incorporated into the 1987–9 Pléiade edition. The American and British editions, though in the same number of volumes, take different pagination, but the text remains identical. In most cases, quotation from the original text is immediately followed by the English translation; the exception is a few cases of brief quotation where the meaning of the French or English alone is self-evident.

References

Providing page references to Proust's novel is, inescapably, a complicated and cumbersome affair, exacerbated where, as here, the pagination is different in the two English-language editions. Typically, text in French is followed by a reference, the roman numeral referring to the volume, and the arabic to the page number, as: II, 397. Text in English is followed by volume number in roman, followed by TWO page numbers in arabic, first that of the British edition, then that of the American edition (the latter practically always takes a higher number), as: III, 690/818. References which are allusions where there is no quoted text are in the order French – British – American, as: IV, 615; VI, 438/516. (Note that with this system there is no need for title abbreviations.)

Other frequently mentioned works by Proust, with their abbreviations, are as follows:

Contre Sainte-Beuve (*Against Sainte-Beuve*) (*CSB*).
Correspondance (*Correspondence*) (*Corr.*).
Jean Santeuil (*JS*).
Les Plaisirs et les jours (*Pleasures and Days*) (*PJ*).

(For the editions see the Select Bibliography.)

References to other works are given in full in endnotes to chapters and in the Select Bibliography.

'The Narrator' or 'Marcel'?

It was for long common practice to designate the main character of *A la recherche du temps perdu* 'Marcel'. The justification was the following passage in *La Prisonnière*: 'Elle [Albertine] retrouvait la parole, elle disait: "Mon" ou "Mon chéri", suivis l'un ou l'autre de mon nom de baptême, ce qui, en donnant au narrateur le même prénom qu'à l'auteur de ce livre, eût fait: "Mon Marcel", "Mon chéri Marcel"' (III, 583) ['Then she would find her tongue and say: "My – " or "My darling – " followed by my Christian name, which, if we give the narrator the same name as the author of this book, would be "My Marcel," or "My darling Marcel"' (V, 77/91)]. Although the nomenclature is repeated on III, 663; V, 172/203, nowhere else in the novel does this happen, anonymity being the general rule. (Besides, these passages occur in a section of the novel that Proust left unrevised at his death.) Early commentators doubtless felt that the Narrator 'needed' a name, especially in his role as developing human being. This function can, however, readily be covered by the term 'the Protagonist', when a clear distinction has to be established between the younger and the older Narrator. Most frequently, though, the umbrella-term 'the Narrator' suffices, and indeed reinforces the continuity between all stages of his development.

CHRONOLOGY

1871	10 July: birth, at Auteuil in the Paris suburbs, of Marcel Valentin Louis Eugène Georges Proust, son of Adrien Proust, a distinguished professor of medicine, and Jeanne-Clémence Weil. The father is Catholic, the mother Jewish.
1872	The Proust family takes up residence in the fashionable boulevard Malesherbes (Paris 8ᵉ). Proust will always live in this area, except at the end of his life.
1878–86	Family holidays at Illiers (now Illiers-Combray) in the *département* of Eure-et-Loir.
1882–89	Attends the Lycée Fontanes (renamed Lycée Condorcet in 1883); poor health often keeps him absent.
1888	Proust is strongly influenced by his philosophy teacher, Alphonse Darlu.
1889–90	Proust performs his military service at Orléans, a feat of which he is exceptionally proud.
1890–95	Student years (law and political science). Licence en droit (1893); licence ès lettres (1895).
1891	Co-founds a short-lived journal, *Le Banquet*. Is an active contributor to this and other journals.
1894	Beginning of the Dreyfus affair.
1895	Begins a novel, *Jean Santeuil* (unfinished).
1896	Publication of *Les Plaisirs et les jours*, a collection of stories, essays and miscellaneous pieces.
1897	Proust becomes increasingly enthusiastic about the work of the English writer Ruskin.
1898	Publication of Zola's 'J'accuse'. Proust rallies to the Dreyfus cause.
1900	Death of Ruskin. Proust devotes the next few years to translating (with the help mainly of his mother) and annotating selected works of his. Two trips to Venice. The family moves to the rue de Courcelles.

1902	Artistic trips to Belgium and Holland; sees Vermeer's *View of Delft*.
1903	Death of Proust's father.
1904	*La Bible d'Amiens*, translation of Ruskin.
1905	Death of Proust's mother. He is inconsolable.
1906	Proust moves to 102, boulevard Haussmann. *Sésame et les lys*, translation of Ruskin.
1907–14	Summer holidays at Cabourg, on the Normandy coast.
1908	Writes *Pastiches* of other authors, based on an amusing extortion racket. Begins what is now known as *Contre Sainte-Beuve*, an essay.
1909	The essay transforms itself into a novel: it will eventually become *A la recherche du temps perdu*.
1910	Goes to see the *Ballets russes*. Has his bedroom lined with cork, because of building work in an adjoining apartment.
1911	The novel's title at this time is *Les Intermittences du cœur*. Proust employs a secretary to type up his work, more than 700 pages to date.
1912	Proust seeks a publisher, in vain.
1913	*Du côté de chez Swann* is published by Grasset, at Proust's own expense. The general title of the novel is changed to *A la recherche du temps perdu*.
1914	The second volume of the novel as it then existed is being set up in proof when the outbreak of war stops the printing presses.
1914–18	During the war, with no possibility of publication, Proust vastly expands his novel, notably in respect of the character Albertine.
1915	Publication rights are transferred from Grasset to Gallimard.
1918	Publication of *A l'ombre des jeunes filles en fleurs*.
1919	Proust is forced to move from 102, boulevard Haussmann, firstly to the rue Laurent-Pichat, then to what will turn out to be his final residence, 44, rue Hamelin. He is controversially awarded the *Prix Goncourt*, France's premier literary prize.
1920	Proust is named Chevalier de la légion d'honneur. Publication of *Le Côté de Guermantes I*.
1921	Extracts from the novel are regularly published in journals, mainly *La Nouvelle Revue française*, continuing into 1922. Proust visits an exhibition of Dutch paintings at the Orangerie in May: he sees the *View of Delft* again. *Le Côté de Guermantes II – Sodome et Gomorrhe I* is published.

1922	*Sodome et Gomorrhe* II is published. Proust develops bronchitis, then pneumonia, and dies on 18 November. He is buried in Père Lachaise cemetery on 22 November.
1923	Publication of *Sodome et Gomorrhe* III – *La Prisonnière*.
1924	Publication of *Albertine disparue*.
1927	Publication of *Le Temps retrouvé*.
1952	Publication of *Jean Santeuil*.
1954	Publication of a version of *Contre Sainte-Beuve*.

INTRODUCTION

Received opinion dictates that Proust is a 'difficult' author. Is this really so? After all, everyone knows something about him, even if it is only at second hand. On the level of Proust the person, the (in)famous cork-lined room he inhabited for a number of years is deemed to epitomise an ivory-tower existence far removed from the harshness of everyday life. The fact is, of course, he lived on the bustling street side of a modern building in the heart of the business and social district of the Parisian right bank, and was in rapid and frequent contact with the world outside. He even had a telephone, a means of communication he would memorably immortalise in his novel. Installing the cork was only intended to be a temporary measure, to shield him from builders hammering away in the next apartment. Not much of an ivory tower, really. But the elitist image is surprisingly persistent, and still biases opinion: Proust, in moving in high bourgeois and aristocratic circles, and in dealing with them in his novel, is assumed to be a snob, not an appropriate stance from which to speak with universal authority. And of course his demeanor as a sickly individual, sexually suspect, sleeping during the day and 'working' at night, is frowned upon: these are not features which add up to greatness. Being wealthy, too, is a distinct disadvantage on this score: as one of the 'idle rich', Proust can hardly be expected to speak for the generality of human beings.

In truth, though, the general public knows a lot more about Proust than this comic-strip picture suggests. He is *the* author when it comes to treating the theme of time, time which can be apprehended in unexpected ways, the most spectacular being sudden resurrection of the past, triggered off by tasting a madeleine cake dipped in tea, or by tripping over uneven paving-stones – moments of literary anecdote which have become familiar to those who have never read a word of the novel. Are they so well known because they are great literature, or because the experiences, being so everyday, could easily have been ours? Both perhaps. For if the old notion that *A la recherche du temps perdu* is Proust's scarcely-veiled autobiography has long been superseded, the fact that there is an unusually close proximity between personal experience and the literary expression of it is an attractive proposition for a reader. Far removed from the so-called remoteness of much of Proust's subject-matter, the famous flashes of insight chime with widespread perception, the more so as it is common knowledge that the early sections of the novel dwell on areas of childhood experience which are bound to overlap in essence with many a reader's own memories. Above all, the episode of the goodnight kiss – at first withheld by the Narrator's mother, then granted – has become a celebrated icon of childhood traumas as universally lived.

No one nowadays would waste time trying to prove that Proust the man went through an identical childhood drama, or that later on in his life there was an identifiable day on which he savoured a madeleine and underwent an overwhelming metaphysical vision. The temptation towards autobiographical interpretation – and sometimes it is strong – needs to be eschewed, and these days it routinely is. For although Proust clearly built his fiction out of what he had known in his own life, it is manifest that *A la recherche du temps perdu* is one of those fictions which, once set in motion, behaves according to its own internal rules, and not those of the world outside it. Searching for keys – who *really* was Charles Swann? who *really* was the duchesse de Guermantes? – has long since been considered an idle occupation: even if one can point to real-life individuals who possessed similar traits to those of Proustian characters, this activity can never acquire higher status than that of informed speculation. Today's readers, armed (perhaps unwittingly) with the critical priorities and expectations of recent decades, exercise greater sophistication than that: just as Proust thought Sainte-Beuve's method of judging authors by their personality wrong, so alert readers of the present day cannot allow unprofitable conjecture to enter into evaluation of works of art, whose autonomy is nowadays automatically granted (and applauded).

A particularly instructive feature of *A la recherche du temps perdu* arises from the small roll-call of places the novel moves within: Combray, Paris, Balbec, Doncières, Venice. Not many for a three thousand-page book. And note the mix of real localities and fictional ones: this is a world where the solidity of what is known and verifiable coexists with towns of the imagination which figure on no map one can buy. By being part and parcel of a work of fiction, Paris and Venice, while retaining features which can readily be checked physically, take on fresh substance which springs from the life of the fiction. Likewise, Combray, Balbec and Doncières, even if they are imaginary, assume the solid familiarity of French provincial towns to such an extent that it feels we could go out and check physical features there too.

A wonderful example of this fictional cohabitation of the real and the imaginary – itself a sort of template for the whole novel – occurs early enough on in the novel for many novice readers already to have reached that far. In day-dreaming about catching the train which will, he hopes, one day take him to his desired destination of Balbec, the young Narrator encapsulates so much that is emblematic of his personality, of the novel, and of what may generally be recognised as a Proustian sensibility. The train departs at a fixed time of day, 1.22 in the afternoon, but in doing so it 'opens out' time as it advances in space, permitting desires and fantasies to be gratified, in the Narrator's case visiting places which in his mind have acquired mythical status. Not just Balbec, whose fantastical 'Persian' church is the avidly wished-for goal, but the real towns through which the train progresses, each of them possessing poetic dimensions invented by the Narrator's imagination alone: Benodet, for example, 'nom à peine amarré que semble vouloir entraîner la rivière au milieu des algues' (I, 382) ['a name scarcely moored that the river seemed to be striving to drag down into the tangle of its algae' (I, 468/553)]; or Pont-Aven, 'envolée blanche et rose de l'aile d'une coiffe légère qui se reflète en tremblant dans une eau verdie de canal' (ibid.) ['pink-white flash of the wing of a lightly posed coif, tremulously reflected in the greenish waters of a canal' (ibid.)]. And the order in which the places traversed are listed carries another, but similarly poetic, message: at first the itinerary is via Bayeux, Coutances, Vitré, Questambert, Pontorson, Balbec, Lannion, Lamballe, Benodet, Pont-Aven and Quimperlé (I, 379; I, 464/549); the second time, the order is jumbled (I, 381–2; I, 468/553). But whatever the order, a cursory glance at a map of Normandy and Brittany would tell one that not even the bravest of trains could hope to take in all of these places, irrespective of the order. Of course, mention of Balbec here provides the key: this is a voyage which, although seemingly traversing areas of reality, is essentially a journey into realms of the imagination. This is confusion to a purpose, and that purpose is the ongoing construction of a wholly self-defining fictional world, in which the imaginary life of an individual (the Narrator) is mapped onto verifiable and objective realities.

The element of confusion is there right from the outset, of course: just a few pages into the novel, the Narrator baldly lists the localities in which he has occupied rooms, but the reader, having no experience thus far of what will be a potent mix of the real and the imaginary, can only feel perplexed in the face of what has not yet been explained. And this insistence is only one of many such examples one could quote from the opening of A la recherche du temps perdu – famously, a byword for vagueness and obscurity. Some early commentators attributed this to a poor writing technique. But nowadays Proust's fame tells us that the uncertainties of this opening are willed, and are part of a carefully organised literary strategy, one which withholds as much as it discloses. In a way, the reader's initial difficulties are also the Narrator's, so closely do we accompany his emergent being. They are even, by extension, the novel's itself, stuttering into existence as it does in a series of disjointed trial efforts. In all cases, sense needs to be made out of chaos. But if a certain brand of difficulty is in some degree inscribed within the very fabric of *A la recherche du temps perdu*, it has also to be said that there are counterbalancing features of great comfort, 'welcoming' aspects which rarely hit the headlines. Paramount amongst these must be the reader's development in intimate tandem with the Narrator's. This proximity is more often than not taken for granted, as is the simple trajectory the novel pursues – the unfolding of a life in all the ups and downs of a sort we ourselves know all too well. Empathy is acquired in the very process of reading and continuing to read.

The physical appearance of the novel repeats this same combination of the difficult and the easy. Its stupendous length is, of course, a formidable challenge; but the very title, in its wonderfully transcendent directness, positively demands investigation. Then the titles of the various volumes, combining as they do hints at characters one will encounter (Swann, the Guermantes, Albertine) and at aspects of narrative development (*La Prisonnière*, *Albertine disparue*, *Le Temps retrouvé*), tantalise by being simultaneously informative in what they reveal and sketchy in what they leave unexplained (who are the 'jeunes filles'? what lies behind the biblical *Sodome et Gomorrhe*?). Closer in, there are smaller subdivisions which are reassuring ('Combray', 'Un amour de Swann') but then there are also headings which are decidedly unhelpful. *Le Côté de Guermantes*, for instance, is divided into two parts: part I, consisting of about 300 pages, has no sub-headings. But part II, some 280 pages long, is subdivided into two chapters, each of which is prefaced by a summary of its contents: chapter one is only about thirty pages long; chapter two, some 240. Why this imbalance? And why does the short part II, chapter one get a list of contents when the much longer part I gets none? A mystery. But even when the contents are supplied, the result is scarcely what one might today call 'user-friendly'. Take, for example, the summary of part II, chapter two:

> Visite d'Albertine. – Perspective d'un riche mariage pour quelques amis de Saint-Loup. – L'esprit des Guermantes devant la princesse de Parme. – Etrange visite à M. de Charlus. – Je comprends de moins en moins son caractère. – Les souliers rouges de la duchesse. (II, 1987)

> [A visit from Albertine – Prospect of rich brides for certain friends of Saint-Loup – The wit of the Guermantes as displayed before the Princesse de Parme

– A strange visit to M. de Charlus – His character puzzles me more and more
– The duchess's red shoes.] (Omitted from the current English editions; translation taken from earlier editions.)

What a curious way to signpost 240 pages of text!

After registering initial bafflement, the reader can at least cling onto the names of characters with whom he or she is becoming familiar; but even so, how their activities are to fill out so many pages, given the thinnest imaginable indications, is impossible to predict. And the registers of each notation are puzzlingly disparate: what could be less helpful than 'A visit from Albertine'? Why not an element of evaluation such as occurs when the Narrator intriguingly anticipates about Charlus? And what about the ridiculously bathetic effect of 'The duchess's red shoes'? But by now the alert reader knows not to expect short-cuts from an author who has hitherto abundantly displayed his greater interest in respecting the idiosyncratic unfolding of impressions than in providing an initial explanatory framework. In this respect, the confused opening pages of *A la recherche du temps perdu* stand as a sort of motto for the whole novel. So the innocuous-sounding 'Visit from Albertine' is probably going to reveal very much deeper involvement on the part of the Narrator than the bland words convey; and the 'more and more', qualifying puzzlement about Charlus, looks as if with him the Narrator is further advanced on the path of acquaintanceship, if not of knowledge. But how? As for 'The duchess's red shoes', those who know the anecdote alluded to will draw in breath at the mere reading of these words: their perfunctoriness masks one of the great episodes of the novel, a scene where Proust's characters, in their interaction, provide one of the hardest-hitting analyses of human behaviour, of an exceptional degree of profundity. (The episode is partially dealt with in Chapter 9 of this *Companion*; but for the full effect the reader needs to stalk ahead to its powerful location at the end of *Le Côté de Guermantes*.)

So, if Proust's novel appears weird and wonderful from the outside, that is largely because the inner goings-on heavily dictate the structural appearance. The moral is: the sooner one enters the world of the text, the better. This is where critical works such as the present one come in: while not in any way attempting to substitute for the novel – each contributor will prove that that is impossible – outside help can facilitate access from within, as it were. Our *Companion* is just what it claims to be – an accompaniment taken on a voyage of discovery. If, like the Narrator on his own imagined – then realised – train-journey into Normandy and Brittany, the potential reader of Proust has an approximate idea of the geography which lies ahead, then the staging-posts which each of our chapters represent can only help in giving body to that geography. And again, as in the novel, the order in which places are passed through is variable: while we present the chapters in an order which follows a certain sort of logic, that is not to say it is the only possible logic. On the contrary, Proustian fluidity almost demands selective gleaning. Sometimes, familiar textual territory is re-traversed: that is because the landscape of Proust's novel is criss-crossed with intersecting tracks, and famous quotations operate as so many junctions which redirect trajectories along fresh lines.

Once embarked on the journey, the reader of *A la recherche du temps perdu* soon learns what to look out for, without the assistance of specialist guides. For getting to know Proust is not the acquisition of a bundle of facts, it is familiarity with a world of the imagination in which one gradually feels at home, easy in the company of a Narrator who is as normal – and as eccentric – as ourselves. It is the growing realisation that humanity is a frail, yet durable thing, subject to an enormous range of vicissitudes, but obedient also to recurrent laws. It is the recognition that life, drab though vast swathes of it may be, can be transfigured in rare moments of insight. It is above all the acknowledgement, in our intimate association with the Narrator, that what is humble and what is sublime cohabit in indissoluble symbiosis. For if there is just one lesson one retains from a reading of Proust it is that what seems trivial is often what is most significant and revelatory. And if experiences of transcending time represent events of great moment, so too do the duchess's red shoes.

I

CYNTHIA GAMBLE

From *Belle Epoque* to First World War: the social panorama

A la recherche du temps perdu spans the period in France between the 1870s and the years of the 1914–18 war, together with an ill-defined post-war period: this represents more or less Proust's own life (1871–1922). Navigational aids are sparse in this work of fiction which is essentially non-linear and which moves rapidly and often imperceptibly backwards and for-wards as in cinematographic flashbacks, but there are occasionally some markers to help the reader traverse the political and social seas. Balzac's aim as a novelist had been to paint a sociological canvas of his time, to produce an inventory of French society in the first half of the nineteenth century. Proust, however, observes and analyses essentially the interior world of his characters set against a background of selected exterior, actual events which provide an authentic sociological backcloth to his novel in the period com-mencing some twenty years after Balzac's death. As early as 1894, in his introduction to his first published work *Les Plaisirs et les jours*, he identified the best vantage point for observing social behaviour as from within an enclosed space, in this case Noah's Ark: 'Je compris alors que jamais Noé ne put si bien voir le monde que de l'arche, malgré qu'elle fût close et qu'il fît nuit sur la terre' (*JS*, p.6). ['Then it was I understood that Noah could never have had so clear a view of the world as when he gazed upon it from within his ark, sealed though it was, and when darkness was over all the earth'].[1] Proust's technique is to portray, throughout the whole of *A la recherche du temps perdu*, an interplay between life and fiction, the encounter between reality and imagination, what can be called 'l'imaginaire'. So successful is this method that boundaries become blurred and the reader may easily be lulled into believing that a fictional character, such as Mme Verdurin, actu-ally existed.

The *Belle Epoque*, so-called retrospectively – Vincent Cronin suggests that the term was current from the 1920s[2] – is akin to 'the good old days', a golden age which never really existed, or a period which, if it did exist, did so for the affluent classes. It is chronologically ill-defined but is generally regarded as that period of euphoria at its zenith in the centenary year of 1900 and the years of insouciance preceding the outbreak of the First World War. The expression immediately triggers an impression which has been deliberately cultivated of luxurious, carefree living, especially in Paris, of a romanticised, idyllic vision of a hedonistic society with great wealth and much leisure. It reflected a lost paradise, and bathed in a romantic afterglow in contrast to the horrors and grim realities of the slaughter of the war. To what extent is this true and how is this period depicted in *A la recherche du temps perdu*?

A main character who is present throughout, is the courtesan Odette de Crécy (who ascends in society through her sexual favours with wealthy men), later to become Mme Swann and subsequently Mme de Forcheville: the sense of stability she gives to the novel by her continued, yet changing presence, allows Proust to attach temporal markers to and around her. In 'Un amour de Swann', the love affair between Charles Swann, the Jewish dilettante, writer *manqué*, art collector, wealthy man about town, son of a stockbroker, and Odette de Crécy is analysed. A moment when Swann's passion is intensified is his receipt of an impassioned letter from Odette, written at midday, from the non-fictional, fashionable Parisian restaurant *La Maison Dorée*, at 1 rue Lafitte in the 9th *arrondissement*, and beginning: 'Mon ami, ma main tremble si fort que je peux à peine écrire . . .' (I, 222) ['My dear, my hand trembles so that I can scarcely write . . .' (I, 271/319)]. That particular day, Swann recalls, was the day of a charity event in aid of those who had suffered in the floods in the coastal province of Murcia in South East Spain. In reality, the flooding occurred between 14 and 15 October 1879, and a charity ball, presided by the Queen of Spain, was held at the Hippodrome in Paris on 18 December 1879. The day of the ball was also the very day when Odette had been with another of her lovers, the Comte de Forcheville, a fact which she half reveals and half conceals when under interrogation by her jealous suitor Charles Swann (I, 364–5; I, 446/526–7).

Many years later in wartime and post-war Paris, in *Le Temps retrouvé*, the Narrator, on encountering Odette, now Mme de Forcheville, superimposes on her ageing body – she is soon described as being 'gaga' (IV, 530; VI, 325/383) – the memory of her youthfulness at the time of the Paris Exhibition of 1878 (IV, 526; VI, 321/377) and also his preferred image of her as the extremely elegant, fashionably dressed Mme Swann, in her carriage, in the Allée des Acacias in the Bois de Boulogne in 1892 (IV, 528; VI, 323/380). But on another occasion Mme Swann is depicted in the same Allée des Acacias, being pursued not by Charles Swann but by the Narrator of *A la recherche du temps perdu*, who is eager for a glimpse of Mme Swann, the mother of Gilberte with whom he is in love. He overhears an un-named man, in the crowd, boast that he had slept with Odette, in fact on the very day on which President Mac-Mahon resigned, that is to say, 30 January 1879 (I, 413; I, 505/597). Mac-Mahon, with monarchist tendencies, was elected President of the French Republic in 1873, and Proust uses his period of office between 1873–9 to situate certain events in his novel and thereby give it also a greater sense of authenticity. Odette's early life of pleasure, in Baden-Baden, Nice and the Côte d'Azur, and her sexual relationship with Uncle Adolphe, the Narrator's uncle, before her marriage to Swann, belong to that period (I, 307–8; I, 376–7/444–5). Mac-Mahon is presented in Proust's novel as a cousin of the fictional Mme de Villeparisis (II, 46; III, 305/360).

We can, therefore, place the *demi-mondaine* Odette de Crécy in the 1870s, and as Mme Swann she was already the mother of a precocious daughter, Gilberte, by 1892, and a well-known society hostess by 1896 at the time of the visit of the Russian Tsar Nicolas II to Paris (I, 533; II, 134/159). Mme Swann finds herself in the middle of a *cause célèbre*, the question of the innocence or guilt of the wrongly accused French army officer, Captain Dreyfus, in the late 1890s. As Mme de Forcheville, and also the mistress of the aged Duc de Guermantes to whom she is shamelessly unfaithful, Odette remains a monument to the *Belle Epoque*, at the very end of Proust's novel.

This fairly long time-scale, although imprecise, enables Proust to chart the rise and fall of fortunes, families and values, and to show the fragility and collapse of a hedonistic upper-class society living an illusion of being impregnable. No one is prepared for any adversity, and any impending danger or sign of mortality is rejected: when Swann, seriously ill with cancer, announces to the Duc and Duchesse de Guermantes that he has only three or four months to live, his remark is brushed aside as being preposterous (II, 882–4; III, 689–91/817–19). Similarly, the death of Dechambre, Mme Verdurin's favourite pianist, is a taboo subject in her *salon* (III, 288; IV, 340/399). Death, in this pre-war society of the *Belle Epoque*, is something which the bourgeoisie and aristocracy depicted by Proust prefer, if possible, to ignore and is, therefore, not prominent in his novel, with the striking exception of the long account of the illness and death of the Narrator's grandmother.

Salons

The *salons* formed an important part of French society and Proust owed much of his literary and social success to the important network of influential contacts he made there. He was a regular visitor to 12, avenue Hoche, the *salon* of Mme Arman de Caillavet, mistress of the writer Anatole France, and soon became a close friend of Mme de Caillavet's son, Gaston. He also frequented the glittering *salon* of the painter Madeleine Lemaire in the rue de Monceau where he first met Comte Robert de Montesquiou. Few people are spared in his acerbic vignettes of the *salons*. In *A la recherche du temps perdu*, through the *salons* in particular, Proust depicts the preoccupations and attitudes of much of upper-class, and aspiring upper-class society, toward political events such as the Dreyfus affair. There are, broadly, two contrasting sets of *salons*, that of the upwardly mobile bourgeoisie of Mme Verdurin, and those of the aristocracy, the Guermantes family.

Mme Verdurin is first described at the beginning of 'Un amour de Swann' as 'vertueuse et d'une respectable famille bourgeoise excessivement riche et entièrement obscure avec laquelle elle avait peu à peu cessé volontairement toute relation' (I, 185) ['a thoroughly virtuous woman who came of a respectable middle-class family, excessively rich and wholly undistinguished, with which she had gradually and of her own accord severed all connection' (I, 225/265)]. Through ruthless control over her guests, through single-mindedness, a degree of *savoir-faire*, a superficial but nevertheless adequate knowledge of art and politics, Mme Verdurin manages to acquire a varied assortment of followers at her first *salon* in the rue Montalivet in the 8th *arrondissement*, not far from the Elysée Palace (III, 706–7; V, 225/265). These include fictional characters such as the painter Elstir, the musician Vinteuil, Professor Brichot, Dr Cottard and many others. She moves astutely with the times, favouring intelligence and the arts, whereas the Guermantes *salons* despise intelligence and tend to ossify. Her *salon* evolves as a Temple of Music (III, 263; IV, 309/363): Mme Verdurin is a fervent supporter of Wagner, Russian Ballet, Nijinsky and Stravinsky (III, 140; IV,165/193), music that was fashionable in Paris, driven by the prevailing spirit of Franco-Russian *rapprochement* favoured at governmental level. There was a Russian pavilion, among others, at the Great Exhibition of 1900, and the Alexander III bridge across the Seine was inaugurated in the same year in honour of the Emperor who had signed the Franco-Russian alliance. Russian Ballet became the craze, for Diaghilev had promoted his troupe vigorously in Paris, even persuading the Comte and Comtesse Greffulhe and other wealthy patrons to provide financial support for the performances. The dazzling Russian Ballet season opened in Paris in May 1909 and continued on a regular basis for several years. Proust, with his close friend the composer Reynaldo Hahn, saw a performance of *Scheherazade*, choreographed by Baskt and Fokine, with music by Rimsky-Korsakov, on the opening night, 4 June 1910, when Nijinsky was the slave, and Ida Rubinstein the Sultan's favourite wife. It was described as an orgy never before witnessed, the stage a bright green tent with shadowy blue doors and a huge orange carpet. The sheer exoticism of this highly visual, wild circus act, with accentuated actions and thrills, was vividly captured by Hahn in his account published in *Le Journal* of 10 June 1910 (*Corr.* x, 114–15). Invited by Comtesse Greffulhe, Proust also attended a performance of the ballet *Cléopâtre*, at the Paris Opera on 11 June 1910, starring Ida Rubinstein and Nijinsky. Hahn was fêted by Diaghilev in Saint-Petersburg in March 1911 when he first played the music of his new composition *Le Dieu bleu*. Stravinsky's *Rite of Spring* was first performed at the Théâtre des Champs-Elysées in 1913. The uncertain sexual identity, characteristic of the Ballets russes, and the transvestism of the Paris Music Hall, were intriguing stage developments which Proust incorporated into his novel, particularly in his construction of Odette. The latter is revealed through Elstir's painting *Miss Sacripant* as having been a transvestite music-hall actress.[3]

Ridiculous as Mme Verdurin may appear at times in Proust's novel, such as when she feigns a cold in her head and neuralgia as the consequences of listening to Vinteuil's sonata (I, 203; I, 247/291), and has her nose greased with the far from pleasant smelling 'rhino-goménol', a decongestant and antiseptic ointment which Proust himself frequently used,[4] as a preventative measure (III, 745; V, 271/320), or when Proust depicts her as some strange bird from a zoo, on a lofty perch, emitting sounds in an indistinct and garbling manner (I, 202; I, 246/290), she nevertheless succeeds in drawing attention not only to herself, but to this new music which she patronises and publicises, thereby encouraging artistic activity and commerce and reinforcing her position in society. There is a superb portrait of Mme Verdurin's role in relation to the Ballets russes: 'depuis que le goût [du public] se détournait de l'art raisonnable et français d'un Bergotte et s'éprenait surtout de musiques exotiques, Mme Verdurin, sorte de correspondant attitré à Paris de tous les artistes étrangers, allait bientôt, à côté de la ravissante princesse Yourbeletieff, servir de vieille fée Carabosse, mais toute-puissante, aux danseurs russes' (III, 741) ['now that the public taste had begun to turn from the rational Gallic art of Bergotte and was developing a taste for exotic forms of music, Mme Verdurin, a sort of accredited representative in Paris of all foreign artists, would soon be making her appearance, by the side of the exquisite Princess Yourbeletieff, as an aged Fairy Godmother, grim but all-powerful, to the Russian dancers' (V, 266–7/314)]. After the Ballet, the dancers, their director, their designers, the composers Stravinsky and Richard Strauss, would repair to Mme Verdurin's for an exquisite supper, where gossip and discussions, for example about *Scheherazade*, would continue. In this description, Proust interweaves fact and fiction so effortlessly that Mme Verdurin acquires a reality which increases her authenticity.

In contrast to Mme Verdurin, the large Guermantes family, hostile to the bourgeoisie, have the strongest position in the aristocratic world of *Belle Epoque* Paris society, generally known as the Faubourg Saint-Germain. Geographically, the Faubourg Saint-Germain is the area comprising the 7th *arrondissement*, on the left bank of the Seine. Why, therefore, does Proust situate the Guermantes *salon* on the right bank? This is a source of puzzlement to the young Narrator. 'Il est vrai que mon esprit était embarrassé par certaines difficultés, et la présence du corps de Jésus-Christ dans l'hostie ne me semblait pas un mystère plus obscur que ce premier salon du Faubourg situé sur la rive droite . . .' (II, 330) ['It is true that my mind was perplexed by certain difficulties, and the presence of the body of Jesus Christ in the host seemed to me no more obscure a mystery than this leading house in the Faubourg being situated on the right bank of the river . . .' (III, 26/30)]. An examination of a fragment of Proust's manuscript not included in the main body of the published text of *A la recherche du temps perdu* reveals that the 'leading house' is in fact situated partly in the Faubourg Saint-Germain and partly elsewhere: '. . . alors que l'entrée de notre escalier à deux mètres de l'hôtel Guermantes était à cent lieues du faubourg Saint-Germain, en revanche le paillasson d'entrée de cet hôtel . . . faisait essentiellement partie du plus pur faubourg Saint-Germain' (II, 1065) ['the entrance to our staircase, two yards from the hôtel Guermantes, was a long way from the Faubourg Saint-Germain, whereas the doormat at the entrance to their house . . . was firmly part of the genuine Faubourg Saint-Germain']. This is an indicator of how the old Faubourg Saint-Germain is changing and extending both socially and geographically, spilling onto the Right Bank and the Faubourg Saint-Honoré, a phenomenon which Proust charts throughout his novel.

The Faubourg Saint-Germain is both a state of mind and an exclusive group generally comprising royalists, nationalists, Catholics and anti-Dreyfusards, that many, including the Narrator of *A la recherche du temps perdu* at the beginning, aspire to join, believing it to be the pinnacle of society. The Duchesse de Guermantes is regarded as having 'le premier *salon*, la première maison du faubourg Saint-Germain' (II, 328) ['the most exclusive drawing-room, the leading house in the Faubourg Saint-Germain' (III, 24/28)]. However, at the very end of the novel we witness the collapse of the old aristocratic and exclusive house of Guermantes, 'comme une douairière gâteuse' (IV, 535) ['like some senile dowager' (VI, 331/390)], or like a machine whose enfeebled, broken springs can no longer keep out the crowds. A revolution, as well as an evolution, has taken place in the structure of Proust's society in post-war, post-*Belle Epoque* Paris, and the hostess at the final Guermantes *salon,* at the 'matinée chez la princesse de Guermantes', is none other than the upstart, at times vulgar, bourgeois Mme Verdurin who has finally achieved her ambition to penetrate the Guermantes coterie through marriage, but who is presiding over a *salon* not in the coveted Faubourg Saint-Germain, but in the less well-regarded 16th *arrondissement.* Proust's canvas of the wasted, futile lives of all the dilettanti at that afternoon gathering is a masterly portrayal of the decomposition of upper-class society and enables his Narrator to take the decisive step in his life, that of becoming a writer and of realising that he had already accumulated the very material of his book that he was about to write.

Entertainment and leisure

The fascination for a visual and live spectacle, on stage, was part of Parisian life in the *Belle Epoque.* The rise of the Ballets russes had been preceded by the rise of 'le Music-Hall' (the English word was introduced into French in 1862). The area around Montmartre, the hill-top village as it was at the end of the nineteenth century, was becoming a mecca for artists, musicians and poets. The famous night-club and dance hall *Le Moulin Rouge,* inaugurated in 1889, was ensured a strange kind of immortality in the colourful, sometimes licentious posters by Toulouse-Lautrec. The *Folies-Bergère,* in the rue Richer, originally opened as a theatre in 1869: it was later enlarged and developed a repertory of pantomime, acrobatic displays, ballets and light opera. The *Olympia* Music Hall at 28, boulevard des Capucines, close to the Opéra, was also a flourishing venue for popular music and night-time entertainment from the end of the century. In Proust's novel, the *Olympia* is loosely associated with the prostitution, sadism and sado-masochism depicted in Jupien's homosexual brothel in wartime Paris (IV, 392, 404; VI, 152/179, 166/196), and is invoked in the course of bawdy conversations on at least two occasions. Julot's 'godmother' is 'la dame qui tient le chalet de nécessité un peu plus bas que l'Olympia' (IV, 392) ['the woman who looks after the toilets just beyond the Olympia' (VI, 151/178)]. Charlus obtains additional sadistic pleasure by his crude linguistic flagellation of a male protégé accusing him of infidelity: '"Toi, c'est dégoûtant, je t'ai aperçu devant l'Olympia avec deux cartons. C'est pour te faire donner du 'pèze'"' (IV, 404) ['"You're disgusting, you are, I saw you outside the Olympia with two tarts. After a bit of brass, no doubt"' (VI, 166/196)]. The 'taverne de l'*Olympia*' is a favourite haunt of Proust's character Rachel, the dancer (II, 461; III, 183/215). There were cabarets such as the *Chat Noir,* where Charlus, in Proust's novel, claimed he had taken Odette (I, 310; I, 380/449):

it was Montmartre's most renowned artistic cabaret in the 1890s, situated at 12, rue Victor Massé, not far from the busy Place Pigalle. *Les Variétés*, the theatre on the boulevard Montmartre, was well-known from about 1870 for its variety shows, and was recorded by the genre painter Jean Béraud in his famous painting *Devant les Variétés*, with the elegantly dressed wealthy ladies and gentlemen of the period, and the Morris column in the distance announcing forthcoming entertainment, perhaps *Le Testament de César Girodet* by A. Belot and E. Villetard, or Sophocles' *Oedipus Rex*, or *Les Diamants de la Couronne* or *Domino Noir*, comic operas by Scribe and Auber, all of which the young Narrator found fascinating (I, 73; I, 86/101). Adam's comic opera *Le Chalet* was also popular and is one of the Duc de Guermantes' favourite works (II, 781; III, 567/673).

An integral part of *A la recherche du temps perdu* is the theatrical panorama and the juxtapositioning and involvement of real-life and fictional players. In his hierarchy of talent, the Narrator places Sarah Bernhardt just before La Berma, the fictional tragedienne who plays the role of Phèdre in Racine's eponymous play and whose performance so much disappoints the young Narrator. The beginning of Swann's frequenting the Verdurin *salon* is given historical authenticity by his promise to obtain a 'coupe-file' (I, 212) ['a special pass' (I, 259/304)] for Mme Verdurin for the re-opening of the play *Les Danicheff*, by the Russian-born writer Pierre de Corvin-Kroukowsky, which took place at the Paris theatre of Porte-Saint-Martin in 1884.

Through the fictional, female Jewish character known simply as Rachel (she has no surname, but her name is identical to the real-life French actress Rachel (1821–58), thus creating some confusion for the reader), a Parisian music hall actress, mistress of the aristocrat Saint-Loup, prostitute, 'une énigme, un véritable sphinx'(II, 578) ['an enigma, a regular sphinx' (III, 323/382)], Proust explores the underworld or the seedy side of the *Belle Epoque*. Rachel is first introduced working as a prostitute in a heterosexual brothel: that is where the Narrator first encounters her (I, 566–7; II, 174/206). This is also the brothel to which the Narrator has donated furniture which had belonged to his aunt Léonie in Combray and in particular a divan, a most appropriate and useful item for such an establishment. Rachel is depicted on stage (II, 472–3; III, 196/231) and 'au promenoir des Folies-Bergère' (II, 578) ['in the promenade at the Folies-Bergère' (III, 323/382)]. To the uninitiated reader, this may appear an innocent kind of stroll. The 'promenoir' at the *Folies-Bergère* did exist, and was the equivalent of the famous, or rather infamous, promenade at the Empire Theatre Music Hall, Leicester Square, in London, notorious as the place at the back of the theatre, usually next to a bar, where high-class prostitutes paraded, particularly during the interval. Manet captured and immortalised the atmosphere of such a bar with his painting of 1882, *A Bar at the Folies-Bergère*. At the end of Proust's novel, Rachel has risen in society to become a close friend of the Duchesse de Guermantes, pandering to high society's 'constant thirst for novelty to entertain themselves, for people who were interesting and even a little notorious'.[5] Similarly, Mistinguett and Louise Balthy are the real-life music hall actresses, singers and dancers whom the Duchesse de Guermantes finds 'adorables' (IV, 571; VI, 380/447).

Another leisure and social activity is centered on hotel life. There are two grand hotels in *A la recherche du temps perdu*: the fictional Grand Hôtel de la Plage at Balbec, and the authentic Ritz on the Place Vendôme in Paris, which opened in 1898, the first hotel to install private baths.

The Grand Hôtel de la Plage at Balbec is modelled on opulent hotels which Proust had known, but in particular the new Grand Hôtel at Cabourg, on the Normandy coast, some six to seven hours from Paris by train via Mézidon.[6] It had re-opened in 1907 in a blaze of publicity emphasising 'le Modern Style' and its Casino, bathing facilities, golf course, gardens.[7] The Narrator's room at Balbec is like a show bedroom at an Ideal Home exhibition with its colourful and modern décor; Ripolin, then a new gloss paint, was being advertised on posters in 1898. 'Celle [ma chambre] du Grand Hôtel de la Plage, à Balbec, dont les murs passés au ripolin contenaient, comme les parois polies d'une piscine où l'eau bleuit, un air pur, azuré et salin . . . et sur trois côtés . . . des bibliothèques basses, à vitrines en glace'(I, 376) ['my room in the Grand Hôtel de la Plage, at Balbec, the ripolin-painted walls of which enclosed, like the polished sides of a bathing-pool in which the water glows blue, a finer air, pure, azure-tinted, saline . . . and . . . on three sides of it, a series of low book-cases with glass fronts' (I, 461/545). Yet his bedroom does not seem to have en-suite facilities, for there is a basin-stand and a servant brings hot water for his ablutions (II, 33–4; II, 289–90/341–2). In contrast, the Narrator's family apartment in Paris has two bathrooms (III, 520; V, 2/3).

The luxurious life-style of the leisured classes on vacation at Balbec, typified by Andrée's husband in 'l'audace frénétique qu'il portait jadis, à Balbec, aux sports, au jeu, à tous les excès de table' (IV, 310) ['the frenzied daring which he had shown in the old days at Balbec, in sport, in gambling, in excesses of eating and drinking' (VI, 50/59)] was brought to a close at the onset of the Great War when the Grand Hôtel Cabourg was requisitioned and transformed into a military hospital. In Proust's novel, Charlus has turned his large house into a military hospital, and the manager of the Grand

Hôtel, Balbec, ends up in a concentration camp (IV, 387, 325; VI, 146/172, 69/81).

Proust was an *habitué* of the Ritz and it is therefore surprising that this famous hotel does not have a more prominent presence in his novel. For the fictional Albertine, it is the place which provides her with exotic, sensual ice-creams, in taste and shape 'des colonnes Vendôme de glace . . ., des obélisques de framboise' (III, 636) ['Vendôme Columns of ice . . ., raspberry obelisks' (V, 140/165). For the fictional Robert de Saint-Loup, when on leave from the front, the Ritz provides the setting for an imaginary farce acted by characters in their night attire (IV, 338; VI, 85/100). For Swann, the Ritz was not an exclusive place 'puisque tout le monde peut y aller en payant' (IV, 543) ['since anybody can go to these places who pays' (VI, 343/404)]. His lofty position was guaranteed by his membership of select clubs, such as the Jockey. The theme of social exclusivity, be it the tightly-knit family group in Combray, the 'little clan' at the Verdurins', or the Faubourg Saint-Germain, is abundantly represented throughout Proust's novel.

Speed of change

Turner's painting *Rain, Steam and Speed*, of 1844, was a precursor to Claude Monet's *Gare Saint-Lazare* of 1877: both depicted the emerging mode of rail travel, together with a hint of the accompanying problem of pollution. The railways had developed at a fast pace in France and by 1894, when Proust was 23 years old, there were about 24,000 miles of railways, offering 1st, 2nd and 3rd class travel, owned by the Government (le Réseau de l'Etat), six large companies and a considerable number of smaller ones.[8] Sometimes there were two stations in the same town belonging to different companies as at Cabourg, where the Gare de l'Etat was next to the Gare départementale (Gruyer, *Normandie*, p.321). The London–Paris rail and boat service in 1899 via Calais or Boulogne provided up to five services a day, with a journey time of about eight hours.[9]

The medieval town of Combray first appears, not really from a cup of tea, as the Narrator poetically claims (I, 47; I, 55/64), but 'de loin, à dix lieues à la ronde, vu du chemin de fer' (I, 47) ['at a distance, from a twenty-mile radius, as we used to see it from the railway' (I, 56/65)]. Proust provides snapshots of the poetry of emerging rail transport in his novel. As the Narrator and his grandmother journey to the fictional seaside resort of Balbec, we glimpse 'le bar du train' with its friendly barman and attendants (II, 12; II, 264/312), and 'la fenêtre dont nous avions abaissé le rideau qui ne remplissait pas tout le cadre de la vitre, de sorte que le soleil pouvait glisser sur le chêne ciré de la portière et le drap de la banquette' (*ibid.*) ['the window, the blind of which, though we had lowered it, did not completely cover the glass, so that the sun could shed on the polished oak of the door and the cloth of the seat' (*ibid.*)].

Railway stations are, for the Narrator, both marvellous and tragic places. Proust demonstrates the particular social function of the little halts on the slower lines – almost a mini-*salon* – and in a letter to Mme de Maugny recalled some of the social activities at Thonon station: 'A Thonon, long arrêt, on serrait la main d'un tel qui était venu accompagner ses invités, d'un autre voulant acheter les journaux, de beaucoup que j'ai toujours soupçonnés de n'avoir rien d'autre à faire là que retrouver des gens de connaissance. Une forme de vie mondaine comme une autre que cet arrêt à la gare de Thonon' (*Corr.* XIX, p.538). ['At Thonon there was a long wait, while the passengers shook hands with someone who was seeing his guests off, or another who's come to buy newspapers, or a good many who, I always suspected, came only as an excuse to chat with their acquaintances. The stop at Thonon was a form of social life like any other.']¹⁰ Proust fully developed the theme of railway stops as the setting for social intercourse in his novel (see III, 494–5: IV, 590–2/695–7). On a more modest level, bicycles were all the rage: Béraud's famous painting *Au chalet du cycle au Bois de Boulogne* captures this *joie de vivre* and shows off female cycling attire. In Proust's novel, the energetic, sports-loving Albertine is closely associated with bicycles (II, 146, 151–3; II, 426/503, 431–3/509–12).

Norman Davies, in *Europe: A History*, has conveyed the speed of change of this *fin de siècle* in his observation: 'In 1895 Henry James, the American novelist living in Europe, acquired electric lighting; in 1896 he rode a bicycle; in 1897 he wrote on a typewriter. And that was in a period which a British Royal Commission had called "the Great Depression"'.¹¹

Two major displays of grandeur in Paris, the Great Exhibitions of 1889 and 1900, encapsulated a sense of pride in the technological achievements of the time, the importance of the French capital as an influential city on the world stage, and France as a dominant, colonial power. The centrepiece of the 1889 exhibition was the controversial and impressive Eiffel Tower, that iron structure built to commemorate the centenary of the French Revolution: it was equipped with lifts and at its inauguration was illuminated by a vast array of gas lights. Posters advertised railway tickets at special rates to encourage crowds to marvel at this phenomenon. The Polish pianist, composer and politician, virtuoso interpreter of Chopin, Ignace Paderewski, came to Paris for this exhibition and played before thousands on Bastille Day, as well as performing at private recitals in the homes of the wealthy. In Proust's novel, Paderewski's name is dropped casually at Mme Verdurin's *salon*, but his prowess is not really recognised by Mme Verdurin, who considered his talent to be inferior to that of the second-rate fictional pianist Dechambre (III, 289; IV, 341/400).

The Great Exhibition of 1900 epitomised the optimism and excitement of experiencing the birth of a new century. Not only did it portray French achievements and discoveries, but tried to be representative of the universe, with Paris at the centre. Proust's friend, the artist Jacques-Emile Blanche, conveyed this spirit of universal brotherhood in his painting, *André Gide et ses amis au café maure de l'Exposition universelle de 1900*, now in the Musée des Beaux-Arts at Rouen. The catalogue of the 1900 Exhibition presents a breathtaking variety of stands, palaces (such as the palaces of the French and English Colonies, even the palace of England), entertainments, exotic restaurants, pavilions, including the heavy and proud promotion of the State tobacco and matches industry employing 16,660 workers in its twenty-one factories in a country where 990 grams of tobacco were consumed per person per year. The new-found uses of electricity were promoted – electric clocks, railways, signals, detonators, mines, civil engineering, medicine, telegraph and telephone systems – and displayed prominently in the eighty-metre high Palace of Electricity, a monument to Progress and 'le Génie de l'Electricité'. In *A la recherche du temps perdu*, the news, on the good authority of the electrician Mildé (whose shop specialising in electrical goods opened in 1900 at 52, rue du Faubourg Saint-Honoré: it is identified in I, 1416), that Mme Verdurin's recently acquired town house will have the luxury of electricity, with electric lights with lampshades, causes a stir (I, 596; II, 211/249). In his bedroom in Paris with a fireplace but no central heating, Proust's Narrator has a 'poire électrique au-dessus de [son] lit' (III, 521–2) [an 'electric push . . . hung above [his] bed' (V, 4/4)]. The Grand Hôtel de Balbec is equipped with electricity, 'les sources électriques faisant sourdre à flots la lumière dans la grande salle à manger' (II, 41) ['hidden springs of electricity flooding the great dining-room with light' (II, 299/353).

There were fifty-six public telephone booths at the Exhibition, as well as a telephone service on the first and second floors of the Eiffel Tower. This represented an impressive display of this new invention, for subscribers in France of 1900 numbered only 40,000, of whom more than half, 22,468, were in Paris.[12] The Wagram and Gutenberg telephone exchanges in Paris are mentioned in *A la recherche du temps perdu* (II, 435; III, 151/178). The novelty of the possibility of having a private telephone incites the fictional Mme Cottard, generally a rather naive woman, to foresee its disadvantages: 'Le premier amusement passé, cela doit être un vrai casse-tête' (I, 596) ['Once the first excitement is over, it must be a real headache' (II, 211/250)], as well as the luxury it affords of being able to place an order for delivery without going out. In *Le Côté de Guermantes*, there is a reference to the Narrator's parents having had a private telephone at home for a short while (II, 422; III, 136/160). Without the telephone at home, to which one subscribed, and of course electricity, Proust would not have been able to have a 'théâtrophone' enabling him to hear live performances of works such as Chabrier's *Gwendoline*, or Wagner's *Meistersinger* from the Paris Opera, or Debussy's *Pelléas et Mélisande*, libretto by Maeterlinck, from the Opéra-Comique (*Corr.* XI, 294; *Corr.* X, 250). A théâtrophone network, operated by the 'Compagnie du théâtrophone' with its main exchange in the rue Louis-le-Grand, analogous to the telephone network, connected some Paris theatres, in particular the Opéra, Opéra-Comique and Le Théâtre Français, with individual subscribers' homes. Powerful microphones and horn-shaped loudspeakers placed on the stage transmitted the performance via telephone lines. In London a similar device called an electrophone was used to transmit theatre performances to subscribers, but the service was not successful and was short-lived.[13]

Tensions and upheavals

The *salons* were, to some extent, a microcosm of the tensions in French society at the time. In particular, the Dreyfus affair which had repercussions throughout France, and beyond, created conflict within the small social groups of the *salons*, thus reflecting the national situation.

The reverberations of the Dreyfus affair continued after Dreyfus's acquittal, as Proust himself observes: 'l'affaire Dreyfus était pourtant terminée depuis longtemps, mais vingt ans après on en parlait encore' (III, 548) ['The Dreyfus case was long since over, but twenty years later people would still talk about it' (V, 36/42)]. Proust underestimated its impact, for Eric Cahm has demonstrated in the epilogue to his study of the Affair that it is still a sensitive topic today:[14] Winock also maintains that 'the Affair has produced a phenomenon of remanence lasting to our own time'.[15]

The Dreyfus affair is extremely complex: secrecy, suspicions, hatred, prejudice and some unexplained deaths helped to conceal the truth. In brief, an army officer, Captain Alfred Dreyfus, a wealthy Jew, originally from Mulhouse, in Alsace, was wrongly accused of releasing secret information concerned with national defence to the German military attaché in Paris in the form of a written document known as the *bordereau*. He was arrested in 1894 as a spy, and sentenced by court martial to be deported to the remote Devil's Island (L'Ile du Diable), off the coast of French Guyana, in South

America. The writer Emile Zola publicly took up Dreyfus's case in a famous open letter to the President of the French Republic, Félix Faure, published in the radical newspaper *L'Aurore*, on the front page, under the heading 'J'Accuse . . . !' Zola attacked the army cover-up and asserted Dreyfus's innocence. In *L'Aurore*, there was an 'Intellectuals' Manifesto' demanding a retrial and Proust was one of the signatories, along with the writers André Gide and Anatole France. Zola was tried – 'L'Affaire Zola' was blazoned on the front cover of the newspaper *Le Petit Journal* on 20 February 1898 – and sentenced to a year's imprisonment and a fine for writing this incitement. He escaped to exile in England for a year. A revision of Dreyfus' case took place in August 1899 in Rennes, in the heart of traditional and Catholic Brittany, after Colonel Henry had been found guilty of forging evidence. Henry was sent to prison where he committed suicide. Dreyfus was nevertheless found 'guilty but with extenuating circumstances', and sentenced to ten years' imprisonment. He was eventually pardoned and set free, but the verdict was only finally quashed in 1906, by which time Dreyfus was a broken man. The long campaign against Dreyfus, waged on the whole by Catholics, anti-Semites and nationalists, was partly responsible for the anti-clerical reaction which ensued.

In Mme Straus's *salon*, as early as October 1897, Joseph Reinach, himself of Jewish origin, author of the monumental seven-volume work *Histoire de l'affaire Dreyfus* and politician – he was *député* for the Basses-Alpes at the time of the Dreyfus affair, having been elected in 1889 – had proclaimed his firm belief in Dreyfus's innocence. The effect was electric on those present, some of whom left as a sign of disagreement. Mme Straus's *salon*, like Mme Verdurin's in Proust's novel, became the headquarters of a pro-Dreyfus faction. The real Joseph Reinach, Emile Zola, Colonel Picquart, Clemenceau, Labori and Anatole France gather at the *salon* of the fictional Mme Verdurin (III, 144, 741; IV, 169/199, V, 267/315).

'L'Affaire', as it came to be known, stirred up emotions and furious passions, and ensured that people could not remain indifferent to the plight of one of their countrymen. People were divided into the Dreyfusards and anti-Dreyfusards, sometimes changing allegiance through expediency. As Léon Blum recalled: 'On était dreyfusard ou on ne l'était pas.'[16] A wave of anti-semitism had been fostered by Etienne Drumont (1844–1917) through his book *La France juive* of 1886, and his anti-semitic daily newspaper *La Libre Parole* (1892–1910) which generally carried propaganda denouncing Jews, Protestants and 'métèques', a pejorative word for undesirable immigrants, while promoting the Catholic church and 'France for the French'.

Proust, the son of a Jewish mother and a Catholic father, with a very wide circle of Catholic, Jewish and Protestant friends and contacts, experienced the entire Dreyfus affair at first hand. In spite of his own father's position as an anti-Dreyfusard, Proust openly and courageously took the side of Dreyfus and campaigned on his behalf from a very early stage, and also for Picquart (*Corr.* II, 251). Proust, in a letter of 1919 to Paul Souday, the official critic for the newspaper *Le Temps*, proudly declared: 'Je crois bien avoir été le premier dreyfusard, puisque c'est moi qui suis allé demander sa signature à Anatole France' (*Corr.* XVIII, pp.535–6) ['I do believe I was the first Dreyfusard, since I was the one who asked Anatole France to sign the petition': my translation]. In *La Prisonnière*, when the discussion centres on Dreyfus at the Guermantes', the Narrator wishes to avoid confrontation and quickly steers the conversation to the subject of dresses (III, 551; V, 39/46). Recanati interprets this behaviour by the Narrator as a tendency to avoid argument, and as if he was an outsider or afraid.[17] I do not believe the Narrator was afraid: he was emulating the diplomatic behaviour of his mother who, in *Le Côté de Guermantes*, had remained silent about her opinions on Dreyfus. The Narrator is as much pro-Dreyfus as his father is anti-Dreyfus, a state which causes a temporary rift: 'Il ne me reparla pas de huit jours quand il apprit que j'avais suivi une ligne de conduite différente' (II, 450) ['He refused to speak to me for a week after learning that I had chosen to take a different line' (III, 169/200)].

Proust, who as a novelist was conceptually and stylistically in many ways diametrically opposed to Zola, supported Zola's political stance without faltering. He even attended Zola's trial, and transposed his presence through the Jewish character Bloch in *A la recherche du temps perdu*. Bloch attends several hearings of Zola's trial which he describes as a 'beautiful dream' (II, 531; III, 266/315: translation altered). He is totally engrossed in the trial, but not to the extent of forgetting his nutritional needs: 'Il arrivait là le matin, pour n'en sortir que le soir, avec une provision de sandwiches et une bouteille de café, comme au concours général ou aux compositions de baccalauréat' (*ibid.*) ['He would arrive there in the morning and stay until the court rose, with a supply of sandwiches and a flask of coffee, as though for the final examination for a degree' (*ibid.*)]. In Proust's novel, the fictional Mme Verdurin is seated next to the real Mme Zola at Zola's trial 'aux pieds du tribunal, aux séances de la Cour d'assises' (III, 741) ['immediately below the judges' bench, during the trial in the Assize Court' (V, 267/315)] and in the evening she entertains at her home Picquart and Fernand Labori, Zola's lawyer (III, 742; V, 268/316): all this in order to have a more prominent and important position in society.[18]

Contributing to the changing social panorama were the anti-clerical laws – which Sprinker believes to be a backlash against Catholic anti-Semitism and anti-Dreyfusism[19] – such as the expulsion of religious congregations, introduced by Emile Combes when he was Président du Conseil (Prime Minister) between 1902 and 1905, culminating in the act of separation of the Church and State on 9 December 1905. Proust himself took a strong public stance against the proposed legislation which he eloquently denounced, invoking the support of Ruskin and Emile Mâle, in his article in *Le Figaro* of 16 August 1904 entitled 'La Mort des Cathédrales' (*CSB*, pp. 141–9). Although this Church versus State debate does not percolate into his novel to the same extent as the Dreyfus Affair and the Great War, echoes of it are apparent. The new Mayor of Combray is anti-clerical: 'un maire radical à Combray, qui ne salue même pas le curé' (IV, 255) ['a Radical mayor now at Combray, who doesn't even lift his hat to the priest' (V, 779/920)]. Charlus remarks on how unlikely such anti-clerical measures had seemed: 'Les républicains les plus sages pensaient qu'il était fou de faire la séparation de l'Eglise' (IV, 376) ['The most prudent republicans thought that it was mad to separate the Church from the State' (VI, 132/156)].

The Narrator returns twice to Paris in wartime after a stay in a sanatorium. These breaks are a useful device, enabling him to distance himself from Paris and to see the capital with fresh and rested eyes, as well as to witness the effects of war sometime after its commencement and after an interval of two years, in 1916, and on a third occasion after the war (IV, 433; VI, 202/238).

The effects of war are apparent. There is a brief mention of a lack of coal and light: the Louvre and all other museums are closed: lights have to be turned off promptly at 9.30 pm and restaurants closed. There are constant 'Taube' raids on the city as well as Zeppelin and Gotha raids.[20] The dark city was periodically lightened by 'les projecteurs [qui] se remuaient sans cesse, flairant l'ennemi, le cernant de leurs lumières jusqu'au moment où les avions aiguillés bondiraient en chasse pour le saisir' (IV, 338) ['the searchlights [which] strayed ceaselessly to and fro, scenting the enemy, encircling him with their beams until the moment when the aeroplanes should be unleashed to bound after him in pursuit and seize him' (VI, 84/99–100)]. Shelling and blazing buildings do not deter the Narrator. In the blackness, he stumbles against dustbins: clocks have been put forward as a daylight saving device, a law decreed in June 1916 in the face of much opposition as the editors of the Pléiade edition explain (IV, 1219). There are special police regulations in force and hotels are purported to be full of spies.[21]

Comte Robert de Saint-Loup is killed in action. Charlie Morel, after working as a Press Officer, joined the army, but was later arrested as a deserter, then sent back to the front. The image of dying soldiers, engaged in the act of writing as their last earthly task, goads the Narrator into tackling his inability to write his novel (see IV, 616, 620; VI, 439/517, 445/524).

In spite of these deprivations, deaths, war casualties, slaughter, the sickening insouciance of high society, of its women in particular, the *Belle Epoque* continues. As the Narrator remarks: 'La vie continuait presque semblable pour bien des personnes qui ont figuré dans ce récit' (IV, 351) ['Life continued almost unchanged for many of these who have played a part in this story' (VI, 101/119)]. The Verdurins give dinner-parties and their *salon* becomes a political *salon*. Mme Verdurin, almost a Marie-Antoinette figure, continues to take great selfish pleasure in her regular morning *croissant* which she has obtained on prescription from Dr Cottard for her migraine, indulging in a luxury in a city where people queue for bread and coal rations, while she superficially sympathises with the sinking of the *Lusitania*, the British liner, one of the great casualties of the war, torpedoed off the Irish coast on 7 May 1915 by a German submarine with the loss of twelve hundred lives (IV, 352; VI, 102/120).

The so-called *Belle Epoque* was a period of rapid change and technological advances. The speed of communications in transport – bicycles, railways, omnibuses and aeroplanes – and in telecommunications, such as the telegraph and telephone, was rapid. Alongside these developments, there was political and social instability, such as the Dreyfus Affair which rocked French society and created divisions. The Catholic church and the French State were to separate irreparably in 1905. Diseases such as cholera, tuberculosis, typhoid fever (IV, 459; VI, 234/276) were rife: drug addiction was becoming common and in Proust's novel the Vicomtesse de Saint-Fiacre has become unrecognisable and a physical wreck due to her dependence on cocaine and other drugs (IV, 523; VI, 315/371). Brothels and promiscuity encouraged the spread of syphilis which at the time was very difficult to treat. The First World War, which killed and wounded millions of men, in which gas was used for the first time, in which soldiers endured miles of stinking, flooded trenches, shattered any latent illusions of permanent prosperity and happiness.

NOTES

1 Quoted by André Maurois, *The Quest for Proust*, translated by Gerard Hopkins (Harmondsworth: Penguin Books in association with Jonathan Cape, 1962), p.87.

2 Vincent Cronin, *Paris on the Eve: 1900–1914* (London: Collins, 1989), p.17.

3 For a fuller discussion of this point, see Cynthia J. Gamble, 'Zipporah: a Ruskinian enigma appropriated by Marcel Proust', in *Word & Image*, vol.15, no. 4, October–December 1999, pp.392–4.

4 François-Bernard Michel, *Proust et les écrivains devant la mort* (Paris: Grasset, 1995), pp.89–93.

5 Seth L. Wolitz, *The Proustian Community* (New York University Press, 1971), p.155.

6 Paul Gruyer, *Normandie*, Collection des Guides-Joanne (Paris: Hachette, 1912), p.319.

7 Christian Péchenard, *Proust à Cabourg* (Paris: Quai Voltaire, 1992), pp.28–30.

8 Karl Baedeker, *Northern France from Belgium and the English Channel to the Loire excluding Paris and its Environs. Handbook for Travellers* (Leipsic: Baedeker; London: Dulau, 1894), p.xv.

9 See advertisement in *La Chronique des Arts et de la Curiosité*, 23 September 1899, p.280.

10 Quoted in George Painter, *Marcel Proust* (Harmondsworth: Penguin Books, 1983), p.229.

11 Norman Davies, *Europe: A History* (London: Pimlico, 1997), p.781. See in particular chapters x and xi.

12 *La Grande Encyclopédie*, Tome 30, 1887–1902.

13 See Asa Briggs, *The Birth of Broadcasting* (Oxford University Press, 1995), I, 39.

14 Eric Cahm, *The Dreyfus Affair in French Society and Politics* (London and New York: Longman, 1996), pp.185–93.

15 Michel Winock, trans. Jane Marie Todd, *Nationalism, Anti-Semitism, and Fascism in France* (Stanford: University Press, 1998), p.111.

16 Léon Blum, *Souvenirs sur l'Affaire* (Paris: Gallimard, 1993 [1935]), p.34.

17 Jean Recanati, *Profils juifs de Marcel Proust* (Paris: Editions Buchet/Chastel, 1979), p.71.

18 Proust provided a much more comprehensive and documentary account of Zola's trial through the eyes of the young man Jean (Santeuil), in some of the fragments which were entitled *Jean Santeuil* by Bernard de Fallois in 1952. (See *JS*, pp.620–7, 649–51 and also *Jean Santeuil*, translated by Gerard Hopkins, preface by André Maurois (Harmondsworth: Penguin, 1985), pp.350–3 for one of the extracts.)

19 Michael Sprinker, *History and Ideology in Proust* (London: Verso, 1998), p.111.

20 References to the preceding allusions are as follows: IV, 311; VI, 52/61. IV, 302; VI, 41/48. IV, 313; VI, 54/64. IV, 330; VI, 74–5/88. IV, 337–8; VI, 83–4/98–9. IV, 341, 356; VI, 89/105, VI, 108/127.

21 References to the preceding allusions are as follows: IV, 412–13; VI, 176–7/207–8. IV, 341–2; VI, 89/105. IV, 312–15; VI, 53–6/62–6.

2

WILLIAM C. CARTER

The vast structure of recollection: from life to literature

In Paris, on Saturday, 3 September 1870, as news of the humiliating defeat of the French by the invading Prussian army at Sedan spread throughout the capital, Dr Adrien Proust, a middle-aged Catholic bachelor, a grocer's son originally from the small provincial town of Illiers, married Jeanne Weil, the Jewish daughter of a wealthy Parisian family. At twenty-one, the beautiful, dark-haired woman was fifteen years younger than the bridegroom. No one knows how they met, but it is likely they were introduced at a government sponsored event or social gathering. Adrien had recently risen to the top ranks in public health administration and Jeanne's family had many connections in official circles.

Marcel was born the following July at Uncle Louis Weil's estate at Auteuil where Jeanne's family usually spent the summer months. The house, built of quarrystones, was large, with spacious rooms, including a drawing room with a grand piano and a billiard room where the family sometimes slept to keep cool during heat waves.[1] In fine weather Louis and his guests enjoyed the large garden with a pond surrounded by hawthorn trees, whose blossoms Marcel was also to admire in his other uncle, Jules Amiot's garden in Illiers.

Marcel's mother possessed a lively mind, an unfailing sense of humour, a profound appreciation of literature and music, combined with common sense and a firm belief in traditional bourgeois values. Her influence would be the most important in Proust's life. Jeanne and her mother, Adèle, supervised his cultural education, exposing him to what they considered the best works in literature. In *Jean Santeuil*, the mother initiates Jean into the love of poetry by reading to him from Lamartine's *Méditations*, Corneille's *Horace* and Hugo's *Contemplations*. Jean's mother believes that good books, even if poorly understood at first, provide the child's mind with healthy nourishment that will later benefit him. When Marcel was older, his mother and grandmother read with him the great seventeenth-century works, of which he acquired a special understanding and appreciation. He came to love the tragedies of Jean Racine, whose masterpiece *Phèdre* in its depiction of obsessive, destructive jealousy haunts the pages of *In Search of Lost Time*.

Adrien's sister, Élisabeth, had married Jules Amiot, who operated a successful notions shop in Illiers at 14, place du Marché, opposite the church of Saint-Jacques. It was to the Amiots' house in the rue du Saint-Esprit that Adrien returned with his wife and two young sons, Marcel and Robert, during the Easter holidays, when the town was at its best, offering wild flowers and trees in bloom that Marcel adored. The Prousts travelled by rail from Paris to Chartres, where they changed trains for the short ride to Illiers. Seen from afar as the train approached, Illiers was contained in its steeple, just as is Combray in the *Search*:

> Combray, de loin . . . n'était qu'une église résumant la ville, la représentant, parlant d'elle et pour elle aux lointains, et, quand on approchait, tenant serrés autour de sa haute mante sombre, en plein champ, contre le vent, comme une pastoure ses brebis, les dos laineux et gris des maisons rassemblées.   (1, 47)

> [Combray at a distance . . . was no more than a church epitomising the town, representing it, speaking of it and for it to the horizon, and as one drew near, gathering close about its long dark cloak, sheltering from the wind, on the open plain, as a shepherdess gathers her sheep, the woolly grey backs of its huddled houses.]
>   (1, 56/65)

Jules indulged his passion for horticulture by creating a large pleasure garden, just beyond the banks of the gently flowing Loir River. He called it the Pré Catelan, after a section of the Bois de Boulogne in Paris. On the south end of the garden a magnificent row of hawthorn trees rose up a slope, leading to a large white gate that opened onto fields of blue cornflowers and brilliant red poppies fanning out to the west and south on the plain towards Méréglise and the château of Tansonville. The Pré Catelan became the model in *Swann's Way* for Charles Swann's park at Tansonville near Combray.[2] It must have seemed natural to Marcel, who often played in the Bois near Auteuil, for his Illiers uncle to name his own garden after the one in Paris. The name held in common by the two principal gardens of his childhood may have provided the first linking in Marcel's mind of the two spaces, Auteuil and Illiers, that inspired Combray.

In Illiers, Marcel visited his elderly grandmother Proust who lived in a modest apartment. Relatively little is known about her except that she was an invalid cared for by an old servant, which makes her a more likely model for the hypochondriacal Aunt Léonie in the *Search* than Élisabeth Amiot, generally considered the original. Adrien took his sons on walks to show them where he had played as a child. He pointed out how two different topographies join at Illiers: the Beauce, a flat, windy plain that, as it moves westward, meets Le Perche, whose hilly terrain is ravined by streams rolling down to feed the Loir River. The defining features of Combray's fictional topography approximate those of Illiers where the two walks – one the landscape of an ideal plain, the other a captivating river view – embody, for the child Narrator, two separate worlds.

As Adrien and his boys made their way back from Tansonville, it was the steeple of Saint-Jacques, appearing now and then in the sky as they mounted a hillock or rounded a bend, that beckoned them home. Proust later used a motif from the church's sculpted wood as one of the most powerful symbols of his art. On either wall behind the altar stands a wooden statue of a saint above whose heads are placed scallop shells. Such shells are the emblem of Saint James (Jacques in French) and, in the Middle Ages, were worn by the pilgrims on their way to Santiago de Compostela. The church of Saint Jacques was a stopping point on the route to Spain. The shells also provide the form of the little cakes known as madeleines, symbol of a key revelation in the Narrator's quest to find his vocation as a writer. Proust would remember the connection between the pilgrims and the madeleines, when he described the cakes in the *Search:* 'the little scallop-shell of pastry, so richly sensual under its severe, religious folds' (I, 46; I, 54/63).

On his walks through the river country north of Illiers, Marcel spied on Mirougrain, the large manor house built on a slope overlooking a water-lily pond. Proust remembered the impressions evoked by this mysterious dwelling later when creating the composer Vinteuil's house in the *Search*. He took the name of the old mill, Montjouvin, but used the setting and atmosphere of Mirougrain for the lesbian love scene between Vinteuil's daughter and her friend. The names of the streets, old inns, manor houses and ruined churches of Illiers and its surroundings, such as Tansonville, Méréglise, Montjouvin, Saint-Hilaire, rue de l'Oiseau flesché, were to live in Proust's memory and imagination, until he used them, with slight alterations or none at all, as part of the material out of which he constructed Combray, a place that exists only in his book.

A story that Proust wrote in his early twenties depicts the goodnight kiss drama from his childhood, generally thought to have taken place at Auteuil.[3] In 'La Confession d'une jeune fille' ['A Girl's Confession'], a woman, dying of a self-inflicted gunshot wound, confesses her weakness that led to tragedy. Although she had given up her lewd behaviour to become engaged to a fine young man, she succumbed one evening to the temptations offered by an attractive guest. Her mother, who happened to catch the daughter and visitor in a passionate embrace, fell dead from the shock. As the girl lies dying, she recalls her childhood and the tender, loving relationship with her mother.

Until she reached fifteen, her mother left her every summer at a country home. The child, like Marcel, dreaded more than anything separation from her mother. Before departing, the mother used to spend two days with her, coming each evening to her bed to kiss her goodnight, a custom the mother had to abandon because 'j'y trouvais trop de plaisir et trop de peine, que je ne m'endormais plus à force de la rappeler pour me dire bonsoir encore' (*JS*, p.86) ['it caused me too much pleasure and too much pain, because due to my calling her back to say goodnight again and again I could never go to sleep'].[4] This is the prototype of the crucial goodnight kiss scene in the *Search* that sets in motion the Narrator's long quest to regain his lost will and become a creative person.

In the *Search*, it is the mother's habit to give the child Narrator one last kiss before going to bed. On nights when company prevents her from coming to his room, he is particularly upset. On one such night, he waits up for her and then implores her to remain with him. She does not want to yield to his nervous anxiety, but the usually stern father intervenes and capriciously tells her to stay with the boy. The child, incredulous at the easy violation of a strict rule, feels guilty for having caused his mother to abandon her convictions. He will spend the rest of his life trying to recover the will he lost that night and to expiate the wrong done to his mother. This scene illustrates how Proust eventually learned to make his private demons serve the plot and structure of his novel.

It was probably during the fall visit of 1886 to Illiers that Marcel, at fifteen, knew that he wanted to be a writer. He had brought along Augustin Thierry's history, *The Norman Conquest of England*, considered a masterpiece of historical narration. As he read page after page of vivid, picturesque narration, he was captivated. In an early draft of *Du côté de chez Swann*, Proust evokes this reading in the context of the Narrator's visit to Combray:

> Je lisais dans la 'salle' au coin du feu la 'Conquête de l'Angleterre par les Normands' d'Augustin Thierry; puis quand j'étais fatigué du livre, quelque temps qu'il fît, je sortais: mon corps resté immobile pendant ces heures de lecture où le mouvement de mes idées l'agitait sur place pour ainsi dire, était comme une toupie qui soudain lâchée a besoin de dépenser dans tous les sens la vitesse accumulée.   (*Textes retrouvés*, pp.178–9.)

> [I read, in the 'living room' by the fireside, Augustin Thierry's *The Norman Conquest of England*; then, when I tired of reading, I went out, no matter what the weather: my body, which in the long spell of immobility while reading for hours, during which the movement of my ideas kept it moving in place so to speak, was like a wound up top which, when suddenly released, felt the need to let go, to expend the accumulated energy in every direction.]

>   (Translation mine.)

In the final version, the situation is the same, but the book is unspecified. The Narrator realises, as he walks through the forest, that despite his great desire to express himself as forcefully as the authors he loves, he is incapable of doing so. He expels his pent-up energy and frustrations by shouting and beating the trees with his umbrella. The passage illustrates one of Proust's most successful narrative tricks, used with variations throughout the *Search*: he tells us in dazzling prose about his inability to write!

> Voyant sur l'eau et à la face du mur un pâle sourire répondre au sourire du ciel, je m'écriai dans mon enthousiasme en brandissant mon parapluie refermé: 'Zut, zut, zut, zut.' Mais en même temps je sentis que mon devoir eût été de ne pas m'en tenir à ces mots opaques et de tâcher de voir plus clair dans mon ravissement. (I, 153)

> [Seeing upon the water, and on the surface of the wall, a pallid smile responding to the smiling sky, I cried aloud in my enthusiasm, brandishing my furled umbrella: 'Gosh, gosh, gosh, gosh!' But at the same time I felt that I was in duty bound not to content myself with these unilluminating words, but to endeavour to see more clearly into the sources of my rapture.] (I, 186/219)

The ebullience Marcel felt during such readings created in him an urge to uncover and express the hidden secrets, the profound meaning of the impressions stored up during his walks. And he had made an invaluable discovery: he must devote his life to literature. But how? And what would he write about?

One day while playing in the garden along the Champs-Élysées, Marcel met Marie de Benardaky and fell in love. Once he met Marie, nothing mattered more than the afternoon trek to the garden to find the 'pretty, exuberant' girl with the open, winsome smile whom he remembered as 'the intoxication and despair of my childhood' and one of 'the great loves of my life' (see *Corr.* XVII, 175, 194). In *Jean Santeuil*, where Proust describes his infatuation, Marie appears with her real name (*JS*, p.46). His crush on her evolved into the Narrator's adolescent love for Gilberte.

But Marcel was not attracted solely to girls. He wrote classmates letters expressing affection, recriminations and invitations to have sex (see *Selected Letters*, I, 10–11). Many of his adolescent letters are remarkable because he used them, not simply to express his emotions, but to analyse his feelings and try to comprehend his motivations and those of his classmates. He played roles and assigned different attitudes to his friends. This practice, begun at such a young age, combined with his extraordinary sensitivity, which allowed him to put himself in another's place, served him well when, as a mature writer, he began creating fascinating, multifaceted characters.

After high school, Marcel received invitations to Paris's leading salons where he met many prominent socialites, such as Charles Ephrussi and Charles Haas, both successful Jews who moved at ease in the art world and in high society and who served as models for Charles Swann. At Madeleine Lemaire's salon Proust met aristocrats, artists and political figures. Celebrated actors Sarah Bernhardt and Réjane, both models for the *Search*'s La Berma, often attended, as did writers Pierre Loti, Jules Lemaître and Anatole France. Madeleine, who loved music, offered her guests the occasion to listen to Paris's most celebrated composers. One might hear Camille Saint-Saëns, Jules Massenet, or Gabriel Fauré at the piano playing their own works or accompanying a singer. Here Proust met the darkly handsome Reynaldo Hahn, only nineteen and already successful as a composer and performer. Soon he and Marcel were inseparable. Madeleine, who insisted upon silence during performances, provided the primary model for Proust's domineering hostess Mme Verdurin, who, like Lemaire, refers to the members of her salon as the 'faithful'.

Madeleine introduced Proust to Robert de Montesquiou and begged the conceited, irascible count to be kind to the intimidated youth. Montesquiou, recognising Marcel's potential as an admiring disciple, invited him to call. The count, arbiter of taste and epitome of aristocratic hauteur, poet, artist, and critic, supplied Proust, over the years, with the major ingredients for one of his most famous characters, the disdainful, vituperative, homosexual Baron de Charlus.

Between his twentieth and twenty-fifth birthdays, Proust wrote many stories that were published in reviews or in the volume *Les Plaisirs et les jours*, illustrated by Madeleine Lemaire and prefaced by Anatole France. These stories present important themes that were fully developed and orchestrated in the mature novel. In *L'Indifférent*, a novella about desire, Marcel described the fear of imminent death from suffocation. He likened an asthmatic child's experience of breathlessness to the feeling of panic and doom that overcomes the lover upon learning that the beloved is to depart on a long voyage:

> Un enfant qui depuis sa naissance respire sans y avoir jamais pris garde, ne sait pas combien l'air qui gonfle si doucement sa poitrine . . . est essentiel à sa vie. Vient-il, pendant un accès de fièvre, dans une convulsion, à étouffer? Dans l'effort désespéré de son être, c'est presque pour sa vie, qu'il lutte, c'est pour sa tranquillité perdue qu'il ne retrouvera qu'avec l'air duquel il ne la savait pas inséparable.[5]

> [A child who has been breathing since birth, without being aware of it, does not realise how essential to life is the air that swells his chest so gently . . . But what happens if, during a high fever or a convulsion, he starts to suffocate?

His entire being will struggle desperately to stay alive, to recapture his lost tranquillity that will return only with the air from which, unbeknownst to him, it was inseparable.] (My translation.)

Asthma, first experienced by Proust at age ten, reminded him of the sheer terror that overtook him when he learned that his mother was leaving on a trip and, eventually – when he had become so dependent on her presence – even when she came to kiss him good night. *L'Indifférent* tells the story of Madeleine who falls helplessly in love with Lepré, a man who cannot return her affection. She finally learns that he leads a secret life that explains his indifference to decent women. He can only make love to prostitutes, whom he pursues relentlessly. A similar trait is given to Swann, a highly eligible bachelor who, rather than making a good marriage and settling down, prefers to seduce servant girls.

'Avant la nuit' ['Before Nightfall'], written in 1893, was Proust's first published work about a future major theme in the *Search*: same-sex love. The character Françoise incarnates and legitimises homosexuality; like the heroine of 'La Confession d'une jeune fille', she shoots herself. Before dying, Françoise observes that Socrates, a wise and just man, tolerated homosexuality. After acknowledging the superiority of procreative love, she argues that when the purpose of lovemaking is not procreative, there can be no 'hierarchy among sterile loves', and, therefore, it is no more immoral for a woman to find pleasure with another woman than with a man. Françoise's final justification for such love is aesthetic. Since both female and male bodies can be beautiful, there is no reason why 'une femme vraiment artiste ne serait pas amoureuse d'une femme. Chez les natures vraiment artistes l'attraction ou la répulsion physique est modifiée par la contemplation du beau' (*JS*, p.170) ['a woman who is truly an artist should not fall in love with another woman. Among those with truly artistic natures, physical attraction or repulsion is modified by the contemplation of beauty': my translation]. These justifications for homosexual desire are refined and expanded in the *Search*, where Proust became the first novelist to depict the continuum of human sexual expression.

In these early stories, Proust treated themes that he was to develop until they became uniquely his. In 'L'Éventail' ['The Fan'] a lady paints on a fan memories of her salon, a 'little universe . . . that we shall never see again'. This notion of moments rescued from oblivion, illustrated by the minor art of fan painting, states his main theme: time lost – and regained. But, like the fan painter, Proust remained, until he was nearly forty, an artist in a minor genre, rendering exquisite little pieces that might easily go unnoticed.

'La Fin de la jalousie' ['The End of Jealousy'] focuses on another major

Proustian preoccupation. Honoré is in love with Françoise, with whom he has enjoyed a passionate, secret liaison. A gentleman friend tells him that Françoise is easy to possess, but too arduous in her affairs. This remark transforms Honoré, who becomes extremely jealous and interrogates Françoise, who swears she has always been faithful. This story, Proust's favourite from his early years, possesses the dynamics of nearly all the erotic relationships in the *Search*. The two most fully developed of these, Swann's obsession with Odette and the Narrator's with Albertine, follow the pattern of emotions that bind Honoré and Françoise. The lies that Honoré tells Françoise, as he attempts to trick her into making revelations, are the models for Swann's jealous interrogations of Odette and the Narrator's of Albertine.

In 1895, Marcel and Reynaldo, vacationing in Brittany, reached the village of Beg-Meil where, on a hill overlooking the sea, they found a small hotel. It was here that Marcel most likely began drafting *Jean Santeuil*. Proust's encounter with Thomas Alexander Harrison, an American expatriate, inspired the character known as the writer C, aspects of whom Proust would use in the *Search* for Elstir who, like Harrison, is a painter.[6] A text combining Proust's impressions of Beg-Meil and Lake Geneva sketches a key theme: the phenomenon of memory ignited by a physical sensation, the examination of which leads him to conclude that our true nature lies outside time. One day Jean is driving through farmland near Geneva, when he suddenly sees the lake:

> En apercevant ainsi la mer (c'est presque la mer à cette heure-là) au bout de la route . . . Jean s'est aussitôt souvenu. Et voici qu'il la voit belle, qu'il en sent le charme, de cette mer d'autrefois, en la retrouvant là devant lui. Et soudain toute cette vie de là-bas qu'il croyait inutile et inutilisée lui apparaît charmante et belle . . . quand le soleil baissait avec la mer devant soi.   (*JS*, pp.398–9)

> [Looking at the sea (at this hour it had almost the appearance of the sea) at the end of the road . . . Jean suddenly remembered. He saw it before him as the very sea he once had known, and felt its charm. In a flash, that life in Brittany which he had thought useless and unusable, appeared before his eyes in all its charm and beauty . . . when the sun was setting and the sea stretched out before him.][7]

Then he wonders about the nature of the extraordinary phenomenon he is experiencing and sees that what the poet needs to feed his imagination is memory experienced in the present, containing both the past and now. Jean then recalls a similar experience, provoked by the smell of a seaside villa where he and his family had vacationed:

> Toute cette vie, toutes ses attentes, ses ennuis, sa faim, son sommeil, son insomnie, ses projets, ses tentatives de jouissance esthétique et leur échec, ses essais

de jouissance sensuelle . . . ses essais de captation d'une personne qui plaît . . .
cette odeur a enveloppé tout cela.   (*JS*, p.400)

[The whole of that period of my life, with its hopes, its worries, its hungers, its
hours of sleep or sleeplessness, its efforts to find joy in art – which ended in
failure – its experiments in sensual gratification . . . its attempts to win the love
of someone who had taken my fancy . . . all were caught up and made present
in that smell.]   (p.408)

Shortly after 25 December 1898, Proust wrote to thank Marie Nordlinger
for her Christmas card. In his meditative letter he touched on topics that preoccupied him and would form the philosophical underpinnings of his future
work: the soul and its encasement in the body, the passage of time and,
through time, the slow, unconscious accumulation of memories, largely
ignored by the superficial, egotistical self. Sounding the depths of his being,
Proust perceived only a faint echo indicating the unknown treasures that
might lie buried beneath the sands of time. The scent of tea and mimosa fur-
nishes the sesame that opened, at least briefly in 1898, the door to the treasure trove. He spoke first about Christmas cards and other symbols and why
we need them:

Si nous n'étions que des êtres de raison nous ne croirions pas aux anniversaires,
aux fêtes, aux reliques, aux tombeaux. Mais comme nous sommes faits aussi
d'un peu de matière, nous aimons à croire qu'elle est quelque chose aussi dans
la réalité et nous aimons que ce qui tient de la place dans notre cœur en ait aussi
une petite autour de nous, qu'elle ait, comme notre âme l'a en notre corps, son
symbole matériel. Et puis au fur et à mesure que Noël perd pour nous de sa
vérité comme anniversaire, par la douce émanation des souvenirs accumulés il
prend une réalité de plus en plus vive, où la lumière des bougies . . . l'odeur de
ses mandarines imbibant la chaleur des chambres, la gaité de ses froids et de
ses feux, les parfums du thé et des mimosas nous réapparaissent enduits du miel
délicieux de notre personnalité que nous y avons inconsciemment déposée
pendant des années, alors que – fascinés par des buts égoïstes – nous ne la sen-
tions pas, et maintenant tout d'un coup elle nous fait battre le cœur.
                                                      (*Corr*. ii, 269–70)

[If we were creatures only of reason, we would not believe in anniversaries,
holidays, relics or tombs. But since we are also made up in some part of matter
we like to believe that it too has a certain reality and we want what holds a
place in our hearts to have some small place in the world around us and to have
its material symbol, as our soul has in our body. And while little by little
Christmas has lost its truth for us as an anniversary, it has at the same time,
through the gentle emanation of accumulated memories, taken on a more and
more living reality, in which candlelight . . . the smell of its tangerines imbib-
ing the warmth of heated rooms, the gaiety of its cold and its fires, the scent of

tea and mimosa, return to us overlaid with the delectable honey of our personality, which we have unconsciously been depositing over the years during which – engrossed in selfish pursuits – we paid no attention to it, and now suddenly it sets our hearts to beating.]   (*Selected Letters* I, 180)

Proust must have recognised the importance of these insights, since he transposed them for a scene in *Jean Santeuil* inspired by another of his muses, the young and beautiful poet Anna de Noailles, to whom he gave the fictional name Vicomtesse Gaspard de Réveillon. Proust attempted to state the importance of such intoxicating, fleeting episodes, like the one evoked by tea and mimosa, that inspire creativity:

> Nos poèmes étant précisément la commémoration de nos minutes inspirées, lesquelles sont déjà souvent une sorte de commémoration de tout ce que notre être a laissé de lui-même dans des minutes passées, essence intime de nous-même que nous répandons sans la connaître, mais qu'un parfum senti alors, une même lumière tombant dans la chambre, nous rend tout d'un coup jusqu'à nous en enivrer et à nous laisser indifférents à la vie réelle dans laquelle nous ne la sentons jamais, à moins que cette vie ne soit en même temps une vie passée, de sorte que dégagés un instant de la tyrannie du présent, nous sentons quelque chose qui dépasse l'heure actuelle, l'essence de nous-même.
>
> (*JS*, p.521)

> [Poems being precisely the commemoration of our inspired moments which in themselves are often a sort of communication of all that our being has left of itself in moments past, the concentrated essence of ourselves which we exude without realising that we are doing so, which a perfume smelled in that past time, a remembered light shining into our room, will suddenly bring back so vividly, that it fills us with . . . intoxication, so that we become completely indifferent to what is usually called 'real life', in which it never visits us unless that life be at the same time a past life, so that freed for a moment from the tyranny of the present, we feel something that spreads out beyond the actual minute, the essence of our being.]
>
> (p.464; 'the essence of our being' is omitted from the English translation.)

In the *Search*, Proust turns this around, as hinted here, and says that moments of vivid, spontaneous memory and their conscious application in the creative process form the real life and that our daily life in its habitual, vain actions is a life lived on the surface, and hence, a life lost.

The letter to Marie and the draft in *Jean Santeuil* where Lake Geneva recalls Beg-Meil are Proust's first known gropings for the elucidation of the key moment in his novel: the experience he called involuntary memory. These early attempts to describe and comprehend this phenomenon indicate there was not one extraordinary moment in Proust's life when he bit into a madeleine and, in a frenzy of inspiration, began writing the *Search*. Proust recognised, as early as *Jean Santeuil*, that the key to his work lay submerged in the past. He saw the rich potential of such experiences, saying they were 'alive on a higher level than memory or than the present so that they have not the flatness of pictures but the rounded fullness of reality, the imprecision of feeling' (*Jean Santeuil*, p.409). But he was years away from discovering how to make them serve a novel's plot. Around 1899, unable to create a plot and find the right point of view, he abandoned *Jean Santeuil*.

From 1900–05 Proust translated John Ruskin's *The Bible of Amiens* and *Sesame and Lilies*. This arduous work, entailing the study of French history, geography, architecture and the Bible, proved crucial to the development of Proust's own style and aesthetics. In 'Sur la lecture' ['On Reading'], the preface to his translation of *Sesame and Lilies*, Proust wrote: 'Il n'y a peut-être pas de jours de notre enfance que nous ayons si pleinement vécus que ceux que nous avons cru laisser sans les vivre, ceux que nous avons passés avec un livre préféré' (*CSB*, p.160) ['There are perhaps no days of our childhood we lived so fully as those we believe we let slip by without having lived them, those we spent with a favorite book'].[8] Books were more than words on paper; the novels he had loved in childhood held the power to evoke the places in which he had first read them: 's'il nous arrive encore aujourd'hui de feuilleter ces livres d'autrefois, ce n'est pas que comme les seuls calendriers que nous ayons gardés des jours enfuis, et avec l'espoir de voir reflétés sur leurs pages les demeures et les étangs qui n'existent plus'(*CSB*, p.160) ['If we still happen today to leaf through those books of another time, it is for no other reason than that they are the only calendars we have kept of days that have vanished, and we hope to see reflected on their pages the dwellings and the ponds which no longer exist'].[9] The beginning of the preface, with its shifts in time and place, is an early sketch for the first paragraph of the *Search*, where the Narrator in bed, falling asleep while reading, is uncertain of where he is, who he is, and even what he is, since in his slumbering state he confuses his own identity with that of the book he is trying to read. The preface ends with another resurrection of the past. Readers of the preface cannot have known – nor could Proust himself – that they were being given a foretaste of Combray.

On New Year's Day, 1908, Mme Straus gave Proust five little notebooks from a smart stationery shop. Thanking her in a February letter, he indicated that he had a new project and was eager to 'settle down to a fairly long piece of work' (*Selected Letters* II, p.348).The first of these notebooks, known as *Le Carnet de 1908*, bears annotations for various projects that slowly converge and lead to the *Search*.[10] One episode, evoking childhood memories, shows his little brother Robert being forced to part with his pet kid. Robert was eventually written out of the story altogether and the lengthy scene reduced to twenty-five lines when the Narrator bids farewell to his beloved hawthorns at Combray (I, 143; I, 173–4/203–4). Other autobiographical elements are found here. The Narrator's mother, encouraging him to be brave while she is away, quotes inspiring passages about courage from Latin and French authors. For several years, Proust made entries in the notebook regarding topics and themes, lists of names that might serve for characters, and sensations: odours of rooms, bed sheets, grass, perfume, soap, food, capable of reviving the past. The *Carnet of 1908* served as a memo pad and, later, as an inventory of sections already written. As the 1908 text progressed from essay to fiction, the theme of homosexual love, nearly absent from *Jean Santeuil*, became a major topic. In the *Search* Proust analyses erotic love in heterosexual and homosexual couples, showing that the obsessions of desire and jealousy are the same and doomed to failure because they are based on illusions.

In July, Proust listed the six episodes he had written (*Le Carnet de 1908*, p.56). The first was 'Robert and the Kid', followed by 'the Villebon Way and the Méséglise Way'. The two place names, the first from a château near Illiers and the other from a nearby village, indicate he had found the 'two ways', one of the major unifying elements of the *Search*. Another key episode was the mother's goodnight kiss. The last episode on the list concludes the story: 'What I learned from the Villebon Way and the Méséglise Way'. Proust had conceived an apprentice novel, in which the neurotically dependent Narrator grows up to explore the two ways of his world – that of the landed gentry and Paris salons – fails to find happiness in erotic love, and explores the world of homosexuality. Proust's novel would be circular in time and space. As a child the Narrator believed the two ways led in different directions and must remain forever separated, but as an adult, he discovers the ways are joined by a circular path. Having completed his quest, the Protagonist understands, at last, the true nature of his experience, is fully endowed as a creative person and ready to write the ideal version of the story we have just read.

However, Proust's latest efforts to write a novel were again undermined by self-doubt. Overwhelmed by all that he wanted to say and his inability to shape and focus the material, he felt a sense of urgency: 'Warnings of death. Soon you will not be able to say all that.' Then Proust judged himself severely: 'Laziness or doubt or impotency taking refuge in the lack of certainty over the art form.' He was stymied by the same challenges regarding plot, genre, and structure that had made him abandon *Jean Santeuil*. He asked the questions left unanswered a decade earlier: 'Must I make of it a novel, a philosophical study, am I a novelist?' (*Le Carnet de 1908*, pp.60–1).

Before he felt confident that he had found his story, Proust made one more detour in pursuing his goal, this time by way of Sainte-Beuve. In late 1908,

Proust bought a quantity of school notebooks. By August 1909, he had written nearly 700 pages of an essay attacking the eminent critic's method and legacy. Some of these drafts anticipate the *Search*. By mid-December Proust found himself at an impasse. He wrote to Georges de Lauris and Anna de Noailles, whose literary judgement he trusted, and asked each to indicate the better of two ideas for attacking Sainte-Beuve:

> La chose s'est bâtie dans mon esprit de deux façons différentes . . . La première est l'essai classique, l'Essai de Taine en mille fois moins bien (sauf le contenu qui est je crois nouveau). La deuxième commence par un récit du matin . . . Maman vient me voir près de mon lit, je lui dis que j'ai l'idée d'une étude sur Sainte-Beuve, je la lui soumets et la lui développe.   (*Corr.* VIII, 320–1)

> [The idea has taken shape in my mind in two different ways . . . The first would be a classical essay, an essay in the manner of Taine, only a thousand times less good (except for the content which I think is new). The second begins with an account of a morning, my waking up and Mama coming to my bedside; I tell her I have an idea for a study of Sainte-Beuve; I submit it to her and develop it.]   (*Selected Letters* II, 416)

In drafts for the introduction to *Against Sainte-Beuve*, Proust wrote that his old cook 'offered me a cup of tea, a thing I never drink. And as chance would have, she brought me some slices of dry toast.' As soon as he dipped the toast in the tea and tasted it 'je ressentis un trouble, des odeurs de géraniums, d'orangers, une sensation d'extraordinaire lumière, de bonheur'. ['Something came over me – the smell of geraniums and orange-blossoms, a sensation of extraordinary radiance and happiness.'] He concentrated on the taste of the toast and tea 'qui semblait produire tant de merveilles, quand soudain les cloisons ébranlées de ma mémoire cédèrent, et ce furent les étés que je passais dans la maison de campagne . . . Alors je me rappelai . . .' (*CSB*, p.212) ['which seemed responsible for all these marvels; then suddenly the shaken partitions in my memory gave way, and into my conscious mind there rushed the summers I had spent in the . . . house in the country. And then I remembered'].[11]

In his critical remarks about Sainte-Beuve, Proust is writing as himself in a fictional situation, imagining a conversation with his mother. This invented setting for a real person (Proust) commenting on another real person and his work (Sainte-Beuve) served as the incubator for the emergence of the Narrator's full voice. In the *Sainte-Beuve* passages describing involuntary memory, Proust began to transmute his lived experience and his invented ones into the Narrator's life. We can see the transition from essayist to novelist in many notations from *Le Carnet de 1908*. A strange but remarkably fecund symbiosis is being created in which Proust is himself and not himself as the Narrator. Although highly autobiographical, the *Search* is a true novel. The Narrator, who resembles Proust in many ways, is different in others. Although remarkably well informed about homosexuality, he desires only women. His mother, unlike Jeanne Proust, is not Jewish nor is the hero's father a distinguished medical luminary. By the time he finished his novel, Proust would have created what is perhaps the richest narrative voice in literature, a voice that speaks both as child and as man, as actor and as subject, and that weaves effortlessly between the present, past and future.

While writing about his dilemma as an author, Proust had been tracing, without seeing it, the answer to the question that had tortured him for so long. The *Search* is about a man who cannot write and spends his life pursuing the wrong paths (lost time, wasted time), until at the very end, ill, discouraged, and growing old, he discovers that his vocation is to write the experience of his life – now that he understands it at last and can transpose it into a work of fiction. This moment of illumination is described in *Time Regained*:

> Alors, moins éclatante sans doute que celle qui m'avait fait apercevoir que l'œuvre d'art était le seul moyen de retrouver le Temps perdu, une nouvelle lumière se fit en moi. Et je compris que tous ces matériaux de l'œuvre littéraire, c'était ma vie passée; je compris qu'ils étaient venus à moi, dans les plaisirs frivoles, dans la paresse, dans la tendresse, dans la douleur, emmagasinés par moi, sans que je devinasse plus leur destination, leur survivance même, que la graine mettant en réserve tous les aliments qui nourriront la plante . . . je me trouvais avoir vécu pour elle sans le savoir, sans que ma vie me parût devoir entrer jamais en contact avec ces livres que j'aurais voulu écrire et pour lesquels, quand je me mettais autrefois à ma table, je ne trouvais pas de sujet. Ainsi toute ma vie jusqu'à ce jour aurait pu et n'aurait pas pu être résumée sous ce titre: Une vocation. (IV, 478)

> [And then a new light, less dazzling, no doubt, than that other illumination which had made me perceive that the work of art was the sole means of rediscovering Lost Time, shone suddenly within me. And I understood that all these materials for a work of literature were simply my past life, I understood that they had come to me, in frivolous pleasures, in indolence, in tenderness, in unhappiness, and that I had stored them up without divining the purpose for which they were destined or even their continued existence any more than a seed does when it forms within itself a reserve of all the nutritious substances from which it will feed a plant . . . I began to perceive that I had lived for the sake of the plant without knowing it, without ever realising that my life needed to come into contact with those books which I had wanted to write and for which, when in the past I had sat down at my table to begin, I had been unable to find a subject. And thus my whole life up to the present day might and yet might not have been summed up under the title: A Vocation.] (VI, 258–9/304)

In 1909, while vacationing at Cabourg, Proust wrote Mme Straus and told her: '. . . I've just begun – and finished – a whole long book' (*Selected Letters* II, 445–6). This 'whole long book' was the earliest draft of the *Search*, the opening section 'Combray', which establishes the major characters, locations, themes, and the conclusion, in which the Narrator understands the lessons from his apprenticeship. The most important word in the letter is 'finished'. Since the days when he struggled unsuccessfully to complete *Jean Santeuil*, Proust had never been able to finish any work of fiction because he lacked the story and point of view. He had at last found the ideal structure for his narrative skills. Proust never composed in a linear manner or according to an outline. He always worked like a mosaicist, taking a particular scene, anecdote, impression, image, and crafting it to completion. In his manuscripts, there are many notes to himself about such bits, 'To be placed somewhere', or, if a remark or trait, to give it to a certain character or perhaps to another. As he composed and orchestrated the rich Proustian music, the structure expanded to include the war years and the Albertine cycle, partly influenced by his love for the doomed chauffeur Alfred Agostinelli.

In the summer of 1911, Proust wrote René Gimpel, who had connections with the Japanese art world, to inquire if he knew

> le petit jeu japonais . . . qui consiste à mettre des petits papiers dans l'eau [lesquels] se contournent devenant des bonshommes etc. Pourriez-vous demander à des Japonais comment cela s'appelle, mais surtout si cela se fait quelquefois dans du *thé*, si cela se fait dans de l'eau indifféremment chaude ou froide, et dans les plus compliqués s'il peut y avoir des *maisons*, des *arbres*, *des personnages*, enfin quoi. (*Corr.* x, 321. Proust's emphasis.)

> [the little Japanese . . . game that consists in soaking little scraps of paper in water which then twist themselves round and turn into little men, etc. Could you ask someone Japanese what it's called, and especially whether it's sometimes done with *tea*, whether it's done with either hot or cold water, and in the more complicated ones whether there can be *houses*, *trees*, *persons*, or what have you.] (*Selected Letters* III, 43–4, and n. 1. Proust's emphasis.)

Proust had returned to the image of tea and toast (from the essay on Sainte-Beuve) for the passage on involuntary memory, adding the madeleine dipped in tea and expanding the metaphoric role of the Japanese pellets to explain this phenomenon that revived the past. He intended to place the scene in the Combray section where it is the first such episode. He was curious about the pellets' capacity to form houses and people because when the Narrator bites into the tea-soaked cake, the sensations that overwhelm him evoke the entire village from his lost youth:

Et comme dans ce jeu où les Japonais s'amusent à tremper dans un bol de porcelaine rempli d'eau, de petits morceaux de papier jusque-là indistincts qui, à peine y sont-ils plongés s'étirent, se contournent, se colorent, se différencient, deviennent des fleurs, des maisons, des personnages consistants et reconnaissables, de même maintenant toutes les fleurs de notre jardin et celles du parc de M. Swann, et les nymphéas de la Vivonne, et les bonnes gens du village et leurs petits logis et l'église et tout Combray et ses environs, tout cela qui prend forme et solidité, est sorti de ma tasse de thé. (I, 47)

[And as in the game wherein the Japanese amuse themselves by filling a porcelain bowl with water and steeping in it little pieces of paper which until then are without character or form, but, the moment they become wet, stretch and twist and take on colour and distinctive shape, become flowers or houses or people, solid and recognisable, so in that moment all the flowers in our garden and in M. Swann's park, and the water-lilies on the Vivonne and the good folk of the village and their little dwellings and the parish church and the whole of Combray and its surroundings, taking shape and solidity, sprang into being, town and gardens alike, from my cup of tea.] (I, 54–5/64)

The conclusion of the madeleine scene summarises the experience of involuntary memory, the means by which the Narrator can regain his past, whose elements he will, upon the discovery of his vocation, examine, comprehend, enrich and transpose into a work of art:

Quand d'un passé ancien rien ne subsiste, après la mort des êtres, après la destruction des choses, seules, plus frêles mais plus vivaces, plus immatérielles, plus persistantes, plus fidèles, l'odeur et la saveur restent encore longtemps, comme des âmes, à se rappeler, à attendre, à espérer, sur la ruine de tout le reste, à porter sans fléchir, sur leur gouttelette presque impalpable, l'édifice immense du souvenir. (I, 46)

[When from a long-distant past nothing subsists, after the people are dead, after the things are broken and scattered, taste and smell alone, more fragile but more enduring, more immaterial, more persistent, more faithful, remain poised a long time, like souls, remembering, waiting, hoping, amid the ruins of all the rest; and bear unflinchingly, in the tiny and almost impalpable drop of their essence, the vast structure of recollection.] (I, 54/63–4)

NOTES

1 See Denise Mayer, 'Le Jardin de Marcel Proust', *Cahiers Marcel Proust,* nouvelle série 12, *Études proustiennes* 5 (1984), 14.
2 In 1971, on the centennial of Proust's birth, Illiers officially changed its name to Illiers-Combray, in a brilliant public-relations initiative and unique example of reality yielding to fiction.
3 In a letter written after his mother's death, Proust recalled his 'childhood when

she would refuse to come back ten times and tell me goodnight before going out for the evening'. See *Corr.* VI, 28.

4 Marcel Proust, *Pleasures and Regrets*, trans. Louise Varese (New York: Crown, 1948), p.32.

5 *L'Indifférent*, introduced and edited by Philip Kolb (Paris: Gallimard, 1978), pp.42–3. By coincidence, the last sentence quoted contains two words that are the keys to the *Search*: loss and recapture.

6 Philip Kolb, 'Historique du premier roman de Proust', in *Saggi e ricerche di letteratura francese*, IV, 1963, 224.

7 *Jean Santeuil*, trans. Gerard Hopkins (New York: Simon and Schuster, 1956), p.408.

8 *On Reading Ruskin* (New Haven: Yale University Press, 1987), p.99. Translation slightly modified.

9 *On Reading Ruskin*, pp.99–100.

10 *Le Carnet de 1908* transcribed and edited by Philip Kolb, *Cahiers Marcel Proust*, nouvelle série 8, 1976.

11 See Marcel Proust, *On Art and Literature*, trans. Sylvia Townsend Warner and with an introduction by Terence Kilmartin (New York: Carroll and Graf, 1997), p.19. See also *Against Sainte-Beuve and Other Essays*, translated with an introduction and notes by John Sturrock (Harmondsworth: Penguin, 1988), pp.3–4.

3

DIANE R. LEONARD

Ruskin and the cathedral of lost souls

When Proust announced to Marie Nordlinger in December of 1899 that he had begun working on something different from what he usually did, dealing with Ruskin and certain cathedrals, he could scarcely have imagined upon what a long road he was embarking, or where it would lead him. Perhaps without realising it, he had closed the early period of his literary apprenticeship and begun a new era in which he would exercise his talents as a critic and translator, rather than as a creative writer. Before this second period was completed, Proust would publish two translations of Ruskin's works, and various articles and reviews about him. Though it might seem that this labour of erudition was a detour from his main path as a writer, and though he often chafed under the constraints it imposed on his creative imagination, it was in fact his Ruskin work that paradoxically led him to the discovery of a form for the narrative he was later to write, *A la recherche du temps perdu*.

Proust had made his literary début in 1893 with the publication of *Les Plaisirs et les jours*, a collection of texts that were largely traditional in form, cast in the classical and symbolist moulds he had inherited from his immediate literary predecessors. When he later embarked upon writing a novel, he again tried to shape it within the framework of conventional nineteenth-century forms, the autobiographical novel and the *Bildungsroman*, or novel of growth and self-discovery. It seems likely that the reason he never finished this narrative (published posthumously under the title *Jean Santeuil*) was his dissatisfaction with its structure. It was only after the years he spent working on his Ruskin translations and articles that he would take up again some of the autobiographical materials of this text and shape them into a new form, providing within the narrative itself the aesthetic theory which explained and justified it.

Both the theory and the form were inspired by the works of John Ruskin (1819–1900). At first glance, it may appear somewhat paradoxical that the ideas of an English writer on the visual arts should have such an impact on a young French novelist. Ruskin, however, was no ordinary 'art critic', but a towering literary figure who influenced the writers and thinkers of an entire generation, including those as distant as Tolstoy and Gandhi. Moreover, throughout his voluminous body of writings he elaborated a rich and complex theory of art, exploring the creative process, the nature, function and formation of the artist, and the social and spiritual context most conducive to artistic creation. Whether in his five-volume *Modern Painters* (1843–60) in defence of the English painter, J.M.W. Turner, or his three-volume *The Stones of Venice* (1851–3), a reading of Venetian history through its architecture, or even the social and economic studies he published in his later years, Ruskin's texts were primarily focused on art and the conditions through which it is nurtured. It is easy to see, then, why Proust felt drawn to this work, and how he might have come to believe that a period of 'apprenticeship' with Ruskin would help him become the artist he aspired to be.

The origins of Proust's interest in Ruskin are shrouded in obscurity. It is probable that he encountered his work through Paul Desjardins, his professor at the Ecole des Sciences Politiques whose *Bulletin de l'Union pour l'Action Morale* was the first to publish French translations of Ruskin's writings (brief extracts that began appearing in 1893). The earliest concrete information we have about Proust's Ruskin undertakings is provided by Marie Nordlinger, who has recorded that '. . . when I first met Marcel in Paris in the winter of 1896, in the home of my cousin Reynaldo Hahn, he had read everything by Ruskin that had been translated into French.'[1]

Ironically, it was Ruskin's death on 20 January 1900 that formed the occasion for Proust's first publication about him – a brief obituary that begins with the dramatic announcement, 'Ruskin est mort' ['Ruskin is dead'] (*CSB*, p.439). At the same time Proust revealed in a letter to Marie Nordlinger his belief in the continued life of Ruskin's spirit:

> . . . Mais quand j'ai appris la mort de Ruskin j'ai voulu exprimer à vous plutôt qu'à tout autre ma tristesse, tristesse saine d'ailleurs et bien pleine de consolation, car je sens combien c'est peu que la mort en voyant combien vit avec force ce mort, combien je l'admire, l'écoute, cherche à le comprendre et lui obéir plus qu'à bien des vivants . . .
> (*Corr.* II, 384)

> [. . . But when I learned of Ruskin's death I wished to express to you rather than to any other my sadness, a sadness which is however healthy and full of consolation, because I feel how insignificant death is in seeing with what force this dead man lives, how much I admire him, listen to him, seek to understand him and to obey him more than many of the living . . .][2]

In a second short essay, 'Pèlerinages ruskiniens en France' ['Ruskinian Pilgrimages in France'], Proust urges his fellow countrymen to honour

Ruskin's memory by making pilgrimages to the places '. . . qui gardent son âme . . . ' ['which retain his soul'] (*CSB*, p.441). In the same spirit, he characterises Ruskin's books as material vehicles that prolong the life of his ideas after the destruction of his 'cerveau périssable' ['perishable brain'] (*CSB*, p.443).

Though Ruskin's body had perished, his soul lived on, incarnated in the places he had loved and the works he had written. By visiting these places and reading his works, Proust believed, one might seek out Ruskin's soul; by writing about the places and translating his works, one might transmit his soul to others. It was in this spirit that Proust undertook both his own Ruskinian pilgrimages – to Amiens, Rouen and Venice – and his translations of *The Bible of Amiens* and *Sesame and Lilies*.

In two long essays Proust wrote on Ruskin in 1900, he set about trying to transmit Ruskin's 'soul' by conducting his readers on pilgrimages to the places Ruskin had loved. In 'Ruskin à Notre-Dame d'Amiens' (*CSB*, pp.69–105), he takes his readers to the cathedral that Ruskin had called 'The Bible of Amiens'. Ruskin had written his *Bible* in order to restore the lost language of figuralism in which the Gothic cathedral was inscribed, and which had been forgotten in his own time. Figuralism or typology – an exegetical method that was the dominant mode of interpretation throughout the Christian middle ages – held that the Bible must be read on four levels: literal, figural, moral and anagogical. On the latter three levels, the signs to be interpreted were not words, but the things which the words signified. These things were to be read as a kind of picture-language, a set of hieroglyphics whose meanings were disclosed through their visual forms. The cathedrals of the middle ages, too, had been inscribed in this picture-language of figuralism – what Ruskin called 'the language of every graven stone and every glowing window'.[3] In his book on Amiens, therefore, Ruskin gave lessons in how to 'read' its sculptures by presenting a kind of literary guided tour through the cathedral.

In his own essay on Amiens, Proust adopts Ruskin's metaphor of the Cathedral as a Bible, referring to it as '. . . une sorte de livre ouvert, écrit dans une langue solennelle où chaque caractère est une œuvre d'art . . .' (*CSB*, p.104) ['. . . a kind of open book, written in a solemn language where each character is a work of art . . .'] (p. 27).[4] In imitation of Ruskin, he gives lessons in how to 'read' the figural language of this cathedral/book, quoting frequently from Ruskin's text. At the same time, he follows another aspect of Ruskin's thought: his insistence on the necessity for the artist to render the 'truth of impression'. For Proust repeatedly weaves around Ruskin's text a record of his own impressions of the cathedral, thus re-inscribing it within a different sort of language of figures.

We can see an example of this re-inscription in Proust's lengthy discussion of the statue of the Vierge Dorée at the south portal of the cathedral. He begins by citing Ruskin's text:

> . . . And, coming quite up to the porch, everybody must like the pretty French Madonna in the middle of it, with her head a little aside, and her nimbus switched a little aside too, like a becoming bonnet. A Madonna in decadence she is, though, for all, or rather by reason of all, her prettiness, and her gay soubrette's smile . . .   (XXXIII, 128)

Proust transposes Ruskin's description into an account of his own impressions in approaching the cathedral. He begins by humanising the statue of the Virgin, whom he presents as yielding graciously to the sun's caresses. He then emphasises her persistence over thirty years in Ruskin's memory:

> Sans doute, si, – comme on l'a dit – à l'extrême vieillesse, la pensée déserta la tête de Ruskin . . . parmi les formes familières qui traversèrent encore la confuse rêverie du vieillard . . . tenez pour probable qu'il y eut la Vierge Dorée. Redevenue maternelle, comme le sculpteur d'Amiens l'a représentée, tenant dans ses bras la divine enfance, elle dut être comme la nourrice que laisse seule rester à son chevet celui qu'elle a longtemps bercé . . .   (CSB, p.84)

> [No doubt, if, as has been asserted, Ruskin's mind wandered in his extreme old age . . . among the familiar forms that still ran through the confused reverie of the aged man . . . the Vierge Dorée must surely have been present. Maternal again, as the sculptor of Amiens portrayed her, holding the divine child in her arms, she must have been like the nurse whom alone the one she rocked in the cradle for so long allows to remain at his bedside . . .]   (pp.14–15)

Thus Proust metamorphoses the Vierge Dorée into various human forms – from a flirtatious soubrette into a maternal figure, and finally into a nurse for the aged Ruskin. Her survival in Ruskin's memory through so many years is placed in stark contrast to the rapid degeneration of his physical being.

In the long meditation on the Vierge Dorée that follows, Proust transposes the decay attributed to the physical body of Ruskin into the crumbling of her statue at the cathedral door:

> . . . ces aubépines sculptées sont encore en fleurs. Mais ce printemps médiéval, si longtemps prolongé, ne sera pas éternel et le vent des siècles a déjà effeuillé devant l'église . . . quelques-unes de ses roses de pierre. Un jour sans doute aussi le sourire de la Vierge Dorée . . . cessera, par l'effritement des pierres qu'il écarte gracieusement . . .   (CSB, p.85)

> [. . . this sculpted hawthorn is still in bloom. But this medieval springtime, pro-longed for so long, will not be eternal, and the wind of the centuries has already stripped from the front of the church . . . some of its stone roses. One day, no

doubt, the smile of the Vierge Dorée . . . will also cease, because of the erosion
of the stones which it gracefully scatters . . .]   (pp.15–16)

Here Proust presents the same paradox of the survival of an artist's
thought despite the disintegration of the material in which it is expressed –
summed up in the oxymoron of the 'medieval springtime', and rendered
vivid in the image of the crumbling stone of the roses and of the Virgin's
smile.

Proust finds the 'gay soubrette's smile', which Ruskin had regarded as a
defect, to be a mark of the Virgin's individuality that allows him to love her
as a person. He links this individuality to her rootedness in a particular place,
and to the fact that she bears a name that is emphasised by being cried aloud
on the train taking him to the site where she is located. He associates the
Vierge Dorée's particularity with her condition as a physical rooted being,
worn away by the elements over time. It seems to be this very materiality
which makes her akin to him, makes of her a friend whose absence will evoke
sadness:

> . . . C'est une belle amie que nous devons laisser sur la place mélancolique de
> province d'où personne n'a pu réussir à l'emmener, et où, pour d'autres yeux
> que les nôtres, elle continuera à recevoir en pleine figure le vent et le soleil
> d'Amiens, à laisser les petits moineaux se poser avec un sûr instinct de la déco-
> ration au creux de sa main accueillante, ou picorer les étamines de pierre des
> aubépines antiques qui lui font depuis tant de siècles une parure jeune . . .
> (CSB, p.86)

> [. . . She is a beautiful friend we must leave at the melancholy provincial square
> from which no one has ever succeeded in taking her away, and where, for eyes
> other than ours, she will continue to receive directly on her face the wind and
> sun of Amiens and to let the little sparrows alight with a sure instinct of scenic
> effect in the hollow of her welcoming hand, or pick at the stone stamens of the
> antique hawthorn that has been her youthful attire for so many centuries . . .]
> (pp.16–17)

He concludes his reading of the statue by comparing her with the Mona Lisa:
in his bedroom, he says, a photograph of the latter keeps only the beauty of
a masterpiece, while the photo of the Vierge Dorée has 'la mélancolie d'un
souvenir' (CSB, p.86).

Thus Proust has woven together his impressions of the statue's distinctive
smile, of her fixed location in the geographical region from which her stone
was cut, of her being named like a person, of her existence as a physical
entity subject to the erosion of time – all of which result in her making a
claim on his emotions and therefore on his memory, as she had on Ruskin's.
By 'reading' the Vierge Dorée in light of the impressions she made on him

during his pilgrimages, he has transformed her statue into a character in a brief narrative, as well as a figure for the survival of the artist's thought.

In his second long essay of 1900, 'John Ruskin' (*CSB*, pp.105–41), Proust tells of another pilgrimage he had made, this time to the Cathedral of Rouen to see a small carving Ruskin described in *The Seven Lamps of Architecture*. Ruskin had pointed out the carving as representative of the vitality of medieval architecture, and had illustrated his text with a drawing of it. Proust cites Ruskin's passage on this 'petite figure':

> . . . the fellow is vexed and puzzled in his malice; and his hand is pressed hard on his cheek bone, and the flesh of the cheek is *wrinkled* under the eye by the pressure . . . considering it as a mere filling of an interstice on the outside of a cathedral gate, and as one of more than three hundred . . . it proves very noble vitality in the art of the time. (VIII, 217)

As he had done with the Vierge Dorée, Proust elaborates these few lines into a narrative of several pages, weaving around the small kernel of Ruskin's text intricate layerings of his own impressions. He begins by explaining the reason for his pilgrimage:

> . . . j'allai à Rouen comme obéissant à une pensée testamentaire, et comme si Ruskin en mourant avait en quelque sorte confié à ses lecteurs la pauvre créature à qui il avait en parlant d'elle rendu la vie et qui venait, sans le savoir, de perdre à tout jamais celui qui avait fait autant pour elle que son premier sculpteur . . . (*CSB*, p.125)

> [. . . I went to Rouen, as if obeying a dying wish, and as if Ruskin, upon dying, had in some way entrusted to his readers the poor creature to which he had given life again by speaking of it, and which, unknowingly, had just lost forever the person who had done for it as much as its first sculptor . . .] (p.45)

He tells the story of his search for the carving, recounting his difficulty in identifying the tiny figure among the crowd of sculptures on the cathedral portal, followed by his delight as his companion recognises it. He then presents the figure in a different context than Ruskin had given it, a context shaped by his concern with Ruskin's death:

> . . . L'artiste mort depuis des siècles a laissé là, entre des milliers d'autres, cette petite personne qui meurt un peu chaque jour, et qui était morte depuis bien longtemps, perdue au milieu de la foule des autres, à jamais . . . (*CSB*, p.125)

> [. . . The artist, who died centuries ago, left there, among thousands of others, this little person who dies a little more each day, and has been dead for a really long time, forever lost in the midst of the crowd . . .] (p.45)

Proust then introduces Ruskin as an actor in this story: inspired by the sight of a sculpted scene above the portal depicting the Last Judgment, he assimilates Ruskin to the image of the archangel who resurrects the dead, and the little figure to one of the saved who re-assumes bodily form:

> . . . Tel qu'au jour du Jugement, qui non loin de là est figuré, il fait entendre en ses paroles comme la trompette de l'archange et il dit: 'Ceux qui ont vécu vivront, la matière n'est rien.' Et, en effet, telle que les morts que non loin le tympan figure, réveillés à la trompette de l'archange, soulevés, ayant repris leur forme, reconnaissables, vivants, voici que la petite figure a revécu et retrouvé son regard . . . (*CSB*, p.126)

> [. . . As on the Day of Judgment, which is represented near by, his words resound like the archangel's trumpet, and he says, 'Those who have lived will live, matter is nothing.' And, in fact, like the dead whom, not far away, the tympanum represents awakening at the sound of the archangel's trumpet, arising, having recovered their forms, recognizable, alive, the figurine is now alive again and has recovered its look . . .] (p.46)

In noticing and pointing out the little figure, Ruskin had resurrected the soul of its dead sculptor, had 'reincarnated' it by taking it into his own consciousness. By writing about the figure and drawing it, he had transmitted the sculptor's soul to his readers. In finding the little figure in his turn, Proust implies, he himself is resurrecting Ruskin:

> . . . J'ai été touché en la retrouvant là, et, en effet, rien ne meurt de ce qui a vécu, pas plus la pensée du sculpteur que la pensée de Ruskin. (*CSB*, p.126)

> [. . . I was touched on finding [it] there again; nothing therefore dies that has survived, no more the sculptor's thought than Ruskin's thought.] (p.46)

Thus Proust makes of this preservation and transmission of the artist's soul through art a figure of the Christian concept of death and resurrection: the artist's soul 'dies' when his work falls into oblivion, but is 'resurrected' when it is again held in human consciousness, and thus given a new 'reincarnation'.

These texts on the little figure and the Vierge Dorée prefigure Proust's meditations on the resurrective power of memory and art in the *Recherche*, and elements from each of them would later re-appear there. For in addition to transmitting Ruskin's soul through these essays, Proust was also in the process of discovering new narrative possibilities. By weaving his brief stories around these sculptures, he had not only resurrected Ruskin, but had also taken the first steps towards creating his own cathedral-novel.

The Bible of Amiens

Proust's translations of Ruskin's texts were another means through which he sought to transmit Ruskin's soul. He explains his belief in this sort of transmission in a letter he wrote to Georges Goyau in 1904, thanking him for his review of *La Bible d'Amiens*, which had recently appeared:

> Vous savez quelle admiration j'ai pour Ruskin. Et comme je crois que chacun de nous a charge des âmes qu'il aime particulièrement, charge de les faire connaître et aimer, de leur éviter le froissement des malentendus et la nuit, l'obscurité comme on dit, de l'oubli, vous savez de quelles mains – scrupuleuses – mais pieuses aussi et aussi douces que j'ai pu – j'ai touché à celle-là . . .
>
> (*Corr.* IV, 399)

> [You know what admiration I have for Ruskin. And since I believe that each of us has charge of the souls that he particularly loves, charge of making them known and loved, of avoiding for them the slights of misunderstandings, and the night, the obscurity as they say, of oblivion, you know with what hands – scrupulous – but pious also and as gently as I could – I have touched that soul . . .]

There could be no doubt that Proust was scrupulously painstaking in his translation. Since he did not know English very well, at least at the outset of his work, and since Ruskin's prose in *The Bible of Amiens* is often complex and idiosyncratic, he availed himself of the assistance of various people: his mother, who apparently made rough drafts of passages to serve as his point of departure; Marie Nordlinger, who was his chief consultant for the subtleties of English meanings; and also Reynaldo Hahn, Antoine Bibesco, Robert d'Humières and Douglas Ainslie, among others. Yet despite this daunting array of helpers, it is clear that Proust laboured over every word of the translation himself, as he insisted in a 1903 letter to Constantin de Brancovan:

> . . . depuis quatre ans que je travaille sur la *Bible d'Amiens* je la sais entière-ment par cœur et elle a pris pour moi ce degré d'assimilation complète, de transparence absolue, où se voient seulement les nébuleuses qui tiennent non à l'insuffisance de notre regard, mais à l'irréductible obscurité de la pensée con-templée . . . Je ne prétends pas savoir l'anglais. Je prétends savoir Ruskin . . .
>
> (*Corr.* III, 220–1)

> [. . . during the four years that I have worked on *The Bible of Amiens* I have learned it entirely by heart and it has taken on for me that degree of complete assimilation, of absolute transparence, in which only those mists are seen which arise, not from the inadequacy of our sight, but from the irreducible obscurity of the thought contemplated . . . I do not claim to know English. I claim to know Ruskin . . .]

In fact, Proust's knowledge of English and of Ruskin grew rapidly during this period. For he was not only translating *The Bible of Amiens*, but also annotating it with relevant passages from other Ruskin texts. Thus he must have read widely in Ruskin's work in English, since very little of it had been translated into French. Indeed, Proust's copious footnotes demonstrate clearly that he had first-hand knowledge of the English texts of virtually all of Ruskin's major works, since he himself had translated most of the passages cited.[5] In the 'Avant-Propos' to his preface, he explains that these abundant annotations were intended to furnish a kind of 'sounding board' for the reader, in which a given idea in *The Bible of Amiens* would reverberate through all the other Ruskin works in which it appeared – yet another means of transmitting Ruskin's soul.

In addition to the 'Avant-Propos', the preface consisted of Proust's 1900 essays, 'John Ruskin' and 'Ruskin à Notre-Dame d'Amiens', along with a 'Post-Scriptum' written in 1903. In the 'Post-Scriptum', Proust gives a brief record of another of his Ruskinian pilgrimages of 1900, the one he made to Venice. Here he presents a different version of reading a cathedral when he describes his own reactions to reading Ruskin's *The Stones of Venice* inside St Mark's Church:

> . . . l'émotion que j'éprouvais à lire là cette page . . . était très grande et n'était pourtant peut-être pas très pure. Comme la joie de voir les belles figures mystérieuses s'augmentait, mais s'altérait du plaisir en quelque sorte d'érudition que j'éprouvais à comprendre les textes apparus en lettres byzantines à coté de leurs fronts nimbés, de même la beauté des images de Ruskin était avivée et corrompue par l'orgueil de se référer au texte sacré. . . .   (CSB, p.133)

> [. . . the emotion I felt, as I was reading this page . . . was great, and yet perhaps not very pure. In the same manner as the joy of seeing the beautiful, mysterious figures increased, but was altered in some way by the pleasure of erudition that I experienced upon understanding the text that . . . appeared in Byzantine letters around their haloed brows, so in the same way the beauty of Ruskin's images was intensified and corrupted by the pride of referring to the sacred text . . .]   (p.53)

This text occurs within a passage in which Proust accuses Ruskin of idolatry. He illustrates that idolatry by placing the images of the mosaics inside St Mark's in opposition to the Byzantine inscriptions accompanying them. He thus implicitly contrasts St Mark's with the Cathedral of Amiens: in the Gothic cathedral, there was no explanatory text, but only the 'language of every graven stone and every glowing window'; in the Byzantine church, by contrast, the figures in the mosaics are identified by labels bearing their names and their stories, thus diverting the spectator's attention away from reading the figures towards deciphering the letters. Proust points out a similar problem in *The Stones of Venice*, where he finds that the beauty of Ruskin's images is corrupted by the didactic effect of the Biblical citations accompanying them. In both cases, the distracting presence of the explanatory text hinders the readers or spectators from reading the images.

Ironically, Proust himself is in a similar situation here: despite the fact that he is reading inside St Mark's, he is reading the text of Ruskin, rather than the figural language of the mosaics. Moreover, the inscriptions on the mosaics prevent him from having that innocence of the eye indispensable to the truth of impression. He thus is staging a conflict that takes place within himself: his struggle to wrest his impressions free from the erudition he has gained through reading Ruskin. Proust is not rejecting Ruskin here through his charge of idolatry: rather, he is rejecting the exegetical side of Ruskin's thought in order to follow its artistic side. In other words, he is renouncing his own role as exegete in order to become an artist.

Sesame and Lilies

In the preface to his second Ruskin translation, *Sésame et les lys*,[6] Proust presents a text on Venice from which he has erased all Ruskinian inscriptions. Instead of describing St Mark's Church, he concludes his essay with a text on the Piazzetta columns entirely composed of his impressions:

> . . . belles étrangères venues d'Orient sur la mer qu'elles regardent au loin et qui vient mourir à leurs pieds, et qui toutes deux, sans comprendre les propos échangés autour d'elles dans une langue qui n'est pas celle de leur pays, sur cette place publique où brille encore leur sourire distrait, continuent à attarder au milieu de nous leurs jours du XIIe siècle qu'elles intercalent dans notre aujourd'hui . . .
> (*Sésame*, p.57)

> [. . . beautiful strangers come from the Orient over the sea at which they gaze in the distance and which comes to die at their feet, and who both, without understanding the conversations going on around them in a language which is not that of their country, on this public square where their heedless smile still shines, keep on prolonging in our midst their days of the twelfth century, which they interpose in our today . . .]
> (p.128)

Ruskin had presented these columns at great length in *St Mark's Rest*, which Proust had read during his Venetian pilgrimage. Here, however, Proust does not mention Ruskin's name, nor does he give citations from his book, as he had done in his 1900 essays. Rather, he concentrates on describing his own impressions, and leaves it to the reader who knows the works of Ruskin to identify the text. He thus puts into practice an idea that Ruskin himself had elaborated in *Sesame and Lilies*:

> . . . And be sure also, if the author is worth anything, that you will not get at his meaning all at once . . . Not that he does not say what he means, and in strong words too; but he cannot say it all; and what is more strange, *will* not, but in a hidden way and in parables . . . I cannot quite see the reason of this,

nor analyse that cruel reticence in the breasts of wise men which makes them always hide their deeper thought. They do not give it you by way of help, but of reward; and will make themselves sure that you deserve it before they allow you to reach it . . . (XVIII, 63–4)

Apparently Proust was struck by this passage, for he comments on it in a footnote, observing that a beautiful book is characterised by '. . . sa noble atmosphère de silence, ce merveilleux vernis qui brille du sacrifice de tout ce qu'on n'a pas dit . . . '(*Sésame*, p.85, n.1) ['. . . its noble atmosphere of silence, that marvellous varnish which shines with the sacrifice of all that has not been said . . .'] (p.153).

By not mentioning Ruskin in his description of the columns, Proust has followed his counsel to conceal the meaning of his text in order to render it more difficult of access. Instead of giving us an inscription bearing Ruskin's name, he has presented us with a figure of him. Anonymous, Ruskin penetrates his text like the Piazzetta columns penetrate the present. Like them, he is 'un étranger', speaking a language which is not that of this country, or even of this time, the lost language of figures. The columns serve to mark the space in the text where Ruskin exists. Their silence is the silence of his absence, the silence that makes the text shine with the sacrifice of all that has not been said.

Ruskin in the 'Recherche'

During the period of his Ruskin translations, Proust had found the conception of narrative structure which he was seeking. In *The Bible of Amiens*, he had encountered the idea of reading a cathedral like a book – therefore, why could not he, as a writer, create a book that could be read as a cathedral? He had amused himself by sketching for Reynaldo Hahn humorous drawings of stained-glass windows and cathedral statues depicting Reynaldo and himself as characters in brief narrative situations.[7] It was only a short step from that point to conceiving of a 'cathedral-novel' – a narrative constructed like a cathedral, inscribed in a figural picture-language.

On the other hand, he had discovered in *Sesame* the idea of presenting his text 'in a hidden way and in parables'. Perhaps it was for this reason that he decided to delete explicit references to his cathedral-novel in the *Recherche*, as he reveals in a 1919 letter to Jean de Gaigneron:

> . . . vous ne lisez pas seulement le livre imprimé que j'ai publié, mais le livre inconnu que j'aurais voulu écrire. Et quand vous me parlez de cathédrales, je ne peux pas ne pas être ému d'une intuition qui vous permet de deviner ce que je n'ai jamais dit à personne et que j'écris ici pour la première fois: c'est que j'avais voulu donner à chaque partie de mon livre le titre: Porche I, Vitraux de l'abside etc. . . J'ai renoncé tout de suite à ces titres d'architecture parce que je

les trouvais trop prétentieux mais je suis touché que vous les retrouviez par une sorte de divination de l'intelligence.   (*Corr.* XVIII, 359)

[. . . you read not only the printed book that I have published, but also the unknown book that I would have wished to write. And when you speak to me of cathedrals, I can't help but be moved by your intuition that permits you to divine what I have never said to anyone and am writing here for the first time: that I wished to give to each part of my book the title: Porch I, Stained-Glass Windows of the apse, etc. . . I immediately gave up these architectural titles because I found them too pretentious, but I am touched that you discovered them by a sort of divination of the intellect.]

These architectural titles were not the only features of his text that Proust deleted: early manuscript versions of the *Recherche* show that he also removed various references to Ruskin.[8] These references cluster especially within the segments on the trip to Balbec (in early drafts a Ruskinian pilgrimage to Amiens) and the section on Venice (another explicitly Ruskinian pilgrimage). Though the reader can still perceive faint traces of the original outlines of these materials, the deletion of Ruskin references in the final version serves to throw a veil over the initial conception, leaving it up to the reader to discover Ruskin's presence there.

Among the Ruskin materials thus veiled in the *Recherche* are the 'petite figure' and the Vierge Dorée. The 1900 text on the little figure, for example, re-appears in the guise of the petite madeleine scene in 'Combray'. After remarking that his past is virtually dead for him, the Narrator asks, 'Dead forever?' and then makes the following reflection:

Je trouve très raisonnable la croyance celtique que les âmes de ceux que nous avons perdus sont captives dans quelque être inférieur, dans une bête, un végétal, une chose inanimée, perdues en effet pour nous jusqu'au jour, qui pour beaucoup ne vient jamais, où nous nous trouvons passer près de l'arbre, entrer en possession de l'objet qui est leur prison. Alors elles tressaillent, nous appellent, et sitôt que nous les avons reconnues, l'enchantement est brisé. Délivrées par nous, elles ont vaincu la mort et reviennent vivre avec nous.   (I, 43–4)

[I feel that there is much to be said for the Celtic belief that the souls of those whom we have lost are held captive in some inferior being, in an animal, in a plant, in some inanimate object, and thus effectively lost to us until the day (which to many never comes) when we happen to pass by the tree or to obtain possession of the object which forms their prison. Then they start and tremble, they call us by our name, and as soon as we have recognised their voice the spell is broken. Delivered by us, they have overcome death and return to share our life.]   (I, 50–1/59)

Just as the soul of the medieval sculptor, incarnated in the little figure, is lost until the figure is recognised and brought to life in someone's consciousness, so the soul of the Narrator's past is lost to him until he finds the object in which it is incarnated and identifies it, raising it from the dead by bringing it back to life in his memory.

This passage, of course, serves as a prelude to the resurrection of Combray in the Narrator's consciousness. After tasting the madeleine soaked in tea, the Narrator goes through an arduous struggle, searching deep within his memory to identify the visual image connected to the taste. And suddenly he finds the 'petite figure' carved within the cathedral of his mind, lost there among so many other figures inscribed by his past impressions: it is that scallop-shell figure of the petite madeleine that Tante Léonie used to dip in her tea for him on Sunday mornings. The shape of the madeleine is itself suggestive, moulded as it is in the form of a 'coquille de Saint-Jacques' (scallop-shell). For Saint-Jacques is the patron saint of pilgrims, and who is to say whether Proust may not have thus encoded in his text an oblique reference to another pilgrimage he had made – to Rouen, in search of a different little figure, equally lost?

The Vierge Dorée re-appears in the *Recherche* as the statue of the Virgin on the porch of Balbec Church (originally the Cathedral of Amiens). In the Balbec episode, however, she undergoes an ironic metamorphosis, for the Narrator finds her disguised as a little old woman in stone, '. . . soumise à la tyrannie du Particulier . . .' (II, 20) ['. . . subjected to the tyranny of the Particular . . .' II, 274/324]. Thus the particularity which Proust had shown to be the basis for the Vierge Dorée's survival in memory is seen as a negative attribute by this youthful Narrator, who has not yet learned to 'read' the sculptures of a cathedral. It is only later, when Elstir deciphers the figures of Balbec Church for him *à la* Ruskin, that he will discover its lost language.

The outlines of the Vierge Dorée may also be seen to underly the whole theme of the reversibility of characters and statues in the *Recherche*. Just as she was transfigured from statue to human in Proust's essay, so in the narrative various characters are hardened into stone, becoming sculptural. This theme begins in 'Combray' with the description of Tante Léonie in terms suggestive of a statue: '. . . Elle tendait à mes lèvres son triste front pâle et fade . . . où les vertèbres transparaissaient comme les pointes d'une couronne d'épines . . .' (I, 51–2) ['. . . She would hold out for me to kiss her sad, pale, lacklustre forehead . . . through which the bones shone like the points of a crown of thorns . . .' I, 61/71]. The Narrator describes Françoise a few lines later as '. . . immobile et debout dans l'encadrement de la petite porte du corridor comme une statue de sainte dans sa niche . . .' (I, 52) ['. . . motionless and erect, framed in the small doorway of the corridor like the statue of a saint in its niche . . .' I, 61/71].

The description of the church of Saint-André-des-Champs seems designed specifically to draw the reader's attention to this theme of the reversibility of statues and characters. Not only does the statue of a saint on its porch resemble the peasant-girls of the countryside, but the Narrator recognises among its Gothic sculptures the visage of young Théodore:

> . . . comme si les visages de pierre sculptée, grisâtres et nus, ainsi que sont les bois en hiver, n'étaient qu'un ensommeillement, qu'une réserve, prête à refleurir dans la vie en innombrables visages populaires, révérends et futés comme celui de Théodore, enluminés de la rougeur d'une pomme mûre . . .   (I, 149)

> [. . . as though those carved stone faces, naked and grey as trees in winter, were, like them, asleep only, storing up life and waiting to flower again in countless plebeian faces, reverent and cunning as the face of Théodore, and glowing with the ruddy brilliance of ripe apples.]   (I, 181/213)

Here the sculpted stone faces, 'grisâtres et nus', echo the stone visage of the little figure, and, like his, are only 'ensommeillés', holding in reserve the souls that are ready to re-flower.

All of these sculpturesque characters prefigure the crowd of crumbling stone statues into which the aged characters have metamorphosed when the Narrator encounters them many years later at the 'matinée' of the Princesse de Guermantes in the final volume. Thus the lineaments of the cathedral-novel, traced in filigree in the opening sections of the *Recherche*, are brought into clearer focus at the end, as the statue-like aspect of its characters is foregrounded: they have hardened into stone during the ageing process, and their sculptural features are now eroded by time, like the crumbling smile of the Vierge Dorée.

At the same time that the outlines of the cathedral-novel are sharpened, the aesthetic theory that informs it is unveiled. When the Narrator enters the Guermantes' courtyard and stumbles on the uneven paving stones, he finds at once both the 'Open Sesame' to his treasury of memories and the key to the construction of his narrative. As he waits in the Guermantes' library to enter the party, he meditates on the conception of his work, the main themes of which are Ruskinian: impressions are imprinted in 'figures' on the mind of the Narrator, where they are stratified in layers in his memory and, being 'lost' to consciousness, must be 'found' and 'resurrected' by his involuntary memory, then identified and 'translated' by his intelligence. Proust has thus combined Ruskin's insistence on the priority of the 'truth of impression' with his discussions of reading the 'lost language' of figures. But he has interiorised this figural language to make it part of an inner cathedral of the mind, built up over time by the layered inscriptions of the years.

Proust's cathedral-novel itself functions in the same manner: by laying down impressions in the reader's mind – magic-lantern projections on the walls of his consciousness – which become layered in memory in a vertical 'fourth dimension' where they co-exist simultaneously, like the stratifications of different centuries in the Church of Combray. Thus the narrative's 'architecture' is built up from the fugitive and ethereal impressions projected successively by the text as we read, just as the notes of the Vinteuil sonata, liquid and ceaselessly overlapping, harden in Swann's memory:

> . . . Ainsi à peine la sensation délicieuse que Swann avait ressentie était-elle expirée, que sa mémoire lui en avait fourni séance tenante une transcription sommaire et provisoire . . . Il . . . avait devant lui cette chose qui n'est plus de la musique pure, qui est du dessin, de l'architecture, de la pensée . . . (1, 206)

> [. . . And so, scarcely had the exquisite sensation which Swann had experienced died away, before his memory had furnished him with an immediate transcript . . . He . . . had before him something that was no longer pure music, but rather design, architecture, thought . . .] (1, 251/295–6)

Similarly, Proust's narrative, which we encounter during our reading experience as a sequence of transitory and flowing impressions, becomes design, architecture, thought in our memory – taking on shape and solidity, like the towns and gardens of Combray that spring into being from the Narrator's cup of tea.

From the moment that the Narrator enters the Guermantes' courtyard in the final episode, disparate elements of the text begin to coalesce into a subtle suggestion of a cathedral: the uneven paving stones form the floor, the projections of Time's magic lantern serve as the stained-glass windows, the characters sculpted and eroded by time are the statues, and the Narrator (the bell ringing in his ears) forms the steeple. For the Narrator finds that he has become taller than a church steeple, touching simultaneously many distant epochs in that inconceivable fourth dimension of Time. The Church of Combray has travelled through the ages of the text to become the fourth-dimensional cathedral-novel of the *Recherche* itself.

When we make our pilgrimages through Proust's cathedral, however, we will not find Ruskin among these statues, just as Proust, on his pilgrimage to the Cathedral of Amiens, could not find his statue on the porch:

> . . . Et maintenant nous avons beau nous arrêter devant les statues d'Isaïe, de Jérémie[,] d'Ezéchiel et de Daniel . . . il y . . . a un [prophète] de plus qui n'est pas ici et dont pourtant nous ne pouvons pas dire qu'il est absent, car nous l'y voyons partout. C'est Ruskin: si sa statue n'est pas à la porte de la cathédrale, elle est à l'entrée de notre cœur . . . (CSB, p.105)

[. . . And now we stop in vain before the statues of Isaiah, Jeremiah, Ezekiel and Daniel . . . there is one more [prophet] who is not here and of whom, moreover, we cannot say that he is absent, for we see him everywhere. It is Ruskin: if his statue is not at the cathedral door, it is at the entrance to our heart . . .] (p.28)

Ruskin was nowhere in the Cathedral of Amiens because he was everywhere, his soul infusing all the sculptures he had described. In the same way, Ruskin's 'soul' lives on in the *Recherche* through various reincarnations of the figures he had loved, though he himself is virtually absent there. It is we who must recognise these veiled figures, by reading them through the lenses of Ruskin's works. When we have called them by their names, their enchantment will be broken, and they will be delivered from their captivity in the text. Then the vast cathedral that they ornament may take on shape and solidity in our consciousness, its crumbling stones sculpted with a multitude of expressive faces in which Ruskin's thought is incarnated. Ruskin had to remain 'perdu' in the *Recherche* in order that his soul might be 'retrouvée': only thus could he dwell at the entrance to our hearts.

NOTES

1 Marie Nordlinger-Riefstahl, 'Proust and Ruskin', in *Marcel Proust: An Exhibition of Manuscripts, Books, Pictures and Photographs* (Manchester: Whitworth Art Gallery, 1956), pp.5–6.

2 All translations of Proust's letters are my own.

3 *The Works of John Ruskin*, edited by E.T. Cook and Alexander Wedderburn (London: George Allen, 1903–12), XXXIII, 170. All references to Ruskin's texts are to this edition.

4 *On Reading Ruskin* translated and edited by Jean Autret, William Burford, and Phillip J. Wolfe (New Haven: Yale University Press, 1987). All page numbers appearing in parentheses following English translations of Proust's essays refer to this text.

5 Jean Autret concludes that Proust's notes to *La Bible d'Amiens* show he had read at least as many as twenty-three Ruskin texts in the original – including such large and complex works as *Modern Painters*, *The Stones of Venice*, *Praeterita*, and *Fors Clavigera*, and that most of the passages he cites from them had not appeared before in French. See Jean Autret, *L'Influence de Ruskin sur la vie, les idées et l'œuvre de Marcel Proust* (Geneva: Droz, 1955), pp.57–8.

6 *Sésame et les lys. Des trésors des rois. Des jardins des reines.* (Paris: Mercure de France, 1906).

7 Some of these sketches are reproduced in Marcel Proust, *Lettres à Reynaldo Hahn*, présentées, datées et annotées par Philip Kolb (Paris: Gallimard, 1956).

8 See Jo Yoshida, 'Proust contre Ruskin: la genèse de deux voyages dans la *Recherche* d'après des brouillons inédits', dissertation, Université de Paris IV, 1978. 2 vols.

4

MARION SCHMID

The birth and development of *A la recherche du temps perdu*

Of the many areas of Proust scholarship, the one that has probably most enriched our knowledge of *A la recherche du temps perdu* consists of the wealth of genetic and textual studies on the novel carried out over the past thirty years.[1] It now seems generally agreed that the long history of the novel's conception, elaboration and publication is not only fascinating and rewarding in its own right, but also enlightens our understanding and appreciation of Proust's work, giving a glimpse into the mind of one of the great masters of modern writing. In this chapter, I will outline the various compositional stages the novel underwent in the fourteen years of its development between January 1908, when Proust began to jot down ideas for a new fictional project, and November 1922, when – already terminally ill – he envisaged a highly controversial reorganisation of the novel's penultimate volume, *Albertine disparue*.

From 'Contre Sainte-Beuve' to the novel of remembrance (1908–1909)

The year 1908 is generally considered as the starting point for the *Recherche*. Proust is thirty-six years old and virtually unknown as a writer. He has published a collection of short stories, portraits and poems, *Les Plaisirs et les jours* (1896), two annotated translations of Ruskin, *La Bible d'Amiens* (1904) and *Sésame et les lys* (1906), as well as a series of articles and reviews, but has produced no fiction since 1899, when he abandoned his novel *Jean Santeuil*. We do not know precisely what made him return to novelistic writing in the early months of 1908. What is certain, however, is that, from January onwards, he was firmly embarked upon a new project, which, together with a series of literary pastiches, was to occupy him until the summer. Drafts for this period have been lost, but, if we are to believe Bernard de Fallois, the first editor (1954) of *Contre Sainte-Beuve*, there used to be seventy-five manuscript folios comprising six major episodes, all of which were taken up in the later *Recherche*. They contained a description of

Venice, a stay at the seaside, an encounter with a number of young girls, the traumatic bedtime at Combray, the poetic nature of names, and even the two 'ways' (later called 'le côté de Méséglise' and 'le côté de Guermantes') which, in the published novel, symbolise the social division between the bourgeoisie and the aristocracy (see *CSB*, p.14).[2] Fallois has included two extracts from the lost drafts, 'Robert et le chevreau' ['Robert and the young goat'] and 'Les hortensias normands' ['The Norman hydrangeas'] in his *Contre Sainte-Beuve*. In addition, we have a progress report, which largely corresponds to his description of the seventy-five folios, drawn up by Proust himself in a little notebook known as *Carnet 1* or *Carnet de 1908*, a document that is very closely linked to the genesis of the *Recherche*. It contains numerous notes for the unnamed novel on which Proust was working that year, including a brief plan for a second part which already encapsulates the central theme of *La Prisonnière*: 'Dans la 2e partie du roman la jeune fille sera ruinée, je l'entretiendrai sans chercher à la posséder par impuissance du bonheur' (*Carnet de 1908*, p.49) ['In the second part of the novel, the young girl is ruined: I shall support her, but won't seek to possess her, because happiness is impossible'].[3] What needs to be remembered, then, is that in the first few months of 1908 Proust was working on a novelistic project which already strongly anticipated the future *Recherche*. In so far as we are aware, however, the drafts for this project did not yet form a continuous text, nor was there any developed plan or framework which would have allowed Proust to eventually draw them together into a coherent narrative.

The novel sketched out between January and July 1908 seems to have faltered during the course of the summer. By the autumn, Proust turned his attention to another project which, as we know from his correspondence, had interested him at least since spring: an essay against the critic Sainte-Beuve.[4] He initially hesitated between a traditional essay and a dialogue between a first-person narrator and his mother which was to combine literary criticism with narration proper. The Sainte-Beuve project in the form of a dialogue is outlined on a set of loose sheets, catalogued as *Proust 45* by the Bibliothèque Nationale, and in a number of drafts in *Carnet 1*. It was developed in a series of ten draft notebooks, the so-called *Cahiers Contre Sainte-Beuve*, written between the end of 1908 and spring 1909. These *Cahiers* are the most important documents that remain of the novel's early genesis. It is in them that the planned essay against Sainte-Beuve was gradually transformed into the novel of remembrance and that one can trace the actual 'birth' of the *Recherche*.

Let us clarify from the outset that the *Cahiers Contre Sainte-Beuve* did at no time form a coherent, linear text, despite the misleading impression given by the two editions to date: Bernard de Fallois' *Contre Sainte-Beuve* of 1954, and Pierre Clarac and Yves Sandre's of 1971. Neither is there a continuous version of the *Sainte-Beuve* in the form of a narrative (the version that Fallois has artificially put together) nor in the form of a traditional essay (Clarac and Sandre's version). The ten notebooks contain narrative as well as theoretical parts, none of which build into an organised whole. Proust (and this is particularly surprising given the scale of his writing), apparently worked without any precise plan in mind. He characteristically began a project by jotting down short fragments of text, which at first seem to have little or no connection, but which already show a distinct concern for style and expression reflected in the numerous deletions and revisions that characterise his manuscripts. His creative approach was essentially thematic: he worked around an idea, character, or place, giving little attention to chronology and plot; only at a later stage, when he had a clearer vision of his project, did he assemble hitherto disparate fragments into a more coherent sequence by means of a sophisticated 'cut and paste' technique not dissimilar to the 'montage' used by modern film makers. His method thus combines a considerable amount of heuristic exploration in the first stages of the genesis, when the text is allowed to develop more or less organically, with a subsequent phase of more systematic reorganisation when the textual material is shaped into an articulate narrative. The practice of constant recycling of earlier fragments and of restructuring his material gave Proust's drafts a unique flexibility and elasticity, which allowed him to incorporate vast textual expansions even at a relatively advanced stage of the novel's evolution.

The different stages of *Contre Sainte-Beuve* can be reconstructed as follows: between November 1908 and February 1909, Proust sketched out fragments for a Sainte-Beuve narrative which, from March onwards, developed into a genuine novel. The narrative was initially planned in two parts: first, a morning scene when a sleepless man reminisces over the past and, second, a discussion between this man and his mother about an article on Sainte-Beuve that he is intending to write. In the first notebooks, we find fragments of a story in which a first-person Narrator, who has been ill for some time and sleeps only during the day, awaits the morning, when his mother will wish him a good night. Half asleep, he remembers various rooms he has occupied in the past. When the mother finally appears, she gives him *Le Figaro* which contains an article he wrote a while ago and which has eventually been published.

Proust initially had considerable difficulties finding a link between the different fragments. A solution presented itself, when, in *Cahier 3* (November–December 1908), after numerous attempts, he eventually introduced a complex temporal framework based on 'then' (i.e. the time when the Narrator still led a 'normal' way of life, sleeping during the night) versus 'now' (the present, when he sleeps during the day), which reconciled the disparate time levels and introduced a structure of retrospection that was to become instrumental in transforming the Sainte-Beuve narrative into a genuine novel.

Between January and February 1909, Proust expanded on the first part of his narrative, introducing a number of new characters and motifs, which rapidly expanded beyond the framework set out in the first notebooks. In *Cahier 5*, the third of the Sainte-Beuve series, the intimate family scenario sketched out in the first drafts quite literally exploded: a number of new characters enter the scene, amongst them an anonymous count and countess (the future Guermantes), a florist who keeps a little shop in the count's house in Paris (the future Jupien), Mme de Villeparisis and her great-nephew Montargis (the future Saint-Loup), as well as a certain Mlle Quimperlé, who captivates the Narrator's attention. The setting extends from Paris to an unnamed seaside resort where the hero spends his summer holidays (the future Balbec). The rapid extension of fictional characters and dramatic space that occurred at this stage of the manuscripts, clearly shows that the novelistic parts were taking on a momentum of their own, which was threatening to eclipse the Sainte-Beuve project. As Claudine Quémar has pointed out in a seminal essay: 'Proust était comme entraîné au-delà de son récit initial, vers le genre romanesque, par le dynamisme même de son écriture'[5] ['It was as if the sheer force of Proust's writing had carried him beyond his initial narrative toward the novelistic genre'].

It is in *Cahier 4* (March 1909) that Proust scholars tend to place the transition from the Sainte-Beuve narrative to the novel. From this point on, the novelistic parts expanded beyond return and the great outlines of the future *Recherche* began to appear. Proust simultaneously developed fragments on Combray, on the hero's infatuation with the Countess in Paris, and on the seaside. A number of social constellations emerged: the intimate world of the Narrator and his family; Swann, his mistress, and the Verdurin circle; the Guermantes, Mme de Villeparisis, and her nephew Montargis; a number of anonymous girls whom the hero observes from his bedroom window or contemplates in public. The hero's interest in young women or, more precisely, his quest for sexual initiation soon emerged as a major theme in the drafts. In *Cahier 36* he is in turn infatuated with the enigmatic chambermaid of Baroness Picpus (who had quite a considerable role in the early drafts), a young woman he mistakes for a prostitute but who turns out to be his early love, Gilberte, the aristocratic Mlle de Quimperlé whom we already know from an earlier draft, and a beautiful stranger who sexually provokes him at a ball. The female characters in early drafts, as Antoine Compagnon remarks, clearly show Proust's affinities with fin-de-siècle 'decadent' art and literature: the chambermaid, who, we learn in due course, has been permanently disfigured in a liner accident, is an incarnation of Medusa, the corrupted beauty, whilst the young provocative stranger is Salome, the dangerous youthful temptress. The decadent couple disappeared from the manuscripts with the creation of Albertine in 1914; it was replaced by another pair, Albertine and Morel, who no longer represent two facets of heterosexual desire, but, instead, explore male and female homosexuality.[6]

It is important to note that in 1909 only male homosexuality, but not its female counterpart, is present in the drafts. The homosexual theme developed around M. de Guercy, the later Charlus, who was first introduced in *Cahier 7*. The hero's discovery of Guercy's sexual preferences leads into a reflection on homosexuals being a cursed 'race': Proust at some length discusses their suffering and behaviour before likening them to the persecuted race of Israel. This fragment is an early nucleus for the famous analogy between homosexuals and Jews we know from *Sodome et Gomorrhe I*. In *Cahier 6*, the penultimate notebook of the Sainte-Beuve series, Proust emphasised the homosexual theme by 'classifying' the different types of male homosexuals in a piece of text entitled 'La race des tantes' ['The queer race'], which again prefigures the overture of *Sodome et Gomorrhe*.

So, in spring 1909, Proust had fragments for the future *Du côté de chez Swann*, *A l'ombre des jeunes filles en fleurs*, *Le Côté de Guermantes* and *Sodome et Gomorrhe*, but none of them was envisaged as a whole text. He had also introduced virtually all of the novel's main characters with the exception of Legrandin, the Cambremer family, Bloch, M. de Norpois, the four artists (Vinteuil, Elstir, Bergotte and the actress La Berma) and, most importantly, Albertine. Some, such as a pianist who eventually became Morel, were still anonymous and under-developed, whilst others like Reynaldo Hahn (Proust's composer friend who figures in early fragments thus underlining the strongly autobiographical dimension of the work), and Hubert de Guerchy, the homosexual cousin of M. de Guerchy or Guercy, disappeared from the text at a later stage of composition (see I, xlvii). The crucial question that arises in view of this already considerable fictional universe is of course: what has happened to the *Contre Sainte-Beuve* project?

We have seen that the first part of the novel grew rapidly between March and June 1909. It would, however, be wrong to think that notebooks of this period were exclusively dedicated to fiction. We still find critical and aesthetic texts that were apparently intended for the last, theoretical, part, the conversation between the Narrator and his mother on Sainte-Beuve and a number of other authors: Balzac, Nerval, Baudelaire. The conversation with the mother remained in the manuscripts until the invention of the famous

'Bal de têtes' (the Narrator's discovery of the destructive force of time), in spring 1910, which was to form the novel's new ending, and the elaboration of the chapter entitled 'L'Adoration perpétuelle' between 1910 and 1911, which provided a new aesthetic conclusion, replacing the *matinée* between Narrator and mother with the *matinée* at the residence of the princesse de Guermantes (ibid.). The original division of the novel into a first fictional and a second theoretical part in the form of a conversation, then, continued to exist beyond the *Cahiers Contre Sainte-Beuve*. Crucially, however, the theoretical fragments, which were to form the conclusion to Proust's hybrid work, were temporarily abandoned in the summer of 1909, when the author began to draft a first continuous version of 'Combray'.

The development of the 'Cahiers Contre Sainte-Beuve' (1909–1911)

From June 1909 onwards, Proust developed the ten *Cahiers Contre Sainte-Beuve* whilst at the same time composing new episodes. First of all, on the basis of earlier sketches, he established a continuous version of 'Combray', selecting only those fragments that relate to this part of the novel and assembling them into a coherent narrative. This practice of taking up earlier fragments and merging them into a continuous textual sequence in so-called 'cahiers de montage' is characteristic of Proust's work from the beginning of summer 1909. He continued to work thematically, whilst at the same time becoming increasingly concerned with the narrative organisation of his text.

In mid-August Proust approached Alfred Vallette, the director of the *Mercure de France*, about publication of his novel, which, significantly, at this stage was still called 'Contre Sainte-Beuve. Souvenir d'une matinée' ['Against Sainte-Beuve. Memories of a Morning']. Proust's idea was to publish the first narrative part in instalments, and the second theoretical part in book form. Vallette declined after a few days without even soliciting the manuscript. Undeterred by this, and another refusal from the publisher Calmann-Lévy, Proust turned to Gaston Calmette, director of *Le Figaro*, who promised to serialise his novel as requested. In view of this publication, Proust first prepared a fair copy, then, in November 1909, a typescript for 'Combray', continuing to make corrections and additions on both of these documents. To his great disappointment, however, Calmette went back on his initial agreement, eventually forcing him to retrieve his manuscript in July 1910. By that time the novel had already taken on such proportions that the author opted against publication in two halves (one in instalments, the other in book form) and decided instead to publish the novel as a whole. Between November 1909 and the summer of 1911, partly due to the various rejections he had undergone, he developed a first complete version of the novel with the exception of the radical changes entailed by the invention of Albertine in 1914.

The progress made in the manuscripts between 1909 and 1911 can be roughly outlined as follows: on the basis of the *Cahiers Contre Sainte-Beuve*, Proust composed drafts for Combray, Paris and Querqueville (the future Balbec). He added to the various love stories in his novel, reworking and expanding drafts on Gilberte, Odette and the young girls at the seaside, invented a new female character (Maria, a young woman of Dutch descent, whose relations with the hero anticipate those with Albertine) and introduced the various artists we know from the published work. Whilst continuing to work thematically, Proust also increasingly concentrated on individual parts of his work. He put together a continuous version of what was to become 'Un Amour de Swann', which already contains virtually all the episodes of the future text, but is not yet separated off from the rest of *Du côté de chez Swann*. After a series of draft notebooks that develop the love stories, we find drafts and montages for Querqueville and for *Guermantes* (*Cahiers* 38, 13, 30, 37, 51, 13, 49), which, between April/May and September 1910, were assembled into a continuous version in *Cahiers* 39 to 43 and 49. Finally, between 1910 and 1911, *Le Temps retrouvé* also began to take shape: a first continuous version figures in *Cahiers* 58 and 57. *Le Temps retrouvé* is the ultimate stage of the *Contre Sainte-Beuve* project, which, as has already been said, Proust never completed in its initial form, but which was not abandoned altogether either. What happened is that the theoretical fragments pertaining to the Sainte-Beuve project were eventually transposed into the last two chapters of *Le Temps retrouvé*.[7] The aesthetic reflections which belonged to the conversation with the mother were integrated into the penultimate chapter entitled 'L'Adoration perpétuelle', which was sketched out in 1911, whilst the chapter called 'Le Bal de têtes', first sketched out in 1910 and developed between 1910–11, became the novel's new conclusion. This development was roughly contemporaneous with a second montage for 'Combray' and a manuscript draft for 'Un Amour de Swann' (in which the Swann story is separated from 'Combray'), confirming what Proust himself had maintained throughout his life: that the beginning and the ending of his novel had been written at the same time.[8]

The novel in 1911, the choice of a title, and the quest for a publisher

In 1911 a first version of the novel, which could have filled two big volumes, existed in the form of typescripts and drafts. It covered the future *Du Côté de chez Swann*, parts of *A l'ombre des jeunes filles en fleurs* (without

Albertine) and of *Le Côté de Guermantes*, drafts on homosexuality revolving around Charlus, as well as numerous drafts for *Le Temps retrouvé*.[9]

Early in 1912, Proust began to realise that a single volume might not be sufficient for his ever-growing text. In two letters dated March, he hesitates between one long volume of 800 or 900 pages and two volumes of 400 pages each (see *Corr.* XI, 68, 76). By April or May he already planned two volumes of 700 pages each, to be published under an overall title plus individual titles for each volume (*Corr.* XI, 118). The first ideas for the overall title were, as Jean-Yves Tadié has pointed out, still distinctly *fin-de-siècle*, but they already showed Proust's preoccupation with the past which characterises the novel as a whole: 'Les Stalactites du passé' ['Stalactites of the Past'], 'Le Visiteur du Passé' ['The Visitor of the Past'], 'Les Reflets du Temps' ['Reflections of Time'] are amongst the fifteen or so titles Proust suggests to Reynaldo Hahn in a letter dated from the first part of 1912 (*Corr.* XI, 151). In October, he first introduced the opposition between *Le Temps perdu* and *Le Temps retrouvé* in his titles for the two volumes. The overall title is *Les Intermittences du cœur* (*Corr.* XI, 257). In November, he envisaged three volumes: *Le Temps perdu*, *L'Adoration perpétuelle* (or possibly *A l'ombre des jeunes filles en fleurs* which is given as an alternative title in a letter to Gallimard) and *Le Temps retrouvé*; the overall title remains *Les Intermittences du cœur*.[10] In May 1913, finally, he first mentioned the title *A la recherche du temps perdu* in a letter to Bernard Grasset (*Corr.* XII, 176). The first volume is called *Du côté de chez Swann*; the second (and Proust still hesitated about this), *Le Côté de Guermantes*; the third remained *Le Temps retrouvé*. The reason for changing the overall title to *A la recherche du temps perdu* was apparently that Proust did not want his *Les Intermittences du cœur* to be confused with a novel by Binet-Valmer, *Le Cœur en désordre*, that had been published in November 1912 (see Tadié, *Marcel Proust*, pp.701–2).

Proust was soon to find out that publication was to prove infinitely more difficult than the choice of a title. The story of his various rejections is well known: the publisher Fasquelle turned down the manuscript for *Du côté de chez Swann* on 24 December 1912, following a devastating report from Jacques Madeleine, who famously complained: 'Au bout de sept cent douze pages de ce manuscrit . . . on n'a aucune, aucune notion de ce dont il s'agit. Qu'est-ce que tout cela vient faire? Qu'est-ce que tout cela signifie? Où tout cela veut-il mener? – Impossible d'en rien savoir! Impossible d'en pouvoir rien dire!' (see Tadié, *Marcel Proust*, pp.684–5) ['At the end of seven hundred and twelve pages, one has absolutely no idea what this manuscript is about. What is it trying to achieve? What does it mean? Where is it trying to head? Impossible to answer any of these questions! Impossible to say anything about it!']. The prestigious *Nouvelle Revue Française* showed little more understanding for Proust's work: the reading committee under the direction of André Gide refused *Du côté de chez Swann* apparently without even having read it. Jean Schlumberger, an influential member of the committee, later commented that the *NRF* was discouraged by the size of the manuscript and by Proust's reputation of being a snob (see Tadié, *Marcel Proust*, p.686). The final blow to Proust's self-esteem came from the publishing director of Ollendorff, a man called Humblot, on whom the subtleties of *Du côté de chez Swann* seem to have been totally wasted: 'Je suis peut-être bouché à l'émeri, mais je ne puis comprendre qu'un monsieur puisse employer trente pages à décrire comment il se tourne et se retourne dans son lit avant de trouver le sommeil' (see Tadié, *Marcel Proust*, p.689) ['Perhaps I am as thick as two short planks, but I cannot understand how a man can take thirty pages to describe how he turns round in his bed before he finally falls asleep']. A frustrated and humiliated Proust eventually submitted his manuscript to the progressive young publisher Bernard Grasset who accepted it at the author's own expense.

Du côté de chez Swann went on sale on 14 November 1913. The volume was initially to end with the Narrator's first trip to the seaside, but, for editorial reasons, this ending was shifted to the planned second volume, provisionally entitled *Le Côté de Guermantes*. *Du côté de chez Swann*, as in the current edition, ended with the episode in the autumnal Bois de Boulogne where the Narrator reminisces over the lost past. A press release published by Grasset in November 1913 introduced *Du côté de chez Swann* as the first volume of a trilogy entitled *A la recherche du temps perdu*, to be followed in 1914 by volumes II: *Le Côté de Guermantes* and III: *Le Temps retrouvé*. The second volume was to cover material which, in the final edition, corresponds to *A l'ombre des jeunes filles en fleurs* (but, crucially, without the group of young girls) and most of *Le Côté de Guermantes I*. It was to begin with the Narrator's visits to Mme Swann and end with a chapter on Mme de Villeparisis's salon. The last volume, *Le Temps retrouvé*, on the other hand, was to contain the Narrator's encounters with the young girls at the seaside as well as a number of chapters which, in due course, were transposed to *Le Côté de Guermantes*, *Sodome et Gomorrhe*, *Albertine disparue* and *Le Temps retrouvé*. They included: a chapter on the princesse de Guermantes, on M. de Charlus and the Verdurin circle, the death of the grandmother and the narrator's realisation of her loss, the Giotto frescoes in Padua, Mme de Cambremer, Robert de Saint-Loup's marriage, and finally, the closing chapter entitled 'L'Adoration perpétuelle' ['The Perpetual Adoration'] (cited in Tadié, *Marcel Proust*, p.703). Less than a year later, this table of contents together with Proust's planned structure for the novel, had become obsolete: the introduction of the Albertine story and the outbreak of the First World War overthrew the planned three-part structure and entailed a considerable reorganisation of the novel's plot.

The novel in 1914

In 1913, as we have just seen, Proust was working on a trilogy, whose first volume was out in print whilst the following two existed partly in proof, partly typed, partly in manuscript form. What was to become *A l'ombre des jeunes filles en fleurs* was still intermingled with *Le Côté de Guermantes*. The most striking difference between the novel of 1913 and the novel we know, however, is that Albertine was still absent from the plot, as is evidenced by the table of contents cited above. The creation of what is commonly called the 'Albertine cycle' (i.e. *La Prisonnière* and *La Fugitive*) in 1914, together with the outbreak of the First World War (which considerably delayed the publication of the planned subsequent volumes and gave Proust ample time to revise and develop his manuscript), affected the novel in the most unexpected and radical way: the initially planned three-volume structure broke its boundaries, giving way to four new volumes developing over the next eight years, which made the novel double in size. This enormous expansion happened essentially at the centre of the novel, whilst the beginning (*Du côté de chez Swann*) and the ending (*Le Temps retrouvé*) largely preserved their original outline: Proust drafted new sketches for Balbec which, together with the already existing ones, were assembled into one single volume, *A l'ombre des jeunes filles en fleurs*, which pushed *Le Côté de Guermantes* to the third place in the sequel. On the basis of already existing drafts on homosexuality he developed the *Sodome et Gomorrhe* cycle which, as the genesis and the volume titles he chose in 1922 show, also includes *La Prisonnière* and *La Fugitive*. The two parts of *Sodome et Gomorrhe* centred around Charlus' homosexuality thus found their counterpart in the two volumes centred around Albertine's lesbianism.

The character Albertine first appeared in a notebook dated spring 1913 (see Tadié, *Marcel Proust*, p.717). Her name replaces that of Maria, the young Dutch woman with whom the hero is infatuated in Balbec, and whom we know from earlier drafts. It was, however, only in 1914 that the novel began to undergo the drastic changes I have briefly sketched: Proust first of all introduced the group of young girls together with the newly invented Albertine, into the first holiday in Balbec (they initially did not appear before the second holiday). He then considerably developed the first two trips at the expense of a third sojourn planned for the beginning of *Le Temps retrouvé*, and inserted Albertine's visits to the hero in Paris, which were to figure in the future *Le Côté de Guermantes II* (see Tadié, *Marcel Proust*, p.711). The first drafts for the Albertine cycle proper, that is to say for *La Prisonnière* and *La Fugitive*, were written between 1914 and 1915. They are inseparable from the trauma of jealousy, loss, and death which Proust suffered in 1914 and to which we must now turn.

In May 1913, Alfred Agostinelli, who had been one of his chauffeurs in Cabourg, moved into Proust's home in the capacity of his new personal secretary. Up to that date, as Jean-Yves Tadié has commented, Proust's life and work were complementing each other; from then on they began to intersect (see Tadié, *Marcel Proust*, p.717). The stormy relationship between Proust and his young secretary was of brief duration: in December 1913, Agostinelli left Paris without prior warning. Proust, in an acute state of anxiety and desperation, made various attempts to call the young man back, but to no avail. On 30 May, Agostinelli, who had taken flying lessons under the name Marcel Swann, was killed in a plane crash near Antibes. The parallels between Alfred Agostinelli and the fictional character Albertine in the novel are of course striking. Whilst it would be reductive to see the Albertine novel as a mere projection of Proust's relations with Agostinelli (we should not forget that the theme of the kept woman which dominates *La Prisonnière* was already present in early fragments in 1908, and was explored even earlier in 'Avant la Nuit' and *Jean Santeuil*), it cannot be denied that the experience of death, mourning and eventually oblivion that Proust suffered following the young man's death gave his novel a new direction, and, ultimately, a new dimension, that would have been inconceivable without the tragic events of 1914.

In the first months of 1914, Proust began to write drafts for the future *La Prisonnière*, followed by drafts for *La Fugitive*. A first full draft of the Albertine cycle was ready in 1915. The development of the Albertine story is inseparable from that of *Sodome et Gomorrhe*, which, as mentioned earlier, forms its early counterpart. Drafts for *Sodome et Gomorrhe*, *La Prisonnière* and *La Fugitive* are contained in *Cahiers* 52, 72, 53, 73, 55, 56 and 74. Proust continued his practice of reusing older fragments during the elaboration of the Albertine cycle: the theme of awakening which runs through *La Prisonnière* goes back to the *Cahiers Contre Sainte-Beuve*, as does the article in *Le Figaro* in *La Fugitive;* the trip to Venice and the two marriages stem from the novel of 1911; the first stay with Gilberte at Tansonville, finally, which brings *La Fugitive* to a close, was announced since the publication of *Du côté de chez Swann* in 1913. Albertine's flight and death, as well as the Narrator's mourning and oblivion, which are at the centre of the Albertine cycle, by contrast, are all new. They date from 1914 at the earliest (see Tadié, *Marcel Proust*, pp.720–1).

To briefly summarise, then, in 1915 *A l'ombre des jeunes filles en fleurs* had emerged as a separate volume, *Le Côté de Guermantes* was relegated to the third volume of the sequence; *Sodome et Gomorrhe*, *La Prisonnière* and *La Fugitive* formed a reasonably continuous, albeit far from complete, draft. Finally, *Le Temps retrouvé* was enriched by a whole new chapter, 'Monsieur de Charlus pendant la guerre: ses opinions et ses plaisirs', written largely between 1916 and 1917, some additions dating from the last war year.

In 1916, Proust changed publisher. Grasset's publishing house had been closed since the outbreak of the war, so he eventually accepted an offer from Gallimard to publish the sequel of his novel with the *Nouvelle Revue Française* (who had resumed negotiations in 1914 after the relative success of *Du côté de chez Swann*). In a letter written in May, he informed Gallimard that his novel was to contain a volume entitled *Sodome et Gomorrhe*, which was likely to shock if not the publisher himself, then at least potential readers and critics (see Proust/Gallimard, *Correspondance*, pp.35–6). In 1916 he developed the manuscript for *Sodome et Gomorrhe*, and until about 1917, worked on the drafts for the future *La Prisonnière* and *La Fugitive*. At the beginning of 1917, he explained to Berthe Lemarié, the production manager of the *NRF*, that if necessary, his housekeeper would be able to show his manuscripts to Gallimard. Should the author die unexpectedly, Gallimard could publish the *Recherche* on his own, but should point out to readers that what they had in front of them was only a rough draft (see Proust/Gallimard, *Correspondance*, p.76).

The novel of 1918

At the end of 1918, we have a new detailed outline for the novel, the first since Grasset's press release of 1913. The novel is now planned in five volumes: *Du côté de chez Swann* (already published), *A l'ombre des jeunes filles en fleurs* (in print, but not yet for sale), *Le Côté de Guermantes*, *Sodome et Gomorrhe I*, and *Sodome et Gomorrhe II-Le Temps retrouvé* (cited in Tadié, *Marcel Proust*, pp.782–3). The big difference between the 1918 outline of the novel and the novel we have today is, of course, that *La Prisonnière* and *La Fugitive* do not yet constitute separate volumes. They are merely chapters within *Sodome et Gomorrhe II-Le Temps retrouvé*. When Proust realised in 1922 what proportions his manuscript had taken he subdivided the Sodom cycle further into *Sodome et Gomorrhe III: La Prisonnière* and *Sodome et Gomorrhe IV: La Fugitive*.

In 1919, almost six years after the publication of the first volume of *A la recherche*, Proust's readers were finally able to read the sequel to the novel, *A l'ombre des jeunes filles en fleurs*, which went on sale in June. Gallimard simultaneously published a reprint of *Du côté de chez Swann* (which contained a number of revisions compared to the 1913 Grasset edition) and an edition of *Pastiches et mélanges*. In May 1920, Proust launched a *de luxe* edition of *A l'ombre des jeunes filles en fleurs*, limited to fifty copies at 300 francs each. Every copy contained two proofs with the author's corrections and additions – a delight for bibliophile collectors, but a misfortune for Proust scholars who thus lost a precious research document. *A l'ombre des jeunes filles en fleurs* was not only to offer Proust financial profit; it also finally brought him the success for which he had to wait so long. On 10 December 1919, in what rapidly amounted to a public controversy, he was awarded the Prix Goncourt for *A l'ombre des jeunes filles en fleurs*, ahead of Roland Dorgelès's far more popular war novel *Les Croix de bois*. The press was quick to denounce Proust's relatively advanced age (Jean de Pierrefeu in an article in the *Journal des Débats* calls him a 'talent d'outre-tombe'), his relations with the Goncourt Jury, and perhaps most importantly, his inactivity during the war (see Tadié, *Marcel Proust*, p.829).

In October 1920, *Le Côté de Guermantes I* came out in print. In the course of 1921, Proust made a number of pre-publications in magazines such as the *NRF* and the *Revue hebdomadaire*. In May, *Le Côté de Guermantes II-Sodome I* went on sale. Over the summer, Proust worked on *Sodome et Gomorrhe II*, which was published in April 1922. From the autumn of 1921 until his death, he concentrated mainly on *La Prisonnière* and *La Fugitive*, whilst also correcting the proofs for *Sodome et Gomorrhe II* at the beginning of 1922. In May, the title *La Prisonnière* was mentioned for the first time (see *Corr.* XXI, 197). *Albertine disparue* was substituted for the original *La Fugitive* (which parallels *La Prisonnière*) in July, after Proust discovered the translation of a collection of poems by the Bengali poet and Nobel Laureate Rabindranath Tagore equally entitled *La Fugitive*. In spring 1922, Proust, who is also working on *Le Temps retrouvé*, tells his housekeeper Céleste Albaret that he has put the word 'Fin' to his manuscript and adds 'Maintenant, je peux mourir' ['Now I can die'].

'Albertine disparue'

Proust's health began to decline seriously in September 1922. Despite a severe bronchitis, the after-effects of which were to claim his life on 18 November, he continued to work on the Albertine cycle, correcting the manuscript for *La Prisonnière* and *Albertine disparue*, contrary to his doctor's advice. On 7 November, Gallimard acknowledges receipt of the typescript for *La Prisonnière*. Between 7 and 17 November, Proust concentrated on *Albertine disparue*, which he was anxious to submit to his publisher as quickly as possible. It is during these ten days that he made a radical change to *Albertine disparue*, which, when it was belatedly discovered in 1986, has both shaken and divided the scholarly community: on a previously unknown typescript found by Claude Mauriac after the death of Proust's niece, Suzy Mante-Proust, the author has eliminated approximately two thirds of *Albertine disparue*. On folio 648 of the typescript we find in his own hand: 'NB. Au bas de cette page finit le chapitre 1er d'"Albertine disparue". De 648 à 898 rien, j'ai tout ôté. Donc nous sautons de 648 au chapitre II d'Albertine disparue. Sautons sans transition au chapitre deux 898'[11] ['NB. The first chapter of 'Albertine disparue' ends at the bottom of this page. From 648 to 898 – nothing, I have got rid of everything. Thus we jump from 648 to Chapter II of Albertine disparue. Let's jump to Chapter two, 898, without transition']. This little marginal note has highly disturbing consequences: it annihilates the largest and arguably most important part of *Albertine disparue*: the hero's investigations into his mistress's homosexuality. Proust did not simply omit this big chunk of text, but also changed the place where Albertine suffers her fatal riding accident from Touraine to Montjouvain. The rationale behind this change is clear: Albertine has gone to Montjouvain to see Mlle Vinteuil or her enigmatic lesbian friend. Her homosexuality is thus clear from the beginning, making the long speculations and investigations about her sexual inclinations and adventures that fill the rest of the text redundant (see Tadié, *Marcel Proust*, p.904). Why should Proust have made such drastic changes of plot and story only a few days before his death? Several hypotheses have been advanced. Giovanni Macchia has suggested that the truncated version of *Albertine disparue* was not actually intended for the novel, but for a pre-publication in *Les Œuvres libres*. His hypothesis is contradicted by the typescript itself where, again on folio 648, we find in the hand of Céléste Albaret, who occasionally acted as Proust's secretary: 'si M. Gallimard aime mieux avoir un volume plus long' ['if Mr Gallimard prefers a longer volume'] indicating clearly that Proust was preparing his typescript for the *NRF* and not for *Les Œuvres libres*. Nathalie Mauriac-Dyer has more convincingly argued that Proust decided to shorten the second part of the Albertine story in order to make it a proper counterpart to *Sodome et Gomorrhe III-La Prisonnière*. She also asserts that Proust was intending to reuse the omitted material in a later volume entitled *Sodome et Gomorrhe IV*. Jean Milly, finally, claims that the shortened typescript was only an interim solution: Proust, anxious to get on with the novel's publication, decided to send only those parts of *Albertine disparue* that he had already corrected to Gallimard, and to temporarily suppress the rest. According to Milly, he trusted that Gallimard and his team would complete the volume on the basis of his manuscripts. Mauriac-Dyer, following her hypothesis, has published an edition of the shortened typescript with Grasset in 1987, whilst Jean Milly has edited a full version of *Albertine disparue*, which uses all the various documents available, for Honoré Champion in 1992.

The amendments Proust impressed upon *Albertine disparue* so shortly before his death raise an important question: what form would the novel as a whole have taken had Proust's work not been cut short so tragically? Would it have expanded further, as it had done so drastically during the war years? Was Proust's writing potentially endless and without conclusion like that of the other great master of Modernity, to whom he is sometimes compared, Robert Musil? The post-modern fascination with the unfinished, which has dominated literary discourses for some time now, should not blind us to a number of facts about Proust's writing: first, unlike Musil who failed to bring his novel to a close because he was getting embroiled in too many contradictory endings, Proust had a beginning and an ending for his project from a very early stage; the expansion that occurred during the war years, as has already been said, came from the centre of the novel, whilst the beginning and the ending remained largely untouched. Second, Proust was anxious to ensure publication, as is evidenced in his letter to Berthe Lemarié of 1917, and even, if one were to endorse Milly's argument, in his changes to the typescript of *Albertine disparue*. Third, and perhaps most important, he had less and less opportunity to make changes to his novel as publication advanced: in 1922, only *La Prisonnière*, *Albertine disparue* and *Le Temps retrouvé* were still open for alterations; all the other volumes were out in print. It is likely that, had he had the time, Proust would have ironed out the various inconsistencies that remain in the volumes published after his death (most famously, the reappearance of characters that have died a few hundred pages earlier). He might also have tightened and reorganised the plot, created yet more links and echoes between individual episodes, and even introduced new scenes. He would, however, not have been able to make any far-reaching changes to the novel's overall framework; in 1922, this was simply no longer an option because of the stage of publication he had reached.

Rather than speculating what the novel might have become, we should perhaps give more attention to how it became what it is, to use a title by Nietzsche. The work of numerous researchers, most notably the *Equipe Proust* at the *Institut des Textes et Manuscrits Modernes*, Paris, has given us a fascinating insight into the *Recherche*'s formidably complex genesis as well as into Proust's idiosyncratic (though, as I have attempted to show, by no means unsystematic) writing practice. Thanks to the new Pléiade edition of the novel we are now in the privileged position to have first hand access to a vast corpus of manuscripts previously reserved for the specialist. For the reader who has explored the preparatory drafts for *A la recherche du temps perdu*, the novel will undoubtedly never be the same again. The wealth of earlier, often alternative versions, provides a once-familiar novel with a new depth of virtuality, returning it into its very own dimension: time.[12]

NOTES

1 Proust's manuscripts have been available for scholarly enquiry since 1962, when the Bibliothèque Nationale, Paris, purchased the quasi-totality of his drafts, typescripts and corrected proofs from his niece Suzy Mante-Proust. In 1972, a *Centre d'études proustiennes* was founded which, under the direction of Bernard Brun, has done ground-breaking research on the genesis of the *Recherche*. Their work is published in the annual journal *Bulletin d'informations proustiennes*. There are also a number of monographs on the genesis of the novel, most notably Maurice Bardèche, *Marcel Proust romancier*, 2 vols. (Paris: Les Sept Couleurs, 1971), Alison Winton, *Proust's Additions. The Making of 'A la recherche du temps perdu'*, 2 vols. (Cambridge University Press, 1977), Anthony Pugh, *The Birth of 'A la recherche du temps perdu'* (Lexington, KY: French Forum Publishers, 1987), and my *Processes of Literary Creation. Flaubert and Proust* (Oxford: Legenda, 1998). An excellent synthesis of the novel's genesis is given in Jean-Yves Tadié's introduction for the new Pléiade edition (Paris: Gallimard, 1987–89) and in his recent biography *Marcel Proust* (Paris: Gallimard, 1996). In this chapter, I shall refer mainly to the latter.

2 See *Contre Sainte-Beuve, suivi de Nouveaux mélanges*, ed. Bernard de Fallois (Paris: Gallimard, 1954), p.14.

3 All translations are my own.

4 In an often quoted letter to Louis d'Albufera, dated 5 or 6 May 1908, Proust cites a number of projects he is working on at that moment, amongst them an essay on Sainte-Beuve and Flaubert. See *Corr.* VIII, 112–13.

5 'Autour de trois avant-textes de l'"Ouverture" de la *Recherche*: Nouvelles approches des problèmes du *Contre Sainte-Beuve*', *Bulletin d'informations proustiennes*, 3 (1976), 7–39 (p.21).

6 Antoine Compagnon, *Proust entre deux siècles* (Paris: Seuil, 1989), pp.125–6.

7 On the genesis of *Le Temps retrouvé* see Bernard Brun, '*Le Temps retrouvé* dans les avant-textes de *Combray*', *Bulletin d'informations proustiennes*, 12 (1981), 7–23.

8 See Jean-Yves Tadié, *Marcel Proust* (Paris: Gallimard, 1996), p.672.

9 For a more detailed description of the novel in 1911, see Jean-Yves Tadié, *Marcel Proust*, pp.673–4.

10 Marcel Proust/Gaston Gallimard, *Correspondance*, ed. Pascal Fouché (Paris: Gallimard, 1989), p.17.

11 Cited by Jean Milly, 'Problèmes génétiques et éditoriaux à propos d'*Albertine disparue*', in *Ecrire sans fin*, eds. Rainer Warning and Jean Milly (Paris: CNRS Éditions, 1996), pp.51–77 (p. 60). My discussion of the controversy around *Albertine disparue* is based mainly on this article.

12 I would like to thank my friends Jane Yeoman, Mario Longtin and Siân Williams for their helpful comments on a draft of this chapter.

5

ROGER SHATTUCK

Lost and found: the structure of Proust's novel

Near the middle of 'Combray', the opening section of Proust's *Search*, the Narrator describes the exceptional after-dinner walks the Protagonist[1] and his parents used to take on beautiful May evenings. His father would lead them far out into the countryside as darkness was falling and then suddenly ask, 'Where are we?' (I, 113; I, 136/160). After his mother invariably acknowledged that she was utterly lost, her amused husband would point out that they were standing right in front of their lower garden gate: by a gently circuitous route, he had led them home in the dark. 'You're extraordinary!' the wife would exclaim admiringly. The Protagonist would stand silent, attentive to how the forbidding world of unfamiliar shadows around him was now transforming itself under his feet into the welcoming garden of his childhood.

No novelist could compose such an incident of getting lost and finding one's way again without thinking about how to tell a story and its effect on the reader. In this case, the father's surefooted navigation stands for Proust's confidence about the direction and outcome of his story. 'You may think you've lost your way in my narrative, but I know exactly where I'm taking you.' We are, of course, still close to the opening.

More than a decade later, Proust could not be so sure of himself. His novel had grown to immense and as yet unascertainable length, and, in his declining health, he was far from certain he could hold the whole enterprise together. A few months before he died, he wrote to his editor and publisher, Gaston Gallimard, that he had no trouble composing, writing down his narrative. 'But patching things together and tying up the loose ends, that's more than I can handle' (*Corr.* xx, 500). Proust added that the struggle to maintain the form of his story was obliging him to leave out some of his best passages. The responsibility of having events turn out as planned seemed to exceed his capacities at this late date.

Between these extreme expressions of confidence and despair about giving coherent shape to his creation, Proust offers us in the novel a more nuanced passage on the subject. The teenage Protagonist has developed a cult-like admiration for the prose style of a much talked about author, Bergotte. He speaks of this admiration to the Marquis de Norpois, an eminent ex-ambassador who comes to dine with his parents. Norpois does not prevaricate in his response. 'Mon Dieu, dit M. de Norpois . . . je ne partage pas cette manière de voir. Bergotte est ce que j'appelle un joueur de flûte; il faut reconnaître du reste qu'il en joue agréablement . . . Mais enfin ce n'est que cela, et cela n'est pas grand'chose. Jamais on ne trouve dans ses ouvrages sans muscles ce qu'on pourrait nommer la charpente. Pas d'action – ou si peu – mais surtout pas de portée'(I, 464) ['"Good Heavens!" exclaimed M. de Norpois . . . "I do not share your son's point of view. Bergotte is what I call a flute-player . . . But when all is said, there's no more to it than that. Nowhere does one find in his flaccid works what one might call structure. No action – or very little – but above all no range"' (II, 51–2/60–1)]. Insofar as Norpois is presented as a man of wide experience and culture, his opinion carries weight against the Protagonist's immature infatuation. Insofar as we come to see Norpois as an opinionated old fool, we dismiss his opinion about Bergotte and literature. Insofar as we reach a more balanced view of Norpois' intelligence, we realise that he has put his finger on the two aspects of writing that preoccupied Proust: structure [*charpente*] and significance [*portée*]. One of Proust's most spontaneous expressions of feeling in his correspondence comes in the opening sentence of his response to Jacques Rivière's letter on first reading 'Swann's Way'. 'Finally, I have found a reader who can discern that my book is a dogmatic whole and a construction' (*Corr.* XIII, 98).

Now, how does one 'construct' or hold together or find a unity for a story that runs to 3,000 pages? Especially if it was originally a small fraction of that size? It will be worth looking for a moment at the narrative conventions that human beings have evolved over the thousands of years we have been telling stories to one another. I shall have to simplify a highly complex history. We elaborate and enlarge a few glorious episodes out of history into *epics*, from the *Odyssey* to *War and Peace*. Their narrative mass arises from a collective experience. We create a character both stereotypic and eccentric and send him or her out on a life of endlessly renewed adventure called the *picaresque* novel. *Don Quixote* belongs to this genre. We call *Bildungs-roman* the extended story of how a protagonist's mind and character develop and finally mature through a series of experiences. We recognise novelists like Balzac whose overall ambition appears to be the near-total portrait of contemporary society. This is the domain of *realism* or *naturalism*. And we honour in works such as Dante's *Divine Comedy* and Melville's *Moby Dick* the prolonged and detailed story of a *quest*, of a journey with a single ambitious goal.

All of these conventions will hold and shape a series of events and episodes encompassing great length. Proust was familiar with them all, and they all contributed elements to the "construction" on which he worked so hard. A reader will not be wasting time to examine carefully to what extent each of these conventional narrative structures is embedded in the *Search*. But there is an aspect of Proust's novel that impels me to proceed differently.

The opening six pages of 'Combray' furnish little information as to when or where these 'swirling and confused evocations' (I, 7; I, 6/7) are taking place, who is speaking, and where we are going. The reader is precipitated into a great fall backward in time to an era before Adam and Eve, before the cavemen, all the way to 'nothingness' [*néant*] on the third page. We are abandoned to the point of elimination from the universe. But this unidentified consciousness survives, miraculously pulls itself together again, and carefully describes to us in thirty pages the famous scene of the goodnight kiss, fully particularised in time, place and persons. Now we know precisely where we are. We have come through.

The movement I am describing, a narrative sequence of 'lost and found', recurs immediately in the *madeleine* episode, which brings back the whole conglomerate mass of the Protagonist's childhood in Combray. Then in later sections of the novel, which move the scene to Paris, to Balbec, and elsewhere, he (and we readers) get lost again. This time our wandering in the wilderness will be prolonged for thirty years and two thousand pages, relieved by occasional glimpses of hoped for rewards and by the earnest pursuit of shallow goals such as social success and love. The most fundamental movement of the action, twice repeated after the opening, each time on an expanded scale, is also a construction: a boy-man becomes lost, meanders, and finds his way again. One might identify it as the Prodigal Son parable, except that in the *Search* there is no loving father at the end to take him in.

What I am calling the 'lost and found' structure takes place in narrative time and can also be contemplated as an abstract shape removed from time. It entails along the way ignorance, revelation, discovery, misguidance, error, drifting, corruption, resolve, patience, impatience and salvation. The basic form of the novel is not something static that lifts the action out of time and contingency. The structure maintains a strong yet fluctuating forward movement, even when we are lost. One grasps it better on reading.

Having made such a sweeping claim about the overall shape and movement of the *Search*, I want to come back to the novel itself as it unfolds for the reader and to the way Proust employs a variety of building procedures and structural devices as he goes along.

I have already discussed the opening pages. It is as if we are shown a film of something blurred, which gradually comes into focus as a bedroom with boy and mother. After a lengthy shot of that scene, the camera pulls back into an establishing shot revealing 'all Combray' with its church and environs and family and neighbours. Here the Narrator (whose voice we hear telling the Protagonist's story because it is his own, and who has achieved near total recall) has infinite reserves of things to record about his earlier life in Combray. How does he choose and arrange them into a mere 150 pages?

Proust uses two utterly simple organising devices, which hover halfway between description and narrative. He tells us what happens every Sunday in Aunt Léonie's household, a dependable routine of conversations and meals, and then what happens on Saturday's slightly modified schedule. These tiny domestic provincial events are given near epic status, like life at Versailles. Then the Narrator switches from the calendar to geography to hold the story together. We learn that all Combray is divided into two parts, into two possible directions in which the family may take its daily walk. These two 'ways' open up the countryside and their neighbours as neatly as Sunday and Saturday open up the household for inspection. We see Combray as vividly as a glass-enclosed ant hill.

Now, 200 pages into the novel, the Narrator, whose voice has told us of his (i.e., the Protagonist's) childhood in Combray, enters again in his own person. He says he will reach back before his own childhood to recount what he has learned about an earlier love affair of their chic Combray neighbour, Swann. Why this apparent digression into the past? Why introduce a 200-page subplot about Swann just when the Protagonist's story should begin in earnest? Because Swann's character and experience will reveal many similarities to his (I, 191; I, 232/273). Perhaps because Proust had these remarkable pages all written and ready in a drawer. And surely because this extended flashback has the narrative effect described in the French proverb, *reculer pour mieux sauter*: Fall back to make a better leap. As the only freestanding unit within the full novel, 'Swann in Love' works as an internal replica or miniature of the whole, a microcosm that leads into the macrocosm that surrounds it. In all sections of the book, the Narrator feels free to intervene and to observe about an incident: 'we shall see' how it relates to later developments (e.g. I, 462; II, 49/58). 'Swann in Love', rather than hanging apart from the larger mass to which it is appended, implies everywhere: 'We shall see' how this story about Swann will shed light on later events.

The internal construction of 'Swann in Love', because of its smaller scale and third person narrative concentrated on two characters engaged in a love affair, differs from that of the *Search* as a whole. A rewarding and challenging project for a reader or student is to diagram or make a flowchart of the novella. Many different representations are possible, most of them tending towards a line or graph tracing the fluctuations and modifications of Swann's feelings towards Odette. Indifference, dependence, deprivation, happiness, habit, jealousy, obsession, and indifference again form into a dynamic curve. Proust gives that curve a pronounced shape by having the two moments of most intense feeling coincide, not with love scenes, but with social scenes, an evening at the Verdurins at which Swann unexpectedly fails to find Odette, and the concert at Mme de Saint-Euverte's at which the music obliges him to relive the trajectory of his unstable infatuation. 'Swann in Love' carefully read with responsiveness to its endless variations and sinuosities, conveys a sense of physical shape, like a curve with two peaks. At this order of magnitude, Proust's sense of form seems unerring.

And now, after 400 pages of finding the focus, consisting of scenes of the Protagonist's early childhood and of Swann's preparatory interlude, the story is launched. The Protagonist starts growing up and branching out and groping his way. He goes to new places, he meets new characters. Does anything hold all these incidents together other than the thread of his responsive yet bumbling personality? How do we and he make it through the next two thousand pages? Has the novel become merely episodic? The résumés now included in all editions of the novel will guide us through the outward incidents as they pass and the major subjects examined. But because Proust never shows us all of a character at once or all the consequences of an incident at that moment, we, like the Protagonist, have to pick our way through an essentially piecemeal universe.

Across the extended basins and plateaus of the middle section, the *Search* sustains its forward motion on the basis of three areas of investigation and one overall direction. The Protagonist sets about with unequal success to enter elite society, to find a way to love and be loved by Albertine, and to discover his relation to art. All three actions move towards disenchantment with the goal sought. The central steppes of this vast narrative trace a downward curve through these three false scents of society, love and art. Commenting on the Protagonist's miraculously vivid childhood in Combray, the Narrator states categorically (at its close):

C'est parce que je croyais aux choses, aux êtres, tandis que je parcourais [les deux côtés], que les choses, les êtres qu'ils m'ont fait connaître sont les seuls que je prenne encore au sérieux et qui me donnent encore de la joie. (I, 182)

[It is because I believed in things and in people, while I walked along those paths that the things and the people they made known to me are the only ones that I still take seriously and that still bring me joy.] (I, 221/260)

The Protagonist *believed* in the world of Combray. He had faith in its reality and its integrity. Once out in the wide world, unprotected by family and household routines and the magic spell of childhood, he gradually ceases to believe. He loses his faith in everything except those early memories. He tries in vain to restore his faith (II, 680–1; III, 446/529). In the last sections, he is fully deprived of his childhood faith in the world, though still deeply aware of its earlier power (IV, 123, 436; VI, 619/730–1, 205/241–2). The book follows a downward trajectory.

Before I examine further how Proust carries the Protagonist and us through two thousand middle pages of the *Search* and deposits us on the farther shore, it is worth looking at the metaphors Proust employs to refer to structure, to stand for the process of creating a graspable unity out of an overwhelming variety of materials covering more than forty years. These metaphors relate indirectly to the traditional forms of the novel discussed earlier. But they are more personal and more specific.

Early in 'Combray', the first scene to be given a detailed description after Aunt Léonie's top-floor room is the ancient village church of Saint-Hilaire. Its sturdy architecture, handsome stained-glass windows, secret crypt and distinguished bell tower belong to an edifice more imposing and more ordered than any other in the village. The articulation of parts from porch to sanctuary offers us the first representation of form and structure in the book. That quiet symbolism in the opening pages becomes explicit at the close, where the Narrator refers to 'building [his book] up like a church' (IV, 610; VI, 431/507). But the Narrator insists also on two much more down-to-earth metaphors for making a work of literature, both of them linked to the servant figure of Françoise: dressmaking (II, 10; II, 261–2/308–9) and cooking (IV, 610–12; VI, 431–3/507–9). Throughout the novel, Françoise is praised as a true artist in these two domestic domains. Writing a book bears many resemblances to combining swatches of cloth into a dress, and to blending selected ingredients into a *bœuf mode*.

Proust refers to two other major domains as forms of order that relate to a work of art. Geology with its layering of deposits and stable formations serves as an image of the past held in place for our later inspection. In dramatic contrast, music, particularly in its attention to development, variation and recapitulation, presents a far more dynamic version of form than geology. But, after his years of visiting cathedrals and translating Ruskin, Proust remained faithful to the metaphor of the church as the ideal of structure. For him, however, a church expresses not a stable form like geology but a dynamic form like music. The Narrator describes the successive styles followed in building the Combray church. Thus it records motion in time and becomes a 'ship sailing through the centuries from bay to bay, from chapel to chapel' (1, 60; 1, 71/83. Translation altered.). Structure here maintains and displays a dimension in time, gradual change and prolonged construction. Both characteristics belong to the *Search*.

Launched now onto the wide interior sea of the middle sections of the novel, Proust has given himself a form, an itinerary of remarkable flexibility. He appears to be at the mercy of the winds and currents he meets. But as I stated in my opening pages, he has signalled his reader and written to his friends and informed interviewers: the end is already in place, he knows his destination, and he can attain it. Within reasonable limits, therefore, he can extend the voyage, add new ports of call, change course and speed. The Protagonist moves through the middle sections of his life and his novel somewhat as Odysseus does, delayed by distractions, impediments, luxurious surroundings and spellbinding women to the point of despair and no return. Like Homer, Proust knows how to play out his story. The Protagonist's goodnight kiss episode is built on a foundation of patience in waiting for his mother. In the *madeleine* sequence, the Narrator has to force himself to look again several times into himself and to relax his mind before he connects with the elusive memory trace of tea and cake.

This narrative of postponement and delay, if properly conducted, leads to an effect we learn very early to expect from a story: suspense. Will the messenger arrive in time? Will the ship reach the harbour despite all obstacles? Proust knows his trade and gives us many clues. In Combray, Aunt Léonie has become deeply dependent on Eulalie's regular Sunday visit. But the hour of her visit is uncertain, a circumstance that has important consequences. 'If unduly prolonged, the rapture [*volupté*] of waiting for Eulalie became a torture.' If her visit came too late, it 'would almost make [Aunt Léonie] ill' (1, 69–70; 1, 82/96). The narrative art of timing, that is, knowing how to structure a story in time, prevents the sheer pleasure of suspense from turning into irritation or boredom. Proust started with a book of some 500 pages and expanded it to 3,000 without, for responsive readers, exceeding that limit. Other readers will disagree and argue that Proust far overshoots narrative limits and does not deserve comparison with Homer.

What I have written so far might incline a reader to conclude that, in regard to structure, Proust took great care to place the beginning and the end of his novel in alignment with one another, and then threw everything else into a loose and capacious middle. Because of the book's length and number of places and characters and social levels, it can be difficult for the reader to locate himself in the narrative landscape. But I wish to demonstrate that in the central reaches Proust has not lost control, is not just throwing out one incident after another. I would even argue that the novel has a 'middle' as clearly marked as the beginning and the end. These middle 500 pages present in a very ordered way within this partial *Bildungsroman* the Protagonist's triple rite of passage into maturity and into a new perspective on his goal in life.

The major scenes in the middle section take place in an alternating order similar to the montage of a film. The order of things seems to arise both from contrast and from chronology. First, the Protagonist witnesses from close up the illness and death of his beloved grandmother without registering their effect on his deepest self (II, 609–41; III, 359–97/425–71). When he is invited to an elegant sit-down dinner at the Duc and Duchesse de Guermantes', his fantasies about the magic world of aristocracy wither into disenchantment at their empty rituals (II, 709–836; III, 480–632/570–750: it is the longest sustained scene in the book). From a window, the Protagonist observes the homosexual encounter of the imposing Baron de Charlus, a Guermantes, and Jupien, a tailor, and his eyes are opened to understand the Baron's aggressive and enigmatic behaviour (III, 3–33; IV, 1–38/ 1–44). Climbing even higher socially, he attends an immense reception at the Prince and Princesse de Guermantes' and finds himself surrounded by homosexuals and by discussions of the Dreyfus affair (III, 34–122; IV, 39–143/45–168). And finally, travelling to the seaside resort of Balbec, the Protagonist, first in a dream and then at the sight of apple trees in full bloom with their roots in the spring mud, responds both to the terrible loss of his grandmother and to her survival as a moral and almost physical presence in his life (III, 148–78; IV, 174–209/204–45).

These 500 middle pages recount, in the two short framing sequences about the grandmother, the Protagonist's first encounter with the death of a beloved family figure. That split incident of delayed action frames the two scenes depicting the sumptuous yet empty rewards of social ambition. Centered in this double frame sits the scene that Proust always referred to as 'indecent': the explicit revelation of Charlus as a homosexual predator. From here on the direction of the novel becomes unmistakable, a long decline until the story comes to a standstill before the new beginning of the closing sequence. At the furthest extent of his narrative reach, Proust has constructed a sequence of scenes forming a 500-page unit that serves as the novel's pivot, its turning, its evident midpoint. If one opens the book at random in these areas, one may find no paragraph breaks, no dialogue, just uninterrupted prose made up of startlingly lengthy sentences. Nevertheless, any given page occupies its place in a larger overall structure of postponement and divulgence, of beginning and middle and end. The scale, the distance between points travelled, remains very large. The 120-page dinner scene at the Duc and Duchesse de Guermantes' ranges as far afield as Kant's philosophy and café-concert performances. But each page and each scene has its appointed place within this wide narrative aperture.

Keeping faith with this slow-motion overall structure will help readers to reach 'the end'. By the end, I mean the last 200 pages, which stand apart as clearly as the first 200 pages of 'Combray'. During the thirteen plus years he spent composing the *Search*, Proust insisted on the close, almost symmetrical relation of beginning and end. They were written together. They fit together. They draw the form of the book together. I believe one can perceive that the first pages describe a divergent movement like the delta of a river. They move from the tiny swirl of an unfocused consciousness to the 'patch' of a single bedroom scene, to 'all Combray', and finally to the world at large. In a loosely opposite sequence, the closing pages lead back, in a converging funnel-like movement, towards a very limited point. This final sequence needs clarification.

The abruptly interrupted sentence on page IV, 433 (VI, 201/237) represents not an ordinary ellipsis or omission but a genuine breakdown, a dramatic incapacity on the Narrator's part (and perhaps Proust's) to continue. The language of rhetoric has a concise term for this kind of interruption: *aposiopesis*. The Narrator cannot go on. The words come to a sudden halt in the middle of an awkward digression on the dire effects of the recent war. One receives the impression, deliberate, I believe, and even if not, strikingly effective, of a maniac disabled in the middle of a rant.

The ensuing line break represents a total silence and a gap of several years. And appropriately, when the narrative begins again, the first words refer to a *maison de santé*, a mental hospital or insane asylum. The Protagonist has lost his wits as well as his way. What finds and saves him, like a harbour awaiting his arrival, is the other end of the great narrative arch sketched out but not used at the beginning of the tale. From the world of darkness and loss, he comes back to Paris. Numbly and somewhat mechanically he goes to a concert-reception at the Prince and Princesse de Guermantes'. This regathering of the cast, like a curtain call, corresponds to the opening sequence describing life in Combray. The first tableau of the Guermantes' salon then closes down its aperture to concentrate on a single figure, Mlle de Saint-Loup. The two 'ways' of the novel converge and become reconciled in her Swann-Guermantes parentage. She represents a crossroads in a forest, the living symbol of the overall narrative movement towards reconciliation. And her sixteen-year-old reality 'goads' the Protagonist, after so many years of drifting, to find the resolve to set to work, to become the Narrator of his own story, to recognise not only all his former friends but himself in her. 'She was like my own youth' (IV, 609; VI, 430/507).

At the point where the Protagonist becomes the Narrator, the narrative we are reading lapses back one last step to the uncertain condition of 'vertigo' (IV, 624; VI, 451/531). This last stage of the novel corresponds to the opening stage, three thousand pages earlier, of a consciousness caught within a swirl of dreams and memories, 'the kaleidoscope of darkness' (I, 4; I, 2/2). Between them lies a long quest and most of a lifetime.

No, the story does not end exactly where it began. But Proust carried out his original plan to relate how the Protagonist becomes lost for years and years, constructively lost, like the youngest son in a fairy tale performing the onerous tasks that will transform his life, until he finds the path that will set him back on his way. The last scene of self-recognition in the figure of a young girl also reveals to him his vocation (literature), his subject (his own story), his narrative perspective (lived Time), and the resolve to carry it all out.

The closest structural parallel to the *Search* lies in an American story that derives from German folklore and has attained folk status for us. The greatest difference is that Washington Irving wrote his twenty-page tale 'to make a long story short'. Proust moved in the opposite direction in regard to length. But just recall a few details of 'Rip Van Winkle' (1819). The dreamy Rip has 'an insuperable aversion to all kinds of profitable labor' and lives in terror of his termagant wife. When he flees to the woods, a twenty-year sleep descends on Rip. He returns to his village an old man and a stranger. When his own son is pointed out to him (the counterpart of Mlle de Saint-Loup), Rip 'doubted his own identity'. It takes an old woman, after peering into his face to confirm to everyone, including Rip, 'It is himself.' Yet some uncertainty remains whether he 'is out of his head' with his tale of old Dutchmen playing bowls in the mountains. Rip ends up a patriarch sitting at the inn door. Inevitably and appropriately, 'he used to tell his story to every stranger that arrived at Mr. Doolittle's hotel'.

To my knowledge, Proust did not read Irving and did not know Rip's story. Thus the parallel becomes all the more striking. The motif of departure and long delayed return leads both protagonists to behold contingent time not in abstract but in vividly physical terms, not only decrepitude and foot-long beards, but a young person who embodies the elapsed time. Both the Protagonist and Rip are painted as frivolous idlers who waste their best years. But where Rip merely settles into a comfortable niche as an old fogey with one story to tell, the Protagonist, having recognised himself and his tale, dedicates the rest of his life to transforming his story into a literary work. What Rip cannot even imagine the Protagonist discovers and embraces: a calling, a purpose. But the outward shape of the two tales is similar, though very different in scale.

Replying to his friend Henry James who called on the novel 'to represent life' ('The Art of Fiction'), Robert Louis Stevenson drew a succinct contrast between the two. 'Life is monstrous, infinite, illogical, abrupt, and poignant; a work of art, in comparison, is neat, finite, self-contained, rational, flowing, and emasculate' ('A Humble Remonstrance'). Stevenson's description of life applies more aptly to the *Search* than does his description of a work of art. And it is true that many circumstances, from sheer length to prose style to indeterminacy of character may leave the impression that Proust's novel is as overwhelming and as shapeless as life itself. But though Proust claimed to have difficulty patching the narrative parts of his novel together, he succeeded in doing so. He gave it not one but a number of sturdy structures. The unity of the *Search*, what I discern as the 'lost and found' saga adapted also in the Prodigal Son parable and in 'Rip Van Winkle', is finally equal to its length. To discover it brings great reward.

NOTE

1 In Chapter two of my *Proust's Way* (New York: Norton; London: Penguin The Allen Lane Press, 2000), I explain why I favour the convention of referring to the first person protagonist of Proust's novel as 'Marcel'. In order to avoid confusion over names in this collection, and to honour our editor's wish for consistency, I here accept the convention of saying 'the Protagonist' when referring to the central personage of the *Search*.

6

BRIAN ROGERS

Proust's Narrator

Men who produce works of genius are not those who live in the most delicate atmosphere, but those who have had the power . . . to make use of their personality as a mirror, in such a way that their life, however unimportant it may be, is reflected by it, genius consisting in the reflective power of the writer and not in the intrinsic quality of the scene reflected.

A l'ombre des jeunes filles en fleurs

Proust's Narrator is the successor to a long line of heroes in European fiction who mirror the author's sensibility and reflect his conception of reality. This mirror is different however. The central character in *A la recherche du temps perdu* is more akin to Flaubert's and Stendhal's characters who reflect their inner vision of the world outside them, than to the robust actors of *La Comédie humaine* whose physical image is inseparable from the reality they represent. The psychological analysis of Proust's fictional hero reaches into the cocoon of sensations, impressions and reflections which inform his view of himself as an artist. It is they which furnish the key to the Narrator's personality. If we wish to understand him we must look into his mirror, share the images swirling around in his imagination and unravel the process by which they form patterns which will turn into a work of artistic creation. The path down which the reader is led is the same as that which the central character himself follows without realising it. The originality of the portrait lies in the fact that the novelist he becomes at the end of *A la recherche du temps perdu* relives his transformation and shares it with the reader without damaging the chrysalis from which he is emerging.

Who, then, is the Narrator? His body, his mind, his senses seem to exist only when Proust shares with us his reactions to certain stimuli. When they are not present, he ceases to function. It is as though he had ceased to exist. Large empty spaces are concealed beneath the pages of *A la recherche* which other novelists fill with information irrelevant to Proust. The spark is rekindled only when the Narrator finds himself asking questions containing the stuff from which he will construct a novel. Is the physical world forever beyond his reach? What is the mysterious nature of certain objects which seem to possess a meaning of their own? Are they in some way connected to himself? What are these unexpected messages he sometimes receives, partly from people and places, more often in response to unsolicited signs and clues, the significance of which is obscure and of no interest to anyone but himself? What are people really like, since it is so difficult to form a consistent image of them as they move in Time and Space? Do they cease to exist or change into something else when he cannot visualise them, like the places he imagines, so different from those with which he comes in contact? The portrait of the Narrator is made up almost entirely of these questions and of the answers he supplies as he moves from childhood to maturity. Likewise the plot, pared down to the suspicion that many of the solutions he is seeking are to be found in the works of great artists and that his desire to follow their example will probably remain unfulfilled.

To understand the Narrator is therefore to understand Proust's novel. Fortunately, the reader has many ways of gaining access to his individuality. The first and most recognisable, especially for anyone familiar with the traditions Proust inherited from predecessors like Stendhal and Balzac, is the not inconsiderable importance given to the external circumstances of the hero's life. Disembodied though he is, the character belongs to a recognisable period in France's history between the end of the Second Empire and the aftermath of the First World War, that is to say between about 1870 and the early 1920s. Most of Proust's biographers agree that he drew considerably on his life and times when constructing the fragile outer shell of his protagonist. Few readers today, however, are inclined to fall into the trap of identifying the Narrator with the author or of enjoying *A la recherche* simply as an historical chronicle, mentally 'fleshing out' the Narrator. The social backdrop invites comparison with the France of Balzac, Flaubert and Zola it is true, and gives a certain solidity to the hero but is less Proust's tribute to the social novel of the nineteenth century than a means of exploring the first stage in the Narrator's evolution in society as an embryonic artist.

The second path open to the reader is to accept Proust's invitation to share the Narrator's deepest response to the messages he receives from the outer world. The poetic fabric of the novel is not confined to the famous transcriptions of real and fictional works of art. It plays a dramatic part during the whole of the Narrator's story and the style in which it is written is a counterpoint to the meagre drama of his life. His intense mental activity, to which the reader is always privy, leaves little trace on the physical events supporting it but the Narrator's inner tensions, his doubts about the value of the impressions and sensations he shares with the reader, the imperious calls of a superior intelligence almost convincing him that they are of little significance, this silent dialogue only surfaces in the final chapters, where it takes precedence over everything else. For a novel whose subject is the nature of art and the artist, *A la recherche* is remarkable for the paucity of fictionalised debates on aesthetics, unlike the novels of Anatole France where they play a major part. It is nevertheless the unspoken conversation between the man and the artist-in-waiting which provides the second level of characterisation: the metamorphosis of a man into a novelist.

The third path is the most original. This final key to the Narrator's consciousness lies in the construction of *A la recherche* and in the techniques which give a special resonance to the voice expressing the character's perception of himself. The structure of Proust's novel is like a gigantic mirror reflecting the kaleidoscope of a lifetime's images, a glass in which the reader is shown colours, shapes and volumes gradually emerging. The process he is asked to grasp – the reader does so instinctively – is the same as that which the Narrator and, according to Proust, every artist, novelist, painter or musician experiences as he wrests from within himself, embraces and transmits his deepest and most consistent impression of the outside world.

The artist in society

The first mirror image of the Narrator most closely resembles, then, those to be found in Proust's predecessors. Many elements of the portraits in *A la recherche* are adapted from the worlds of Balzac, Flaubert, Stendhal, Hardy, Dostoievski, Saint-Simon, Molière, Barbey d'Aurevilly and Anatole France, to mention only some examples. The Narrator's artistic vocation is moulded in part by his relationships with other people and hampered or impelled by the classic interweaving of personalities which is the particular genius of the French novel. The fictional characters in *A la recherche* function, too, as mirrors, distorting or complementing the images forming in the Narrator's mind, changing shape and consistency until they achieve the only permanence to which they can aspire: the accumulation of conflicting, superimposed images reflected in the mirror of another's consciousness.

These characters are broadly divided into two categories: those whose reflection is more or less consistent with the Narrator's own evolving vision, and those who refract a light so alien, so hostile – but sometimes so hypnotic – that they cause him to doubt the validity or relevance to any artistic vocation of his inner world. In the first group, of course, are the fictional artists of *A la recherche*, Vinteuil, Elstir and, until his decline and death, the novelist Bergotte. In the second group are Mme Verdurin, one of the true monsters of the novel and the most important female character after Albertine; Albertine herself, a malign Goddess of Time and Space distorting the

Narrator's view of the world far more than Charlus, Mme de Guermantes or Bloch, false prophets who, apart from the latter, are all artists potentially as original as the Narrator.

In between these contrasting mirrors stands the ambiguous figure of Swann, so convincing a reflection of the Narrator that only at the conclusion of the novel does he reveal himself as the mere skeleton of the novelist the latter has become. The structure of *A la recherche* and the Narrator's temptation to give Swann an importance he only partially deserves are devices used by Proust to define what the central character is not. It is a process already used by Thomas Hardy. The memory of Swann's affair with Odette and the Narrator's subsequent experience when he falls in love with Albertine recall the superimposable narratives of the English writer whose originality, according to Proust, lies in the shifting geometry of a fictional world where apparently recurring lines illustrate the variations of a mind at different moments in his life.[1] Adapting this technique, Proust draws a comparison between the Narrator and Swann which eventually convinces the latter of the true nature of the artist. Swann was deluded in searching for the essence of Odette in the music of Vinteuil and the paintings of Botticelli. When in turn he falls in love, like Swann and, like him, listens to the composer's music, the Narrator discovers the eternal reflections of an experience which his friend had glimpsed but impatiently discarded. More importantly, the tantalising image of Swann proves that there is no alter ego, no doppelgänger in the life of the artist. Apart from the value of suffering, Proust's Narrator discards many of the conceptions of the artist found in romantic literature: the friendship of a kindred spirit in the guise of Swann or Saint-Loup, the reflection of unnamed aspirations in the ideal woman. But for a long time he is unable to disentangle the shapes and colours the medieval craftsmen gave to her ancestors in the stained glass window of the Combray church from the fascinating Duchesse de Guermantes, the superficial hostess he meets at dinner parties, just as the sense of Time and History culled from his reading of Saint-Simon's *Mémoires*, Tallemant des Réaux's *Historiettes* and the novels of Balzac and Barbey d'Aurevilly, is cruelly distorted when he makes the acquaintance of the descendants of the greatest families in France.

One image is so fascinating, so strange that it almost takes precedence over all the others. It was much worked over by Proust in the sections of *A la recherche* composed or rewritten during the War. What is this unnamed, perhaps unnameable world so familiar that it reaches deep into the Narrator's earliest childhood memories and reappears in moments of intense distress? Charlus offers him a reflection of the world he will discover in another form in the mirror of Albertine. It contains an inverted picture, as it were, of the Narrator's final vision of reality, one where the intangible essence he will discover is tantalisingly locked away forever in the material world. This truly infernal vision is illustrated in *Sodome et Gomorrhe*, *La Prisonnière* and *Albertine disparue* by the subterranean regions of homosexual love.[2] It is a region presided over by the Baron de Charlus according to whom it is a Holy of Holies, like that described in the Old Testament or recreated by Racine in his Biblical play *Esther*. It contains hidden rooms and corridors, he says, like those being rediscovered at the beginning of the century during the restoration of Versailles. 'Vous savez,' the Baron confides in an early draft of his attempted seduction of the Narrator, 'que depuis qu'il y a un nouveau conservateur à Versailles, on a découvert tous les jours dans ce Palais Enchanté, d'abord des meubles, des pendules, des bustes, des tableaux . . . une salle entière avec de merveilleux panneaux, un escalier peint par Lebrun, des châteaux inconnus dans le château'[3] ['You know, since the arrival of a new curator at Versailles, every day there are discoveries in this Enchanted Palace: furniture, clocks, busts, paintings . . . an entire room with marvellous panels, a staircase painted by Lebrun, unknown castles within the castle']. In the final version of the conversation Charlus is actually made to speak in the voice of one of the characters in Racine's play, *Esther*, inviting the Narrator, not into the fabled palace of Ahasuerus in which her drama will unfold, but into the sumptuous home of the Princesse de Guermantes over which the Baron stands guard.[4] The Narrator's reaction, however, is to stamp on Charlus's hat. His experience with Albertine is less comic. It is only after the death of his bisexual lover that he can view with some equanimity the spectacle of the scion of another ancient family, the descendant of the Cambremers whom he had known during his tortured affair with Albertine, accepting the Baron's offer to marry Mlle d'Oléron, the niece of Charlus' homosexual lover, Jupien (IV, 236; V, 756/893).

Many of the portraits in *A la recherche*, like the description of places and events, contain coded references to writers the Narrator is reading or has read and to painters and musicians to whom he is drawn. One of the functions of the subterranean language of quotation in the novel is to highlight the influence, good or bad, the predecessors of the future novelist exert on his vocation and, in particular, on the evolution of the style which will express his vision.[5] The venerable Marquise de Villeparisis, for example, is a mirror containing among other things the dangerous reflection of Sainte-Beuve's criticism and his false conception of art. Her advice to the Narrator during their rides in the countryside around Balbec to be wary of Vigny, Balzac and Musset is a parody of the nineteenth century critic's *Causeries du lundi*, while the tone of her rebuke and the inflexions of her voice are a pastiche of Sainte-Beuve's friend and admirer, Mme de Boigne, whose *Mémoires* Proust had read and criticised in 1907 (see II, 70, 80–2; II, 334/395, 347–9/410–12).[6] The

verve with which the old lady debunks Chateaubriand is a mixture of the
anecdotal criticism Proust condemned in his *Contre Sainte-Beuve* and the
spiteful reminiscences of Mme de Boigne. The story the Marquise tells of
Chateaubriand's celebrated evocations of moonlight is the rewriting of the
latter's ironic chronicle of a real social occasion on which the poet gave a
reading of *Les Abencérages*. 'Quant aux phrases de Chateaubriand sur le
clair de lune', Mme de Villeparisis declares, referring to a passage in the
Voyage d'Italie entitled 'Promenade dans Rome au clair de lune', 'elles étaient
tout simplement devenues une charge à la maison' ['As for his fine phrases
about the moon, they had quite simply become a family joke'], her intention
being, like that of Sainte-Beuve and Mme de Boigne, to destroy the reputation of the artist by criticising the man.[7] This aspect of the Narrator's aesthetic evolution through pastiche and cryptic allusion is still one of the least
appreciated or researched features in *A la recherche*.

It is in part through the tensions set up by quotations such as these and
the more visible reflections offered by the mirror-characters that the
Narrator's vocation is honed and determined. No sooner, for example, does
he discover affinities between the mature painting of Elstir and his own pro-
pensity to analogy and quotation than he is faced with real, if comically
expressed objections to his notion of the continuity and renewal of art. The
Duc de Guermantes's realist attitude to painting, although he seems unaware
of it, is the expression of a philosophical view current in the late nineteenth
century and the opposite of Proust's. A canvas of Elstir's showing a contemporary 'fête populaire' reminds the Narrator of Carpaccio's landscapes, an
intuition confirmed by the presence of the artist's patron in contemporary
dress on the margins of the scene, which deliberately alludes to the
Renaissance artist's manner. 'Avec son air endimanché,' the Duke kindly
informs his socially inexperienced guest, and unaware of the homage paid
by Elstir's quotation of his predecessor's work as he renews the genre, 'il fait
un drôle d'effet' (II, 790) ['With his Sunday-go-to-meeting look he creates a
distinctly odd effect' (III, 578/686)].

No fictional character mirrors the Narrator's vision of art and reality as
closely as Elstir, Vinteuil and Bergotte. So long as he considers them merely
as friends or acquaintances, even the latter seem alien to his vocation and he
makes little attempt to cultivate the society of artists. Like Sainte-Beuve, he
sometimes falls into the trap of judging them by their behaviour. Vinteuil dies
during the childhood of the Narrator who, like Swann, can for a long time
see little connection between the music and the eccentric neighbour he recalls
from childhood, or with his discovery of Vinteuil's daughter's sadistic treatment of her father's memory after he dies (I, 157–63; I, 190–8/224–33).
Bergotte, he learns, conducts a semi-incestuous affair behind his wife's back,

is guilty of mental cruelty and suspected of financial dishonesty. It is only at his grandmother's insistence that the Narrator agrees to visit Elstir in his hideous modern villa by the sea, where he is as interested in the painter's colourful past as in his pictures, even using his new friend to make the acquaintance of Albertine. When he questions the artists he does come to know about their work, their verbal explanations appear as opaque as the young Elstir's cryptic appreciation of a fellow painter, which delighted Mme Verdurin and her guests so long ago. 'Ça a l'air de rien,' he would expound to the *petit clan*, 'pas plus moyen de découvrir le truc que dans *La Ronde* ou *Les Régentes* . . . Tout y est, mais non, je vous jure' (I, 250) ['It looks as though it was done with nothing at all . . . No more chance of discovering the trick than there is in the "Night Watch" or the "Female Regents". . . It's all there – but really, I swear it"' (I, 306/361)]. Mme Verdurin was no more capable of seizing the importance of his reference to Rembrandt as a means of understanding the new painter's style than the young Narrator, unable still to grasp the message conveyed by the mature Elstir's advice to explore his dreams. What does he mean by asserting 'ce qui guérit, ce n'est pas moins de rêve, mais plus de rêve, mais tout le rêve'? (II, 199) ['The cure . . . is not to dream less but to dream more, to dream all the time' (II, 488/577)]. Only at the end of *A la recherche* does the Narrator appreciate the value of the painter's advice which seemed to contradict Bergotte, who exhorted him to prize the gift of intelligence. Has the mirror dimmed, which the ageing novelist kindly offers to his gaze? 'Je crois que c'est assez vrai,' is all that he will say when asked about his own work, 'c'est assez exact, cela peut être utile', but his notion of intelligence is still luminous, if only the Narrator had seen it (I, 546) ['I think it's more or less true, more or less accurate; it may be of some value perhaps' (II, 150/178)]. All the same, the artist in society when he talks about his art is a poor reflector of his work.

Those who make a profession of criticising or appreciating art, the authorities the Narrator consults like Brichot, the Sorbonne professor, Bloch, the ambitious writer of articles and reviews or Norpois, who has met all the eminent men of his day, hold up mirrors to reality and its artistic expression so diverse that their images form a meaningless blur. They hardly give focus to the Narrator's own confused pictures of Berma in the title role of *Phèdre*, his contradictory perceptions of the church at Balbec and the Cotentin coastline. Like those of each succeeding generation of commentators, their reflections on art and reality contradict each other sometimes – it would seem – for the satisfaction of showing exactly the opposite of what had previously seemed real. Some project a microscopic view of art and prefer Musset's short stories to his poetry, Molière's Italian comedies to *L'Avare* and a horn passage in *Tristan and Isolde* to the *Ring* cycle. Others like the Duchesse de

Guermantes, admired in social circles for her advanced views, adopt strange magnifying glasses, as on the famous occasion when she astonished her guests by informing them she would rather see the paintings of Frans Hals from the top of a tram than not at all (II, 813; III, 606/718). It is only when the Narrator looks closely for himself into the mirror of the works themselves that he discovers the images he is looking for.

The transcription of the Narrator's inner world

The second path to our understanding of the Narrator is composed of the silent dialogue taking place between the man and the novelist he has yet to become. It occurs when he converses not with others, but with himself and, if we listen carefully, includes fragments or sketches of his future novel. Some of them retain the imprint of other artists, most are linked to the vision of the world he tentatively described in his childhood. Still others reflect images which as yet have no definitive verbal equivalent. This mute dialogue is a revolutionary means of fictional characterisation and reappears in some form in many of the great novels of the twentieth century, extending the realm of psychological analysis to embrace a commentary on mental worlds in evolution. Writers of other essays in this book deal more fully with the sources of pain and pleasure accompanying the Narrator's conversation with himself. It is recalled here principally to show how the words and phrases slowly forming in his mind contribute to the portrayal of the central character of *A la recherche*.

Glimpses of the world they describe are clustered in groups at the beginning and the end of his story, recapitulated in the 'overtures' which introduce the pictures developing in each individual volume and strung together as congruent images link them all: impressions of bird-song in the 'overture' to *Le Côté de Guermantes I* giving expression to memories of forgotten spring-times; a taste of chocolate creating a phrase capturing the sensation of mornings in a country town in the prelude to the second chapter of *Guermantes II*; sounds of a tram performing a similar function in the first chapter of *Sodome et Gomorrhe II*; old feelings of loss at the start of *Albertine disparue* translated into a metaphor containing the memory of the dead grandmother; a train returning to its point of departure at the beginning of Chapter II of the same volume; in Chapter III the roofs of Venice at the heart of an image recalling the Sunday markets of Combray; the resurrection of childhood in the madeleine sequence in *Du côté de chez Swann* turning into the narrative of *A la recherche*; the illumination of a life towards the end of *Le Temps retrouvé* becoming the kernel of the Narrator's long-awaited novel. We realise the importance of this dialogue when it altogether replaces the fictional setting of the Princesse de Guermantes's final *matinée*. But it has been there from the beginning, punctuated by the Narrator's conversations with artists of the past and present. Phrases from the novels of Bergotte colour the childhood episodes; memories of the painting of Elstir and the music of Vinteuil give a particular tone to the social episodes in *Le Côté de Guermantes II* and the story of Albertine. Beneath the surface of the Narrator's external activity we listen to his questions and share his discovery of words and images.

The first sketch, the embryonic precursor to the Narrator's completed novel is inserted, like the madeleine episode from which it springs, in *Du côté de chez Swann*. Taking as its subject the spires of Martinville, it appears as the prose poem quoted in inverted commas in 'Combray'. Its reappearance some years later as an article submitted to the *Figaro* and its eventual emergence as the seed of a still incomplete work of art are one of the most important keys to the Narrator's inner world.

This leitmotif, as important a narrative device as the repeated references to involuntary memory, had its origin in a real experience crucial to Proust's decision to begin work on *A la Recherche*. In 1907, a year before he began writing notes for his novel, he described the sensation of driving down the steep hill into Caen and seeing the spires of the abbey church of Saint-Etienne and the tower of Saint-Pierre change places in a kind of dance as his car wound its way down towards the plain stretching inland from the sea. So strong was his impression that he made it the subject of an article published in the *Figaro* in November.[8] The circumstances of the experience were modified and introduced as the dance of the fictional spires of Martinville and the real tower of Vieuxvicq, giving the reader his first glimpse of the future novelist's transcription of the world. Referred to as a 'petit morceau' in *Du côté de chez Swann* (I, 179) ['little fragment' (I, 217/255)], it is superseded in *A l'ombre des jeunes filles en fleurs* by a long article containing allusions to Elstir's painting. Submitted to the *Figaro*, it does not appear for some time and is anxiously awaited in *Le Côté de Guermantes II* and *La Prisonnière*. Although we never read it, the fictional article is one of the measures Proust gives the reader of the Narrator's desire to give permanent expression to his view of reality but also of his uncertainty about the vehicle he should adopt. Little more than a child when he composed the Martinville piece (which he keeps jealously to himself), he is only a young man when the *Figaro* article is published (IV, 148; V, 649/766). Disappointed by the form in which it communicates his vision, he decides to rewrite it. The equivalent of Proust's *Contre Sainte-Beuve*, the article combines personal experience with aesthetic criticism. Worse, it is a piece of journalism, the relationship established between the writer and his reader being nothing compared to the silent communion the Narrator enjoys with great artists. It is with difficulty, none-theless, that he resists the temptation to send copies of the newspaper to his friends, but realises that the 'conversation' which would ensue would be no more satisfying than the dialogue Sainte-Beuve held with the readers of the *Constitutionnel* in the nineteenth century, offering the same empty pleasure as the leading articles of Bergotte in the *Figaro* today. It is on the advice of Odette that the old novelist has fallen into the trap of regarding literature as inferior to life. 'Est-ce que vous trouvez que ce qu'il écrit n'est pas bien' ['Do you mean you don't think what he writes is any good?' (II, 179/212)] she protests, adding in her anglicised French, he is 'the right man in the right place' (I, 571).

Clumsily communicated, the experience expressed in the article neverthe-less contains the essence of the Narrator's evolving vision of the world. It is the kernel of the memories evoked by the madeleine and the cornerstone of his future novel. As he resumes his questioning of the artists he admires, he realises that they share the same ideals. Norpois was right in noticing simi-larities between his childhood scribble – 'je l'avais dit,' he remembers saying when he showed it to the great man, 'mais je n'en pensais pas un mot' ['I had indeed said so, but I did not mean a word of it' (II, 52/62)] – and the novels of Bergotte (I, 465). Not because, as Norpois put it, it is a pale imitation of the novelist's style but because it expresses the same conception of literature, the same conviction that style and not ideas communicates an artist's vision. The accumulation of metaphors in the Martinville sketch reaches into the deep enduring memory recounted more prosaically in the narrative of the goodnight kiss when, as a frightened child, he demanded comfort and reas-surance from his mother. Transformed into images, the three church spires encapsulate the sense of foreboding, of isolation and loss following the joyous light of day, the dark side of the magical world of Combray, and introduce the implacable rhythm of anguish at nightfall, repeated through-out his life, which permeates his vision of the world. The volumes hidden below the surface of Elstir's landscapes, the ethereal regions in Vinteuil's music reflecting a light which has vanished from the earth are undiscovered parts of the same universe which, the Narrator slowly realises, he has been seeking to recreate since childhood when it emerged briefly in his earliest composition. Elstir and Vinteuil cannot show it precisely in the way in which he saw it: their colours and shapes have different patterns. In Elstir's paint-ings, the pink sky of twilight he had seen behind the Martinville spires as they faded into dusk is the colour of dawn tinting the sky with hope, and the bells ringing out in Vinteuil's music are not the ones the Narrator still hears in his dreams. Pursuing his dialogue with these great masters, he neverthe-less learns that without realising it he has been clumsily following in their wake. The early Vinteuil sonata and the mythological pictures he discovers in the Guermantes's gallery are the equivalent of his own first sketch, the initial steps – 'délicieux mais bien frêles' – towards later, triumphal master-pieces. The confident translation of the artist's inner world starts with images as naïve and as deeply-rooted as those he had hurriedly jotted down in Dr Percepied's carriage. Even La Berma, who had disappointed him when as a child he did not understand the greatness of her art, encompasses in the lines her body traces on the stage the transcendental reality he had captured for himself on the occasion when the three golden pivots of the spires turned into a translucent substance and gave birth to a cluster of images refracting 'le rayon central et prisonnier qui les traverse' ['the imprisoned, central ray that pierces through them' (I, 179, II, 348; I, 217/255; III, 48/56)].

The Author-Narrator

The tensions contained in the Narrator's inner dialogues are resolved in *Le Temps retrouvé*, the origin of the third track the reader is invited to explore in his search for the central character in Proust's novel. *A la recherche* is not only his spiritual autobiography, a kaleidoscope of mirrors reflecting his transformation into an artist. It is a statement of the author's conception of art and a commentary on his work. Like a palimpsest visible beneath the surface of the narrative lies the essence of its creator. Like him the reader looks back at the end of the book on the life evoked in the previous volumes and discovers the meaning which has turned it into a work of art.

The form and structure of *A la recherche* are examined in the previous chapter. Its strange architecture was largely designed to give particular focus to the first-person narrative in which it is cast and to lend a special function to the voice bringing the Narrator and his story to life. This focus and the functions it performs are the technical means by which Proust ensures both the reader's contribution to the creation of his hero and his participation in the act of creation which is the climax of the novel.

A voice is all that the reader has at his disposal. The guiding hand of the omniscient author has apparently been abandoned. How can this 'I', alter-nately emerging from a web of dreamlike memories and impressions, and submerged in the cluster of hours, years and places belonging to another's consciousness, how can this disembodied voice help the reader perform a task no other novelist had previously demanded? Jagged shards of memory reflect separate images of somebody whose essence seems hidden in a blur of impressions akin to the changing colours of the kaleidoscope referred to in the opening pages of the novel. The function of the 'I' is to communicate the unique quality of separate facets of this person as they appear and disappear and to submerge them simultaneously in the mass of sensations and impressions which together constitute his being. Challenged to perform a similar process of creation, the reader is given the material which changes the 'I' into a novelist.

The choice of first-person narrative solved the question of both the reader's and the Narrator's perspective. When contemplating the focus he wished to give one day to the story of Albertine, the Narrator himself decided that it ought to be written 'from within' in order to reproduce his own subjective view, which no outsider could share:

> Bien vite je me dis: 'On peut tout ramener, en effet, si on en considère l'aspect social, au plus courant des faits divers : du dehors, c'est peut-être ainsi que je le verrais . . . Mais il y a autre chose que ces faits qu'on raconte . . . il y a peut-être du mystère dans la vie de tous les jours.' Il m'était possible de le négliger concernant la vie des autres, mais celle d'Albertine et la mienne, je la vivais par le dedans. (III, 866)

> [Very soon I said to myself: 'One can of course reduce everything, if one regards it in its social aspect, to the most commonplace item of newspaper gossip . . . But there is something beyond those facts that are reported . . . , there is perhaps an element of mystery in everyday life.' It was possible for me to neglect it in the lives of other people, but Albertine's life and my own I was living from within.] (V, 416/490–1)

For that reason, when he includes 'Un amour de Swann' among his memories, the Narrator writes this part of his story in the third person. Swann is so like the Narrator that the reader is not unduly concerned by the subterfuge which allows him to enter, like the Narrator apparently, the skin of the fictional character, sharing without knowing it images of Swann which, in fact, reflect the Narrator's vision of the world. The reader follows his advice in the rest of the novel, however, and recreates the protagonist of *A la recherche from within*. The peculiar properties of Proust's use of first-person narrative allow the reader both to remain largely unaware of the meaning of many of the signs in the novel indicating that the childhood vocation has not been lost, and to participate in the miracle of *Le Temps retrouvé*, discovering in his memory of the pages he has been reading the equivalent of the geological upheaval taking place in the Narrator's mind.

This trick is achieved by the use of two simultaneous but separate viewpoints which fuse only at the end of the novel. The double internal focalisation of *A la recherche* permits the reader to share the Narrator's perspective on his life as he sees and lives it *from within*, and at the same time views it *from without* as he discovers in it the material for his novel. One focalisation reproduces the sensation of a rich muddle of experience as it occurs, the second extracts from it the essence of a work of art. The two focalisations converge and separate during the course of the narrative before becoming one in the ideal form of the Narrator's projected novel. His life is consequently seen by the reader both through the eyes of the person resuscitated in the memories which are the fabric of *A la recherche*, and in the mind of the narrator-novelist recreating him. Each of the Narrator's experiences retains in consequence its authentic reverberations. Encased like a jewel in the sensations accompanying it as it unfolds, his life is further enriched by the echoes it produces in the mind of the artist reliving and recreating it. It accrues associations and falls into patterns which possess meanings sometimes different, always richer than at the original moment which remains intact, the origin of a seemingly endless chain of reflections and interrogations. In the space between these focalisations, Proust has situated the essence of the Narrator's character and personality. The reader's perception of him is not identical to the perspective of the author-Narrator, who looks back with irony, humour and sometimes embarrassment on his former self; nor is he held irrevocably to the point of view of the man who has yet to achieve his goal. The richness and the complexity of the Narrator are contained in a style which captures the ebb and flow of two perspectives on a single being searching for and discovering himself. So it is that, like the Narrator in 'Combray', the reader learns that experience, especially that of reading, must be detached from and remain connected to the contingencies surrounding it, if he is to capture its significance.

It is for this reason that the most important image offered by the Narrator to the reader of *A la recherche* contains the reader's own reflection. If it is recognisable, so is the portrait of the Narrator. If the reader sees the characters of the novel in the colours and shapes they assume for the evolving artist, the portrait of the Narrator is a true likeness. Is the Princess of Luxembourg a stem entwined with the tendrils of her scarf, the Marquis de Cambremer a victim seeking divine recognition for his martyrdom, Saint-Loup a luminous vein of opal running through rough stone, M. de Stermaria a traveller in a hurry furtively consuming his chicken in a station buffet, the guests at the Grand Hôtel inhabitants of Dante's Underworld and the reception clerks their judges? Are the street sellers the chorus from *Boris Godunov*, the flower girl a figure in a painting of David and Goliath, the Embassy officials acolytes accompanying their priest in the Temple of Jerusalem?[9] If so, the Narrator's mirror is not inaccurate. Has Proust encouraged the reader to rewrite the world according to the novelist's aesthetic principles, discovering the rich, invisible geometry supporting the characters he encounters, rearranging the lines and surfaces of their bodies which conceal, instead of expressing, their reality? If so, the reader has added in his imagination fresh pages of his own to the Narrator's novel. Perhaps he is more like Swann and needs personal reasons for recognising the grotesque nature of characters he would rather take for granted. It is probably too much to expect every reader to see the world through the eyes of the child, who grows up seeing reflections of Old Masters in his friends or, in the hated enemy he meets in the final episode of *Le Temps retrouvé*, the vision of an aged beggar, a grotesque snowman, an insect in a mummified chrysalis and the ferocious hero of Mme de Ségur's novel *Général Dourakine* reduced to infancy (IV, 501; VI, 288/339). More likely he will find in his imagination personal reflections of the landscape of Combray and Balbec, of the countryside smells invading Léonie's apartment, personal equivalents of the bedroom described at the beginning of *A la recherche*, the cradle of the novel we are about to read, in summer the precarious haven of a tomtit on a wind-tossed branch, in winter a sea-swallow's nest snuggling in dry land (I, 7–8; I, 6–7/7–8).

The Narrator is not Marcel Proust. He often borrows the eyes and ears of the author and seems to possess the same encyclopaedic culture. But he is only a character in a story and his story contains only one event, the decision to write a book. In all probability it will contain little the reader has not already learned about him as he turns the final page of *A la recherche du temps perdu*. His novel will contain 'cette réalité loin de laquelle nous vivons . . . cette réalité que nous risquerions fort bien de mourir sans avoir connue, et qui est tout simplement notre vie' (IV, 474) ['that reality, remote from our daily preoccupations . . . that reality which it is very easy for us to die without ever having known and which is, quite simply, our life' (VI, 253/298)]. Why should we care? The reader must take on trust what the Narrator chooses to tell us about himself. He has no name, we have no clear idea what he looks like. For long stretches of his book he disappears from view, leaving the reader to eavesdrop on the conversations of people who seem oblivious of this man's existence. He is passive and transparent, everywhere and nowhere, sometimes a spy, often a voyeur turning up in unlikely situations, a disembodied presence unlike that in any novel before. But the mirror he offers the reader is so fascinating that we not only enter the world reflected in it, we inhabit the Narrator's body, see everything through his eyes, and share his sensibility.

NOTES

1 Proust's analysis of the 'admirable geometrical parallelism' of *A Pair of Blue Eyes*, *The Well-Beloved* and *Jude the Obscure* is contained in the *Carnet de 1908* (p. 114), and is the basis for the Narrator's discussion of the novelist in *La Prisonnière*. He disliked *Far from the Madding Crowd*, but confided to Robert de

Billy that *The Well-Beloved* presented similarities with his novel, in a letter dated 1910 (*Corr.* x, 54).

2 The Narrator's discovery of the infernal regions inhabited by Albertine and her friends is discussed in Brian Rogers, *Le Dessous des cartes. Proust et Barbey d'Aurevilly* (Paris: Champion, 2000).

3 The manuscript version is reproduced in II, 1818 (not in the English editions). Trans. R. Bales.

4 See also II, 893 (not in the translations). Proust alludes to the conversation in *Esther* which takes place before the gates of Ahasuerus' palace, in which Esther reveals her true identity (Racine, *Esther*, III, i).

5 The function of Proust's encoded references is discussed in Annick Bouillaguet, *L'Imitation cryptée: Proust lecteur de Balzac et de Flaubert* (Paris: Champion, 2000).

6 The origin of the conversation with Mme de Villeparisis is discussed in my article 'Deux sources littéraires d'*A la recherche du temps perdu*: l'évolution d'un personnage', in *Cahiers Marcel Proust* XII (Paris: Gallimard, 1984), 53–68.

7 See *Mémoires de la comtesse de Boigne née d'Osmond*, édition présentée et annotée par Jean-Claude Berchet. 2 vols. (Paris: Le Temps retrouvé, Mercure de France, 1999), I, 285–6.

8 A facsimile of the original article, together with photographs showing the spires of Caen at the beginning of the century, is reproduced in the *Album Proust* (Paris: Pléiade, 1965), pp.222–3.

9 The references for these allusions are: II, 24, 40, 59, 88; III, 64, 257, 624 (II, 279/329, 298/352, 320/377, 356/420; IV, 75/87, 302/355, V, 126/148).

7

The unconscious

Proust's inquiry into the nature of the unconscious in *A la recherche du temps perdu* begins on the first page, with the Narrator's loss of his identity in the book he is reading. An insomniac, he wakes in the middle of the night, so disoriented he does not even know who he is. Feeling 'plus dénué que l'homme des cavernes' ['more destitute than a cave-dweller'] he has 'seulement dans sa simplicité première, le sentiment de l'existence comme il peut frémir au fond d'un animal' (1, 5) ['only the most rudimentary sense of existence, such as may lurk and flicker in the depths of an animal's consciousness' (1, 4/4)]. Having stripped him of his identity, sleep – and its absence – has carried him to man's beginnings. In fact, it has reduced him to the core of existence itself. But sleep has also carried away his furniture, his room, everything of which he was only 'une petite partie et à l'insensibilité duquel [il allait] vite [s']unir' (1, 4) ['an insignificant part and whose insensibility [he] should very soon return to share' (1, 2/3)]. He has fallen into 'le néant' (1, 5) ['the abyss of not-being' (1, 4/4)] from which, he says, he could never escape by himself. Memory arrives to pull him out of the abyss and is already working to rebuild 'les traits originaux de [son] moi' (1, 6) ['the original components of [his] ego' (1, 4/5)]. In the first four pages Proust has given a metaphorical description of the *tabula rasa* from which the quest for the lost treasure of the Narrator's identity begins. Memory, already a companion in the search, has only just begun the foundation for what will become 'l'édifice immense du souvenir'(1, 46) ['the vast structure of recollection' (1, 54/64)] that, as the Narrator will discover, actually holds the very treasure he has lost.

In the same few opening pages, with the loss of an internal, subjective reality founded on a solid notion of self, the Narrator also loses the external reality of an objective world anchored in fixed notions of time and space: 'Un homme qui dort, tient en cercle autour de lui le fil des heures, l'ordre des années et des mondes' (1, 5) ['When a man is asleep, he has in a circle round him the chain of the hours, the sequence of the years, the order of the heavenly host' (1, 3/4)]. If the chain had held, he would not have needed the help memory brings. The 'kaléidoscope de l'obscurité' (1, 4) ['shifting kaleidoscope of darkness' (1, 2/2)] that surrounds him is less a source of certainty than the illusory projections of his magic lantern onto the walls of his childhood bedroom. The realities of subject and object are, in fact, bound together, but it is the latter that depends on the former for a solid foundation rather than the reverse: 'Peut-être l'immobilité des choses autour de nous est-elle imposée par notre certitude que ce sont elles et non pas d'autres par l'immobilité de notre pensée en face d'elles' (1, 6) ['Perhaps the immobility of the things that surround us is forced upon them by our conviction that they are themselves and not anything else, by the immobility of our conception of them' (1, 4/5)]. A tension has already been established between the subjective, internal world of sleep and dreams and the objective, external world of conscious order that 'endows the unconscious life with a validity which almost, if not indeed totally, equates it with the world of wakefulness'.[1] The search for the essence of the one, then, is also the search for the essence of the other. In penetrating the mystery of his lost identity, the lost reality of the objective world will also be revealed. Memory holds two lost treasures.

The search for the essence of man's nature is not new. Nor are the assumptions on which it is based, that is, first, that there is a core nature to be found, and second, that it can be reached and understood. The Socratic 'know thyself' is as dynamic an imperative today as it was generations ago. Descartes gave the self a foundation in reason and, from it, posited man's existence in his 'I think therefore I am'. Combined with Cartesian mathematics and Newtonian physics, a coherent world-view based on the capacity of man's reason to perceive the laws governing a causal, mathematically ordered universe is created. Man and world are united through the laws that govern the universe and the ability to know them. Rousseau disagreed. Inspiration and imagination define man, not reason. For the French Romantics this inspired, imaginative self had little or no use for objective, precise observations of either itself or the world. By the end of the nineteenth century this world-view is doing battle with a world-view that emphasised man's reason and the ability of his senses to perceive objectively a mathematically ordered universe. The Symbolists' view of a world clouded in obscurity, veiled by appearances that must be penetrated by the artist's creative imagination to reveal its hidden order provided yet another path in the search. By Proust's time German philosophy was influencing the Sorbonne with its emphasis on scientific objectivity and exactitude. Combined with German Romanticism, with Schopenhauer's eastern, mystical view of man and world, a positivistic light is being shed on the mysteries of both the external, physical world and the metaphysical world of the psyche, the latter taking place at research institutes such as that run by Charcot at the Salpêtrière in Paris.

The newly emerging form of inquiry known as psychology faced many of the fundamental difficulties encountered in the Narrator's search. They must both deal with the inescapable paradox of any effort to observe man's metaphysical nature in an objective, scientific fashion. The basic problems of the subject-object relationship, seemingly resolved by a careful positioning of the observer so as not to influence the natural sequence of events taking place, become much more complex. The tidy positivistic world-view, based on fixed references in time and space disintegrates into a messy, disorienting eddy of relativity. Instead of one stationary observer and one unmoving observed there is a plurality of people and perspectives, both temporal and spatial. Is the best field of inquiry to be found not in an 'objective' penetrating of someone else's psyche but rather in a 'subjective' probing into one's own inner darkness? But how can one observe oneself without letting oneself know what is happening and thereby ruining the experiment? Even if intelligence, reason and objectivity are possible means of penetration, can they bring the treasure up, can they shed their light on it without changing it? Can it be expressed in logical, scientific terminology? Is there even an essence to be found?

Proust's knowledge of psychology came from several sources. His father worked at Charcot's institute in Paris. Thanks to Charcot, Proust would have come into contact with ideas that also influenced Freud who was a medical student at the Parisian institute of 'psycho-physiology'. Critics have also seen a possible influence in Proust's cousin by marriage, Henri Bergson. Other critics have disagreed, maintaining that Proust had a limited knowledge of Bergson's writings.[2] Proust himself, while acknowledging a common interest, said that he would have called his novel 'bergsonian' instead of 'une suite de *romans de l'inconscient*' ['a series of novels of the unconscious'] if he thought that it would have been correct to do so.[3] Anne Henry has argued that several German philosophers influenced Proust: Schelling, Schlegel, Kant and, most importantly, Schopenhauer.[4] For Proust, the opposition is not a mechanistic one between body and soul, as it appears in Bergson's works. It is, rather, a Schopenhauerian one between Nature and soul. Many terms often attributed to Bergson, including Proust's famous distinction between voluntary and involuntary memory, are derived from Schopenhauer. What is clear from these and other possible influences (including Théodule Ribot, Pierre Janet and Edouard Brissaud) is that Proust's theories – philosophical and psychological – are reflections of the intellectual spirit of the times.

There have been many comparisons between Proust and his contemporary, Freud, who is said to have 'discovered' the unconscious: 'If Freud's discovery had to be summed up in a single word, that word would without doubt have to be "unconscious"'.[5] The Narrator's quest makes him a frequent traveller down what Freud in his *The Interpretation of Dreams* called 'the royal road to a knowledge of the unconscious'.[6] He relishes the ride and often describes those fluid moments during which sleep provides the transportation between the conscious and the unconscious self. He is even a collector of various types of sleep, a cultivator of dreams in the only soil available, his own self: 'En faisant varier l'heure, l'endroit où on s'endort, en provoquant le sommeil d'une manière artificielle, ou au contraire en revenant pour un jour au sommeil – le plus étrange de tous pour quiconque a l'habitude de dormir avec des soporifiques – on arrive à obtenir des variétés de sommeil mille fois plus nombreuses que, jardinier, on n'obtiendrait de variétés d'œillets ou de roses' (III, 631) ['By varying the hour and the place in which we go to sleep, by wooing sleep in an artificial manner, or on the contrary by returning for a day to normal sleep – the strangest kind of all to whomsoever is in the habit of putting himself to sleep with soporifics – we succeed in producing a thousand times as many varieties of sleep as a gardener could produce of carnations or roses' (V, 133–4/157)].

One of the most commonly applied Freudian approaches uses his notion of infantile sexuality and the Oedipus complex. In short, the Narrator's childhood need for his mother's goodnight kiss – and its refusal – explains his later, obsessively jealous love for Albertine. The Freudian critics find strong support from the Narrator's own self-analysing: 'Malheureusement . . . le baiser qu'Albertine me donnerait en me quittant, bien différent du baiser habituel, ne me calmerait pas plus qu'autrefois celui de ma mère quand elle était fâchée . . .' (III, 595) ['Unfortunately . . . the kiss that Albertine would give me when she left me for the night, very different from her usual kiss, would no more soothe me than my mother's kiss had soothed me long ago, on days when she was vexed with me . . .' (V, 91–2/108)]. The effects of this demystification of the Romantic notion of love cannot be overestimated. Love is no longer a metaphysical ideal, it is a natural phenomenon. The psychologist and artist now have a 'scientific' tool they can use, an 'objective' perspective from which they can study the manifestations of sexual desire and a terminology with which they can theorise about and express its nature and its origin. However, while it is true that the Narrator's love for Albertine reveals the Proustian unconscious, to stop here, at an unconscious based on a libidinous, oedipal force manifesting itself as sexual appetite would place a superficial limitation on not only the Proustian, but also the Freudian unconscious: 'In fact, although the chief properties of the system *Ucs.*[the unconscious] reappear in the agency of the id, the other agencies of ego and superego also have an unconscious origin and an unconscious portion ascribed to them . . .' (Laplanche and Pontalis, *The Language of psycho-Analysis*, p.476). As for the Proustian unconscious, it is 'an unconscious so enlarged and so copious as to make the Freudian unconscious seem a miserably stunted affair'.[7]

Freud and Proust share the belief that the unconscious is repressed. Both describe the unconscious topographically as being located beneath the social, conscious self. The Narrator is constantly searching for those revealing moments in human conduct, for any cracks in the conscious constructs that might reveal the hidden unconscious. Like a psychologist, the Narrator observes 'Freudian slips' wherever and whenever he can. These observations are, in fact, an essential part of his vocation as an artist: 'Les êtres les plus bêtes, par leurs gestes, leurs propos, leurs sentiments involontairement exprimés, manifestent des lois qu'ils ne perçoivent pas, mais que l'artiste surprend en eux' (IV, 480) ['The stupidest people, in their gestures, their remarks, the sentiments which they involuntarily express, manifest laws which they do not themselves perceive but which the artist surprises in them' (VI, 261/307)]. But should one stop here, accepting the Narrator's theorising, his own self-analysis as accurate, even though the observations are of a subject that is aware it is being observed and whose actions are being recorded? Can even the Narrator's hypothesising based on his many observations of other people's actions be trusted? Or, like the Narrator, must the reader also look behind any conscious, rational explanations for hidden, unconscious motives? Even if one were tempted to remain here, accepting a general, undifferentiated sexual desire as the manifestation of a libidinous unconscious, both Freud and Proust go on to describe this desire as being sado-masochistic. In the Narrator's hypothesising about the causes of someone's actions, statements, gestures, writings, looks, etc., Proust provides 'a complex phenomenology for mental processes – those associated with bisexuality, jealousy and sado-masochism, for instance – upon which Freud performed certain of his most adventurous pieces of theoretical modelling' (Bowie, *Freud, Proust and Lacan*, p.69). The Narrator can also be quite succinct, as when he states, 'J'appelle ici amour une torture réciproque' (III, 617) ['Here I mean by love reciprocal torture' (V, 117/137)]. Jealousy and its incessant need to know and possess completely another person makes Proustian love 'un mal inguérissable, comme ces diathèses où le rhumatisme ne laisse quelque répit que pour faire place à des migraines épileptiformes' (III, 593) ['an incurable malady, like those diathetic states in which rheumatism affords the sufferer a brief respite only to be replaced by epileptiform headaches' (V, 89/105)].

While love supplies little in the way of knowledge or truth about the other person, it does offer a focus for the Narrator's search. A 'soif de savoir' (III, 593) ['a thirst for knowledge' (V, 90/106)], jealousy causes the narrator to suffer, bringing him closer to the depths of his own unconscious: 'La souffrance ici . . . a pour siège une couche plus profonde du cœur' (III, 595) ['The anguish then . . . has its seat in a deeper layer of the heart' (V, 92/108)]. Jealousy even brings the Narrator closer to Evil itself: 'La jalousie est aussi un démon qui ne peut être exorcé. . . . Fussions-nous arrivés . . . à garder perpétuellement celle que nous aimons, l'Esprit du Mal prendrait une autre forme' (III, 611) ['Jealousy is moreover a demon that cannot be exorcised. . . . Even if we could succeed . . . in keeping the beloved for ever, the Spirit of Evil would then adopt another form' (V, 110/129)]. The Narrator's 'thirst for knowledge' is more insatiable than any simple sexual appetite. He and Freud both share the Platonic urge to arrive at the essence of self and world, the theorist's desire for origins [that] is written into the book of Nature as the prototype of all desire' (Bowie, *Freud, Proust and Lacan*, p.80). Though the Narrator's pain is quite real and his efforts to imprison Albertine dominate a large part of the novel, the sado-masochistic aspect of the relationship remains essentially metaphysical. His observations of Mlle Vinteuil and then Charlus provide the physical manifestation of man's homosexual, androgynous and sado-masochistic nature and his 'thirst' will not be satisfied until he finally follows Charlus into the sexual hell of Jupien's male brothel.

Strange as it may seem, Proust's choice of Charlus as human specimen for his observations reflects the prevailing view of the nature of man at that time. In his *Three Essays*, Freud discusses man's biological heritage and, like Proust, concludes that 'homosexuality, far from being a psychological predisposition of certain individuals within human society, is part of man's archaic biological inheritance' (Bowie, *Freud, Proust and Lacan*, p.78). With his choice of Charlus, the Narrator's quest has not taken him to the fringes of human nature, but to its essence. His scientific quest is now also mythic: 'So in order to recapture lost time in art, in order to make his book a history of the race as well as a history of an individual life, the Narrator must rediscover and exploit in his novel something of, on the mythic level, the androgyny of primal humanity and, on the scientific level, the hermaphroditism of the first plants and animals; and then he must show how the two relate. This he does in *Sodome I* in the . . . courtship of Charlus and Jupien.'[8] For the Narrator Charlus represents 'un admirable effort inconscient de la nature' (III, 23) ('an admirable though unconscious effort on the part of nature' (IV, 25/30)] and thus, like his botanical observations, will have 'une conséquence sur toute une partie inconsciente de l'œuvre littéraire' (III, 5) ['a conclusion that bore upon a whole unconscious element of literary production' (IV, 3/4].

If it can be said that Freud 'discovered' the unconscious, then it can also be said that Proust 'created' it in *A la recherche du temps perdu*.

Armed with the most modern scientific discoveries of the time, the Narrator constantly probes the mysteries of man and world. Practical and theoretical, physical and natural, all of the sciences employed are aimed at penetrating anything that may come between the Narrator and the essence of self and world. The developments in the glass industry, for instance, greatly expanded man's observational abilities.[9] They led to an unprecedented use of the microscope in the medical sciences, allowing increasingly precise observations in such fields as that of Proust's father, the epidemiologist Adrien Proust. The same improvements in the quality of lenses also helped to expand the astronomer's vision outward with larger, more powerful telescopes. Heretofore unseen worlds were revealed on both the microscopic and the macroscopic levels. Developments in glass and iron brought about the perfection and proliferation of aquariums, allowing both the naturalist and sightseers to view the inhabitants of the undersea world under 'natural' conditions. These developments also resulted in architectural innovations, such as the large bay window of the restaurant of the Grand Hôtel at Cabourg (Balbec in Proust's novel). This turns the dining room itself into a large aquarium for the Narrator, offering the opportunity for 'quelque écrivain, quelque amateur d'ichtyologie humaine' ['some writer, some student of human ichthyology'] to observe the human species in its natural element. By noting particular traits, such as 'les mâchoires de vieux monstres féminins se refermer sur un morceau de nourriture engloutie' ['the jaws of old feminine monstrosities close over a mouthful of submerged food'], the species can be classed 'par race, par caractères innés et aussi par ces caractères acquis' ['by race, by innate characteristics, as well as those acquired characteristics']. Through the observation of individual specimens such as 'la vieille dame serbe dont l'appendice buccal est d'un grand poisson de mer' ['an old Serbian lady whose buccal appendage is that of a great sea-fish'], the species can be traced back to its origins – in this case, to the 'eaux douces du faubourg Saint-Germain' (II, 42) ['the fresh waters of the Faubourg Saint-Germain' (II, 300/354)].

Walls have become windows. The observer is brought closer to this little world and is given a possible post of unobserved observation from outside the aquarium/dining room (although in this case this 'amateur' is imagined by the Narrator, one of the objects of observation). Proximity would seem to replace isolation. But this is not the case, as seen when the Narrator, just arriving at the Grand Hôtel, perceives another little enclosed world in the form of several old men who are staring sternly at him from behind the closed glass partition of a reading room. Instead of providing a possible respite for the Narrator's sense of isolation and uncertainty, his observation of the members of the little world of the reading room observing him and their imagined happiness at being part of the select few who have the right to read there in tranquillity only results in terror at the thought that his grandmother might make him go in and wait for her all alone. (II, 24; II, 279/329). Even when he has managed to participate in one of these enclosed worlds as he has in the dining room the Narrator finds the security and sense of belonging that he imagined to be illusory. All of these glass instruments (magic lanterns, kaleidoscopes, microscopes, telescopes, windows and aquariums) will be used metaphorically to describe the Narrator's research not only into the physical nature of the world and man, but also into the human psyche. While some can be said to be 'scientific' – involved in the rational, conscious, orderly collection through objective observation of classifiable data referring to a world fixed in time and space – they all ultimately point out a very modern awareness of the limits of such perceptual knowledge.[10]

The Narrator's use of botanical images to describe people and their actions is as pervasive as that of ocular imagery.[11] It permits the Narrator to have both an objective spatial and moral perspective regarding the people he is observing: 'A défaut de contemplation de géologue, j'avais au moins celle du botaniste et regardais par les volets de l'escalier le petit arbuste de la duchesse et la plante précieuse' (III, 3) ['Failing the geologist's field of contemplation I had at least that of the botanist, and was peering through the shutters of the staircase window at the Duchess's little tree and her precious plant' (IV, 1–2/2)]. One can no more make moral judgements concerning people than a botanist would a plant under study. Both are devoid of conscious will. Both are following the same laws, unconsciously obeying forces that control and unite life: 'Les lois du monde végétal sont gouvernées par des lois de plus en plus hautes' (III, 5) ['The laws of the vegetable kingdom are themselves governed by increasingly higher laws' (IV, 3/3)]. Nor can the reader judge the morality of the Narrator. The original cause of his presence is carefully established as one of a botanist, doing objective, scientific research – a morally unobjectionable activity – and not a pursuit of a voyeuristic, even sado-masochistic pleasure. The only reason that he begins observing the homosexual encounter between Charlus and Jupien is that they drew the attention of his scientific curiosity. As with the pollination of a plant by an insect, it is only a 'hasard providentiel' (III, 4) ['providential hazard' (IV, 2/2)] that brought this exotic pair of representatives of the human race together at a time and place that coincided with the Narrator's clearly detached scientific observations. This participation as unobserved observer, separate from and having no influence on the event, is an essential part of the claim to objectivity of the positivistic perspective. The homology created between this human, homosexual encounter and the botanical one between flower and insect is fundamental to the metaphorical bridge the Narrator establishes between objective, scientific certainty and his own probing of the laws that govern man's psyche. With the encounter of Jupien and Charlus the Narrator becomes a 'herborisateur humain' (III, 30) ['human herbalist' (IV, 33/39)] and can make his observations objectively, without disturbing the plant-people in their natural habitat and thereby ruining the possibility that 'les lois d'un art secret' (III, 6) ['the laws of an occult art' (IV, 5/5)] might be revealed to him.

The Narrator is now better positioned to observe the human species than the 'amateur ichthyologist' he imagined standing outside the window of the restaurant of the Grand Hôtel. Through unconscious expressions and gestures his specimens reveal their inner, feminine natures that, like Galatea, are trying to escape from 'l'inconscient de ce corps d'homme où elle est enfermée' (III, 22) ['the unconscious mass of this male body in which she is imprisoned' (IV, 24/28)]. They are so much a part of the chain of being that the Narrator sees 'successivement un homme, un homme-oiseau, un homme-poisson, un homme insecte' (III, 8) ['in turn a man, a man-bird, a man-fish, a man-insect' (IV, 7/8)]. The Narrator's approach to understanding the nature of the human species is a mirror-image of Darwin's naturalism. Hoping to discover the laws governing man's biological nature, Darwin looked to animals and plants while, conversely, the Narrator, observing man, sees the predetermined playing out of the same laws that govern the lower orders. They share a belief in the natural unity of all life. Knowing the Guermantes well, the Narrator is also in a better position than the 'amateur' to watch particular specimens of this family from a temporal perspective, allowing him to observe the evolution of the species as some particular traits are manifested through different members of the same family over generations. Charlus and his nephew, Robert de Saint-Loup, exhibit traits that at times suggest either their aristocratic heritage or hidden, homosexual desires that reappear over generations. They are excellent examples of the debate over innate versus acquired traits many medical theorists of Proust's time were having.[12] They also serve to point out some of the difficulties that lie in establishing a causal relationship, another fundamental aspect of the positivistic world-view. Even if the manifestations of their homosexuality may appear different, 'l'hérédité peut n'en être pas moins dans une certaine mesure la loi causale, car l'effet ne ressemble pas toujours à la cause' (III, 91) ['heredity may none the less to a certain extent be responsible, for the effect does not always resemble the cause' (IV, 107/124)].

The scientific discovery of a relationship between cause and effect, though based on carefully made observations, depends on an individual who can interpret the particular data and make the correct connections. Science and magic meet: 'Nos existences sont en réalité, par l'hérédité, aussi pleines de chiffres cabalistiques, de sorts jetés, que s'il y avait vraiment des sorcières' (II, 866) ['Our lives are in truth, owing to heredity, as full of cabalistic ciphers, of horoscopic castings as if sorcerers really existed' (III, 669/793)]. The Narrator finds that the sciences, even the study of the natural history of man, do not reveal anything more certain about the self or world than he found in the frightening flux of his sleepless nights or with the illusory projections of his magic lantern. In order to arrive at more than simply a vague, metaphysical description of the nature of man and the world, however, these scientific approaches must be used in the search. Though they may not lead directly to the one underlying essence of man or world, the Narrator gains not only valuable insight and experience with the most precise and probing scientific tools and methodologies available, he develops a vocabulary to describe man's metaphysical essence that transcends the romantic, intuitively known and vaguely expressed 'Moi'.

It is here, in his careful, minute observations of the words, the gestures, the faces of the people that surround him that the Narrator is also most firmly grounded in the prevailing positivistic attitude of the times. The slightest movement, 'vrai comme s'il était noté sur le cahier d'un anatomiste' ['as truthfully delineated as though it had been recorded in an anatomist's notebook'] is used by the writer to express 'une vérité psychologique' (IV, 479) ['a psychological order' (VI, 260/306)]. But he also uses another, even more penetrating scientific tool to arrive at hidden, psychological laws. While listening to conversations the Narrator is x-raying the mentalities which produced them: 'le dessin des lignes tracées par moi figurait un ensemble de lois psychologiques' (IV, 297) ['the pattern of the lines I had traced took the form of a collection of psychological laws' (VI, 34/40)]. It is the instinct of the artist that draws the general out of the particular, that sees in the insignificant babbling of social parrots, 'les porte-parole d'une loi psychologique' (IV, 479) ['mouthpieces of a psychological law' (VI, 260/306)]. It is 'le jeu des différentes lois psychologiques' (IV, 360) ['the interplay of different psychological laws' (VI, 112/133)] which aids in the flowering of the human race, the precise observations of which supply the Narrator not only with some of his most humorous passages, but also with some of his most insightful comments on the universal characteristics that define man.

It is true that these precise references occur only in the final volume of Proust's novel, Le Temps retrouvé. The term 'inconscient' ['unconscious'] is not used as a noun until the third volume, Le Côté de Guermantes, and the first reference to it in Proust's correspondence does not occur until 1915. (Alden, 'Origins', p.343). The evolution of Proust's thoughts concerning the nature of man's psyche can be seen in two quotes from his novel, one from the first volume, the other from the sixth, *Albertine disparue*. In the first quotation the Narrator's description of memory is purely spatial. He uses geological terms to represent the nature of the formation of memory (much like those used by Darwin in his description of the formation of atolls, which helped prove the age of the earth, giving strength to his theory of evolution): 'Tous ces souvenirs ajoutés les uns aux autres ne formaient qu'une masse, mais non sans qu'on pût distinguer entre eux . . . sinon des fissures, des failles véritables, du moins ces veinures, ces bigarrures de coloration qui, dans certaines roches, dans certains marbres, révèlent des différences d'origine, d'âge, de "formation"' (I, 184) ['All these memories, superimposed upon one another, now formed a single mass, but had not so far coalesced that I could not discern between them . . . if not real fissures, real geological faults, at least in that veining, that variegation of colouring, which in certain rocks, in certain blocks of marble, points to differences of origin, age, and formation' (I, 223/262–3)].

   In *Albertine disparue* the role of the fourth dimension of time is included in his psychological description of memory and its partner 'forgetfulness': 'Comme il y a une géométrie dans l'espace, il y a une psychologie dans le temps, où les calculs d'une psychologie plane ne seraient plus exacts parce qu'on n'y tiendrait pas compte du Temps et d'une des formes qu'il revêt, l'oubli' (IV, 137) ['As there is a geometry in space, so there is psychology in time, in which the calculations of a plane psychology would no longer be accurate because we should not be taking account of Time and one of the forms that it assumes, forgetting' (V, 637/751)]. This introduction of time serves to bend the linear view of memory, much as the introduction of this fourth dimension into physics via Einstein's General Theory of Relativity resulted in the curving of the Newtonian view of space (and, with the advent of quantum physics, in micro-space). The Narrator uses the magic lantern as an objective correlative to describe this internal truth: '. . . ma mémoire [était] comme la courbure des projections de ma lanterne magique . . .' (IV, 110) ['. . . my memory [was like] the curve of the projections of my magic lantern . . .' (V, 605/713)]. As Einstein's theories helped move Euclidean geometry from two ('plane' geometry) and three ('solid' geometry) dimensions into the curvature of his four-dimensional space-time continuum, so do Proust's theories concerning memory – with the introduction of time – result in this new view of psychology.

   Once again, this loss of a fixed frame of reference is as much internal as it is external. Not only is the order in the space-time continuum in flux, affecting the objective set of correlatives, but the subjective apparatus of the self – the single, indivisible subject – is also in doubt. It is now seen as a plurality of selves. The Platonic Ideal, having undergone an amoeba-like division with the Socratic 'know thyself' (and later, with Descartes's dualistic splitting of man into subject and object, knower and known with his 'I think therefore I am') has become a futile attempt to arrest time. It is a slip-sliding plurality of selves based on memories of events taking place in the flux of the space-time continuum. Proust was not alone, however, in believing that these selves hide an indivisible, core self – an unconscious, metaphysical essence beneath the conscious self that lies at the surface, divided by the contingencies of time, space, society, emotions – of any phenomenological situation. In his quest for this essential self the Narrator uses three posts of observation in order to study the manifestations of this metaphysical entity. In the first the observer is separated from the observed. In the second, there is interaction between the two and, in the third, there is fusion.

The first type of observation (separation) has already been presented here, with the Narrator's naturalistic observations of Jupien and Charlus in the courtyard of the hôtel de Guermantes. Even though he does penetrate farther into the home, he is never discovered by the two. Later in the novel the Narrator penetrates even farther, entering the confines of a whole society, itself closed off from the world by Jupien's male brothel – itself hidden in the dark night of a wartime Paris – and is able to observe the spectacle of Charlus's masochism from a corridor outside the room. This sense of having crossed several barriers to arrive at the revelation of a hidden reality reflects his effort to penetrate the levels of conscious will in order to arrive at the hidden unconscious. This association of a horizontal, labyrinthine penetration to a central point with a vertical movement towards the dark depths of the unconscious is a fundamental part of the archetypal view of man's essence.[13] In his observations of both of these scenes the Narrator remains separated both physically and morally. There are no admonitions, no moral imperatives. The spectacle is allowed to continue in its 'natural' process, allowing a rare look at the human species manifesting (on an individual level) its most hidden side, its sexual and sado-masochistic impulses (which, on the larger, national level is quite apparent in war). Again, this conception of the unconscious is Freudian in nature. With sadism the libido is project-ing onto the object of desire its death instinct that lies in the desire that each being has to return to the inorganic, the undifferentiated (Durand, *Les Structures*, p.222).

The second type of observation (interaction) introduces the spectator into the spectacle and results in the loss of a certainty based on reason, logic and objectivity. It is nowhere more apparent than in the Narrator's relationship with Albertine. The bond between cause and effect is relative, as the Narrator learns when trying to arrive at the truth behind Albertine's relationships with her friends: 'Je commençais à me rendre compte que le système des causes nombreuses d'une seule action . . . n'était qu'une sorte de symbole artificiel, voulu, des différents points de vue où on se place' (IV, 194) ['I was beginning to realise that the system of multiple motives for a single action . . . was only a sort of symbol, artificial and premeditated, of the different aspects that an action assumes according to the point of view from which we look at it' (V, 707/834)]. Though every effort is made to imprison Albertine, she escapes. Like any person, she is not an object. She is an agent and, as such, is not subject to 'objective' rules of verification. The person being observed is a dynamic process, not a static object and the involvement of the spectator with the spectacle, far from providing a firm foundation for knowledge, only adds confusion and pain to an already unsettling relationship with the world.

In the third type of observation, there is a fusion between subject and object, between observer and observed. In psychological terms this is referred to as self- or auto-analysis. Having realised the difficulties inherent in any study of the nature of man's unconscious from an external position, from outside the self of an 'other', the only recourse left in the Narrator's quest is to look within himself. However, as we have seen, the awareness of being observed inhibits objective observation of a natural process. Freud, reaching the same conclusion, soon realised that true self-analysis is not possible either.[14] So how, then, can the unconscious be revealed?

It is during an unexpected moment, while the Narrator's attention is distracted from these weighty concerns and is simply tasting the madeleine and herbal tea his mother has brought him that the unconscious reveals itself. He tastes the mixture: 'Un plaisir délicieux m'avait envahi, isolé, sans la notion de sa cause' (I, 44) ['An exquisite pleasure had invaded my senses, something isolated, detached, with no suggestion of its origin' (I, 51/60)]. He asks himself where it came from, what it means, how to seize it? He tries a few more mouthfuls, and realises it lies in himself. He puts down the object, the cup, and turns to himself, to his 'esprit'. The search is now in its hands: 'Je pose la tasse et me tourne vers mon esprit. C'est à lui de trouver la vérité. Mais comment?' (I, 45) ['I put down the cup and examine my own mind. It alone can discover the truth. But how?' (I, 52/61)]. While aware that some internal essence is making itself known, he is also conscious of the difficulties inherent in any retrieval of this treasure. Is it a question of finding the unconscious, or is it created? In a typically Proustian paradox, the answer is yes: 'Grave incertitude, toutes les fois que l'esprit se sent dépassé par lui-même; quand lui, le chercheur, est tout ensemble le pays obscur où il doit chercher et où tout son bagage ne lui sera de rien. Chercher? pas seulement: créer.' (I, 45) ['What an abyss of uncertainty, whenever the mind feels overtaken by itself;

when it, the seeker, is at the same time the dark region through which it must go seeking and where all its equipment will avail it nothing. Seek? More than that: create.' (I, 52/61)]. Freud reaches a similar conclusion. The self is like a slide in a magic lantern. By looking at its projection in a work of art (here, the written word), one can study the nature of the unconscious that produced it (Baudry, *Proust, Freud*, p.103).

What involuntary memory is for Proust, free association is for Freud. Tasting the madeleine and herbal tea arouses an involuntary sensation common to both the present and a past experience. Based on that sensation an involuntary memory is created that will be part of the 'vast structure of recollection' that houses his lost treasure. Common to both a present and a past moment, this sensation places the involuntary memory – and its treasure – outside the contingencies of time. Nor is it a question of finding the cause of the sensation in either the object or the subject. It requires a Hegelian synthesis, a fusion of the two for the sensation to occur. A writer unites the internal, subjective truth of the 'plaisir spécial' with an external, 'objective' truth of some seemingly insignificant object in the world, ties them together in a metaphor, creating a bond as strong as that of causality in the sciences (see IV, 468; VI, 246/290). The prerequisite for this free expression of the unconscious is a temporary setting aside of conscious will and intellect. There must be a state 'of consciousness which [Pierre] Janet called "abaissement du niveau mental", that is to say a certain narrowing of consciousness and a corresponding strengthening of the unconscious'.[15] The subject-object unity of the metaphor is not forced, it is an 'unité qui s'ignorait, donc vitale et non logique . . . né[e] d'une inspiration, non exigé[e] par le développement artificiel d'une thése' (III, 667) ['A unity that was unaware of itself, hence vital and not logical . . . It emerges . . . born of an inspiration, not required by the artificial development of a thesis' (V, 177/208)]. Not only does the experience of the 'plaisir spécial' reveal the unconscious, it frees it in a chance encounter to become a dynamic force uniting man and the world that surrounds him, placing the subject-object relationship outside the contingencies of time, space and causality.

This view of the unconscious is part of the German romantic tradition whose philosophy of art unites self and world in a vitalistic yet quasi-scientific way. Jung participates in this tradition and, through his theory of archetypes, also transcends the contingencies of time, space and causality. In his part of *The Interpretation of Nature and the Psyche*, 'Synchronicity: an Acausal Connection Principle', Jung presents an alternative to the rational view of science. While the latter assumes a unity between reason and intelligence in man's consciousness and a causal order in nature, the Jungian theory of simultaneity compels one 'to assume that there is in the unconscious something like an *a priori* knowledge or immediate presence of events which lacks any causal basis' (Jung and Pauli, *Interpretation*, pp.43–4). The internal, metaphysical world of the psyche is connected to the external, physical world. Both subject and object participate in an underlying unity, supplying a foundation for not only an individual's identity but, through the collective unconscious, the nature of man. Archetypes 'constitute the structure of the collective unconscious. The latter represents a psyche that is identical with itself in all individuals' (Jung and Pauli, *Interpretation*, p.29). As in Proust's paradoxical description of his 'plaisir spécial', where it is not only a question of seeking, but also of creating, Jung's definition of archetypes is based on a Platonic idealism – implying a pre-existing state – and, at the same time, a creative act, without which it would not exist: 'as *a priori* ideal forms, [archetypes] are as much found as invented: they are *discovered* inasmuch as one did not know about their unconscious autonomous existence, and *invented* inasmuch as their presence was inferred from analogous conceptual structures' (Jung and Pauli, *Interpretation*, p.59). Jung's theories have helped shed light on *A la recherche du temps perdu*, from what he called the 'Shadow', or man's dark side that exists in opposition to conscious principles,[16] to the 'discovery' of an interesting numerological archetype, '43'[17] and a geometrical, mandala-like archetype (that is, a symbolic figural pattern) that helps to illustrate the experience of the 'plaisir spécial', to summarise the structure of the novel and to tie the Narrator's individual discoveries to man's universal, collective unconscious.[18]

Though evidence is given to suggest the universality of these archetypes in science, art, philosophy and religion, there cannot be any objective, positivistic proof of their existence. As with the treasure that is revealed in the experience with the madeleine, an archetype is as much created as it is found. In order for the reader to see the unconscious in Proust's novel he must experience it himself. No intellectual treatise can accurately present it, no 'literary scientist' can prove its existence. Its treasure will not be surrendered to any direct, frontal assault by the conscious, reasoning mind. In order to get a true picture of the unconscious in Proust's novel one must first allow it to reveal itself through images, words, any apparently insignificant detail that makes itself known through some unconscious reaction. Much like a child with a game whose picture is only revealed when lines are drawn between seemingly random, meaningless dots, the reader can then use his intelligence to see, to understand for himself the nature of the Proustian unconscious. The image revealed will be not only that of the unconscious in the novel, but also himself: 'En réalité, chaque lecteur est quand il lit le propre lecteur de lui-même. L'ouvrage de l'écrivain n'est qu'une espèce d'instrument optique qu'il offre au lecteur afin de lui permettre de discerner ce que sans ce livre il n'eût peut-être pas vu en soi-même. La reconnaissance en soi-même, par le lecteur, de ce que dit le livre, est la preuve de la vérité de celui-ci, et vice versa' (IV, 489–90) ['In reality every reader is, while he is reading, the reader of his own self. The writer's work is merely a kind of optical instrument which he offers to the reader to enable him to discern what, without his book, he would perhaps never have perceived in himself. And the recognition by the reader in his own self of what the book says is the proof of its veracity, the contrary also being true' (VI, 273/322)]. The quest for the unconscious in *A la recherche du temps perdu* must be made by every reader. It is by nature a personal experience which, if successful, can illuminate not only the novel's depths, but can also reveal the treasure of the reader's own unconscious.

NOTES

1 Richard Bales, *Proust: 'A la recherche du temps perdu'* (London: Grant and Cutler, 1995), p.22.

2 Joyce Megay, *Bergson et Proust: Essai de mise au point de la question de l'influence de Bergson sur Proust* (Paris: Vrin, 1976).

3 Douglas W. Alden, 'Origins of the Unconscious and Subconscious in Proust', *Modern Language Quarterly* 4 (1943), 343–57.

4 Anne Henry, *Marcel Proust: théories pour une esthétique* (Paris: Klincksieck, 1981).

5 J. Laplanche and J.-B. Pontalis, *The Language of Psycho-Analysis*, trans. Donald Nicholson-Smith (New York: W.W. Norton & Co., 1973), p.474.

6 Sigmund Freud, *Standard Edition of the Complete Psychological Works of Sigmund Freud*, trans. James Strachey and Anna Freud (London: The Hogarth Press, 1953–74), V, 608.

7 Malcolm Bowie, *Freud, Proust and Lacan: Theory as Fiction* (Cambridge University Press, 1987), p.10.

8 J. E. Rivers, *Proust and the Art of Love: The Aesthetics of Sexuality in the Life, Times & Art of Marcel Proust* (New York: Columbia University Press, 1981), p.236.

9 David Mendelson, *Le Verre dans l'univers imaginaire de Proust* (Paris: Librairie José Corti, 1968).

10 Roger Shattuck, *Proust's Binoculars* (New York: Random House, 1963), p.145.

11 Samuel Beckett, *Proust* (New York: Grove Press, 1931).

12 J.E. Rivers, *Proust and the Art of Love* p.161.

13 Gilbert Durand, *Les Structures anthropologiques de l'imaginaire: Introduction à l'archétypologie générale* (Paris: Bordas, 1969), p.226.

14 Jean-Louis Baudry, *Proust, Freud et l'autre* (Paris: Les Editions de Minuit, 1984), p.114.

15 Carl Jung and Wolfgang Pauli, *The Interpretation of Nature and the Psyche*, trans. R. F. C. Hull (London: Routledge & Kegan Paul, 1955), p.43.

16 Patrick Brady, "Problematic Individuation in *A la recherche du temps perdu*', *L'Esprit créateur*, XXII, 2 (1982), 19–24.

17 The number 43 occurs in Proust's novel. A room number in Jupien's male brothel

that is referred to five times (IV, 391–4, 419; VI, 151–3, 185/178–81, 218), '43' is part of a psychically cohesive constellation of images. In night-time Paris, further darkened because of the war, the Narrator has followed Charlus into a microcosmic hell which reflects that of the world outside. He has gone to the end of darkness, sadism, death, evil – all archetypes of the unconscious. '43' can also be found in numerous similar contexts, including the beginning pages of Faulkner's *Absalom, Absalom!*, André Breton's *Nadja*, Ian Anderson's 'Hymn 43' (*Aqualung*) and in religious writings such as Valentinus's *Occulta philosophia*.

18 Jack Jordan, *Marcel Proust's 'A la recherche du temps perdu': A Search for Certainty* (Birmingham, Al.: Summa Publications, 1993).

8

JOSHUA LANDY

The texture of Proust's novel

If someone were to suggest that the texture of Proust's novel resembles nothing quite so much as molasses, it would be difficult to dissent with any great conviction. The over-long book, with its over-long sentences, over-long paragraphs, over-long sections and over-long volumes, is as thick and viscous as treacle, and little more transparent; it expands not only in all directions but also, and especially, in every *dimension*, so that its excess is ultimately one of density rather than one of magnitude. And its sweetness, as one of its earliest tasters was quick to point out, is best sampled in very small doses. 'Reading cannot be sustained for more than five or six pages,' writes Jacques Normand; 'one can set down as a positive fact that there will never be a reader hardy enough to follow along for as much as a quarter of an hour, the nature of the author's sentences doing nothing to improve matters.'[1] Forced to compose a report for the Fasquelle publishing house in 1912, the same Normand ends up reduced to exquisite despair. 'After the seven hundred and twelve manuscript pages,' he complains, 'after infinite amounts of misery at being drowned in a sea of inscrutable developments and infinite amounts of maddening impatience at never returning to the surface – one has no notion, none, of what it's all about.'

Still, even the long-suffering Normand grudgingly concedes that the work's apparent weaknesses are amply compensated for by its strengths. From a certain point of view, indeed, they *are* its strengths. The various idiosyncrasies of Proust's style – labyrinthine complexity at every level, chronological confusion, an overwhelming atmosphere of uncertainty – find their justification as the reflection of, or in some cases the impetus to, a particular vision of existence. Specifically, they map or model the structure of the self as Proust sees it, namely as an entity divided not only from the outside world (other minds included) but also from within, into discrete temporal segments which each contain, in turn, a plurality of faculties and drives. They echo Proust's portrait of a four-dimensional psychology; they present the outline of an individual subjectivity, namely that of the Narrator-Protagonist; and they may, finally, be designed to train readers into producing a coherent and unique identity of their own.

Narrative sequence

A first set of perplexities concerns temporal structure. Even leaving aside the issue of *external* chronology (such as a Russian Revolution which seems, here, to take place in 1916), the internal chronology of the novel poses serious problems of its own. It is not always easy, when indeed possible, to reconstruct the sequence of events; thus, for instance, the Protagonist meets the *dame en rose* when, by the Narrator's account, she should already have metamorphosed into the more decorous Mme Swann. What is of still greater significance and mysteriousness is the fact that 'today', the Narrator's present, designates not one period but a minimum of three. The visit to the Bois de Boulogne, after which the Narrator concludes that lost time cannot be regained, takes place 'this November', meaning at most a month ago; yet the Guermantes *matinée*, which convinces him otherwise, is 'aujourd'hui même'; and there are also brief but telling references to a now which post-dates the epiphanic climax and even, as it turns out, outstrips the lifespan of Proust himself. For though Proust would die in 1922, he granted his more fortunate Narrator at least enough longevity to receive a letter from the Baron de Charlus in 1926.[2]

Part of the problem, of course, is that the Narrator does not recount his life story in linear fashion. From the description of a given period he omits details as important as his first sexual experience (I, 568; II, 176/208–9), so that when he later refers back to them, it is often impossible to date their original occurrence. Others, inversely, he reveals ahead of time, only to withhold them from us when the appropriate moment arrives: thus, most shockingly, his account of the long years between Albertine's disappearance and the *matinée Guermantes* fails so much as to mention the madeleine episode (see Genette 1972, p.87), in spite of the fact that it should, by rights, have improved his disconsolate mood. Some memories (such as the first evidence of Albertine's potential bisexuality: III,190; IV, 224/262) jump the queue, impatient to be disposed of. Others, by contrast, are detained temporarily 'for the convenience of the tale', ending up as belated flash-backs: so for example the Narrator delays the revelation of Charlus' homosexuality from the end of *Le Côté de Guermantes* until the beginning of *Sodome et Gomorrhe*, neatly separating two phases of life – that of an interest in the Faubourg Saint-Germain, that of a fascination with homosexuality – which, in reality, overlap.

To be sure, the majority of the narrative, from 'Noms de pays: le nom' onwards, conforms in a broad sense to calendar time. But thanks to the extreme waywardness of the earlier sections, this very conformity is made to look like a conscious stylistic decision. And even when the events we see are presented in order, huge gaps regularly remain between them. Tens, sometimes hundreds of pages are spent on a period of hours (such as the *matinée Guermantes*), while the intervening weeks, months and sometimes years (such as those immediately preceding the *matinée*) are simply overlooked, held off until later, or, as at the end of each visit to Balbec, dealt with in a few lines. To compound our bewilderment, what seemed like a single event often turns out to be the description of a repeated state of affairs, or at least of one event which stands for many. Conversely, a quotidian habit mutates without warning – that is, without surrendering its imperfect tense – into a particular occurrence: 'Tous les soirs je me plaisais à imaginer cette lettre . . . Tout d'un coup, je m'arrêtais effrayé' (I, 402) ['Every evening I would beguile myself by imagining this letter . . . Suddenly I would stop in alarm' (I, 492/581)].[3]

We find ourselves, in short, faced with an exorbitant abundance of material, clustered in scenes which hover uncertainly between events and habits and among which it is frequently difficult to discern clear logical or chronological links. And we cannot even determine in advance which incidents are going to prove important in the long run: by the time the Protagonist receives an impossible telegram from a long-dead Albertine (IV, 220; V, 736/869), we may well have forgotten the idiosyncratic way Gilberte scrawls her signature, a detail casually mentioned some two thousand pages earlier (I, 493; II, 86/101) and responsible, as it turns out, for the confusion. Proust's novel thus saddles its reader with enormous burdens both of memory and of analysis.

To understand the various vicissitudes to which linear time is subject in the novel, we need to turn to the portrait of human interiority it espouses, one in which the overall self ('le moi') is made up of myriad smaller selves ('les moi'). Each minor self is a snapshot of the psyche at a given point in time, capturing in particular the primary object of adherence (Combray, Balbec; Gilberte, Albertine) and the subject's momentary attitude towards it: thus Proust's Protagonist is made up (among other things) of several selves which love Gilberte and even more which love, or (increasingly) distrust, Albertine. As we grow older, so our self expands – grows 'taller', in the Narrator's image (IV, 624; VI, 451/531) – to encompass all the sequential selves accumulating within it. Now these are not just passive memory-traces but also active participants in the psychic apparatus; they are, to borrow a traditional metaphor, citizens of a 'commonwealth', each with full voting rights. Just as in a commonwealth, so in the self a shifting balance among *les moi* can bring about a radical change of government. If we wish, for example, to forget someone, we have only to increase the quantity of *indifférents* within us, allowing them to outweigh all the *passionnés* (IV, 71; V, 559/660. I, 621; II, 241/285). Yet while they may vote as a bloc, the sequential selves have no contact with one another: two moments of love for the same woman are still two moments, irreconcilably distinct (I, 366; I, 448/529). Thus time breaks down into a series of discrete instants, and the self, as a result, fractures into a plurality of segregated *moi*, united only by a fantasy of cohesion.

If, therefore, the narration of the *Recherche* is characterised by a widespread discontinuity, the explanation lies herein. The Narrator's past life – which is also the very substance of his present life, as the opening pages make clear – consists in a collection of mutually isolated phases: at the highest level of the hierarchy, the Combray era, the Doncières era, the Paris era, the Tansonville era; lower down, the period of love for Gilberte, the period of love for Albertine; then within each love the stage of passion, the stage of jealousy, the stage of forgetting; deeper still, the separate 'steps' the passion (for example) makes; and finally the individual days, which keep resurfacing even amid the habitual scenes. And if the Narrator tends to move with improbable freedom in the fourth dimension, it is because all of these moments are available to the mind simultaneously, arrayed, like the notes of a familiar piece of music (III, 874; V, 425/501–2), in space rather than in time.[4] It is not that the mind is indifferent to or incapable of chronological sequencing; the linear thrust of most of Proust's narrative suggests that each minor self knows its precise place, while the deviations from this norm – which stand out all the more against such a conventional background – imply that the various selves, for all their monadic insularity, may yet be subsumed under an overall pattern.

Of course, the pattern we produce has no objective validity, as the texture of the novel makes perfectly clear. What the Narrator gives us is not his whole life story, but only what he remembers at the time of writing; and of what he remembers, only those aspects which, at that moment, seem important to him, because they currently correspond to a sizeable sub-population of selves; and the important aspects, finally, in the order which his mind imposes on them, with artificial partitions – as between high society and homosexuality – often inserted. Hence the anticipations (the Narrator writes, for example, that Albertine 'ignorait certes ce qu'elle *devait être* un jour pour moi' (II, 200–1) ['had certainly no conception of what she *was one day to mean* to me' (II, 490/579)], and the collections, as when we hear several of Albertine's successive alibis all at once (III, 659; V, 167–8/197–8). Hence, too, the omissions and belated revelations: events which may at the time have seemed of immense moment to the Protagonist now find themselves relegated to a lower echelon.

The obvious corollary – that the arrangement, having changed once, may change again – is by no means lost on Proust's Narrator. He knows full well that the only reason he now bothers to mention an intrinsically insignificant and declined invitation which would have brought him into earlier contact with Albertine (I, 615–16; II, 234/277), the only reason it has a place in the story he tells about himself, is that Albertine subsequently went on to become his second great love. And at any moment another equally decisive transformation may occur, sending fresh seismic shocks through the geological strata of his mind, forcing a re-evaluation of much that has gone before. Even the recollection of previously buried memories (for although all our selves sit side by side, not all are immediately accessible to the conscious), or simply the re-interpretation of pre-existing data, like the stock of *faits* and *dires* of Albertine, can dramatically alter the way in which our life as a whole appears to us (III, 594–5; V, 91/107). No one version can ever be considered to be definitive.

And it is this fact which provides a potential explanation for the most serious breach of chronological propriety, namely the multiplication of present moments. There is every indication that the Narrator has already made a number of returns to his account, that the superficially homogeneous narrative of the *Recherche* in fact comprises several superimposed layers, each one deposited by a separate narrating instance. Efforts to reconstruct the overall chronology are repaid by the insight that the novel replicates the structure of the human mind in its very texture: the pages we are reading must, it transpires, have been composed in at least three main stages – or, to put it another way, by three sequential selves. 'Un Amour de Swann' may well have been written early on, at the time of Albertine's 'imprisonment' (see III, 868; V, 418/493). Most of the remainder, by contrast, derives from a period postdating the madeleine experience (since without it the Narrator would lack much of the material for his memoir) but predating the final epiphany: the November marked by a despondent visit to the Bois in the first volume must surely be more or less contemporaneous with the train journey to Paris in the last, a journey on which the Narrator notices exactly the same chiaroscuro on the trees and feels exactly the same creative impotence (I, 415; I, 508/600. IV, 433; VI, 202/238). There is, finally, a third phase of writing in which the fully-enlightened Narrator, between spells of work on his new book – a novel which he almost always refers to as his 'œuvre', by contrast with the autobiographical 'récit' – also completes the latter with an introduction, a conclusion, the occasional transition and perhaps even a revision or two.

And just as the self, on the theoretical model delineated above, breaks down into sub-units and sub-sub-units, so we may discern, even within the reign of a single narrating persona, more local variations. Subtle shifts in tone are detectable across the main body of the novel, from the bright, extroverted shades of the first third to the dark solipsism of the last; its Narrator gradually countenances a greater degree of complexity in the world, acknowledging for example that societies and individuals change in and of themselves, as well as in relation to the observer.[5] Finally, it may even be possible to make out elementary sequential selves in the numerous repetitions or variants of the phrase 'she was dead' in the early portion of *Albertine disparue*: it is as if, on each occasion, the Narrator were breaking the news, as he would put it, to 'quelqu'un des innombrables et humbles moi qui nous composent' (IV, 14) ['one . . . of those innumerable and humble "selves" that compose our personality' (V, 490–1/578–9)]. Proust, in other words, is using the temporal aspect of his narrative to convey an inner four-dimensionality, to make powerfully palpable an existence which not only incorporates a multiplicity of minor selves but also – even when one is merely narrating one's life, and thus barely living it – changes across time.

Point of view

About the visit to the Bois de Boulogne, Proust was unrepentant. 'I am forced to depict errors,' he told Jacques Rivière, 'without feeling obliged to say that I consider them errors.'[6] His Narrator appears to feel much the same way: even in relation to issues about which he must know better, he senses no compulsion to report the facts as they genuinely are, but readily puts forward a view of the Protagonist as if it were his own. He thus informs us without hesitation that Albertine has a mole on her chin, only to correct this, a little further on and with equal conviction, to 'on her cheek, beneath the eye', and then to end up admitting without apology that it has been on her upper lip the whole time.[7] Cases of 'impressionism', in which what we are asked to visualise is the way something strikes an observer (usually the Protagonist) rather than, or at least prior to, the way it actually is, abound in the novel. Just as in Elstir and Dostoevsky (III, 880; V, 432/510) – as well, one might add, as in Stendhal – effects very often precede causes, and inanimate objects (the Martinville steeples, for example, which the young Narrator views from Dr Percepied's carriage: I, 179–80; I, 217–8/255–6) appear to move under their own power.

Now while it is relatively straightforward to read such personifications as mere figures of speech – to interpret what looks like a statement of fact by the Narrator as a ventriloquism of the Protagonist's first impressions – matters are already more complicated in relation to assessments of other characters (is Albertine really bisexual, or is it just a case of the jealous imagination run riot?) and positively bewildering when it comes to appraisals of life in general. Barely a page goes by without the Narrator offering a categorical view (or several) on the nature of personality, society, art, love, friendship and so on. And in spite of our strongest temptations to attribute them to Proust, we are repeatedly forced to recognise that opinions expressed in the *Recherche* are not necessarily those of its writer, indeed not even necessarily those of its most mature Narrator. Just as the 'facts' with which we are presented may really be subjective perceptions, so the 'truths' may belong to one or more of (a) the Protagonist, (b) the Narrator at one or another stage of his development and (c) Proust, there being no obvious discriminating marks between those which are spoken by each.

For one thing, where there is a maxim there is very often a counter-maxim or rather, more accurately put, an alternative *hypothesis*.[8] For another thing, reality tends to be too complicated for reduction to universal laws, with the result that exceptions are legion and sometimes almost instantaneous. Finally, maxims have a way of being gradually revised over the course of the novel. Not that the Narrator explicitly takes up an earlier view, reassesses it, finds it wanting and offers a replacement; no, in general he simply presents his 'truths' one after the other, as if there were no conflict among them. Thus what looks, on the very first page, like a belief in reincarnation turns out to be no more than a colourful way of talking about the discrete phases of a single earthly life, leaving poetic fame as the sole viable path to immortality – until, that is, even the notion of living forever in the collective consciousness of successive generations is rejected as excessively optimistic (IV, 621; VI, 445/524). Often, the refinement follows what one might loosely call a dialectical pattern, with the Narrator (or Protagonist) swinging from extreme position p to extreme position q, its diametric antithesis, only to conclude that p is right but in a q kind of way. Music, to take a crucial example, does not communicate an independently-existing 'divine world' which composers visit from time to time, but neither is it merely an elegant ornamental design; instead design, in music as in art more generally, serves to convey an immanent world which is that of the individual artist.[9]

What we learn from the maxims is not just what they have to tell us in terms of their content – which, after all, is not always to be trusted – but also what their combined structure indicates, namely the image of a mind perpetually caught between two opposite and equally unreliable hypotheses. In other words, over and above the division into sequential time-selves, Proust's subject finds itself riven, at a strictly simultaneous level, into multiple faculties (intellect, sensibility, will) and innumerable unruly drives. The sensibility (or instinct) produces the hypotheses which tend to come closer to the mark, though only because it is more pessimistic; as for the intellect, that purported tracker of truth, it spends its time spinning comforting fantasies and convenient alibis. The objective truth always falls between 'ces deux optiques également déformantes' (I, 577) ['these two perspectives, equally distorting' (II, 187/221)], and our one prospect of attaining it lies in gradually moving the two poles (p and q) closer together, in hopes of their eventual convergence.

There is another, more discreet way in which Proust's idiosyncratic use of maxims points towards a simultaneous division of the self. For it suggests that several different agencies, entirely indistinguishable on the surface, are jointly responsible for their production. If we include the Protagonist (whose voice is, strictly speaking, only heard through that of the Narrator), we may detect at least five narrative instances all sharing, whether implicitly or explicitly, the first-person pronoun. We can tell, to start with, that the Narrator is not exactly equivalent to the Protagonist, since the former knows more about their joint existence, simply by virtue of having lived longer. This Narrator announces his separate presence by ironising or critiquing his former self, by gesturing towards the latter's future (his own past), or by focusing on the act of recollection rather than on the memories themselves (II, 186; II, 472–3/558–9). But he, in turn, must bifurcate into an entity which merely knows more about the Protagonist and one which also knows more about everyone else, namely the omniscient Narrator who, instead of being forced into making hypotheses and deductions, can directly declare, in each case, the facts about a given character's state of mind (that of Bergotte, say, in his final moments: III, 692; V, 207/244). Now while the omniscient Narrator may differ from the locally focalised Narrator, the two share a belief that what they are describing is real; they are therefore distinct from the 'author', that voice which dialogues with the 'reader' (III, 51–2; IV, 60/69–70) and which tells us that nothing we have read, saving one tiny detail, is true. Finally, there is someone who views the novel neither as the Narrator's reality nor as pure fabulation but as the reality of Marcel Proust: this is the persona which describes Tissot's portrait of Charles 'Swann' in such detail that it is impossible not to understand the referent as Charles Haas, which claims to have written *Les Plaisirs et les jours* and translated *Sésame et les lys* from Ruskin's original, and which, sadly enough, is outlived by all the others.[10]

Nor will the various speakers co-operate, any more than will the different faculties within the Narrator-Protagonist's consciousness. The two Narrators clash, for instance, when we are told first what the elegant men in their carriages are saying about Odette and then that there is no way for any of it to be heard (I, 413; I, 505/597). When, on the other hand, it is a question of everything in the novel, with the sole exception of the supremely generous Larivière family (IV, 424; VI, 191/225), being 'fictif', the omniscient Narrator (who can know about, but must believe in the reality of, the Larivières) comes into conflict with the Author. And when, finally, we hear Albertine saying '"Mon" ou "Mon chéri", suivis l'un ou l'autre de mon nom de baptême, ce qui, en donnant au narrateur le même prénom qu'à l'auteur de ce livre, eût fait: "Mon Marcel", "Mon chéri Marcel"' (III, 583) ['"My—" or "My darling—" followed by my Christian name, which, if we give the narrator the same name as the author of this book, would be "My Marcel" or "My darling Marcel"' (V, 77/91)], we are scandalously placed in the simultaneous presence of a Narrator – who treats characters like Albertine as if they were real human beings and himself as someone capable of being addressed by or otherwise interacting with them – and, there is no other way around it, the writer Marcel Proust.

Viewpoint, in short, dramatises a consciousness which is thoroughly fractured within itself, and equally divided, what is more, from the world outside. At every turn, the mind runs up against a 'liséré de perception' (IV, 553) ['barrier of perception' (VI, 357/420)] interposed between it and its objects. If we wish to find the facts, such as the actual location of a beauty-mark on a face, we have to bring a secondary, rational mechanism to bear on the sense data to which we have already given a subjective and indeed thoroughly individual arrangement.[11] And this is partly why Proust's literary impressionism, which gives us both the object and the way it fleetingly appears, does so in reverse order. Proust's point is, however, as much about value as about knowledge: what ultimately counts for us, what constitutes our world, is not matter itself but the way in which our perspective filters it, bringing disparate objects into contact with one another, forging new combinations, and ultimately determining what we consider of worth. The crucial aspect of the Protagonist's development, one might almost say, resides in his realisation that instead of forcing his way through to the facts, at great intellectual and emotional cost and with little informational gain, he should instead be focusing on the agency responsible for their persistent and consistent distortion.

It is here, finally, that we begin to discern, amid the manifold discontinuities, an island of fixity within the Proustian subject. Selfhood, after all, requires that one be both coherent (identical to oneself) and unique (distinct from others); the still point at the centre of the psyche must, in other words, be substantive enough to serve as a locus of differentiation. That still point, which Proust's Narrator calls the 'True Self', turns out to be nothing other than the singular way in which one experiences reality ('la réalité telle que nous l'avons sentie': IV, 459; VI, 235/277). It is both individuating – there are as many perspectives, he speculates, as there are pairs of eyes (III, 696; V, 212/250) – and stable, in as much as a madeleine tastes the same to him today as it did thirty years ago. If the world is 'true for us all and dissimilar to each one of us' (V, 212/250) ['vrai pour nous tous et dissemblable pour chacun' (III, 694)], 'true' here must be understood not in the sense of correspondence to outside fact but instead as denoting a purely internal coherence, a set of immutable laws governing each particular perspective so that precisely the same modifications are always made, in comparable circumstances, on similar material.

What the focalisation in the *Recherche* conveys, then, is not just the structure of subjectivity but the structure of *a* subjectivity, a particular one, that of Proust's Narrator-Protagonist. It is above all to be found in metaphor, since metaphor, by bringing together two objects from different realms, exemplifies the very activity of synthesis which is that of perspective. And indeed the metaphors in the novel (which must not, of course, be taken as unmediatedly Proust's) show a remarkable degree of consistency. Young girls are incessantly assimilated to flowers (as most famously in the title of the second volume) and flowers to young girls.[12]

Proust has, however, a more subtle procedure for indicating the 'world' in which his character lives. We have seen that some of the maxims carry absolute truths (subscribed to, we have to assume, by Proust), and that others are hypotheses provisionally concocted by the Narrator; but there still remain those which, while they do not vary, are also not presented as absolute, and these are the ones which delineate the character's moral universe. We would be ill advised, for example, to imagine that all of the sweeping statements we read about love are supposed to apply to everyone without distinction. The Narrator acknowledges not only that people in general love in different ways (II, 188; II, 476/562) but also that he himself diverges from Swann (who is surely more than the artistically impotent *alter ego* he is usually taken to be) over *la jalousie de l'escalier*, Swann being far quicker to lose interest in the infidelities of a woman he no longer holds dear (IV, 132; V, 630/743). All of the Narrator's apparently categorical claims on the subject (e.g. IV, 72; V, 561/662) must therefore be taken to obtain only for his own experience. And so, in and among the faculties which the Narrator holds in common with all humanity, and subtending his innumerable selves which multiply by the moment, the maxims and metaphors he produces hint at an abiding and identifying perspective, something he can never see for the very good reason that it is always doing the seeing (IV, 48; V, 532/628); something *through* which, and never *at* which, he gazes.

Sentence structure

Chronology may be complicated and viewpoint variable, but if there is one single factor preventing us from reading more than six pages in a sitting then it is, as Jacques Normand was well aware, the notorious structure of the Proustian sentence. Although Proust is perfectly capable of being more concise when he so chooses, the longer periods are so numerous, and their combined effect so powerful, that one has the overwhelming impression of a novel written entirely in distended, convoluted, barely legible blocks. It is not just that they stretch to improbable lengths (a little under three Pléiade pages on one occasion: III, 17–19; IV, 18–21/21–4) but also, and especially, that they tend to grow from the middle,[13] so that in a sense their true dimension is rather one of *depth*. Just as at the macroscopic level, so at the microscopic the external boundaries in Proust are always predetermined – if some of the sentences and indeed the novel as a whole remain 'unfinished', it is not because they lack satisfactory resolutions but because discrepancies and lacunae linger amid the minor clauses – yet in the interstices, dividing a subject from its verb, a cause from its effect or a sub-plot from its dénouement, new material may at any moment muscle its way in, clad in a convenient pair of commas.

When the Narrator, to take a relatively brief example, wishes to describe his physical attraction to Albertine as unabating, he only reaches the second word before having to interrupt the thought to explain why it is of interest, namely that it marks a point of divergence from the Gilberte scenario [1]. But he now has to explain what exactly has changed, which means prefacing the contrast with [2] a general statement and [3] a detail or two about the specific mode of association with Albertine. The sentence may now continue, but it cannot yet end. Three words before the full stop, the Narrator as it were draws himself up short, remembering two very important restrictions: first, that his way of loving may not be universal (he interjects the quasi-ubiquitous 'pour moi', and appends a parenthetical disclaimer for good measure [4,5]); second, that the revelation is occurring to him, like almost all knowledge, after the event [6]. The result reads as follows:

> Pour Albertine, [2] grâce à une vie toute différente ensemble [3] et où n'avait pu se glisser, dans un bloc de pensées où une douloureuse préoccupation maintenait une cohésion permanente, aucune fissure de distraction et d'oubli, son corps vivant n'avait point, [1] comme celui de Gilberte, cessé un jour d'être celui où je trouvais ce que je reconnaissais [6] après coup être [4] pour moi ([5] et qui n'eût pas été pour d'autres) les attraits féminins.   (IV, 84)

> [In Albertine's case, thanks to a wholly different life shared with me where no fissure of distraction or obliviousness had been able to penetrate a block of thoughts in which a painful preoccupation maintained a permanent cohesion, her living body had not, like Gilberte's, ceased one day to be that in which I found what I subsequently recognised as being to me (what they would not have been to other men) the attributes of feminine charm.]   (V, 574/677–8)

A sentence like this one is not a marathon but a Zenonian hundred-yard dash,[14] in which writer and reader alike could easily reach the finish line were it not for the necessity to reach the half-way mark, and before that all the half-way marks in between.

One reason for the unusual intricacy is, of course, that the reality Proust is talking about is unusually intricate, given his remarkable sensitivity for subtle nuances. Not all the sentences, however, are content simply to mirror that reality; instead, some actively attempt to reduce its complexity,[15] and do so by the time-honoured method of collection and division, bringing a pair of items together ('just as . . . so') or marking a line of fissure within what looks like a single item ('sometimes . . . sometimes', 'on the one hand . . .on the other'). The active stance reaches a higher degree of intensity when simplification becomes falsification, when the divided items in question turn out to be more or less continuous (as most famously in the case of the two *côtés*), the collected items radically heterogeneous (as when, to cite a minor example, the servants set themselves to 'regarder tomber la poussière et l'émotion' (I, 88) ['watch the dust . . . and the excitement . . . subside' (I, 105/123)]. Even the proliferating paradoxes which, on the one hand, are an apt reflection of life's enigmas, function, on the other, to scale those enigmas down from a multi-dimensional conundrum to a set of straightforward binary oppositions (III, 421–2; IV, 500–1/588–9). At its limit, style forces an obdurately chaotic material into the merest semblance of order, whether sound pattern as rich as 'petit, trapu, étêté et têtu' (I, 414) – a double-binary permutation of consonants (pt/tt) and vowels (u/-) – or a chiastic construction of the form 'opposées et complémentaires, c'est-à-dire propres à satisfaire nos sens et à faire souffrir notre cœur' (II, 248) ['our opposite and our complement, apt, that is to say, to gratify our senses and to wring our hearts' (II, 548/647)].[16] Occasionally, and most often at moments of the greatest tension for the character, the Narrator's prose even ends up in an alexandrine or a perfect octosyllabic couplet (complete, in the following instance, with internal rhyme):

J'ouvris la fenêtre sans bruit
et m'assis au pied de mon lit . . .   (I, 32)

[Noiselessly I opened the window
and sat down on the foot of my bed . . .]   (I, 36/42)

Inevitably perhaps, one central reality the sentences both reflect and shape is that of the self. In addition to the linguistic reflex 'pour moi', several of the layered qualifiers (*peut-être*, *sans doute*) and associated locutions (*comme si*, *semblait*, *paraissait*) evoke the monadic isolation of a psyche which, when confronted with a potential object of knowledge, is continually thrown back on conjecture. Even when the object concerned is his own interiority, the Narrator finds the predicament equally intractable, so that he is reduced at one stage to reporting, rather hesitantly, that he acted 'soit par duplicité, soit par un surcroît véritable de tendresse' (II, 401) ['perhaps out of duplicity, perhaps in a genuine access of affection' (III, 110/130)]. Such starkly opposed hypotheses also point to another predicament, namely to the existence of twin and rival sources of speculation within the mind, each designed less to track the truth than to exaggerate in its own way. And perhaps the various oppositions, exclusions and concessives which control so many clauses and even developments spanning several pages ('granted *a* . . . but *b*', 'if not *a* . . . then at least *b*', 'not only *a* . . . but also *b*') represent efforts to steer a path between the two extremes. In some cases, furthermore, the hypotheses testify in another way altogether to the synchronic division of personality: there is good reason to suspect that the possibilities listed are not mutually exclusive – that the Protagonist, for example, is sincerely tender *and* guileful at one and the same time – especially since the Narrator believes that individual actions have multiple, sometimes even contradictory, motivations (I, 599; II, 214/253).

Analogously, we often feel the presence of multiple *sequential* selves coursing through the complex prose. Occasionally a group of narrators gathers in a single paragraph, all using different tenses to discuss the Protagonist and each other (III, 185; IV, 218/255–6). Or a sentence describing an act of recollection may contain a present-tense narrator describing the scene today, a past-tense character – such as the 'intermediary subject' who stays up late remembering rooms – and as it were a pluperfect character, object of the latter's memory. 'Puis renaissait [*unfocalised narration*] le souvenir d'une nouvelle attitude; le mur filait [*focalisation through the intermediary subject*] dans une autre direction: j'étais dans ma chambre chez Mme de Saint-Loup, à la campagne; mon Dieu! il est [*focalisation through the Tansonville-era self*] au moins dix heures, on doit avoir fini de dîner!' (I, 6–7) ['Then the memory of a new position would spring up, and the wall would slide away in another direction; I was in my room in Mme de Saint-Loup's house in the country; good heavens, it must be ten o'clock, they will have finished dinner!' (I, 5/6)].[17]

Such moments, in which the entire disposition of a former self returns to a position of dominance within the current self to the point of usurping the latter's voice, do more in fact than just juxtapose diverse geological strata. For when any given pair of sequential selves is brought together, 'notre vrai moi', that *petit personnage intérieur* which feeds on extratemporal essences, eagerly awakens (IV, 451; VI, 224/264). As in involuntary memory, so in certain sentences – a glorious example being the very last of 'Combray I' –

three successive events are implied to take place: a moment of contraction
by analogy, in which a dimensionless point of intersection between two tem-
porally distinct sensory impressions, such as the taste of a madeleine soaked
in tea, indicates the existence of an unchanging perspective subtending both;
a moment of dilation by contiguity, in which everything connected with the
first instance of the impression gradually emerges and the entire plane of a
previous self is restored, complete with the desires and dreams of its era (IV,
453–4; VI, 228/268); and finally a moment in which the true self, measuring
the distance between the two selves thus disclosed – that is, the vast areas of
disparity surrounding the tiny vertex of correspondence – glimpses 'a fragment of time in the pure state' (VI, 224/264) ['un peu de temps à l'état pur'
(IV, 451)].

It is, presumably, this true self which is ultimately responsible for bringing order into the myriad motley *moi* of which the total self is composed.
What Vinteuil's septet teaches the Protagonist is not only that his life is made
up of a series of love affairs, with every affair going through its own diverse
stages, and any given stage incorporating multiple two-dimensional time-
bound selves, but also that events which were, at the time, of great significance to him – a first touch, a first attempted kiss, a first kiss – now serve as
mere 'raw material' (IV:608) ['matière industrielle' (VI, 428/504)] for the
artwork which is his overall being. It is as if the Narrator were taking all the
love letters he had ever received, ordering them by size and colour, and
making a beautiful sculpture out of them. And nothing could more perfectly
render the complex musical 'orchestration' of the total self (II, 691; III,
458/543), combining melody (the diachronic division) and harmony (the
synchronic), than the Proustian sentence with its multi-layered hypotaxis.[18]
Far from being a repository for vast quantities of unruly and heterogeneous
material each sentence already begins to suggest the relative positions of the
items listed, intimating (rather as the anticipations, omissions and belated
revelations do) that *a* is more important than *b*, that all *c*'s are governed by
d.

It almost goes without saying that the relations which hold among the
various constituents of the total self, brought together under the complex set
of hierarchies, are not always logical in nature. Since each sequential self is
an isolated entity, not causally linked to any other sequential self, it is impossible to subsume all such selves under a neat narrative leading towards an
end; the Gilberte interlude is taken not to cause but merely to 'prepare' the
Albertine episode, as if, even from the Protagonist's point of view, one merely
foreshadowed the other. What is more, since 'rien ne se perd' (III, 27)
['nothing is ever lost' (IV, 29/34)], there is always a part of the Protagonist
which is still in love with (the image of) Gilberte even when, to all intents

and purposes, he has 'cured' himself of the attachment (IV, 568; VI, 376/443), and a part which is still, at some level, enthralled by the Guermantes name no matter how many times it has been disenchanted.[19] Even strictly theoretical views are likely to be affected: if the Narrator presents all his maxims, abandoned positions included, in the present tense, it is perhaps because he recognises that in a sense they are all believed in at once, just as opposite hypotheses are simultaneously entertained by disparate parts of the soul. And so the total self will have to incorporate ostensibly abandoned positions, just as Vinteuil incorporates fragments of his earlier works, however weak they are by comparison, into the glorious septet (III, 756; V, 284/335); the several components will be justified not logically but aesthetically, according to their place within the whole which they constitute (II, 826; III, 621/737).[20]

Not least among the seemingly impossible challenges Proust set himself when writing the *Recherche* was that of conveying, in a more or less seamless narrative flow, a vision of the world that is true for all, one which is true only for his Narrator-Protagonist, and one which is true for himself alone. We have seen how sentence structure indicates or reinforces a universally applicable notion of subjectivity ('form', here, being attuned to 'content'), and how the Narrator-Protagonist's individual perspective comes through in the metaphors (form, here, being itself content-laden), as well as in some of the maxims. Now since Proust is left, above all, with the domain of plot, we may speculate that the laws of his unique fictional universe – such as the law of double irony, which states that situations shall in general be as bad as possible, but not *reliably* so, since it is even more cruel to live in hope – are what centrally reflect his own point of view on experience.

However this may be, there is, I propose, still a fourth level of communication at work in the novel. Like the first, it is a type of didacticism, but its function is training, not teaching, its vehicle a set of purely structural features, not a body of accurate doctrine. This level, on which form asserts its maximal autonomy from content, serves two main ends. One is to encourage co-operation among the faculties: since readers possess many different types of attention (III, 210; IV, 246/290), all of which may be deployed simultaneously (I, 83; I, 98–9/115), writing may be so layered as to involve several at once, necessitating an active and multi-tiered engagement with the text. If we are to perform the act of deliberate and conscious self-deception required to see our inner volume as a coherent whole, we need to train our faculties – the intellect which produces pleasing pictures, the will which acts as if they were true, the instinct which senses they are not – to work together. As for the other mission of the Proustian spiritual exercise, it is to impart, as it were, the virtue of patience. By continually forcing us to go back and reread, the narrative repeatedly reminds us – in the foreshadowings and anticipations of the complex chronology, the twists and turns of the syntax – that we cannot know anything (even our own lives) all at once, that enlightenment is always retrospective and often long in coming, if it comes at all.

At times we receive more overt encouragement to retrace our steps, as when the Narrator himself structures an episode (such as the description of Swann's visits, I, 13–23; I, 13–26/16–30) in such a way that he, and we, keep returning to earlier motifs, or structures a sentence to comparable effect. When, for example, the Protagonist suspects Albertine of having been with another woman on his second arrival in Balbec but decides not to confront her just yet, the Narrator tries quite hard to explain:

> *Peut-être l'habitude* que j'avais prise de garder au fond de moi certains désirs, *désir* d'une jeune fille du monde comme celles que je voyais passer de ma fenêtre suivies de leur institutrice, et plus particulièrement de celle dont m'avait parlé Saint-Loup, qui allait dans les maisons de passe, *désir* de belles femmes de chambre et particulièrement de celle de Mme Putbus, *désir* d'aller à la campagne au début du printemps revoir des aubépines, des pommiers en fleur, des tempêtes, *désir* de Venise, *désir* de me mettre au travail, *désir* de mener la vie de tout le monde, *peut-être l'habitude* de conserver en moi, sans assouvissement, tous ces désirs, en me contentant de la promesse faite à moi-même de ne pas oublier de les satisfaire un jour, *peut-être cette habitude* vieille de tant d'années, de l'ajournement perpétuel, de ce que M. de Charlus flétrissait sous le nom de procrastination, était-elle devenue si générale en moi qu'elle s'emparait aussi de mes soupçons jaloux et, tout en me faisant prendre mentalement note que je ne manquerais pas un jour d'avoir une explication avec Albertine au sujet de la jeune fille (peut-être des jeunes filles, cette partie du récit était confuse, effacée, autant dire indéchiffrable, dans ma mémoire) avec laquelle – ou lesquelles – Aimé l'avait rencontrée, me faisait retarder cette explication.
>
> (III, 594)

[*Perhaps the habit* that I had acquired of nursing within me certain desires, *the desire* for a young girl of good family such as those I used to see pass beneath my window escorted by their governesses, and especially for the girl whom Saint-Loup had mentioned to me, the one who frequented houses of ill fame, *the desire* for handsome lady's-maids, and especially for Mme Putbus's, *the desire* to go to the country in early spring to see once again hawthorns, apple-trees in blossom, storms, *the desire* for Venice, *the desire* to settle down to work, *the desire* to live like other people – *perhaps the habit* of storing up all these desires, without assuaging any of them, contenting myself with a promise to myself not to forget to satisfy them one day – *perhaps this habit*, so many years old already, of perpetual postponement, of what M. de Charlus used to castigate under the name of procrastination, had become so prevalent in me

that it took hold of my jealous suspicions also and, while encouraging me to
make a mental note that I would not fail, some day, to have things out with
Albertine as regards the girl, or possibly girls (this part of the story was confused and blurred in my memory and to all intents and purposes indecipher-
able) with whom Aimé had met her, made me also postpone this inquest.]

(v, 90–1/106–7).

This one sentence encapsulates the full range of effects produced by the
deliciously exasperating Proustian texture. Insistence on point of view
emerges in the triply-repeated 'in me', as well as in the cautious 'perhaps' for
speculation about Albertine's activities; and speculation extends, here as
elsewhere, to the Narrator-Protagonist's own behaviour. The relentlessly
repeated *désirs . . . désirs . . . désirs* perfectly captures the multiplicity of
simultaneous drives, some of which, it should be noted, are sediments of old
sequential selves (the desire for hawthorns dates from Combray, the lure of
the Putbus' chambermaid only since Doncières); at the same time we sense
a beginning of order, as a partial hypotaxis divides the groups (women,
places, activities) into sub-groups (chambermaids, daughters of aristocrats)
and these in turn into specific cases (Mlle de l'Orgeville). Above all, however,
the Narrator perfectly matches the Protagonist for tactics of deferral, twice
interrupting and returning to the main line, qualifying his qualifiers. One has
the impression that sentences, in Proust, hardly dare to reach their conclusion, as if they were all too aware that new facts and re-interpretations of
existing data can, at any moment, upset their delicate balance. The total self
is always incomplete, contingent, subject to infinite revision and, to that
extent, fictional; though we need to believe, at least with one part of ourselves, in the fiction.[21]

NOTES

1 Henri Bonnet, 'Le "Rapport" de Jacques Madeleine', *Le Figaro littéraire*, 8
   December 1966, p.15; translation mine. Normand wrote the piece under his
   pseudonym, Jacques Madeleine.
2 For these three present moments, see I, 414; I, 506/598. IV, 622; VI, 447/526. IV,
   383; VI, 141/167 respectively.
3 All italics within quotations are mine.
4 See Georges Poulet, *L'Espace proustien* (Paris: Gallimard, 1963), pp.117–35.
5 See III, 139–40; IV, 164/192 and III, 577; V, 70/83 respectively.
6 See Marcel Proust et Jacques Rivière, ed. Philip Kolb, *Correspondance* (Paris:
   Plon, 1955), pp.2–3.
7 See successively II, 200; II, 489/578. II, 228; II, 524/618. II, 232; II, 529/624–5.
8 See Malcolm Bowie, *Freud, Proust and Lacan: Theory as Fiction* (Cambridge
   University Press, 1987) p.54.

9 For the three successive views on the nature and function of music, see I, 345; I, 422/498. III, 702–3; V, 220/259. III, 761–2; V, 291/343.

10 See III, 705; V, 223/262–3 (Haas). IV, 618; VI, 442/521 (*Les Plaisirs et les jours*). IV, 411; VI, 175/206 (Ruskin).

11 See especially IV, 622; VI, 447–8/527, but also II, 712; III, 484/574.

12 For the recurring metaphor of hawthorns as young girls, see for example I, 111; I, 133/156. I, 138; I, 168/197. II, 275; II, 580/685.

13 See Richard Terdiman, *The Dialectics of Isolation: Self and Society in the French Novel from the Realists to Proust* (New Haven: Yale University Press, 1976), p.181.

14 Zeno of Elea is famous for his paradoxes of motion, one of which suggests that it is impossible to travel from any point A to any point B since it is necessary first to reach a point C half-way in between, but in order to reach point C one must in turn reach another point D, and so on.

15 See Jean Milly, *La Phrase de Proust* (Paris: Larousse, 1975), pp.164–87.

16 Chiasmus: construction in which two pairs of elements are arranged *abba*.

17 See Marcel Muller, *Les Voix narratives dans la 'Recherche du temps perdu'* (Geneva: Droz, 1965), p.79.

18 I am drawing here on the opposition in prose writing between paratactic and hypotactic styles. Writers (like Hemingway) who favour the former tend to place clauses or sentences side by side, giving little indication as to the relationship or relationships which might hold among them. Writers (like Proust) who prefer the latter nest clauses within clauses and sentences within sentences according to a logical (or affective) hierarchy. Thus the hypotactic dictum 'We who are about to die salute you' could be paratactically rewritten 'We are about to die. We salute you'.

19 In *Le Côté de Guermantes* alone, the Protagonist is disenchanted (II, 328; III, 25/29), enchanted (II, 329; III, 26/30), disenchanted (II, 506; III, 237/280), enchanted (II, 670; III, 433/514), disenchanted (II, 813–14; III, 606/719) and finally enchanted again (II, 832; III, 628–29/744–5) within a very short space of time.

20 See Alexander Nehamas, *Nietzsche: Life as Literature* (Cambridge, MA: Harvard University Press, 1985), p.229.

21 I would like to thank the Stanford Humanities Center for funding part of the work on this project, and Matthew Tiews for his always invaluable assistance.

9

HOLLIE MARKLAND HARDER

Proust's human comedy

Within the first thirty-five pages of *A la recherche du temps perdu*, one comic scene threatens the author's entire literary project by calling into question the possibility of communicating through words. In this episode, which directly precedes the *drame du coucher*, the Protagonist's great aunts, Céline and Flora, attempt to acknowledge the case of Asti wine their neighbour, Charles Swann, has sent them. During the meal, when Flora mentions the friendliness of another neighbour, M. Vinteuil, Céline sees an opportunity to express her gratitude: '"Il n'y a pas que M. Vinteuil qui ait des voisins aimables," s'écria ma tante Céline' (1, 25) ['"M. Vinteuil is not the only one who has nice neighbours," cried my aunt Céline' (1, 27/32)]. Flora, determined not to be outdone by her sister, obliquely extends her thanks to Swann after a remark about a *maréchal de France* resembling a bottle of foolishness: '[j]e connais des bouteilles où il y a tout autre chose' (1, 26) ['I know bottles in which there is something very different' (1, 29/34)]. After Swann's departure, when the grandfather scolds the sisters for neglecting to acknowledge the gift, Céline expresses her shock: 'Mais voyons, Swann n'est pas bête, je suis certaine qu'il a apprécié. Je ne pouvais pas lui dire le nombre de bouteilles et le prix du vin!' (1, 34) ['Come, come; Swann isn't a fool. I'm sure he understood. You didn't expect me to tell him the number of bottles, or to guess what he paid for them' (1, 39/46)]. Instead of showcasing the women's mental and verbal agility as they had wished, this comic episode effectively demonstrates the inadequacy of language.

The juxtaposition of different perceptions of a single event is characteristic of the way in which Proust generates comedy in the *Recherche*. Germaine Brée observes that '[l]'humour proustien repose presque toujours, ainsi, sur l'incongruité entre deux aspects d'une situation, telle que, de l'intérieur, elle est sentie et telle qu'en fait, à travers gestes et mots, elle transparaît à extérieur'[1] ['Proust's humor rests almost always upon an incongruity between two aspects of a given situation, its aspect as felt subjectively, and as it appears objectively'].[2] But even as Céline and Flora seem to illustrate the insufficiency of language, the author redeems their words through comedy, using language to communicate its own weaknesses. More importantly, perhaps, Proust uses a literary text – his novel – to demonstrate those failings. This comic strategy confirms Brée's observation that in the *Recherche*, humour is instrumental in showing that communication succeeds only through the medium of art (Brée, *Du temps*, p.149; *Marcel Proust and Deliverance*, p.118). Moreover, Proust's expert use of comedy reveals an intricate network of human foibles and literary art, which simultaneously maps out his version of the *comédie humaine* and reveals his understanding of the aesthetics of everyday life.

The intriguing notion of the *Recherche* as a 'human comedy', however, invites further exploration. Since its origins, comedy has outlined 'the shortcomings of actuality in the name of logical order' in the interest of modifying unacceptable behaviour.[3] Whereas Greek tragedy repeated the sacred stories of ancient myth that addressed life, death and fate, classical Greek comedy exposed deficiencies in social practices, institutions and individuals, thereby anchoring the comic in the domain of the human rather than of the sacred. Originally, then, comedy was not by nature amusement but rather a way to bring social, political, or moral behaviour into line with society's norms. After the Peloponnesian War when the Greeks, as a defeated nation, no longer tolerated sharp criticism of their cultural and social institutions, comedies tended to entertain audiences rather than to denounce their values and habits, giving rise to contemporary associations that unite comedy and entertainment. From its beginnings as a form of societal criticism, the comic evolved into an examination of issues that focused a critical but ultimately accepting eye on moral and social practices (Feibleman, *In Praise*, p.38).

Dante Alighieri combines both critique and humour in *La Divina Commedia*, one of the literary precursors of the notion of the 'human comedy' in Proust's work. The poet pens a strong indictment against the religious, political, social, business and military communities in late medieval Italy, yet his depictions employ a variety of comic tropes such as irony, humour, grotesque comedy and word play. If his gift for the comic most often appears in the *Inferno*, perhaps it is because this volume most clearly articulates the contradictions and hypocrisies of the age, providing fertile ground for the development of humour. The worlds described in Dante's *Purgatorio* and in the *Paradiso* lie beyond the human sphere and therefore beyond the realm of comedy.

Humour in Dante's work frequently arises from situations in which characters' human tendencies have cast them knowingly or unknowingly into an *engrenage* or cog wheel with little chance for escape. In this poet's universe of virtue and vice, the eternal inclination towards sin fuels the *engrenage*. In the *Recherche*, Proust constructs a different kind of cycle where, regardless of class, people tend to repeat certain types of social and moral conduct and clichéed modes of communication. In this tension between repetitive behaviour and the unpredictable nature of human existence, Bergson sees the essence of comedy.[4] In both *La Divina Commedia* and the *Recherche*, a fortunate few manage to break out of this cycle; Dante and Beatrice pass into the realm of the divine just as Proust's protagonist moves into the transcendent realm of literature.

Honoré de Balzac, fulfilling his own prediction that Paris 'peut-être, un jour, aura son DANTE',[5] ['perhaps, will some day find its Dante'],[6] maps out the virtues and vices of early nineteenth-century France in *La Comédie humaine*. His novels, which contain a world in themselves, show that '[n]on seulement les hommes mais encore les événements principaux de la vie, se formulent par des types. Il y a des situations qui se représentent dans toutes les existences, des phases typiques, et c'est là l'une des exactitudes que j'ai le plus cherchées'[7] ['not man alone, but the principal events of life, fall into classes by types. These are situations which occur in every life, typical phases, and this is one of the details I most sought after'].[8] Balzac's insistence here on life as a series of repetitions underscores the mechanical *engrenage* in his novels, placing them squarely in the realm of comedy. Like *La Divina Commedia* and the *Recherche*, Balzac's *comédie* allows characters to escape the repetition of human existence through their success in the limited realm of the material world, whereas Dante and Proust offer their protagonists spiritual or artistic transcendence.

The title of Balzac's work, *La Comédie humaine*, recalls the theatrical origins of the comic genre and therefore the element of the mask. This emblem of dissimulation plays an integral role in the novelist's writing: 'Ce titre est riche de sens dont l'un est plus proprement balzacien: il signifie, en effet, que l'homme vit sous un masque, son visage étant déformé par les idées et les passions'[9] ['This title has a number of meanings but one is more strictly "Balzacian" than the others: it signifies, in effect, that man lives behind a mask, his face being deformed by ideas and passions' (my translation)]. In this sense, *La Comédie humaine* illustrates the idea that '[r]isible sera donc une image qui nous suggérera l'idée d'une société qui se déguise . . . d'une mascarade sociale' (Bergson, *Le Rire*, p.34) ['the notion of a society disguising itself, or of a social masquerade . . . will be laughable' (Bergson, 'Laughter', p.89)]. If masks help characters in Balzac's novels to conceal their motives and interests from each other, the narrator stands eager to reveal to his reader what lies behind the mask, a reflex that Proust finds disappointing: 'au lieu de se contenter d'inspirer le sentiment qu'il veut que nous éprouvions d'une chose, il la qualifie immédiatement' (*CSB*, p.269) ['instead of contenting himself with inspiring the feeling he wants us to have about something, he at once qualifies it' (*Against Sainte-Beuve*, p.63)]. In the *Recherche*, Proust's writing style prompts readers themselves to uncover the multiple facets of characters' personalities and to make sense of their frequently incongruous behaviour.

The reader who takes up that challenge will discover that humour is an integral part of the fabric of the novel. As in other landmarks of Western literature – Cervantes' *Don Quixote*, Rabelais' *Gargantua* and *Pantagruel*, and Montaigne's *Essais*, for example – comic situations in the *Recherche* have a central place: they serve to disrupt and thereby call into question our habitual ways of understanding people, things and events. Reading Proust's novel, we find moments of humour, not only in the depiction of language and social practices, but in the very organisation of the work, in the incisive analysis of art, and even in the treatment of such subjects as homosexuality and Judaism.

First and foremost, comedy actually facilitates the reader's comprehension of the ways in which the plot, the internal patterns and the narrative structure of the book unfold. The basic storyline embodies the sort of repetition which, for Bergson, lends itself to humour (*Le Rire*, p.65; 'Laughter', pp.115–16). When Proust's book opens, the Protagonist is a young boy dreaming of writing a novel, and at the end, he is once again planning his *roman à venir*. At the end of the *Recherche* when the Protagonist is ready to write, he seems as nervous and as awkward as in his youth when he did not know which subject to choose for his book. Moreover, he stumbles onto his eventual topic only because he reconsiders an idea he had previously rejected, namely the vicissitudes of his own life.

Certain structural patterns established early in the novel repeat themselves in the *Recherche*, suggesting that, in a comical way, events cycle through a limited series of situations instead of evolving. For René Girard, the castle-like hierarchy of Combraysian society, for instance, offers a preview of the rigid regulations that govern the Verdurin and the Guermantes salons.[10] As a participant in these diverse social groups, Charles Swann is able to mask his identity in order to fit in everywhere, a skill other characters in the novel display as well. In a more aesthetic realm, the problematic rapport between life and literature also emerges in 'Combray' when the family cook and housekeeper, Françoise, is sent to retrieve a medical book during the delivery of her kitchen helper's baby. The description of the girl's condition evokes stronger emotions in the cook than the real-life event, a situation that will recur when the Protagonist judges his family's mourning for Aunt Léonie to be insufficient compared to expressions of grief in *La Chanson de Roland* (1, 154; 1, 184/216–17). Yet from these experiences as a boy, the Protagonist seems to learn little, if anything, to help him more skilfully negotiate his own place in Parisian society or in the world of art.

In Proust's work, comic moments sometimes emerge from the very unpredictability of life. When Françoise violates her strict *code* by delivering to his mother the Protagonist's plea for a good-night kiss, it appears that rules of acceptable behaviour are not always as absolute as they might seem (1, 28–9; 1, 33/38–9). Moreover, when the overwhelming desire for a kiss threatens to provoke his father's anger, the parents yield to the boy's wishes, underscoring the inconsistency of powerful emotional reactions (1, 35–6; 1, 40–2/ 47–9). Likewise, his encounters with Aunt Léonie, who falsely claims to know everyone in town, reveal that people are not always honest in assessments of themselves (1, 55–8; 1, 65–8/76–9). Yet these experiences do not immediately benefit the Protagonist. Françoise's behaviour does not enable him to anticipate the instability of social and moral principles; his parents' reactions do not prepare him for the emotional blows Albertine will inflict on him; and his contact with Léonie does not facilitate his understanding of Charlus's multiplicity or help him perceive the vanity of the aristocracy and the bourgeoisie.

These comic reversals serve an important function in communicating Proust's notion that unfulfilled expectations may lead to innovative ways of seeing that are free from the constraints of custom, tradition and routine. From childhood on, the Protagonist tends to romanticise people and things he does not know, and his inevitably disappointing real-life experiences are responsible for some of the novel's most comically insightful moments. When he finally visits Balbec church, which he had envisioned perched on a precipice next to a raging sea, he finds it instead in the middle of town, situated near a bank branch and a billiards hall. Because his fantastic imaginings prove to be false, he gains the opportunity to see the church from a new and ultimately more rewarding perspective. With the help of the painter Elstir later in the novel, he learns to see the artistic value of Balbec church, no longer through his romantic notion of what it should look like but rather through the concrete details of its sculpture and architecture, which he had not taken the time to examine closely during his first visit. While such reversals have a comic dimension, they also illustrate that art often can be found in ordinary details, a notion that forms a principal tenet of Proust's aesthetic theory.

Perhaps the most astonishing reversals are reserved for the book's final pages. In the end, Françoise, the family cook, housekeeper and paragon of domestic artistry, emerges as a model of literary creation for the *roman à venir*, and the Protagonist, initially a laughably absent-minded and naive individual, evolves into an astute and observant Narrator. Thanks to these comic inversions, readers are better able to understand the author's notions of art and life because, like the Protagonist, they have participated in a process that may enable them to discover creativity that they have over-looked in their own lives. In the *Recherche*, the author uses humour to dem-onstrate that anyone, including an uneducated cook and a bumbling Protagonist, as well as any reader, can discover art in the everyday world if he or she is willing to examine it with an unprejudiced eye.

Just as art can emerge in unexpected places, Proust demonstrates that humour can develop even in tragic situations, providing comic relief while sharpening the effect of these extreme emotions. During the grandmother's final illness, for example, Françoise tries to cheer the dying woman by brush-ing her hair, but for the Protagonist, the coiffure ends up emphasising her misshapen features. When he leans over to kiss her, he realises that not only has she changed physically for him during her illness, he has changed for her as well: 'elle ne m'avait pas reconnu' (II, 630) ['she had not recognised me' (III, 384/455)]. The Protagonist's emotional isolation is compounded by the brusque entry of the Duc de Guermantes, who places formalities above feel-ings. Oblivious to the family's grief, the duke insists on obeying the rules of courtesy and shaking the hand of the Protagonist's father, a rude and insen-sitive request under the circumstances (II, 632; III, 387–8/458–9). Moreover, Dr Dieulafoy, whom the duke recommends as though he were a product that came with a money-back guarantee, is incapable of saving the grandmother despite the promise of his family name (II, 633; III, 388/459–60). The author's choice to incorporate comic elements into this scene highlights the hopelessness of the grandmother's situation, the helplessness of those trying to ease her suffering, and the foolishness of people who privilege social con-vention over compassion.

The place comedy occupies in the narrative organisation of the *Recherche* stems in part from the gap in knowledge and experience that separates the Narrator from the Protagonist. The former's perspicacious sense of humour underscores how different he is from the young boy at the beginning of the novel, a fact that becomes especially evident when the latter enters the social circles of the Guermantes and the Verdurins. Frequently, however, the Narrator does not intervene to correct the Protagonist's thoughts and impressions, and the initial introduction of characters such as Tiche and Mlle Vinteuil's friend tends to mislead the reader. In a 1914 letter to Jacques Rivière, Proust explains that this comic strategy illustrates the notion that people can never be known completely: 'Mais cette évolution d'une pensée, je n'ai pas voulu l'analyser abstraitement mais la recréer, la faire vivre. Je suis donc forcé de peindre les erreurs, sans croire devoir dire que je les tiens pour des erreurs, tant pis pour moi si le lecteur croit que je les tiens pour la vérité'[11]

['But I did not want to abstractly analyse this evolution of a thought, but rather recreate it, make the reader live it. I am therefore forced to paint errors, without feeling obligated to indicate that I think they are errors. Too bad if the reader believes that I think they are true' (my translation)].

The humour generated in the *Recherche* from the idle talk and ridiculous conduct of society members functions as a social corrective in the Bergsonian tradition. If vanity is the human foible most worthy of remedy (Bergson, *Le Rire*, p.133; 'Laughter', p.173), the Baron de Charlus may be the most poignantly laughable character in the novel because he epitomises the emptiness on which the nobility's claims of superiority are based. When Charlus first sees the Protagonist, his overt stare signals his sexual interest. Yet when introduced to the young man, the baron extends only his third and fourth fingers without meeting his eyes, as though indicating that real interest in him would be below his elevated station in life. Later in the novel, the Protagonist apologises for not understanding the 'forget-me-not' message the baron wanted to communicate to him through a book with a floral border. Charlus uses his class affiliation as a shield for his hurt feelings when he shouts: 'Pensez-vous qu'il soit à votre portée de m'offenser? Vous ne savez donc à qui vous parlez? Croyez-vous que la salive envenimée de cinq cents petits bonshommes de vos amis, juchés les uns sur les autres, arriverait à baver seulement jusqu'à mes augustes orteils?' (II, 846) ['Do you suppose that it is within your power to offend me? You are evidently not aware to whom you are speaking? Do you imagine that the envenomed spittle of five hundred little gentlemen of your type, heaped upon one another, would succeed in slobbering so much as the tips of my august toes?' (III, 645–6/765)]. When the Protagonist eventually manages to enter the salon of the Duchesse de Guermantes and even that of the Princesse de Guermantes, Charlus bellows: 'On n'entre dans ces salons-là que par moi' (III, 40) ['There is no admission to those houses save through me' (IV, 46/53)]. The baron's assertion is comically absurd, of course, because what he deems impossible has already transpired. For all the aristocratic pride and egotism that Charlus manifests at the beginning of the novel, in the end, he becomes a slave to his passions. For the sake of his lover, Morel, the baron endures humiliation at the hand of Mme Verdurin, and in search of sexual pleasure, he submits to physical pain. The discrepancy between the lofty image this aristocrat has of himself and his state at the end of the novel heightens his tragi-comic status.

When the characters' egotism leads to cruelty, their sense of self-importance reaches comically grotesque proportions. For instance, when Françoise plots to get rid of the *fille de cuisine*, the cook's calculated manœuvres are likened to the actions of a wasp that paralyses its prey, leaving it to be eaten bit by bit by hatching larvae (I, 122; I, 147/173). This darkly humorous comparison, which suggests that Françoise must be ridiculously paranoid to detect a potential threat from this defenceless kitchen helper, exposes the cook's selfish use of the girl to perpetuate and strengthen her own position in the household. The exaggerated insensitivity of other characters punctuates the novel as well: Mme Verdurin's attention to her personal comfort and pleasure while eating a croissant completely overshadows any concern she might have for the victims of the Lusitania (IV, 352; VI, 102/120); the Duc de Guermantes refuses to acknowledge the death of a family member for the sake of a social engagement (III, 123; IV, 144/169); and Cottard denies medical care to a bleeding servant in order to prevent mussing his own white vest (III, 273; IV, 321/377). Perhaps the culminating point of Proust's commentary on how social life anaesthetises sensitivity to others is when Mme de Guermantes, in order to attend a social occasion, dismisses the news that her old friend Swann is dying (II, 884; III, 691/819). The dark comedy here stems not only from the absurd choice that is posed between social obligations and the duty owed to a dying friend, but also from Mme de Guermantes' apparent decision to place the colour coordination of her shoes and dress above her friendship with Swann.

The insensitivity that characters show to others also results from their inherent snobbery, which is similarly a target for Proust's humour. Many of the snobs in the *Recherche* display an inordinate and seemingly automatic desire to belong to a particular social group, which, comically, is usually a disappointing lot, rather than the sparkling wits one might expect. Legrandin wants so desperately to maintain his weak connection to the Guermantes that he compromises his old friendship with the Protagonist's family. This eminent family of aristocrats also suffers from a certain *snobisme* because their claim to superiority leads them to mask their contempt for others under the guise of goodwill.[12] Even the lower classes yield to temptations of snobbery, as in the case of Françoise, who, by continually serving asparagus, forces the allergic kitchen helper to leave her job and therefore abandon her attempts to play 'la maîtresse' (I, 121) ['the mistress' (I, 146/171)].

Proust's comic treatment of other mechanical aspects of behaviour in society reveals the characters' intellectual and aesthetic limitations. Léon Pierre-Quint, for example, observes that in the final scene of *Le Temps retrouvé*, habit, physical tics and hackneyed phrases among the guests of the *matinée* seem to have extinguished their creative spark, which, for Proust, is the essence of life: 'le mécanisme a envahi tout leur être'[13] ['the mechanical has invaded their entire being' (my translation)]. Perhaps the most compelling example is Mme Verdurin, who, even as the Princesse de Guermantes, remains obsessed by her wish to create a group of loyal admirers: 'Oui, c'est cela, nous ferons clan! nous ferons clan!' (IV, 561) ['Yes, that's it, we will forgather! we will form a clan!' (VI, 368/433)]. The repetition of the word 'clan', which recalls Mme Verdurin's bourgeois salon, illustrates Bergson's notion of comedy. Moreover, the discrepancy between Mme Verdurin's ambitious personality and her rise to the top of the social ladder provides fertile ground for Proust's humour, which clearly shows that class affiliation alone no longer guarantees culture, intelligence or generosity of spirit.

Just as Proust challenges conventional ideas of how the upper, middle and lower classes conduct themselves, his use of language calls into question traditional ways of communicating. The manner in which Françoise expresses (or fails to express) herself is emblematic of Proust's comic treatment of speech in the *Recherche*. Like Mme Verdurin, Françoise relies to a large degree on habit when she talks, but rather than revealing a *petitesse d'esprit*, her words reflect a decidedly creative use of French grammar and pronunciation. Instead of referring to York ham, she speaks of ham 'de Nev'York' (I, 437) ['from Nev-York' (II, 19/22)] because she cannot imagine both New York, a city whose name is familiar, and York, which she believes to be an incorrect pronunciation. Moreover, she imposes French pronunciation rules, thereby transforming 'new' into 'nev', inventing her own term.

Ironically, Françoise's exaggerated attention to French grammar leads to the creation of new words through the humorous misapplication of rules. In an effort to use the correct feminine noun forms, for instance, she says 'la Sagante' for the princesse de Sagan (II, 504) ['the Sagante' (III, 234/277)] and 'Antoinesse' for the wife of Antoine (II, 324; III, 18/21). These errors are not, as the Narrator observes, so different from words used 'par ces Français de jadis' (*ibid.*) ['by those Frenchmen of olden days' (III, 18/22)]. In fact, Françoise's creativity exhibits a 'génie linguistique' (III, 134) ['genius of language' (IV, 157/184)] similar to that of the sixteenth-century French poets such as Du Bellay who enriched the language through neologisms. Moreover, behind this cook's mistakes, which Proust characterises as a 'perpétuelle erreur qui est précisément la "vie"' (IV, 154) ['perpetual error, which is precisely "life"' (V, 656/775)], lies the essence of creativity, and therefore artistry, in everyday life.

According to André Maurois, Proust's language play is more refined than that of Balzac or Dickens; Balzac's Baron de Nucingen, with his heavy Alsatian accent, and Gaudissart, with his persistent jokes, for example, lack the subtlety of Proust's linguistic comedy (Maurois, *A la recherche*, p.255; *Proust*, p.242). In the *Recherche*, Maurois draws a connection between Proust's manipulation of words and his 'philosophie de la relativité et du néant de la réalité' (*A la recherche*, p.255) ['philosophy of relativity and of the nothingness of reality' (*Proust*, p.242)]. In a sense, words must be moulded to suit one's purposes because they often have no shared sense of meaning, as in the case of Françoise's malapropisms. Although this development may have a detrimental effect on communication, it opens the door to artistic creation through an innovative manner of expressing ideas. Art, according to Proust, is like language in that it can present life from a new perspective. As a result, at the end of *Le Temps retrouvé*, Proust claims that everyday life must be manipulated like language in order to produce art: 'les apparences qu'on observe ont besoin d'être traduites et souvent lues à rebours et péniblement déchiffrées' (IV, 475) ['the observable manifestations need to be translated and, often, to be read backwards and laboriously deciphered' (VI, 254–5/300)]. Negotiating language is essential training for learning to uncover art in the everyday world.

Through an elaborate comparison between the speech patterns of Mme de Guermantes and Françoise, Proust demonstrates how language introduces artistry into the duchess's world as well as into the more humble domain of the cook. The Narrator recognises in both women's speech 'le vieux langage et la vraie prononciation des mots' (III, 544) ['the old speech and the true pronunciation of words' (V, 30/35)]. Despite Mme de Guermantes's aristocratic background, or perhaps because of its long history, her language seems very 'vieille France' (II, 775) ['old world' (III, 560/664)] and her pronunciation 'presque paysanne' (II, 775–6) ['almost peasant' (III, 560/665)]; she articulates her words with 'une âpre et délicieuse saveur terrienne" (*ibid.*) ['a harsh and delicious flavour of the soil' (*ibid.*)] that seems to recall the background of Françoise rather than that of a duchess. Because these two women from opposite ends of the social spectrum use the same kind of language, the linguistic similarities that connect them serve as a humorous reminder of the contingency of class, station and oral expression.

Whereas Mme de Guermantes and Françoise are linked by a shared form of expression, other characters in the *Recherche* demonstrate how the meanings of words can change according to who employs them. The phrase 'en être' ['to be one of us'], for example, creates a comic *double entendre* for the reader aware of its dual meanings. When M. Verdurin tells Charlus, 'Or dès les premiers mots que nous avons échangés, j'ai compris que vous en étiez!' (III, 332) ['Now, from the first words we exchanged, I realized that you were *one of us!*'(IV, 393/463)], the baron, 'qui donnait à cette locution un sens fort différent' (*ibid.*) ['who attached a very different meaning to this expression' (*ibid.*)], believes that M. Verdurin knows his sexual orientation. As their conversation continues, this obvious gap in meaning contributes to the comedy. Later in the novel, however, a new connotation for 'en être' piques Charlus's jealousy. In a letter from Léa to Charlus's lover, Morel, the baron discovers that these correspondents have redefined the term to signify a man who loves both men and women, and even more unsettling, to describe a man who loves *as* women love and who therefore '*is* somehow a woman'.[14]

In other instances, coded language in the *Recherche* may actually slip by the uninitiated reader. These secret languages play the same joke on the readers as on the Protagonist and his fellow characters in the novel, and any humour that results is in direct proportion to the degree to which the character or reader is aware of the code. Jarrod Hayes cites the example of Proust's coded tea references. According to slang dictionaries at the beginning of the twentieth century, he notes, 'having tea' suggests homosexual relations. In the novel, Hayes recognises that it is not clear whether the Narrator or the other characters are aware of the sexual connotations of expressions such as *prendre le thé* [to have tea], *théière* [teapot], or *tasse* [tea cup], but he claims that the book 'does negotiate between sexual knowledge and ignorance on the part of characters and readers, playing on the difference in how much they know to comment on the function of secret codes in the production of sexual knowledge'.[15] Only when readers break the code can they understand the hilarity of unintended communications.

If comedy in Proust's description of language exposes previously hidden mindsets, attitudes and interests, it plays a double role in the author's treatment of themes such as homosexuality and Judaism. Not only does humour draw attention to adherents of these practices, but more importantly, it acts as a vehicle permitting their entry into the *Recherche*. The first thirty pages of *Sodome et Gomorrhe*, for instance, present a grotesquely comic portrayal of Charlus's encounter with Jupien that enables Proust to depict male homosexual behaviour. In a 1912 letter to Eugène Fasquelle, the author cites his innovative comic depiction of Charlus to justify the decision to incorporate this character's homosexuality into the novel. Noting that the baron's portrait incarnates 'quelque chose de neuf (surtout à cause de la façon dont il est traité)' ['something new (especially in the way he is treated)'], Proust claims that 'aucun détail [n'est] choquant (ou alors est sauvé par le comique)' (*Corr.* XI, 256) ['no detail is shocking (but if so is saved by humour)' (*Selected Letters* III, 109)].

The comic value of Charlus and the other homosexual characters extends beyond the originality they bring to the novel; they serve to confirm universal principles of contingency and dissimulation in Proust's human comedy. Although Léon Pierre-Quint asserts that the humour generated by homosexual characters in the *Recherche* stems from an 'instinct maladif [qui] est apparu à Proust comme une idée fixe qui isole l'homme parmi ses semblables et le marque de toutes sortes de ridicules' (Pierre-Quint, *Marcel Proust*, p.287) ['unhealthy instinct [that] seemed to Proust an obsession that isolates an individual among his peers and makes him appear ridiculous' (my translation)], his observation suggests that only homosexuals experience excessive sexual preoccupation. If we accept this notion, we must ignore Swann's obsession with Odette and the Protagonist's extreme feelings for Albertine. Certainly the preoccupations of these male characters isolate them and render them comic figures – not because they are heterosexuals but because they yield to excessive desire. Similarly for Charlus, the comedy generated by his attention to young men comes from his exaggerated interest, not solely from his sexual orientation. As Germaine Brée observes, 'cette comédie ne change pas de nature parce que le baron est homosexuel. Cette particularité accentue, simplement, et dramatise les malentendus et contradictions de tout ordre dont est faite une vie' (*Du temps perdu*, p.142) ['the nature of the comedy does not change because the baron is a homosexual. His peculiarity simply accentuates and dramatizes the various misunderstandings and contradictions which compose life' (*Marcel Proust and Deliverance*, p.112)].

If homosexuality in the *Recherche* can be compared to any dissimulated characteristic that later emerges, it may in fact have significance for the aesthetic purposes of the entire novel. Lawrence R. Schehr confirms that '[r]evealing homosexuality, the hidden meaning of things, would be an exemplary case for the process of artistic revelation that structures much of the novel'.[16] By undermining conventional interpretations of people and things, the presence of homosexual characters in the novel helps reshape our habitual ways of seeing and deriving meaning. In this sense, homosexuality may offer a means of finding unconventional connections between people just as art offers the possibility of discovering nontraditional connections within the sphere of everyday life. This new way of seeing and interpreting the world complements Proust's notion that the purpose of art is to capture each artist's singularly individual point of view: 'Grâce à l'art, au lieu de voir un seul monde, le nôtre, nous le voyons se multiplier, et autant qu'il y a d'artistes originaux, autant nous avons de mondes à notre disposition, plus différents les uns des autres que ceux qui roulent dans l'infini et, bien des siècles après qu'est éteint le foyer dont il émanait, qu'il s'appelât Rembrandt ou Ver Meer, nous envoient encore leur rayon spécial' (IV, 474) ['Thanks to art, instead of seeing one world only, our own, we see that world multiply itself and we have at our disposal as many worlds as there are original artists, worlds more different one from the other than those which revolve in infinite space, worlds which, centuries after the extinction of the fire from which their light first emanated, whether it is called Rembrandt or Vermeer, send us still each one its special radiance'(VI, 254/299)].

Proust's representation of Jewish characters in the *Recherche* contributes in a similar fashion to his unconventional brand of comedy. Jews in the

novel, such as the Protagonist's friend Bloch, frequently are said to epitomise the author's contempt for his own religious heritage. Yet Maya Slater
shows that the unfavourable impression Bloch makes on the Protagonist's
family is surpassed only by the foolish behaviour of the father and the grandfather.[17] Moreover, Bloch's antisemitic commentary in Balbec, described by
some critics as an example of Jewish self-hatred, may illustrate a more
general phenomenon. Immediately preceding Bloch's comments, Robert de
Saint-Loup condemns his own noble background. Believing that he belongs
to a 'caste ignorante et égoïste' (II, 97) ['an ignorant and selfish caste' (II,
366/433)], Saint-Loup 'cherchait sincèrement à ce qu'ils lui pardonnassent
ces origines aristocratiques' (*ibid.*) ['was sincerely anxious that they should
forgive in him that aristocratic origin' (*ibid.*)]. In effect, Bloch's comments
show that he wishes for a similar sort of disassociation from his roots: 'On
ne peut pas faire deux pas sans en rencontrer . . . Je ne suis pas par principe
irréductiblement hostile à la nationalité juive, mais ici il y a pléthore. On
n'entend que "Dis donc, Apraham, chai fu Chakop." On se croirait rue
d'Aboukir' (*ibid.*) ['You can't go a yard without meeting them . . . I am not
in principle irremediably hostile to the Jewish race, but here there is a pleth-
ora of them. You hear nothing but, "I thay, Apraham, I've chust theen
Chacop." You would think you were in the Rue d'Aboukir' (*ibid.*)]. The juxtaposition of the comments of Saint-Loup and Bloch suggests that their rejec-
tion of heritage is not a commentary on their class or religion. Through his
depiction here, Proust focuses not on the actions of Jews or aristocrats per
se but rather on more universal human tendencies.

Like homosexuality, Judaism serves as a model for qualities that emerge
after close scrutiny, and in this way, it also demonstrates the principles of
aesthetic revelation that structure Proust's novel. In her study of Marranos,
Jews whose families were forced to convert to Christianity in the late Middle
Ages, Juliette Hassine recognises a connection between Jewish customs mentioned in the *Recherche* and the efforts by Marranos to maintain their traditions in secret.[18] Hassine claims that these covert practices are intricately
related to Proust's artistic principles because, just as the importance of events
and actions may not be immediately evident in the *Recherche*, the significance of the Marranos' actions also may be concealed initially. For Hassine,
the comical 'asymmetrical Saturdays' in Combray exemplify this process of
dissimulation. When the Protagonist's family eats Saturday lunch at eleven
o'clock, this day of the week, which is also the Jewish sabbath, emerges as a
special occasion. The meal serves to unite the family, as does the sabbath for
Marrano families, but the comedy of the episode is intensified by the erroneous belief of the Protagonist's father that everyone should understand
when he alludes to the family's Saturday schedule. In this situation, words

once again lead to failed communication: 'ce "samedi" n'expliquait rien' (I, 110) ['the word "Saturday" has conveyed nothing' (I, 132/155)]. Moreover, the father's assumption that others would be aware of his family's unusual custom is comic because it reverses the dominant position of Christians and the minority Jewish culture in French society.

Although homosexuals and Jews enter the novel through comedy, they clearly serve a purpose beyond entertainment. By incorporating these groups into all levels of society, Proust shows readers that people and practices cannot be understood solely through categories such as appearance, class or sexual preference. In an episode that anticipates his failed efforts to classify others later in life, the young Protagonist tries to group actors according to their reputations, unaware that their rank will inevitably change after each performance: 'Et, d'après ce qu'on m'avait dit d'eux, je les classais par ordre de talent, dans des listes que je me récitais toute la journée, et qui avaient fini par durcir dans mon cerveau et par le gêner de leur inamovibilité' (I, 73) ['And from what I had been told of them I would arrange them in order of talent in lists which I used to recite to myself all day and which ended up by hardening in my brain and hampering it by their immovability' (I, 87/101)]. In the society Proust has created, where members clearly possess histrionic skills, any effort to categorise them leads to misinterpretation. In this sense, then, homosexuality and Judaism in the *Recherche* represent the opposite of habit and its conventional ways of making connections in the world. This sense of innovation and nonconformity that these practices bring to the novel lays the groundwork for the development of the Protagonist's artistic sensitivity, and in this way, they prepare him for his vocation.

By playing a fundamental role in Proust's conception of art, comedy in the *Recherche* becomes itself the victim of the novel's final comic reversal. Ironically, humour serves to expose the most serious and theoretical aspect of the novel: the notion that art emerges from everyday life rather than philosophical musings. Although Maya Slater claims that the novelist 'insistently reminds us of the grandeur of art, only to contrast it with our banal, everyday world' (Slater, *Humour*, p.165), in effect, Proust's comic comparison of Michelangelo and Françoise, who sculpts beef gelatine rather than marble (I, 435; II, 18/21), underscores the similarities linking the two, not their differences. In this manner, Proust shows readers that art exists in everyday life for those who look in unconventional ways: 'La vraie vie, la vie enfin découverte et éclaircie, la seule vie par conséquent pleinement vécue, c'est la littérature' (IV, 474) ['Real life, life at last laid bare and illuminated – the only life in consequence which can be said to be really lived – is literature' (VI, 253/298)]. Through the comic, Proust prompts the Protagonist and the reader to reexamine life, and the new vision that comedy generates is the equivalent of art: 'Ainsi, qu'il soit peinture, sculpture, poésie ou musique, l'art n'a d'autre objet que d'écarter les symboles pratiquement utiles, les généralités conventionellement et socialement acceptées, enfin tout ce qui nous masque la réalité, pour nous mettre face à face à la réalité même' (Bergson, *Le Rire*, p.120) ['So art, whether it be painting or sculpture, poetry or music, has no other object than to brush aside the utilitarian symbols, the conventional and socially accepted generalities, in short everything that veils reality from us, in order to bring us face to face with reality itself' (Bergson, 'Laughter', p.162)].

In the last analysis, then, Proust uses humour to underscore some of his most intellectual and philosophical ideas. By drawing the reader's attention to the human failings of the characters in his novel, Proust highlights the crucial connection between humour, humanity and art. As it turns out, the subtly comic dinner scene with Céline and Flora in 'Combray' shows readers how errors in comprehension prepare our entry into the world of art. Like Elstir's paintings or Vinteuil's musical compositions, literature can lend us 'd'autres yeux' ['other eyes'] in order to 'voir l'univers avec les yeux d'un autre, de cent autres, de voir les cent univers que chacun d'eux voit, que chacun d'eux est' ['see the universe through the eyes of another, of a hundred others, to see the hundred universes that each of them sees, that each of them is'] which, 'sans l'art, nous ne connaîtrions jamais' (III, 762) ['but for art, we should never know' (V, 291/343)]. Proust's book, which records one person's search to uncover the aesthetic components inherent in everyday life, is essentially an exploration into what makes us human: the meanings we give to words, images, sounds and so on, that serve to express our understanding of the world. The *Recherche* is a human comedy in the sense that it attempts to describe the variety of experiences contained in human existence. Paradoxically, the very thing through which we reveal our weakness, in other words, our inherent difficulty with communication and the constant danger of misinterpretation and misunderstanding, creates our capacity for artistic achievement and underscores its greatness. Indeed, without the human and therefore the comic element in the *Recherche*, no artistic epiphany for the Protagonist – or for the reader – is possible.

NOTES

1 Germaine Brée, *Du temps perdu au temps retrouvé* (Paris: Les Belles Lettres, 1969), p.131.
2 Germaine Brée, *Marcel Proust and Deliverance from Time*, trans. C.J. Richards and A.D. Truitt (New Brunswick, NJ: Rutgers University Press, 1969), p.102.
3 James Feibleman, *In Praise of Comedy: A Study in its Theory and Practice* (New York: Russell and Russell, 1962), p.29.

4 Henri Bergson, *Le Rire: essai sur la signification du comique* (Paris: Presses Universitaires de France, 1940), p.55. In English: 'Laughter', in *Comedy*, ed. Wylie Sypher (Baltimore: Johns Hopkins University Press, 1980), pp.61–190 [p. 107].

5 Honoré de Balzac, *La Fille aux yeux d'or,* in *La Comédie humaine* (Paris: Gallimard, 1976), v, 1039–112.

6 Honoré de Balzac, *The Girl with Golden Eyes,* in *The Works of Honoré de Balzac,* trans. Ellen Marriage and Ernest Dowson (Philadelphia: Avil Publishing Co., 1901), XXIII, 281–357.

7 Honoré de Balzac, 'Avant-propos', in *La Comédie humaine* (Paris: Gallimard, 1976), I, 7–20.

8 Honoré de Balzac, 'Author's Introduction' in *The Works of Honoré de Balzac,* trans. Ellen Marriage and Ernest Dowson (Philadelphia: Avil Publishing Co., 1901), I, lxvi-lxvii.

9 Gaston Zélicourt, *Le Monde de la 'Comédie humaine': clefs pour l'œuvre romanesque de Balzac* (Paris: Seghers, 1979), p.223.

10 René Girard, *Mensonge romantique et vérité romanesque* (Paris: Bernard Grasset, 1961), p.198. In English: *Deceit, Desire, and the Novel,* trans. Yvonne Freccero (Baltimore: Johns Hopkins University Press, 1965), p.202.

11 Marcel Proust et Jacques Rivière: *Correspondance (1914–22),* ed. Philip Kolb (Paris: Plon, 1955), p.3.

12 André Maurois, *A la recherche de Marcel Proust* (Paris: Hachette, 1949), p.247. In English: *Proust: Portrait of a Genius,* trans. Gerard Hopkins (New York: Harper and Brothers, 1950), p.234.

13 Léon Pierre-Quint, *Marcel Proust: sa vie, son œuvre* (Paris: Simon Kra, 1925), p.283.

14 Elisabeth Ladenson, *Proust's Lesbianism* (Ithaca, NY: Cornell University Press, 1999), p.102.

15 Jarrod Hayes, 'Proust in the Tearoom', *PMLA,* 110 (1995), 992–1005 [995].

16 Lawrence R. Schehr, *The Shock of Men: Homosexual Hermeneutics in French Writing* (Stanford University Press, 1995), p.59.

17 Maya Slater, *Humour in the Works of Marcel Proust* (New York: Oxford University Press, 1979), p.46.

18 Juliette Hassine, *Marranisme et hébraïsme dans l'œuvre de Proust* (Paris: Minard, 1994).

10

EDWARD J. HUGHES

Proust and social spaces

... il y a des clichés dans les offices aussi bien que dans les cénacles.

(IV, 428)

... there are clichés in the servants' hall as well as in social coteries.

(VI, 195/230)

The promotion in Proust's novel of inner psychological states is regularly reinforced by the Narrator's pronouncements on their importance. Thus our social life stands ostensibly as inferior to the intricate workings of private memory; time spent in society is deemed wasted, whereas according time to introspective contemplation is commended. The aesthetic solutions proposed in *Le Temps retrouvé* confirm this assumption. The fact that the Narrator, through involuntary memory, rediscovers his private past that is now to be immortalised in the work of art reinforces the view that the internal psychological ruminations of the Narrator should override the social. Reflecting on friendship, which signals the social, the Narrator protests that the self loses its true orientation, becoming 'hospitalisé dans une individualité étrangère' (II, 689) ['hospitalised in an extraneous individuality' (III, 456/541)].

Yet the novel's private histories intersect with a broader public one, as Walter Benjamin was quick to point out.[1] As Vincent Descombes explains, while Proust the theorist rejected the sociological view of human life, 'Proust as novelist, in constructing characters and episodes, shows exceptional sociological flair'.[2] Thus the social rise of figures such as Odette de Crécy and Mme Verdurin and the eventual decline of the Duchesse de Guermantes that are integral to the plot of the novel exemplify the growing ascendancy of the bourgeoisie and the demise of the aristocracy in the course of the Third Republic. To take another example, Proust describes how, prior to the Dreyfus Affair, Jews such as Sir Rufus and Lady Israëls (the latter the aunt of Charles Swann) enjoyed a social eminence that was to disappear with the momentous upheaval ushered in by the Affair. As the Narrator comments:

. . . pareille aux kaléidoscopes qui tournent de temps en temps, la société place successivement de façon différente des éléments qu'on avait crus immuables et compose une autre figure . . . [Avec l'affaire Dreyfus] tout ce qui était juif passa en bas . . . et des nationalistes obscurs montèrent prendre sa place. Le salon le plus brillant de Paris fut celui d'un prince autrichien et ultra-catholique. Qu'au lieu de l'affaire Dreyfus il fût survenu une guerre avec l'Allemagne, le tour du kaléidoscope se fût produit dans un autre sens. (I, 507–8)

[. . . like a kaleidoscope which is every now and again given a turn, society arranges successively in different orders elements which one would have supposed immutable, and composes a new pattern . . . [With the Dreyfus affair] everything Jewish . . . went down, and various obscure nationalists rose to take its place. The most brilliant salon in Paris was that of an ultra-Catholic Austrian prince. If instead of the Dreyfus case there had come a war with Germany, the pattern of the kaleidoscope would have taken a turn in the other direction.] (II, 103/122)

Thus the anti-semitism and germanophobia of late nineteenth- and early twentieth-century French history, acting as conduits for nationalist intolerance, mark reconfigurations of the social kaleidoscope.

But there is another kaleidoscope in Proust's novel, the 'kaléidoscope de l'obscurité' (I, 4) ['kaleidoscope of the darkness' (I, 2/2)] formed by the clusters of private night-time memories and associations in the opening half-dozen pages of 'Combray'. Thus we are able to refer to the two cycles in the novel of introspection and social representation. The intersection between these is captured straightaway in 'Combray', where in addition to the central drama of the bedtime kiss, with its focus on a self-absorbed human subject, we also have the beginnings of an important sociology. For the workings of the clan are explored in an overdetermined manner. Thus while Swann's regular ringing at the door bell solicits within the family circle a falsely naive 'Une visite, qui cela peut-il être?' (I, 14) ['A visitor! Who in the world can it be?' (I, 14/16)], the Narrator, with the detachment of the sociological observer, notes the codes of this closed world. As he writes, the bourgeoisie of that period functions within a system of rigid social classification: '[ils] se faisaient de la société une idée un peu hindoue et la considéraient comme composée de castes fermées' (I, 16) ['[They] took what was almost a Hindu view of society, which they held to consist of sharply defined castes' (I, 16/19)].[3] Thus, while the ritual visits paid by Charles Swann inevitably spell for the boy the pain of separation from the mother – and a return to introspection – they also prompt reflection on social organisation. And that Swann should be depicted dramatically as a stranger, an enemy, an assailant (I, 14; I, 14–15/17–18) feeds, albeit in a mock serious way, the sense of exclusion and inclusion at work within the clan.

Symptomatic of this tribalism is the refusal of the boy's great aunt (as opposed to his grandfather) to concede that Swann might frequent social circles outside this round of bourgeois provincial calls. Seeing class loyalty as a virtue, she jealously dismisses any suggestion that Swann might have a life beyond the narrow circuit of Combray. Thus details of Swann's Protean lifestyle (his hobnobbing with the Prince of Wales, his membership of the exclusive Jockey Club, and his sexual promiscuity in the company of working-class Parisian women) are either unsuspected or dismissed, thereby reinforcing the caste. Disapproval of these social contacts becomes outright taboo in the family's response to Swann's marriage to the courtesan Odette. In mitigation, the Narrator's mother pleads with her husband that they should at least ask Swann about his daughter, Gilberte, but the request is dismissed as being socially inept (1, 22–3; 1, 24–5/28–9). An inhibiting set of social codes thus galvanises the tribe and in this particular instance restricts maternal spontaneity. Decorum acts as an imperious call to social order.

These opening scenes from provincial Combray suggest the clan's rigid sense of social propriety; and the veiled violence and insecurity, the resentments and snobberies that pepper the Narrator's family conversation characterise the self-preservation of a clearly defined social class. When news appears in *Le Figaro* of Swann's private art collection, suggesting his higher social standing, the grandmother's admiring response prompts the defensive outburst from the great aunt that to have one's name in print is distasteful (*ibid.*). Here again, the great-aunt's instinct is to generate within the family 'une condamnation en bloc des opinions de ma grand-mère contre lesquelles elle tâchait de nous solidariser de force avec les siennes' (1, 22) ['a wholesale condemnation of my grandmother's views, against which she hoped to force us into solidarity with her own' (1, 24/28)]. The finding of common cause, the judgemental exclusivism, the vulnerability when confronted with cultural difference all confirm this social conservatism. Not surprisingly, his friend Bloch's suggestion to the boy Narrator that the same great-aunt had been a prostitute in her early years prompts the boy's parents literally to expel him from the family home (1, 92; 1, 110/129), an exclusion which symptomatically marks the jealous safeguarding of social reputation.

In his moments of complicity with this cultural narrowness, the Narrator savours situations when the codes of Combray appear inviolable and even exaggeratedly claustrophobic in their impact. The arrangements for Saturday lunch, whereby the family regularly eats an hour earlier to enable Françoise to get to the afternoon market in neighbouring Roussainville-le-Pin, conform to a fixed pattern that is common knowledge to the insider, while the outsider, unaware of these routines, is labelled a barbarian and mocked for ineptly calling in the hope of speaking to the Narrator's father (I, 110; I, 131–2/154–5). The pleasures of participation, mutuality and intolerance of the Other are the hallmarks of the social group. As the insiders enjoy the self-congratulatory collective ritual, the Narrator observes incisively:

> Le retour de ce samedi asymétrique était un de ces petits événements intérieurs, locaux, presque civiques qui, dans les vies tranquilles et les sociétés fermées, créent une sorte de lien national et deviennent le thème favori des conversations, des plaisanteries, des récits exagérés à plaisir; il eût été le noyau tout prêt pour un cycle légendaire si l'un de nous avait eu la tête épique.   (I, 109)

> [The recurrence of this asymmetrical Saturday was one of those minor events, intra-mural, localised, almost civic, which, in uneventful lives and stable orders of society, create a kind of national tie and become the favourite theme for conversation, for pleasantries, for anecdotes which can be embroidered as the narrator pleases; it would have provided the ready-made kernel for a legendary cycle, had any of us had an epic turn of mind.]   (I, 130–1/153–4)

By stressing collective identification and the shunning of deviation, the Narrator is formulating a key principle of the Combray clan, and, one might add, of sociology, namely that the workings of the group take precedence over human individuality.[4] In the reference to the absence of an epic teller within the family's ranks, there is a double irony: first, in that Proust's Narrator and Françoise (since it is she primarily who goads the others on in her hyperbolic telling and retelling of the tale) prove very able exponents of the art of legend; and second, in that by incorporating this tribal tale into the broader social narrative of the *Recherche* as a prelude to transcending the closed world that it signals, Proust is moving beyond epic and homespun familial certainties to the unpredictable evolutions of contemporary history. As we shall see later, the codes of Combray will succumb to the social revolution precipitated by the First World War.

If Combray is a cocoon, the same preoccupation with social ritual significantly provides the point of entry into the second part of *Du côté de chez Swann*, 'Un amour de Swann'. Here too, the tension that characterises the Verdurin salon, where Swann is courting Odette, is captured in the vocabularies of insiderness and banishment that proliferate in the opening paragraphs of the volume: to the opposition between, on the one hand, the faithful, the recruits, the church and, on the other, rebels and strangers, we can add the overdetermined inwardness with which the group denotes itself: 'Pour faire partie du "petit noyau", du "petit groupe", du "petit clan", une condition était suffisante mais elle était nécessaire: il fallait adhérer tacitement à un Credo . . .' (I, 185) ['To admit you to the "little nucleus," the "little group," the "little clan" at the Verdurins', one condition sufficed, but that one was indispensable: you must give tacit adherence to a Creed . . .' (I, 225/265)]. By associating the social with the religious – the Credo implies a code of binding social practices, obligations and beliefs, and indeed the Narrator refers to the orthodoxy of the little church (*ibid.*) – Proust sees the classification and hierarchy that are intrinsic to the workings of the Verdurin salon. Describing it as being inferior to an aristocratic salon, he observes its paranoid exclusion of most women, who, driven on by 'le démon de la frivolité' (*ibid.*) ['this demon of frivolity'] speculate flirtatiously about life in the more prestigious salons. In addition, he evokes its intolerant and insecure patron Mme Verdurin, who prizes what higher social groups devalue (she calls the prostitute Odette 'une perfection' (I, 188) ['an angel' (I, 228/269)] and castigates the faint-hearted and the wayward as '[les] "ennuyeux" dont on se garait comme de la peste' (I, 186) ['the "boring people" who were to be avoided like the plague' (I, 226/267)]. Crassly, she later casts the First World War in the role of 'une grande "ennuyeuse" qui les faisait lâcher' (IV, 348) ['a great "bore" that caused them to defect' (VI, 97/114)]. Her salon is also the stage for scenes of brutal exclusion: thus the expulsion of one of the 'faithful', the archivist Saniette, is described by the habituees as a fine execution (I, 272–3; I, 333/393); while all the aristocratic titles of the Baron de Charlus cannot save him from humiliating exclusion, after his ill-fated love for the musician Charlie Morel comes to an end. Indeed the preposterous rumour that the baron had been expelled for attempting to rape Morel illustrates the power of the salon to denigrate (III, 822; V, 363/428).

True to the logic that what is possessed is flaunted as superior and what is unobtainable is derided, Mme Verdurin savagely dismisses acts of independence and autonomy, such as Dr Cottard's Easter visit to the Auvergne (I, 187; I, 227/268), and zealously promotes her own salon. We thus find an echo of the Combray household, where the Narrator's elderly relatives dismiss Swann's other lives as improbable, irrelevant, or reflecting bad taste. Swann is a visitor to both of these communities in miniature, breaking in on the Narrator's family at Combray which has its rituals, its logic of 'election and exclusion', as does the Verdurin salon (see Descombes, p.186). In their respective roles, Odette and Swann serve to underwrite and/or undo social value: Odette may be shunned by the Narrator's family in Combray but she is Mme Verdurin's prize possession, while Swann, who is no more than tolerated in the Verdurin salon, is the welcome guest in the Combray home. Proust's point is that the conferring and withholding of social value is integral to the construction of the group.

By the same token, as Mme Verdurin's later acquisition of the title of Princesse de Guermantes confirms, social value is a changing commodity. A measure of Proust's attention to social spaces lies in the fact that the early pages of 'Combray', 'Un amour de Swann', *A l'ombre des jeunes filles en fleurs* and *Le Côté de Guermantes* all dwell on the depiction of social milieus and the hierarchies, inclusions and exclusions that underpin them. In the opening page of *A l'ombre des jeunes filles en fleurs*, the Narrator's father launches into what for the reader of 'Combray' is an unexpected diatribe against Swann. The explanation given is that the new Swann, married to the former courtesan Odette de Crécy, has replaced both the visitor once tamed and assimilated by the Narrator's family in Combray, that is the 'fils Swann' ['young Swann'], and the Swann who frequents the prestigious Jockey Club. In place of what the Narrator trumpets as the modesty of the refined Swann (the inferred value judgement about an upper-class *savoir faire* is clear here), we now have a vulgar, insecure husband who boasts about the dull civil servants that he and his new wife have been entertaining. In the Narrator's memorable formulation, Swann the *déclassé* is like a great artist who will give away a precious painting for nothing but who is annoyed to lose a dime in a game of dominoes (I, 424; II, 2/3). Thus, in dedicating himself obsessively to the pursuit of Odette's social ambitions – temporarily at least, as the text tells us – Swann indirectly demonstrates how the social kaleidoscope works. Moreover, by acquiring the preoccupations of another class, Swann unwittingly shows the relativity of social value.

In important ways, Swann represents social change emblematically. His promiscuity forces him to flit between classes. Inattentive in his dealings with a duchess, he fears being humiliated by a housemaid. Moreover, he is a model of unpredictability and mobility:

> Il ne s'enfermait pas dans l'édifice de ses relations, mais en avait fait, pour pouvoir le reconstruire à pied d'œuvre sur de nouveaux frais partout où une femme lui avait plu, une de ces tentes démontables comme les explorateurs en emportent avec eux. (I, 189–90)

> [He did not immure himself in the edifice of his social relations, but had made of them, so as to be able to set it up afresh upon new foundations wherever a woman might take his fancy, one of those collapsible tents which explorers carry about with them.] (I, 230/271)

Swann is clearly a sexual predator rather than a social revolutionary and yet the model of migration across class boundaries that he provides anticipates the impermanence of a social caste system and exemplifies the power of desire to alter the social landscape.

Swann's erotic itinerary in 'Un amour de Swann' involves a plurality of sites. Self-evidently, the Verdurin salon provides the social space that guarantees him access to Odette: 'Ainsi le simple fonctionnement de cet organisme social qu'était le petit "clan" prenait automatiquement pour Swann des rendez-vous quotidiens avec Odette et lui permettait de feindre une indif-férence à la voir.' (I, 223) ['Thus the simple and regular manifestations of this social organism, the "little clan", automatically provided Swann with a daily rendezvous with Odette, and enabled him to feign indifference to the pros-pect of seeing her' (I, 272/320)]. Yet immediately prior to visiting the salon, Swann has taken a young Parisian working-class woman to the Bois de Boulogne. We thus have the contiguity in the text of the salon and the Bois, before shifting to the wide-open streets of Paris when, discovering that Odette is no longer at the Verdurins, a panic-stricken Swann scours the capital in search of her. The Bois, the salon, and the Parisian boulevards thus become the multiple sites of desire in 'Un amour de Swann'.

The reappearance of the Bois de Boulogne in the closing pages of *Du côté de chez Swann* demonstrates how time as well as location modifies both desire and its social organisation. Here the Narrator recalls years later how in his infatuated youth, he had looked out for Mme Swann. New styles of dress and modes of transport are the tangible signs of the passing years, and yesterday's beautiful women are the aged shadowy figures who walk despair-ingly down the Allée des Acacias. In this autumnal setting, these quintessen-tially social spaces where the Parisian leisured classes regularly parade themselves now return to Nature: 'La nature recommençait à régner sur le Bois d'où s'était envolée l'idée qu'il était le Jardin élyséen de la Femme . . . de gros oiseaux parcouraient rapidement le Bois, comme un bois' (I, 419) ['Nature was resuming its reign over the Bois, from which had vanished all trace of the idea that it was the Elysian Garden of Woman . . . large birds flew swiftly over the Bois, as over a real wood' (I, 512–13/606)]. The effect of this closure to the first volume of the novel is to combine two modes of vision: the one ethnographic, as the Narrator muses on the once-vibrant social space of the Bois (capital B), and the other lyrical and private, with the reflection on death set within the evocation of a return to nature, in the form of the lower-case *bois*. To be more exact, the Narrator here signals his reluc-tance to observe the social evolution, what he terms 'toutes ces parties nou-velles du spectacle' (I, 417) ['all these new components of the spectacle' (I, 510/603)]. This shying away from sociological change coincides with a retreat into private memory, and returns us to the configuration of private and social cycles to which I alluded earlier in the discussion of 'Combray'.

A particular kind of 'society' is represented in Proust's novel by the life of the Faubourg Saint-Germain. That the Guermantes family embodies cultu-ral prestige is already signalled in the early pages of the novel where the nobility and longevity of the Guermantes are celebrated in iconic terms in the Combray church (I, 60, 169; I, 71/82, 205/241). If, for the Protagonist, an aura of inaccessibility whets his appetite for integration into this world, for the Narrator, such social remoteness, together with the distinctions and codes that underpin it, becomes a regular object of study. Michael Finn makes the point that 'the world of social distinctions is expertly noted by Proust, and both participated in and disavowed'.[5] As a participant, the Narrator denigrates the crass snobbery of the Verdurin salon, the better to attribute a sacred character to the Guermantes milieu. In other words, true to the logic of what Pierre Bourdieu terms 'the ideology of charisma' ('Whereas the ideology of charisma regards taste in legitimate culture as a gift of nature, scientific observation shows that cultural needs are the product of upbringing and education'),[6] social superiority is seen as a gift, possessed by the Guermantes and denied to the Verdurins. In this way, Proust appears to endorse the imposition of dominant cultural value.

But Proustian disavowal, to take up the second half of Finn's point, comes in a number of guises. Much is made of the threshold of the Guermantes residence in *Le Côté de Guermantes*. For the young Protagonist, a line of demarcation, imagined and yet very real, separates him from this leading aristocratic household in the Faubourg Saint-Germain. The same impression of forbidden social spaces was conveyed earlier in the novel in respect of the household of Swann and Odette, now Mme Swann. Their home is designated as 'le Sanctuaire' ['the Sanctuary'], the couple leading 'leur vie surnaturelle' ['their supernatural existence'] within what is classed as a fairytale domain (I, 499–500; II, 93–4/111). The religious vocabulary again reinforces the idea of election, with the admission of the few to this defended social space serving as a mark of its prestige.

Yet the Guermantes household, while an altogether more aristocratic sanctuary, also undergoes demystification as the Narrator, focusing on the moment of entry into this exclusive zone, alludes to 'le paillasson des Guermantes étendu de l'autre côté de cet Équateur et dont ma mère avait osé dire, l'ayant aperçu comme moi, un jour que leur porte était ouverte, qu'il était en bien mauvais état' (II, 330) ['spread out on the other side of that Equator, the Guermantes doormat of which my mother had ventured to say, having like myself caught a glimpse of it one day when their door stood open, that it was in a shocking state' (III, 26/31)]. The context requires explanation. First, the Narrator's family have recently moved to live in a wing of the property where the Guermantes live, a move that creates an interface between bourgeois and aristocrats and an opportunity not just for the Narrator to analyse these distinct social worlds. (The aristocratic comings and goings also become a focus of constant attention for the family servant Françoise: II, 316; III, 9/11.) This proximity enables the Narrator to bring about a humorous juxtaposition of bourgeois house pride and aristocratic neglect, as the mother sees and comments on the state of dilapidation of the Guermantes doormat. Alongside this idealisation of the aristocracy, there is also, then, a humorous deflation of social mystique. And that the mother should 'venture to say' parallels, one senses, the Narrator's own urge for detachment. Throwing off the charismatic spell of the Guermantes can assume unlikely forms, as when he likens catching sight of the Faubourg Saint-Germain to being on the high seas, with no chance of landing, and seeing on an exotic coastline 'comme un minaret avancé, comme un premier palmier, comme le commencement de l'industrie ou de la végétation exotiques, le paillasson usé du rivage' (II, 331) ['like a prominent minaret, like the first palm, like the first signs of some exotic industry or vegetation, the well trodden doormat of its shore' (III, 27/32)]. Here the Narrator's improbable colonial metaphor to denote aristocrats living literally in the same building signals witty irreverence rather than adulation. The Guermantes have become transformed into exotica, the social hierarchies of Third Republic Paris have been relativised, and aristocratic mystique undone. In the same spirit, the adolescent Narrator wonders if standing in the garden of the Duchesse de Guermantes really amounts to being in the Faubourg Saint-Germain, just as one might ask if being in the Figuig oasis (in the Moroccan Sahara) equates to being in Africa (*ibid.*).

By calling up colonial spaces and transforming the culture of the revered aristocratic subject into that of its traditionally denigrated Oriental counterpart, Proust signals an end to adoration and the beginnings of an impressionistic ethnography that is not without cultural condescension. Much later in the novel, in *Le Temps retrouvé*, the Narrator returns to the surreal motif of the Saharan dwelling of the Guermantes. Now in his old age, Monsieur de Guermantes has a new mistress, Mme de Forcheville, the former Mme Swann, and in his confused moments of irascibility, he is unsure as to whether he is at home arguing with his wife or in the company of Mme Swann: 'peut-être . . . se croyait-il à l'hôtel de Guermantes, comme ces fauves enchaînés qui se figurent un instant être encore libres dans les déserts de l'Afrique' (IV, 596) ['perhaps . . . he imagined . . . that he was still in his own house, like a wild beast in chains who for a brief second thinks that it is still free in the deserts of Africa' (VI, 413/486)]. In reality, the text concludes, he is in the home of Mme de Forcheville, which is likened to the cage in the Jardin des Plantes, while the hairs on the duke's neck, his submissive posture and his staring, round eyes complete the animal portrait. In Proust's subversive metaphor, where a European aristocracy and Africa coalesce, the spaces of domestic normalcy recall unfettered access to the wild, while infidelity brings its own restrictions and dangers.

The animalisation of the Duke in these closing pages of *A la recherche* enables us to see how Proust's sociology has become a zoology. From the sacralisation of the Guermantes earlier in the novel, the Narrator graduates to a position of disabusement and insight. Yet earlier in the human comedy that is *A la recherche*, the Narrator's zoological spotlight is reversed, as the Princesse de Luxembourg, in her superiority, addresses the young Narrator and his grandmother as though they were endearing animals behind the bars at the Jardin d'Acclimatation. When the princess incongruously buys some bread to be fed to the grandmother by the Protagonist as a young boy, as though the child's desire to nurture were being indulged by the princess' generous gift, the Narrator reflects on what he labels playfully 'un merveilleux progrès de l'évolution, ma grand-mère n'était plus un canard ou une antelope, mais déjà ce que Mme Swann eût appelé un "baby"' (II, 60) ['a miraculous stride in evolution, my grandmother was no longer a duck or an antelope, but had already become what Mme Swann would have called a *"baby"*' (II, 322/380)]. Significantly, what energises the extended metaphorical play is social distinction, and the overlay of zoological evolution suggests a flirtatious reflection on the seeming impregnability of would-be higher social states.

Proust insists that the logic of social hierarchy, with its vindictiveness, recrimination and paranoia, obtains at every level of society. Within the Narrator's household, Françoise emerges as the dominant member of the domestic staff, dealing punitively with the pregnant kitchenmaid (the one who resembled Giotto's Caritas), insisting that she, Françoise, and no one else should tend to the needs of Aunt Léonie, and ensuring, by using every ruse possible, that no kitchenmaid ever stayed long in the household. Like her counterparts in other social classes, then, Françoise practises an art of exclusion and only occasionally does the Narrator succumb to a sentimentalised account of her position.

We can consider in the same light the keeper of the public conveniences at the Champs-Elysées, whom Françoise, exaggerating the extent of the keeper's daughter's marriage into higher society, calls 'une marquise' ['marchioness']. Dismissing the title as a ludicrous figment of Françoise's imagination, the Narrator goes on to demonstrate with searing wit how this bizarre figure, plastered in make-up and wearing a wig, is herself an expert in social inclusion and exclusion. Hence her indulgence for the child Narrator as, gesturing to one of her cubicles, she encourages him: 'Vous ne voulez pas entrer? en voici un tout propre, pour vous ce sera gratis' (I, 484) ['Won't you go inside for a minute? Look, here's a nice clean one, and I shan't charge *you* anything' (II, 75/89)]; while a poorly dressed woman, desperate to relieve herself, is fiercely turned away by the keeper. Triumphantly, the keeper reflects: 'Ce n'est pas le genre d'ici, ça n'a pas de propreté, pas de respect, il aurait fallu que ce soit moi qui passe une heure à nettoyer pour madame. Je ne regrette pas ses deux sous' (II, 607) ['That's not the sort we want here, either; they're not clean, don't treat the place with respect. It'd be me who'd have to spend the next hour cleaning up after her ladyship. I'm not sorry to lose her couple of sous' (III, 357/422)]. That the episode entails a humorous recycling of the social rivalries of the novel's privileged classes is confirmed by the Narrator's ailing grandmother, who, having followed the conversation from one of the cubicles, concludes: 'C'était on ne peut plus Guermantes et petit noyau Verdurin' (*ibid.*) ['Could anything have been more typical of the Guermantes, or the Verdurins and their little clan?']. Thus, in the scenarios of domination sketched by the novel, the norms of the dominant class are valorised by being reproduced within the lower social strata. That the keeper's musings are cheap substitutes for the 'real thing' (she refers to her underground cubicles as her salons or parlours (II, 606; III, 356/421)) is underlined by the milieu in which she operates, the system of primitive bodily functions that she oversees pointing directly to the subversion of social mystique in *A la recherche*. For in the conflation of salon and public convenience, snobbery and veiled scatology, the clear inference is that hierarchy, like the notions of taste and value that underpin it, invades every social space. What we are left with is a sense of rigid social conformity, what Bourdieu in another context sees as a call to order, in which the expectations of the dominant group are internalised and reinforced by the subordinate group.[7]

For the insomniac Narrator of the opening of 'Combray', much of the night is spent recalling his past life in a string of locations: Combray, Balbec, Paris, Doncières and Venice. The evocation of these sites comes to be inseparable from the individual projections and desires not just of the Narrator but of the others who frequent them. Thus, in the case of Paris, the keeper of the public conveniences in the Champs-Elysées may refer proprietorially to 'ce que j'appelle mon petit Paris' (II, 605) ['My own little Paris, I call it' (III, 355/420)]. Belonging to another Paris is the Narrator's Uncle Adolphe, into whose apartment the Narrator is ushered on clearly designated days to avoid overlap with the actresses and courtesans who visit the uncle. On one occasion, the naive nephew arrives unannounced to meet an embarrassed uncle and, for the first time, 'la dame en rose', i.e. the future Mme Swann. The separation between routine family duty and the pursuit of erotic pleasure is unambiguous: '[mon oncle] tâchait autant que possible d'éviter tout trait d'union entre sa famille et ce genre de relations' (I, 75) ['[my uncle] had endeavoured as far as possible to avoid any association of his family with this other class of acquaintance' (I, 89/104)]. While for the uncle, suppression of such a linkage is desirable, what this early episode demonstrates is the regular collision of familial piety and illegal pleasure. And into that template, we can slot examples of the plural uses and significances of social spaces and practices: from the ritual tapping on the wall in the Grand-Hôtel at Balbec between the boy and his grandmother to the same routine, this time in his Paris apartment, between the adult Narrator and Albertine; the donation to a brothel of Aunt Léonie's furniture, which she had bequeathed to the Narrator; the slide from a eucharistic piety to erotic pleasure in the kisses bestowed on the Narrator by his mother and later Albertine.

The divorce and yet also the propinquity between family and erotic experience is evident in 'Combray', where the sadistic scene involving Mlle Vinteuil and her lover at Montjouvain (I, 157–61; I, 190–8/224–33) acts as a counterpoint to a familial and a religious Combray, reflected symbolically in the ritual family walks, Sunday mass and the Combray church. Significantly, this tension returns in the evocation of Venice in *Albertine disparue*, where conscious links are made with Combray, one of the dominant social matrices in the novel. The mother, now mourning the loss of her own mother, is described as a well of affection, no longer holding back as she had at Combray (IV, 202–5; V, 715–18/844–8). The tone is confirmed when the Narrator visits the baptistery of St Mark's in the company of his mother, who appears to be immortalised in the basilica: 'elle y a sa place réservée et immuable comme une mosaïque' (IV, 225) ['she has her place reserved there as immutably as a mosaic' (V, 742/876)]. Ironically, Venice becomes a site in which the Narrator's grandmother is commemorated, even though she had never visited the city. But as the Narrator's mother repeatedly asserts, the grandmother would have adored Venice. The desire for the deceased to return is captured in the pathetic fallacy whereby the Doges' Palace waits loyally and thoughtfully for its revered, long since departed occupants to return, '[sa] muette attente des doges disparus' (IV, 208) ['its mute attendance on its vanished lords' (V, 721/852)] shadowing the mother's patient mourning for her absent mother.

Yet beyond the city's tourist destinations and their capacity to absorb the melancholy of mourning – while primarily it is the mother who pines for her mother, the Narrator is still getting over Albertine – there is another Venice, that of the *campi* (squares) and the abandoned *rii* (narrow side-canals), where the Narrator engages in the pursuit of promiscuous sexual pleasure on those afternoons when not in the company of his mother. As Peter Collier observes: 'Tendentiously, the cultural image of Venice itself is distorted by the gravity of desire.'[8] And if Uncle Adolphe's nephew inherits the former's instinct to preserve the separation between family and hedonism, he has also picked up his lasciviousness, acknowledged in *Albertine disparue* in the Narrator's passionate search for Venetian women. In place of the uncle's Parisian haunts, we have a populous Venice in which the Narrator is guided as though through an oriental maze. It is in the Venice of urchins and market gardeners, humble parish churches and crowds of urban poor that the Narrator thinks feverishly of Albertine's earlier, unfettered sexual predation as well as exercising his own.

This detour via the back streets and non-touristic waterways serves as a prelude to meeting up again with the Mother in the Piazzetta, a symbolic return to high-cultural seriousness. But for the Narrator, this convenient compartmentalisation of the social spaces of the city disintegrates when the mother's decision to leave for Paris coincides with her son's learning that Mme Putbus and her entourage are due to arrive at the hotel that day. This latter news and the prospect of sexual pleasure that it portends awakens in the Narrator the strongest and most destructive of emotions: he talks of his state of febrile agitation, of parental plots to frustrate his pursuit of pleasure, and of a brutal desire to impose his will (IV, 230; V, 748/883). What such mental violence destroys is not only the Narrator's sense of selfhood but also the powerful cultural symbolism of Venice itself:

> Ma solitude irrévocable était . . . totale. Car je me sentais seul, les choses m'é-taient devenues étrangères . . . La ville que j'avais devant moi avait cessé d'être Venise. Sa personnalité, son nom, me paraissaient comme des fictions mensongères que je n'avais plus le courage d'inculquer aux pierres . . . [ce lieu] me contractait sur moi-même . . . (IV, 231)

> [My irrevocable solitude was . . . complete. For I felt myself to be alone; things had become alien to me . . . The town that I saw before me had ceased to be Venice. Its personality, its name, seemed to me to be mendacious fictions which I no longer had the will to impress upon its stones . . . [this place] contracted me into myself . . .] (V, 749/884)

Hence the disintegration both of self-identification and the social spaces of the external world that shape it. The sociological dictum seen earlier, that the group precedes the individual, is here radically contested. As Leo Bersani writes, recognising the social, in this case Venice, depends on the Narrator projecting himself on the city, a projection that becomes impossible with the departure of the mother.[9] As Venice is thus reduced to a heap of stones and water, we are invited to reflect on this undoing of the social subject, precipitated by an alienating desire that society, in the form of the mother, refuses to sanction.

It is instructive to return to the Combray/Venice analogy which the

Narrator underscores at the beginning of the 'Séjour à Venise' section. In aesthetic terms, the two locations are markedly different: the solid, architecturally unspectacular Combray recalls the painter Chardin's down-to-earthness, whereas Venice exudes the grand style of Veronese. Yet in sociological terms, great play is made of the rituals that are common to the two locations – Sunday mornings, the churches of Saint-Hilaire and of San Giorgio Maggiore, the ordinary folk in the street or on the water. Indeed reference to 'le plaisir de descendre dans une rue en fête' (IV, 203) ['the pleasure of stepping down into a festive street' (V, 715–16/845)] signals a literal entry into a social community noted for its cohesiveness and gaiety. But whereas, as Descombes observes, Combray is the place in which everyone knows the Narrator, Venice is not.[10] Moreover, its obliteration following the Narrator's mother's departure represents the temporary dissolution of the social being that is the Narrator. Thus in marked contrast with the carefully constructed social matrix of Combray stands the Venice from which the mother has been evacuated, where the Rialto bridge and the Canal lose their magic, as desire occludes culture. In this apocalyptic scenario, what emerges is the denial of a shared cultural history and the self-identification that goes with it.

If the destruction of Venice is a product of the Narrator's desperate mental projections, it does not prepare the reader for the literal, material destruction of parts of Combray in the First World War, as witnessed and relayed by Gilberte in her letter to the Narrator barely 100 pages later in the novel. The sites of memory celebrated in 'Combray', such as the way of the hawthorns and the bridge over the Vivonne, have become a battleground, with the Germans occupying one half of Combray and the French the other (IV, 335; VI, 81/96). What once appeared fixed social structures have been unceremoniously uprooted. Yet in addition to signalling radical social change, the destruction of these privileged, affectively charged locations spawns a reaffirmation of cultural affiliation. Crucially, the death of Saint-Loup in battle is emblematic both of the social change and the nostalgia it generates. The burial of the aristocratic war hero in the church of Saint Hilaire in Combray reinforces the sense of a collective, social being, the single letter in red on the black funeral draperies standing as the language of tribal affiliation: 'sans initiales de prénoms ni titres, le G du Guermantes que par la mort il était redevenu' (IV, 429) ['without initials or Christian names or titles, the G of the Guermantes that he had again in death become' (VI, 197/232)]. But in merging tribe and dead warrior, the Narrator is also signalling the demise of the aristocracy and the advent of a new social order. As Michael Sprinker writes, nostalgia for the past is channelled via the heroisation of Saint-Loup and the exposure of the bourgeoisie's opportunistic self-promotion in the wake of the armistice (Sprinker, *History and Ideology*, p.166).

Proust's novel provides a social anatomy of the Third French Republic, which came into being in the year of the author's birth. Sprinker makes the point that, while identifying an emergent bourgeois hegemony, *A la recherche* does not foresee the challenges posed to such dominance by the rise of Communism in the inter-war years (*History and Ideology*, p.183). But in the novel's analysis of the social kaleidoscope, we see Descombes' logic of election and exclusion working as a fundamental principle. We have evidence of this in the bourgeois codes of Combray, where insiders pity the barbarians, who are unschooled in the ways of the tribe. Part of the lure of Combray is indeed the shared will to believe that these social strata are unshakeable. Yet the traces of insecurity that impinge on the provincial bourgeoisie become unbridled paranoia in the Verdurin salon, where a similar juxtaposition of the elected and the banished obtains. Entry into the hallowed circles of the Guermantes is as intensely desired by the young Narrator as by Mme Verdurin. But what eventually separates the two is the former's growing disabusement and enabling detachment and the latter's social arrival. Indeed, that Mme Verdurin should eventually become the Princesse de Guermantes is symptomatic of this nervous jockeying for social position and of the upheaval of the First World War.

In her incisive social psychoanalysis of the world of *A la recherche*, Julia Kristeva focuses on expressions of group identity based on nation, religion and sexual orientation.[11] Analysing the France of the Dreyfus Affair and the First World War, she emphasises the tension in the novel between *being* and *being one of* (*être* versus *en être*), drawing out the sado-masochistic power of the clan (the Verdurin salon, as we have seen, provides the perfect paradigm for the *en être* imperative). Kristeva paints a compelling picture of Proust's ambivalence: the pro-Dreyfus campaigner who was nevertheless suspicious of group movements; the contemporary social historian who nevertheless prized *la vie intérieure* as an overriding aesthetic goal; the writer who craved recognition and for whom dubious political affiliation was no barrier to literary collaboration (his dedication of *Le Côté de Guermantes* to Léon Daudet of the right-wing *Action française* illustrates the point).

Located both at the social centre and on the periphery, Proust writes this tension into the figure of Swann, who is simultaneously an insider and an outsider, rubbing shoulders with the Prince of Wales, enthusing about Wagner and Botticelli, and yet, with age, looking like a figure from the Old Testament. The urbane secular European of the *belle époque* is simultaneously the ethnic Jew. Atavism rivals aestheticism, just as elsewhere in the novel, the compulsion to engage in social observation coexists with the workings of interiority.

Like Swann, Proust resists tidy categorisation. His Narrator regularly checks the gregarious impulse, all the better to understand its workings, both within himself and others. In stepping outside social spaces, the Narrator becomes an astute observer of group membership and exclusion. His reflections can be provocatively aloof as his misanthropic zoological portraits of individuals readily confirm. But at the same time he can muster the even-handedness of the social historian, as when he parallels the court of Louis XIV and the home of Aunt Léonie, both of which places are dominated by the despot's banal daily round, 'ce que Saint-Simon appelait la "mécanique" de la vie à Versailles' (I, 117) ['what Saint-Simon called the "mechanics" of life at Versailles' (I, 141/165)].[12] The same capacity for quasi-scientific detachment is picked up by Bourdieu in his reading of *Pastiches et Mélanges*, where Proust asserts that in the area of thought, 'la distinction et la noblesse consistent . . . dans une sorte de franc-maçonnerie d'usages, et dans un héritage de traditions' ['distinction and nobility . . . consist of a freemasonry of customs and a heritage of traditions'].[13] Proust's incisive identification of a confraternity of shared cultural assumptions suggests a detribalised and ultimately subversive mind, alert to the potential inherent in custom and heritage for both self-congratulation and violent exclusion.

NOTES

1 Benjamin explores the socio-historical importance of Proust's work in 'The Image of Proust', in *Illuminations*, trans. Harry Zohn (London: Collins/Fontana, 1973).

2 Vincent Descombes, *Proust: Philosophy of the Novel*, trans. Catherine Chance Macksey (Stanford University Press, 1992), p.10.

3 For an authoritative analysis of Proust's novel seen in its historical context, see Michael Sprinker, *History and Ideology in Proust: 'A la recherche du temps perdu' and the Third French Republic* (Cambridge University Press, 1994).

4 As Descombes reminds us, one of the fundamentals of sociological thinking, as represented by exponents such as Durkheim, Mauss and Dumont, is that the group precedes the individual and that human individuality is not a primary datum (Descombes, p.10).

5 Michael Finn, *Proust, the Body and Literary Form* (Cambridge University Press, 1999), p.86.

6 Pierre Bourdieu, *Distinction: a Social Critique of the Value of Judgement*, trans. Richard Nice (London: Routledge, 1994), p.1.

7 Analysing not only the subordination but also the conservatism of working-class culture, Bourdieu refers to 'the calls to order ('Who does she think she is?' 'That's not for the likes of us') which reaffirm the principle of conformity' (Bourdieu, *Distinction*, p.380).

8 See Chapter 2 of Peter Collier's *Proust and Venice* (Cambridge University Press, 1989), 'Desire, Ideal, Remembrance – the Venetian Syndrome', pp.20–30 (p. 24).

9 See Leo Bersani's incisive analysis of these questions in Chapter 1 of his *Marcel Proust: the Fictions of Life and Art* (New York: Oxford University Press, 1965), 'Fantasies of the Self and the World', pp.21–55.

10 Descombes, p.181. The emphasis is Descombes'. He makes the additional point that the anti-Combray is Balbec, in that no one knows the Narrator in the Norman seaside resort.

11 Julia Kristeva, *Le Temps sensible: Proust et l'expérience littéraire* (Paris: Gallimard, 1994).

12 Proust regularly invokes the acuity of Saint-Simon's social observation, often quoting from his celebrated *Mémoires*.

13 *CSB*, p.189. Quoted in Bourdieu, *Distinction*, p.499.

11

ALISON FINCH

Love, sexuality and friendship

The Narrator's reflections on love, sexuality and friendship are at first sight baldly phrased, universalising and tragic.

> De tous les modes de production de l'amour, de tous les agents de dissémina-tion du mal sacré, il est bien l'un des plus efficaces, ce grand souffle d'agitation qui parfois passe sur nous. Alors l'être avec qui nous nous plaisons à ce moment-là, le sort en est jeté, c'est lui que nous aimerons.   (I, 227)

> [Among all the modes by which love is brought into being, among all the agents which disseminate that blessed bane, there are few so efficacious as this gust of feverish agitation that sweeps over us from time to time. From then the die is cast, the person whose company we enjoy at that moment is the person we shall henceforward love.]   (I, 277/326–7)

> . . . l'acte de la possession physique—où d'ailleurs l'on ne possède rien . . .
>   (I, 230)

> [. . . the act of physical possession (in which, paradoxically, the possessor pos-sesses nothing) . . .]   (I, 281/331)

> l'amitié qui est une simulation puisque, pour quelques raisons morales qu'il le fasse, l'artiste qui renonce à une heure de travail pour une heure de cause-rie avec un ami sait qu'il sacrifie une réalité pour quelque chose qui n'existe pas. . . .   (IV, 454)

> [friendship which is a simulacrum, since, for whatever moral reasons he may do it, the artist who gives up an hour of work for an hour of conversation with a friend knows that he is sacrificing a reality for something that does not exist . . .]   (VI, 228/268)

The prevalence of such statements led critics, for decades after the publica-tion of *A la recherche*, to reconstruct and explain, often at length, Proust's 'psychological theories', in particular those about love. This was under-standable: not only are the Narrator's comments often presented as absolute laws of human behaviour, they also deliberately provoke us to extract them from their fictional context and to erect them into a system. This system appears internally coherent and, more important, supports the widest and most dramatic structure of the novel: that which makes of it a progress through painful illusions to some sort of 'Open Sesame', redemption or – if we do not care to go that far – at least to some firm purpose and sense of renewal. Love, desire, friendship are all snares; the only truth is the art to which the Narrator is now about to dedicate himself.

It would be a misrepresentation of the work to claim that this perspective on it is impermissible. And some of Proust's own statements about his novel (for whatever propagandising reasons he made them) backed up such emphases. In a much-cited letter of 1914, he says he is forced to depict mistakes without feeling obliged to say he holds them to *be* mistakes: so much the worse for him ('tant pis pour moi') if the reader thinks they are the truth.[1] The apogee of this generalising and redemptive view of the affections in Proust came with René Girard's brilliant *Deceit, Desire, and the Novel*.[2] Few tried to quarrel directly with this work, but gradually, after its publication in 1961, studies of love and sexuality in Proust began to take a rather different turn. (Leo Bersani's book of 1965, for example, gave a new steer.)[3]

The problem with Proust criticism of the first four or five decades – much of it excellent and pioneering – was not so much its 'explanations' of Proust's 'system' of love, sexuality and friendship as the large areas it overlooked or played down in its urge to stress the 'goal-directedness' of *A la recherche*. These omissions may briefly (and rather crudely) be summarised as follows. First: failing often to see the infiltration of sexual imagery into Proust's descriptions of physical objects, critics stressed the anguish of desire at the expense of its ecstasy. Second: with a few honourable exceptions, Proust criticism tended to present his reflections on love, sexuality and friendship as if they sprang from nowhere, without locating them in any long-standing French or indeed European literary currents. Third, and related: it did not consider that Proust might be presenting us, not with a picture of the human heart as it always was and will be, but with a historically and politically locatable form of love. Fourth: a majority of critics were embarrassed by Proust's extensive treatment of gay sexuality, and – if they did not frankly ignore this – swung between two extremes: either dismissing it as an excrescence which Proust, had he lived long enough, would eventually have had the sense to trim; or saying, in effect: 'Of course Proust's theory of love was tragic; he was a homosexual; what do you expect?' As for 'Proust's views of friendship', these were usually briefly summarised as an addendum to the rest, and often as self-evidently misanthropic. In this chapter I shall present both the 'traditional' approaches – many of which do provide a useful way into the novel for first-time readers – while at the same time describing and to some extent developing the newer emphases Proust criticism has been adopting since the 1970s.

When Proust's novel was first published, then, some of its most-discussed assertions were those on the subject of love. The Narrator maintains that love is almost always unreciprocal: one partner will infallibly be more attached than the other, and that other will be bored in direct proportion to the passion of the devoted one. The Narrator claims that when we fall in love, our feelings have virtually nothing to do with the obvious characteristics of the other; we even attribute to the loved one both qualities and faults which issue merely from our own imaginations. In other words, we fall in love less as a result of the beauty, kindness or intelligence of the beloved than as a result of our belief that this beloved represents a world into which we wish to penetrate but from which we feel excluded. (Hence Swann's and the Narrator's fear of Odette's and Albertine's possible lesbianism, lesbians forming a 'circle' which excludes still more effectively than would a heterosexual infidelity.) Or, more urgently, we may fall in love on suddenly realising that someone whom, until then, we had judged easily accessible seems to be withdrawing, or is unexpectedly unavailable. The fact that the loved one may appear to everybody except the smitten lover to be devoid of special virtues makes no difference. Thus, if we hear people say, 'I don't know what he or she sees in X', this kind of comment is merely naive. For love is essentially a matter of the imagination. As such, our experience of it provides the clearest illustration of Proust's claim that we are composed of a set of discordant, inconsistent selves. When in love, we can't conceive of not loving that particular person. But the rupture comes; eventually pain gives way to forgetfulness; finally, we can even see the former beloved again and feel nothing but indifference. This, says Proust, is because the self that was in love has died, and along with it the colouring it had been projecting on to the object of its passion. (A central argument of Girard's book is that minor writers tend not to dwell on this transfiguring, distorting capacity of imagination; nor do they show what Proust equally brings out – the way in which desires that we believe to be our own are copied from models we admire.)

These 'mechanisms' are not only to be seen in the most obvious forms of erotic desire. Proust displays the role the imagination plays in all his characters' reactions to others. Not only is it part of what makes inaccessible people attractive; it also accounts for the disappointment that may come in the wake of having finally 'secured' someone (the imagination cannot now work on him or her, for the moment at least). And if Proust is especially interested in the role of the imagination in love, he includes all sorts of love. For instance, he sees snobbery as a form of love, key characteristics being shared by the snob and the infatuated or unhappy lover. The snob attributes to the object of snobbery glamour, mystery and coldness. The snob is as excluded from the charmed circle as the lover is by the unresponsive partner, and accordingly yearns for it all the more. The prime cases of this are Legrandin and the Narrator himself; but one should not make the mistake of limiting snobbery to a wish to mix in upper-class company. Proust shows its presence everywhere: his characters can build up an aura of prestige around anybody – or anything; objects are not of course exempt. (Jean-François Revel entertainingly demonstrates the diverse applications of Proust's views on love and snobbery, suggesting that, for instance, grass-roots members of a political party may be subject to a form of snobbish glamorisation of the leaders of that party.)[4] This need to idolise, whether overtly erotic or not, is central in *A la recherche*. And Proust picks out its presence not merely in what we claim we find attractive, but also in what we claim fills us with horror. If, says Proust, we think of something as diabolical, we are attributing to it, too, mystery, supernatural power, a god-like being; we think of it as fascinatingly different from ourselves. This belief that the world of evil is a dreadful yet thrilling world apart is what, in *A la recherche*, makes for sadism and masochism. Sadism such as that enacted at Montjouvain by Mlle Vinteuil and her partner – masochism such as Charlus's in Jupien's brothel – represent, like snobbery and infatuation, a frenzied attempt to get into an unknown sphere (see I, 158–63; I, 192–8/226–33 and IV, 394; VI, 154/181). This is why Proust is able to say that Mlle Vinteuil might have found the idea of cruelty less exciting if she had been able to see that it exists all around us, not in the form of wilfully violent or melodramatic actions, but in indifference to the pain for which we ourselves are responsible: 'cette indifférence aux souffrances qu'on cause et qui, quelques autres noms qu'on lui donne, est la forme terrible et permanente de la cruauté' (I, 163) ['that indifference to the suffering one causes which, whatever other names one gives it, is the most terrible and lasting form of cruelty' (I, 198/232–3)]. Proust deflates sadistic eroticism as he deflates so many other fantasies.

Proust also famously connects adults' love for partners with children's love for parents: he compares the young Narrator's pain over his mother to Swann's over Odette, and openly generalises about the child's (apparently) unreciprocated yearning for his mother and his belief that, downstairs at dinner, she is partaking of devilishly threatening pleasures ('des plaisirs malfaisants et mortellement tristes' (I, 30) ['pleasures that were baleful and of a mortal sadness' (I, 33/39)]. It is perhaps difficult to be sure whether Proust is saying, 'This experience of love predetermined all the Narrator's future experiences of love' – in other words, making a causal connection, as do Freudians – or whether he is saying, more widely, '*All* love is anguished – the child's love for its parent, as well as the adult's for the loved one'. But since in other areas Proust clearly sees childhood impressions as formative, we should be careful before sanitising or censoring out the implicit causality of the chapter 'Combray'. Proust unobtrusively persuades the reader to judge the bedtime drama, and the previous incidents that made it paradigmatic, as crucial in the formation of the child's personality: he will always associate love with anxiety and will always think of the loved one as enjoying pernicious activities that shut him out.

Such, then, are the main 'ideas about love' extracted from the novel by critics. They also, of course, saw that Proust does not present an unrelievedly tragic picture. Amorous misunderstandings and misadventures can make us not only unhappy but ridiculous: Gilberte pushes snowballs down the neck of her besotted young admirer (I, 392; I, 480/567); in *Sodome et Gomorrhe*, Bloch's homosexual great-uncle Nissim Bernard is beaten up by a 'straight' tomato-faced twin when he thought he was approaching the gay one (III, 248–9; IV, 291–3/342–4). But such comedy seemed to back up rather than adulterate Proust's strong statements about the unreciprocity of all love, and critics often presented these statements as self-evidently controversial, even though most of them had already been mooted, implicitly or explicitly, by earlier authors. To take only French literature: in the seventeenth century, Mme de Lafayette's heroine the princesse de Clèves says to her passionate suitor: 'je crois même que les obstacles ont fait votre constance' ['I even think your constancy was created by the obstacles you met'].[5] At the centre of Racine's tragedies is the supposition that the image of the loved one is unstable and that frustration and jealousy are particularly apt to distort it. In the eighteenth century, Marivaux and Laclos both suggest that love need not be 'spontaneous' but can be worked upon and manipulated, elements of frustration again being important. Proust's more immediate predecessors had also shown the necessity for image-building and for the illusion of unattainability in the creation and continuation of love. Benjamin Constant anticipates Proust in *Adolphe*. So does Stendhal, with his theory of 'crystallization' in *De l'amour*; with the see-sawing of Mathilde's and Julien's love in *Le Rouge et le noir*; and with the comical disappointment of his heroes once the longed-for goal is attained: 'n'est-ce que ça?' ['is that all?']. Flaubert brings out the importance of prior models, especially fictional ones, in the formation of erotic images, and suggests that almost all perception of the loved one arrives through the lenses provided by our culture and its clichés.

Proust's analysis of the child's feeling for its parent is also not an *ex nihilo* creation, uncanny though it is that he should appear to be constructing it in tandem with his contemporary Freud, whom he could not have read. Earlier authors had stressed the lasting influence of family attachments and some had indicated their possible eroticism, whether between siblings or across generations: two examples from many in the previous century are George Sand in *François le champi* (1850) and Stendhal again, in the autobiographical *Vie de Henry Brulard*.[6] More generally, Proust is writing in the wake of a century-and-a-half of writers who emphasise the importance of all childhood impressions, from Rousseau in the eighteenth century to Balzac, Dickens and George Eliot in the nineteenth.

Another current of post-1800 French writing central in Proust's presentation of love is the portrayal of the sensitive, 'unvirile' hero. While many literary historians have discussed the early nineteenth-century 'mal du siècle' – melancholia and passivity – recent feminist critics have been setting this in a longer-term perspective relevant to Proust.[7] Proust's Narrator – delicate, often ill; at Combray, never scuffling with other boys or breaking branches as a sturdier child might – has literary great-grandfathers. One of these, early in the nineteenth century, is Chateaubriand's unpugnacious, wavering René; rather later, there is Stendhal's Julien Sorel, who is slight, might be taken for a girl, is always beaten in public games. Other nineteenth-century heroes, such as Flaubert's unenergetic Frédéric Moreau, could be cited. The physical susceptibility and introspectiveness of Proust's Narrator are part of what makes him an artist; but they also influence – as he himself says – his choice of female 'type': robust, unintellectual, precisely of a kind unlikely to appreciate his qualities at first encounter. Thus the form the Narrator's eroticism takes develops a nineteenth-century trend to revalue illness or strip heroes of traditionally heroic attributes. It is part of what we now think of as modernism, and in his sickliness Proust's Narrator is a hero for our times.

Historically speaking, too, Proust's picture of the 'little band' of girls is datable. The 'new woman' of the 1890s, with her interest in such sports as cycling, tennis and golf (virtually impermissible until then) was a much commented-on and, for some, scandalous phenomenon. Hence the Narrator's interest in the girls would have had a rather different character if not located in the *fin-de-siècle*.[8] And, while critics had already seen that Proust's characters may desire not only those of apparently superior status to themselves, but equally those of 'inferior' class – whom they excitedly suppose to be vulgar or cruel – it is again only recently that they have been trying to relate this very directly to the historical moment at which Proust was writing.[9] This process is bound to continue as a growing number of readers absorb the knowledge provided by the formidable scholarly apparatus of the second Pléiade edition of *A la recherche* (1987–9), whose notes elucidate Proust's topical and historical references.

Nor have commentators always appreciated that, alongside the overtly elegiac laments over eroticism, Proust is both celebrating and gently ironising it through his highly metaphorical descriptions of sense-impressions and

landscape. He is simultaneously paying homage to and deflating the tradition, as old as Western literature, in which landscape is compared to the
woman's body and vice versa. Proust's inventive and exquisite religious and
sexual images – often impossible to disentangle from each other – convey the
Narrator's marvelling in front of the physical and his desire to grasp and
possess it. Thus the novel is full of pleasures both sensuous and sensual.
There will always be an element – even if only in the sheer extravagance of
the sentence-structure – that reminds us that the imagery is a projection of
the mind, but this does not annul the eroticism. Proust is saying in the
manner of a (non-goal-directed) 'moraliste': this is what the wonderful and
foolish mind does with the sexuality of the body.

   Why did so many critics, for so long, stress the 'one-sidedness' of Proust's
depictions of love and did not even consider it worthwhile to try to locate
these in other European traditions? Undoubtedly, it was because for decades
many of them interpreted the novel as a thinly disguised autobiography; and
they then, consciously or unconsciously, transferred their homophobia from
the author to his work. Because Proust was 'different', his view of love had
to be aberrant. All the more must his view of sexuality be 'different' too. This
assumption, whether voiced or implied, was given a boost by George
Painter's popular biography, first published between 1959 and 1965.[10]
Painter, although apparently liberal and even sympathetic in his presentation
of Proust's homosexuality, nevertheless offers highly simplifying and conventional 'explanations' for it; and he is even more simplistic in the argument,
which governs his whole book, that A la recherche, dependent in almost
every respect on Proust's own life, is indeed to be read as autobiographical.

   The best Proust critics did not endorse this latter claim, nor the facile
glosses on homosexuality. Nevertheless, it was not until 1980, when Julius
Rivers published his ground-breaking work on homosexuality in Proust,
that this disguised homophobia in Painter and others began to seem entirely
unacceptable.[11] Rivers pointed out that despite the quantities of writing on
Proust to date, there had so far been no substantial inquiry into his treatment of sexuality. While bringing out Proust's ambivalence towards his own
and others' homosexuality (pardonable, given the harshly punitive attitudes
then operating in most Western countries), Rivers stresses that Proust was
the first major novelist to deal at length with both homosexuality and homophobia, and that he was responsible for introducing the themes into the
mainstream of modern literature. He furthermore argues that the high inci-
dence of homosexuality or bisexuality among Proust's characters is not to be
viewed with discomfort but can on the contrary be seen as 'realistic' in the
light of Alfred Kinsey's researches.[12] Rivers sometimes himself overinterprets

biographical material, and is paradoxically severe in his condemnations of Proust's partial complicity with the prevailing homophobia. But his work, coinciding as it did with the growing movement for gay rights in the West, has helped readers to revaluate large parts of *A la recherche*.

Rivers also tantalisingly floats the possibility of a 'feminist' Proust: a Proust who – not solely to provide further worries for the Narrator – envisages that women may be active in searching out partners, may not be exclusively phallocentric, and may find erotic pleasures outside penetrative sex (Rivers, *Proust and the Art of Love*, p.244). Indeed, the Narrator's fantasies suggest that he is perhaps as envious of Albertine as he is jealous over her. This quasi-feminist aspect of the novel is one that deserves further attention, as do its roots in the nineteenth-century interest in transferrable gender characteristics. And Proust is more radical than Baudelaire and more proto-feminist than Rimbaud in his rewriting of the nineteenth-century aesthetics of disgust, in that, more clearly than they, he brings its sources up to full consciousness – those sources being, he suggests, erotic intolerance and fear of the female genitals. From his very earliest writing (the short story about lesbianism 'Avant la nuit') to *Sodome et Gomorrhe* itself (III, 28; IV, 31/36), Proust argues for the beauty of objects reminiscent of a 'repulsive' femininity like jellyfish or oysters.[13] The argument then develops as follows: if we can find these lovely, surely we can grant the gay man, too, his right to find his objects of desire lovely.

There has also been a new interest recently in those short passages directly highlighting bisexuality. In a sense bisexuality is everywhere in *A la recherche*, not only in Albertine's possible infidelities but in characters' changes from apparent heterosexuality to homosexuality; its ubiquity can even give it the character of the carnival, or of pantomime transvestism/travesty. But Proust, during both composition and revision of the novel, occasionally marks it off with an unusually sharp focus. Thus, in one of those additions to additions – a still later insertion on one of the 'layers' already glued into the manuscript of *La Prisonnière* – Proust stresses the specially confusing quality of bisexuality. It is a torment not only to straights but to 'old-fashioned' gays like Charlus: Proust gives it the status of an emotional, intellectual and verbal challenge all at once.

> Le baron était surtout troublé par ces mots 'en être'. Apres l'avoir d'abord ignoré, il avait enfin, depuis un temps bien long déjà, appris que lui-même 'en était'. Or voici que cette notion qu'il avait acquise se trouvait remise en question . . . Ainsi les êtres qui 'en étaient' n'étaient pas seulement ceux qu'il avait crus, mais toute une immense partie de la planète, composée aussi bien de femmes que d'hommes, d'hommes aimant non seulement les hommes mais les

femmes, et le baron . . . se sentait torturé par une inquiétude de l'intelligence autant que du cœur, devant ce double mystère où il y avait à la fois de l'agrandissement de la jalousie et de l'insuffisance soudaine d'une définition.

(III, 720–1)[14]

[What most disturbed the Baron was the phrase 'one of us'. Ignorant at first of its application, he had eventually, now many moons ago, learned that he himself was 'one of them'. And now this notion that he had acquired was thrown back into question . . . So, to be 'one of them' meant not simply what he had hitherto assumed, but to belong to a whole vast section of the inhabitants of the planet, consisting of women as well as men, of men loving not merely men but women also, and the Baron . . . felt himself tormented by an anxiety of the mind as well as of the heart, born of this twofold mystery which combined an enlargement of the field of his jealousy with the sudden inadequacy of a definition.]   (v, 238/280–1)

And some ninety pages later the Narrator, through Charlus, suggests that bisexuality – or apparent bisexuality – is a new phenomenon, likening it to the advent of Cubism:

Je suis bien vieux jeu, mais je ne comprends pas, dit-il du ton d'un vieux gallican parlant de certaines formes d'ultramontanisme, d'un royaliste libéral parlant de l'Action française, ou d'un disciple de Claude Monet des cubistes.

(III, 811)

['I may be very old-fashioned, but I fail to understand,' he said in the tone of an old Gallican speaking of certain forms of Ultramontanism, of a liberal royalist speaking of the Action Française or of a disciple of Claude Monet speaking of the Cubists.]   (v, 349/411)

Charlus is less panic-stricken here, but his fear is still obvious in the link between bisexuality and religious or political authoritarianism, a link which implies an invasively bullying mode rather than an open or exploratory one. However, we may surmise that the Narrator is stepping in with the third comparison. We do not of course have to agree with Charlus that bisexuality *is* new: in whatever incarnations – teasing, delightful or burlesque – it is to be found in Shakespeare and numerous other writers. Rather, Proust is here linking bisexuality not only with his own aesthetic but with the emergence of modernism in the arts. At the time he was planning and writing his novel, Cubism was developing in Paris. More radically than most previous Western art, Cubism dislodges spectators from a single-perspective stance, and at the same time forces them to consider together the different 'sides' or angles of the painting and try, however vainly, to synthesise their incongruities. Proust has often been compared to the Impressionists, with his interest in blurred dividing-lines and in the interchangeability of solid and liquid, and

Elstir resembles an Impressionist more than other kinds of painter. But Proust also gives us the literary equivalent of Cubism, seemingly cutting up the Narrator's experience into disparate and even contradictory portions. Here, in the Charlus comparison, a modernist aesthetics is inseparable from a 'modern' acceptance of paradoxical or polymorphous sexuality; and increasingly Proust's critics are linking these two aspects of the novel.

Perhaps, however, one area which remains to be explored is that of friendship. Proust uses the words 'ami/e/s' and 'amitié/s' frequently.[15] Sometimes he does so perfectly conventionally. But often his usage is provocative and, in its self-conscious desire to define and redefine friendship, takes its place in an affiliation that goes back to Plato. One important forebear is the seventeenth-century maxim-writer La Rochefoucauld, who returns again and again to 'friendship', presenting it as valued yet slippery:

> Nous ne pouvons rien aimer que par rapport à nous, et nous ne faisons que suivre notre goût et notre plaisir quand nous préférons nos amis à nous-mêmes. C'est néanmoins par cette préférence seule que l'amitié peut être vraie et parfaite. [We can love nothing except in relation to ourselves, and we are merely pursuing our taste and pleasure when we prefer our friends to ourselves. It is nevertheless only through this preference that friendship can be true and perfect.]
>
> La plupart des amis dégoûtent de l'amitié, et la plupart des dévots dégoûtent de la dévotion. [Most friends induce a distaste for friendship, and most devout people induce a distaste for devoutness.]

Still more devastating:

> Dans l'adversité de nos meilleurs amis nous trouvons toujours quelque chose qui ne nous déplaît pas. [In the adversity of our best friends we can always find something which does not displease us.][16]

And La Rochefoucauld may in two successive maxims suggest first that friendship is different from love, then that the two are assimilable:

> Ce qui fait que la plupart des femmes sont peu touchées de l'amitié, c'est qu'elle est fade quand on a senti de l'amour. [Friendship has little impact on most women because it is insipid when one has felt love.]
>
> Dans l'amitié, comme dans l'amour, on est souvent plus heureux par les choses qu'on ignore que par celles que l'on sait. [In friendship, as in love, one is often happier because of what one does not know than because of what one does.] (nos. 440, 441)

In nineteenth-century literature this subject had at times taken on a still more ambiguous character. Balzac, for example, can make it difficult to separate out the strands of feeling in friendship: in *La Fille aux yeux d'or*, Paul de

Manerville is infatuated with his dashing friend Henri de Marsay; in *Illusions perdues*, the friendship between Lucien de Rubempré and David Séchard verges on homosexual love (Lucien is physically girl-like too); in *La Cousine Bette*, Bette's feelings for Valérie are made up of maternity, friendship and love ('elle en avait fait sa fille, son amie, son amour') – Balzac does not seek to give these any hierarchy: all three are present.[17]

Proust develops these and other implications. To look at only his best-known tenet: the opposition he sets up between 'socialising' on the one hand and, on the other, individual fulfilment and the artist's creativity comes straight from Romanticism; indeed, many of the remarks on friendship that critics have read as misanthropic can, on closer inspection, be seen to refer not to friendship in general but to the uniquely difficult choices the *artist* has to make. 'Les êtres qui en ont la possibilité – il est vrai que ce sont les artistes et j'étais convaincu depuis longtemps que je ne le serais jamais – ont aussi le devoir de vivre pour eux-mêmes; or l'amitié leur est une dispense de ce devoir, une abdication de soi' (II, 260) ['People who have the capacity to do so – it is true that such people are artists, and I had long been convinced that I should never be that – also have a duty to live for themselves. And friendship is a dispensation from this duty, an abdication of self' (II, 562/664)]. Or, still more specifically, the statements are views particular to the Narrator: 'je n'éprouvais à me trouver, à causer avec lui [Saint-Loup] – et sans doute c'eût été de même avec tout autre – rien de ce bonheur qu'il m'était au contraire possible de ressentir quand j'étais sans compagnon' (II, 95) ['I felt when I was with him, when I was talking to him – and no doubt it would have been the same with anyone else – none of that happiness which it was possible for me to experience when I was by myself' (II, 364/430)]. Even then, this dismissiveness may be overturned, as when the Narrator, sobbing in desolation after Mme de Stermaria cancels their rendez-vous, finds himself rescued by Saint-Loup and almost in spite of himself – admitting that he is contradicting his own earlier judgements – praises the simple comfort and human warmth of friendship (II, 688–9; III, 455–6/540–1). Proust is not, then, the first great French writer to probe and reinterpret friendship, nor is he as bleak on the issue as has sometimes been assumed.

Can we, again, see any political or historical dimension to his depiction of friendship? The answer is a tentative 'yes'. Far from being a nobly disembodied affinity between kindred spirits, friendship is often a class or caste affair, as we see not only in the case of those whom aristocrats decide to admit to their intimacy but also with Françoise's narrowly-defined criteria for friendship (II, 52; II, 313/369). And if friendship can be betrayed regardless of rank (the middle-class Bloch plagiarises the Narrator's work: IV, 611; VI, 433/510), Proust's demonstration of such treachery is specially cruel where it is a matter of aristocrats' attachments. Mme de Guermantes might some-times have had the illusion that she felt friendship for Swann, in the intoxi-cation ['ivresse'] of their conversation together. Once he is dead, he cannot give her that illusion – and the Narrator is stark: no need to be fancy! – 'il ne le pouvait plus' (IV, 161) ['he could do so no longer'(V, 665/784)].

The Narrator also pinpoints the role of Saint-Loup's republicanism in his friendships. Larded with retrospective irony though this analysis may finally seem, it is still evidently to be taken seriously at the moment of its appear-ance. Saint-Loup's republicanism is not (at least, in the first instance) the phoney 'egalitarianism' of other Proustian nobles: that is, it is not an erotic fetishisation of a supposedly crude or promiscuous lower class, nor a wish to acquire the bourgeois artist who may be able to confer prestige on a salon. It arises, rather, from a genuine intellectual conviction: Saint-Loup is the only socialist in the novel, and his fondness for the Narrator is not only that of the perfect gentlemanly companion but also in part stems from a more political 'comradeship'. Proust suggests that Saint-Loup's behaviour – even down to his physical movements – would have been impossible before the Enlightenment and the French Revolution. It is because Saint-Loup has absorbed the tenets of these that he is able to perform some admirably unselfconscious acrobatics in that memorable scene in which he leaps across restaurant seats and lighting-wires in order to drape a warm coat over the Narrator's shoulders (II, 705; III, 475/563). Commenting on this feat, the Narrator says: Saint-Loup would have been wrong to think that his own contempt of rank was worthless in my eyes. I did not, as he could believe, value him only as an aesthetically pleasing representative of 'aristocratic' grace and nimbleness.

> S'il n'avait pas, comme il avait fait, aimé quelque chose de plus élevé que la souplesse innée de son corps, s'il n'avait pas été si longtemps détaché de l'orgueil nobiliaire, il y eût eu plus d'application et de lourdeur dans son agilité même, une vulgarité importante dans ses manières . . . Pour que le corps de Saint-Loup fût habité par tant d'aristocratie, il fallait que celle-ci eût déserté sa pensée, tenue vers de plus hauts objets, et, résorbé dans son corps, s'y fût fixée en lignes inconscientes et nobles. (II, 708)

> [If he had not (as he steadfastly had) cherished something more lofty than the innate suppleness of his body, if he had not been detached for so long from aristocratic arrogance, there would have been something more studied, more heavy-handed in this very agility, a self-important vulgarity in his manners. . . . In order that Saint-Loup's body should be imbued with so much nobility, the latter had first to desert his mind, which was straining towards higher things, and, reabsorbed into his body, to establish itself there in unconsciously aristo-cratic lines.] (III, 478–9/567–8)

Thus friendship has its politically and historically shaped aspects. However, perhaps the most significant novelty in Proust's treatment of 'amitié' is his large-scale extension of earlier writers' dignified or mischievous twisting of the malleable borders between love and friendship. In this he is helped by the French language: 'aimer' means both 'like' and 'love' and the second meaning of 'ami/e' is 'one who has a sexual relationship with another'. But Proust also constantly stretches the meaning of the word 'amitié' so that it too becomes ambiguous and reinterpretable. ('Amitié' can, rarely, have the same amorous application in French as 'ami', but when it does it is far slyer and more self-consciously euphemistic, as when the Narrator observes that Odette's elegance emanates from 'l'amitié' of a Grand-Duke: I, 77; I, 91/107.)

Proust's intensifying of the word 'amitié' starts as early as the bedtime drama: here the anguish of exclusion from the beloved's pleasures is said to be a floating anguish that may attach itself as easily to filial tenderness or to 'l'amitié pour un camarade' (I, 30) ['affection for a friend' (I, 34/40)]. Particularly, the Narrator recharges the word with eroticism in the relationship with Gilberte, where 'amitié' carries a standard meaning for her but means 'love' for him – not only when he speaks of his feeling to Gilberte herself with deliberate caution, but when he is thinking of it: 'je prenais plus de confiance en la vitalité et en l'avenir de notre amitié' (I, 391) ['I acquired more confidence in the vitality, in the future of [our] friendship' (I, 480/567)]. Saint-Loup is soon to enter the Narrator's life: when he does, he speaks of 'amitié' almost as strongly as the narrator had to Gilberte: 'il disait "notre amitié" comme s'il eût parlé de quelque chose d'important et de délicieux qui eût existé en dehors de nous-mêmes' (II, 95) ['he would say "our friendship" as though he were speaking of some important and delightful thing which had an existence independent of ourselves' (II, 364/430)]; and Saint-Loup writes to the Narrator that 'une des ères les plus importantes de ma vie, celle d'où notre amitié date, a commencé' (II, 223) ['one of the most important periods in my life, that from which our friendship dates, has begun' (II, 518/611)]. Charlus too will tell the young Narrator that he hopes their 'amitié' will one day be a truly great one (II, 588; III, 335/396).

All this by-play lays the ground for further complexities in the Albertine relationship. At the most innocuous level, Albertine's early profession of faith in the 'amitié' between herself and the Narrator will, he says, have serious ('grandes et fâcheuses') consequences. For it gives birth to an almost family feeling, a moral kernel, which will always subsist in his love for her; and in order really to suffer over a woman, you must have believed in her completely (II, 294; II, 604/713). This commentary on the metamorphoses of the amorous into the 'merely' friendly, and back again, runs throughout the Narrator's dealings with Albertine. But there is a more dangerous mobility in the case of Albertine's other relationships: she has been 'friends' with Mlle Vinteuil and *her* 'friend', and we never know whether her other liaisons are companionable, sexual or both.

It is true that at certain moments the Narrator seems to warn us against confusing sexuality and 'amitié'. Charlus 'confondait sa manie avec l'amitié, qui ne lui ressemble en rien' (III, 710) ['confused his ruling passion with friendship, which does not resemble it in the least' (V, 229/270)]; the carnal relations between Mlle Vinteuil and her friend eventually give way to 'une amitié haute et pure' (III, 766) ['a pure and lofty friendship' (V, 295/348)]. But far more often the young Narrator is imagining, and the older one is creating, a world in which there is slippage between asexual and erotic 'friendship'; usually, Proust is not here the 'moralisateur' – he who preaches – but, again, the 'moraliste', he who says: this is how things are. And as elsewhere in the novel, the moral exploration is interwoven with the aesthetic one:

> Changement de perspective pour regarder les êtres, déjà plus frappant dans l'amitié que dans les simples relations sociales . . .　　　　　(III, 258)

> [Such a change of perspective in looking at other people, more striking already in friendship than in merely social relations . . .]　　　　(IV, 303–4/357)

> . . . notre vie, dans sa longueur, n'est pas calculée sur la vie de nos amitiés. Qu'une certaine période de temps s'écoule et l'on voit reparaître . . . des relations d'amitié renouées entre les mêmes personnes qu'autrefois . . .　(IV, 255)

> [. . . our life, in the long run, is not calculated according to the duration of our friendships. Let a certain period of time elapse, and you will see . . . friendships renewed between the same persons as before . . .]　　　　(V, 780/920)

Both the temporal ebb and flow of 'friendship', and its inherent ability to become something else, are yet another demonstration of instability. This demonstration is not without the power to shock, nor is it apolitical. In a society which still paraded hatred of gays, Proust is saying to the reader: look at both your own eroticism and the friendships which you believe are 'free' from it.

NOTES

1　To Jacques Rivière; in *Corr.* XIII, 99–100.
2　*Mensonge romantique et vérité romanesque* (Paris: Grasset, 1961); *Deceit, Desire, and the Novel: Self and Other in Literary Structure*, trans. Y. Freccero (Baltimore: Johns Hopkins University Press, 1976).
3　L. Bersani, *Marcel Proust: The Fictions of Life and of Art* (New York: Oxford University Press, 1965).

4 In *Sur Proust: remarques sur 'A la recherche du temps perdu'* (Paris: Denoël/Gonthier, 1960/70); see Chapter 2, 'Proust contre les snobs'.

5 *La Princesse de Clèves* (Paris: Dent, n.d.), p.221.

6 Published posthumously in 1890 and (in a more complete version) 1913.

7 See especially M. Waller, *The Male Malady: Fictions of Impotence in the French Romantic Novel* (New Brunswick: Rutgers University Press, 1993); also, e.g., D. Kelly, *Fictional Genders: Role and Representation in Nineteenth-Century French Narrative* (Lincoln: University of Nebraska Press, 1989).

8 See, e.g., D. Silverman, 'The "New Woman", feminism, and the decorative arts in fin-de-siècle France', in L. Hunt (ed.), *Eroticism and the Body Politic* (Baltimore: Johns Hopkins University Press, 1991), pp.144–63; J. Beizer, *Ventriloquized Bodies: Narratives of Hysteria in Nineteenth-Century France* (Ithaca: Cornell University Press, 1994), p.256; J.-P. Peter, 'Les médecins et les femmes', in J.-P. Aron (ed.), *Misérable et glorieuse: la femme du XIXe siècle* (n.p.: Fayard, 1980), pp.81–100.

9 See, e.g., J. Canavaggia, *Proust et la politique* (Paris: Nizet, 1986); M. Sprinker, *History and Ideology in Proust: 'A la recherche du temps perdu' and the Third French Republic* (Cambridge University Press, 1994).

10 *Marcel Proust: A Biography* (London: Chatto and Windus, 2 vols.,1959, 1965); frequently reissued.

11 J.E. Rivers, *Proust and the Art of Love: The Aesthetics of Sexuality in the Life, Times and Art of Marcel Proust* (New York: Columbia University Press, 1980). See also G. Stambolian and E. Marks (eds.), *Homosexualities and French Literature* (Ithaca: Cornell University Press, 1979), to which Rivers had contributed a chapter.

12 Kinsey's 1940s and 1950s studies of sexuality found, for example, that at least 50 per cent of American men claim post-pubertal experience of homosexual feeling and/or behaviour. Rivers gives clear summaries of Kinsey's research.

13 Rivers gives a translation of 'Avant la nuit' (pp. 267–71), first published in 1893 but not included by Proust in *Les Plaisirs et les jours*. It is republished in P. Clarac and Y. Sandre (eds.), Marcel Proust, *Jean Santeuil, précédé de Les Plaisirs et les jours* (Paris: Gallimard, 1971). See here M. Riffaterre's essay on the jellyfish ('*méd*use') and the '*med*' tag in *A la recherche*: 'Compelling reader responses', in A. Bennet (ed.), *Reading Reading* (University of Tampere, 1993), pp.85–106.

14 See A. Winton [Finch], *Proust's Additions: The Making of 'A la recherche du temps perdu'* (Cambridge University Press, 1977), 2 vols., I, 294; II, 155.

15 More than 1700 times in *A la recherche*, according to E. Brunet: *Le Vocabulaire de Proust* (Geneva: Slatkine-Champion, 1983), 3 vols.

16 *Réflexions ou sentences et maximes morales, suivi de Réflexions diverses* (Paris: Librairie Générale Française, 1965), nos. 81, 427, 583. (My translation, here and following.)

17 *La Cousine Bette* (Paris: Librairie Générale Française, 1963), p.170.

12

RICHARD BALES

Proust and the fine arts

Few authors foreground the arts quite so comprehensively as Proust; certainly, none made them so central to their own literary production. Proust's whole life was saturated with love of the arts, and so too was to be his great novel: probably no other work of literature celebrates the arts as totally as his, or is so convincing in this pursuit. If one could point to, say, Joyce or Thomas Mann as examples of writers who display a keen awareness of the literary possibilities of incorporating the arts into the fabric of their own work, even their efforts seem small when compared to Proust's.

We are fortunate in possessing a clear picture of Proust's artistic tastes in his youth, and as he grew up. Two general questionnaires which he filled in have survived (*CSB*, pp.335–7), and the entries for the arts make fascinating reading: if, at the age of about fourteen, there is a predictable juvenility about some of his choices (George Sand, the historian Augustin Thierry, Musset, Meissonnier, Mozart, Gounod), there are already signs of the maturity which was to be expressed, fully-fledged, in the questionnaire completed at the age of 21. Here, the list acquires more substance: Anatole France, Pierre Loti, Baudelaire, Vigny, Beethoven, Wagner, Schumann, Leonardo da Vinci, Rembrandt. And, as if to underscore the import of his choices, at the top of the questionnaire Proust has written 'Marcel Proust par lui-même' ['Marcel Proust on himself']. To find confirmation of this development, and of his artistic preoccupations in general, one need only glance at the correspondence of these early years: there is scarcely a letter without some reference to the arts, and many of them attest to the fact that he was a voracious reader both of French and of European literature generally (and some American), always up to date with the latest writing. Add to this the fact that Proust had had the meticulous training in the Classics which was *de rigueur* in the educational programme of the time, and the overall picture of his cultural awareness is impressive indeed.

Being relatively sedentary, Proust had no problem in broadening his literary horizons; what is often easily forgotten, however, is that he made considerable efforts to acquire first-hand knowledge of the other arts, in the shape of visits to exhibitions, to the theatre and to concerts. His adult life is for our purposes rather nicely framed by visits to art galleries which were to result in significant literary responses: a trip to the Louvre in 1895 was to lead to an article on Chardin and Rembrandt, while journeys to the low countries in 1898 and 1902 were to develop his love of Flemish and Dutch painting, and where he was to see Vermeer's *View of Delft*, which he considered the most beautiful painting in the world (*Corr.* xx, 226). It was a painting he was to see again in Paris in May 1921, on the occasion (although he could not have known it at the time) of his very last visit to an art-gallery; and of course he was to feature the *View of Delft* in a famous passage of his novel.

As far as music is concerned, we have seen how considerably Proust's tastes developed in his youth. He seems to have needed little guidance on this score, and if his long-standing friendship with the composer Reynaldo Hahn probably provided easy access to musical circles, it surely had no appreciable effect on already well-established preferences. Proust was resolutely a modernist, and above all a convinced Wagnerian, with all the cultural baggage that that brings with it. References to Wagner abound in the correspondence and in *A la recherche du temps perdu*: he was clearly a key aesthetic figure for Proust, combining as he does breadth of vision, telling specificity of detail and sublimity of expression. At one stage, Proust had even intended to incorporate a performance of *Parsifal* into the clinching final episode of his novel (see IV, 799, 812, 946; not in the English translations): the decision to abandon this idea is a good example of Proust's tendency to reject, wherever possible, external 'support' for the internal logic of his own fiction.

Other musical enthusiasms could be listed, including Debussy's *Pelléas et Mélisande*, which Proust heard on the curious invention called the 'théâtrophone' and whose atmosphere of mystery he found particularly haunting (the correspondence of 1910–11 is especially eloquent here). Then there were the Ballets russes, the great cultural hit of the years preceding the First World War, with their dazzling sets and costumes, colourful modern scores and exotically oriental flavour. Was Proust present at the notorious première of Stravinsky's *Rite of Spring*? We do not know for sure; but he was certainly a regular and enthusiastic attender at these ballets. He even put on concerts of his own, extravagantly paying for a string quartet to come to his apartment at night and play modern French chamber music and the late Beethoven quartets – he was way ahead of the times in his appreciation of these profound works.[1]

All of this musical and artistic activity (and there was much, much more) builds up a picture of a Proust whose tastes were distinctly highbrow; they were, but this does not mean he was an artistic snob. On the contrary, he saw great value in the humbler aspects of the arts. As a young man, he appreciated the music-hall artist Mayol; and within the pages of *A la recherche* he was to find unexpected musical beauties in street-criers' calls.[2] In a characteristically witty early essay in *Les Plaisirs et les jours* entitled 'Éloge de la mauvaise musique' (see *JS*, pp.121–2) ['In praise of bad music'],[3] the opening sentence stands as a sort of manifesto: 'Détestez la mauvaise musique, ne la méprisez pas' ['Detest bad music but do not despise it' (p. 138)]. Such music plays an enormous role in people's lives, a role which is somehow heightened by the music's lack of pretensions. There is an admirable simplicity to it: 'Un cahier de mauvaises romances, usé pour avoir trop servi, doit nous toucher comme un cimetière ou comme un village' (*JS*, p.122) ['A collection of bad Romances worn with constant use should touch us as a cemetery touches us, or a village' (p. 139)]. And remember these words were penned during Proust's supposedly snobbish, young dandy period.

In this same collection of *Les Plaisirs et les jours*, in 'Mondanité et mélomanie de Bouvard et Pécuchet' (*JS*, pp.57–65) ['The Social Ambitions and Musical Tastes of Bouvard and Pécuchet' (pp. 100–112)], Flaubert's fictional buffoons with claims to seriousness take on new life and establish what they see as impeccable criteria of taste. Needless to say, what they really provide is an object-lesson in amateurishness, inflated pretensions and general artistic philistinism. There will be plenty more of this in *A la recherche*! What it is important to note from a reading of this essay is Proust's innate attitude of scepticism towards the notion of hierarchy: so when Bouvard rejects Wagner's early *Lohengrin* and *Tannhäuser* as not being 'advanced' enough, but perversely promotes the even earlier *Rienzi*, he is giving in to a modishness, the mere expression of which proclaims its ridiculous and impermanent nature. In writing as he does, Proust can clearly make fun of such attitudes; but as far as he himself was concerned what mattered was not fashion, but sheer excellence. In many ways, his whole life can be seen as a quest for this ideal.

Certainly, a very great deal of Proust's writing activity in the years leading up to 1900 is devoted to consideration of artistic topics of one sort or another. Generally brief articles or reviews, these texts deal with contemporary poets, dramatists and novelists (often friends), with art exhibitions, with musical events, or with questions of a general aesthetic nature (see *CSB*, pp.338–423). The two sets of poems included in *Les Plaisirs et les jours*, entitled 'Portraits de peintres' and 'Portraits de musiciens' (not in the translation) are well worth dwelling on. Clearly deriving from the model of Baudelaire's 'Les Phares' ['The Beacons'], they are examples of art about art, evoking not specific pictures or pieces of music, but providing a general meditation on the chosen painter's or composer's special world, in an attempt to recreate what it feels like to be in close contact with those worlds. Although Proust was surprisingly ungifted as a poet, these verses, for all their gaucheness, are truly redolent of their subject-matter, and point forward to later articulation of artistic material with a view to promoting its transcendent features.

This preoccupation is highlighted even more in an article Proust wrote in 1895, but which was not published until long after his death: in 'Chardin et Rembrandt' (*CSB*, pp.372–82),[4] he tackles the manner in which great artists open the eyes of their beholders to deeper implications than just contemplation of subject-matter. The pleasure one experiences in a still-life by Chardin is thus 'dégagé de l'instant, approfondi, éternisé' (p.374) ['released from the moment, made timeless and profound' (p.123)], language and sentiments which anticipate Proust's later years. Beauty resides not in objects themselves; if it did, it would not be 'si profonde et si mystérieuse' (p.380) ['as profound nor as mysterious' (pp.129–30)]. As for creative acts, they do not proceed from obedience to rules, but from 'une puissance incompréhensible et obscure, et qu'on ne fortifie pas en l'éclairant' (p.382/131) ['an obscure and incomprehensible power, which we do not make stronger by elucidating it' (p.131)]. An altogether remarkable foretaste of the mature writer.

But in these early years Proust was essentially a miniaturist, and such acute insights as we get, perhaps especially in this area of the arts, are tantalising in their brevity. Even *Jean Santeuil*, a would-be novel of potential breadth, suffers from fragmentariness, and is notably short on artistic scrutiny. But with the fillip provided by the discovery of Ruskin's ideas, Proust finds a new expansiveness, a quality particularly useful in laying forth and analysing questions of an aesthetic nature. Certainly the introductions and annotations to his translations of *Sesame and Lilies* and *The Bible of Amiens* speak with an authority which combines a wide range of artistic reference with an assured overall coherence in aesthetic matters. This was clearly the way Proust was going to develop as a writer.

The Ruskin prefaces were essentially *essays*, a *genre* which enjoyed a high profile in the 1900s (Maeterlinck, for example, was an outstanding proponent, much read), and Proust's *Pastiches* of this period fall into the same category. This is important, because the next substantial text he was to write was nothing less than the so-called *Contre Sainte-Beuve*, in other words the harbinger of *A la recherche*. The whole programme of the *Contre Sainte-Beuve* is an aesthetic one: attacking Sainte-Beuve's concentration on the personality of the writer, and replacing it with analysis which respects the autonomy of the work of art. We are not yet in the realms of fiction, so what we have are studies of real, exemplary, writers: full-blooded, penetrating analyses of Nerval, Baudelaire and Balzac which foreground the 'interior vision' of the writer, the 'profound laws' which inform his work, his 'spiritual world', and the way in which they 'donnent pour nous une sorte de valeur littéraire à mille choses de la vie qui jusque-là nous paraissaient trop contingentes' ['give a sort of literary value to countless things in life which had hitherto seemed to us too contingent'] (*CSB*, pp.234/25, 237/28, 252/44, 276/68). Proust never ceases to build on his criticism of Sainte-Beuve's blinkered view of literature, and to privilege expression not just of literature's visionary aspect, but also of how that vision is communicated to the reader, and – most importantly – shared by him or her.

Once one moves into the pages of *A la recherche*, the range of artistic reference becomes vast: aside from the cultivated voice of the Narrator himself – and he is never short on artistic comparisons and allusions – any number of characters express themselves on artistic matters, often not very happily. But the Narrator's immediate family provides a sound enthusiast in the shape of his grandmother (so close to him as a person in all ways): when it comes to choosing a present for the boy, and she selects books by Musset, Rousseau, and George Sand's sexually daring *Indiana*, other members of the family, outraged, force her to substitute something less emotionally advanced. Her reason for falling back on Sand's rustic novels rests on a question of quality: 'Ma fille, disait-elle à maman, je ne pourrais me décider à donner à cet enfant quelque chose de mal écrit' (I, 39) ['"My dear," she had said to Mamma, "I could not bring myself to give the child anything that was not well written"' (I, 45/53)]. So too when she buys him pictures of famous monuments or sites to hang on his wall, she exercises her impeccable taste by ensuring that these pictures are reproductions of paintings depicting those places by, say, Corot, Hubert Robert, or Turner: this enables her to introduce 'plusieurs "épaisseurs" d'art' (I, 40) ['Several "thicknesses" of art' (I, 46/54)]. Her guiding principle clearly is that one cannot have too much of a good thing – a general enthusiasm for the arts which is keenly shared by her grandson.

In choosing the pictures just mentioned, she makes an important link to someone outside of the family: she consults Swann, a supposed expert in such areas. Now Swann is clearly an important role model for the Narrator, and any artistic input he can provide is bound to be received with seriousness. His cultivated sensibility is there for all to see, and his knowledgeability is mightily impressive: who else would have the wit and flair to compare the kitchen-girl at Combray to a painting by Giotto (I, 80; I, 94–5/110–12)? And the fact that he is writing a book on Vermeer only adds to his perceived unimpeachability in the field of art. But we soon see (notably in the flash-back of 'Un amour de Swann') that he is deeply flawed in this area. Perhaps his Giotto comparison *was* witty, but what does it really say about Giotto? Precious little. In coupling together a great artist and a humble girl, Swann is essentially only name-dropping. He famously takes the procedure a degree further in identifying his lover Odette with Botticelli's *Zipporah* in the Sistine Chapel, and putting a reproduction of the painting on his desk where others put a photograph of their wife (I, 220–1; I, 270/318). In reducing high art to a single point of reference, using it as it were anecdotally, he betrays art itself, by debasing it where it should be elevated. Similarly, when it comes to music, he channels his sensitivity in a direction unprofitable to the music itself: in arrogating a little phrase of Vinteuil's *Sonata* for his personal 'use' – he makes it into the 'national anthem' of his love for Odette (I, 215; I, 262/308) – he is extending the Botticelli misappropriation technique. This time, however, his own suspect procedures rebound on him: after falling out of love with Odette, he hears the little phrase again in a state of unprepared-ness, and in being confronted with associations of lost happiness ('les refrains oubliés du bonheur' ['the forgotten strains of happiness']) finds himself the victim of a 'déchirante souffrance' (I, 339) ['[an apparition] . . . so agonisingly painful' (I, 415/490)]. This is obviously not the sort of artis-tic path the Narrator should choose to follow.

Nor, in spite of much distraction, does he. For him, the arts always take first place; his attitude right from the start is that they contain something which it is important for him to learn. So, in one of the many glimpses we get of the boy in Combray engaged in reading, he feels 'ma croyance en la richesse philosophique, en la beauté du livre que je lisais, et mon désir de me les approprier, quel que fût ce livre' (I, 83) ['my belief in the philosophic rich-ness and beauty of the book I was reading, and my desire to appropriate them for myself, whatever the book might be' (I, 99/115)]. There is a clear sense of symbiosis in the act of reading, a form of communion. Although the analysis is provided by the older Narrator looking back on his youth, the reader receives a particularly fresh and close impression of the excitement felt by the boy. The fictional novelist Bergotte, for example,

> exprimait toute une philosophie nouvelle pour moi par de merveilleuses images dont on aurait dit que c'était elles qui avaient éveillé ce chant de harpes qui s'élevait alors et à l'accompagnement duquel elles donnaient quelque chose de sublime. Un de ces passages de Bergotte, le troisième ou le quatrième que j'eusse isolé du reste, me donna une joie incomparable à celle que j'avais trouvée au premier, une joie que je me sentis éprouver en une région plus pro-fonde de moi-même, plus unie, plus vaste, d'où les obstacles et les séparations semblaient avoir été enlevés. (I, 93)

[would express a whole system of philosophy, new to me, by the use of marvellous images that one felt must be the inspiration for the harp-song which then arose and to which they provided a sublime accompaniment. One of these passages of Bergotte, the third or fourth which I had detached from the rest, filled me with a joy to which the meagre joy I had tasted in the first passage bore no comparison, a joy that I felt I was experiencing in a deeper, vaster, more integral part of myself, from which all obstacles and partitions seemed to have been swept away.]   (I, 111/130)

The account is shot through with vocabulary of an appropriately intense emotional immediacy, utilising extremes of depth and elevation which will become more and more familiar to the reader each time the Narrator waxes lyrical in his close encounters of an artistic kind.

We are not given any extended examples of Bergotte's writing, but we get a clear idea of what readers, and not just the Narrator, like in Bergotte: his 'flux mélodique' ['melodic flow'], the 'expressions anciennes' ['old-fashioned phrases'] he uses, combined with common, simple ones, and 'une certaine brusquerie, un accent presque rauque' which he voices in sad sections (I, 94) ['a sort of roughness, a tone that was almost harsh' (I, 112/131)]. The Narrator especially appreciates those purple passages where Bergotte dwells on the beauty of his subject-matter, perhaps to the detriment of the storyline: 'il faisait dans une image exploser cette beauté jusqu'à moi' (*ibid.*) ['by some piece of imagery he would make their beauty explode into my consciousness (*ibid.*)]. The boy's enthusiasm for Bergotte is total, but predictably, and like so many of his preferences, it comes under serious attack, here in the shape of Monsieur de Norpois, a pompous diplomat colleague of the Narrator's father. On hearing that the boy is very keen on Bergotte, Norpois registers his disapproval, labelling the writer a mere 'joueur de flûte' (I, 464) ['flute-player' (II, 51/61)], and proclaiming that in the modern day 'il y a des tâches plus urgentes que d'agencer des mots d'une façon harmonieuse' (I, 465) ['there are tasks more urgent than the manipulation of words in a harmonious manner' (II, 52/61)]. Shortly before this, Norpois had given a silent reception to the Narrator's own youthful prose-poem (I, 447; II, 30/35), and now with his damning of Bergotte, the boy feels 'consterné, réduit' (I, 466) ['dismayed, diminished' (II, 54/63)], his ambitions wrecked: 'je sentis une fois de plus ma nullité intellectuelle et que je n'étais pas né pour la littérature' (I, 466) ['I felt conscious once again of my intellectual nullity and that I was not cut out for the literary life' (II, 53/63)].

It is all a question of self-confidence, an area in which the Narrator is dismally lacking: essentially, he is an idealist, and is naturally vulnerable to seemingly authoritative subversion of his ideals. In the case of Bergotte, the author is himself an agent when it comes to the process of disillusion which sets in when the high idealism can no longer be sustained. Having at first fantasised about Bergotte's being a 'vieillard infiniment sage et presque divin' (I, 402) ['that infinitely wise, almost divine old man' (I, 493/582)], the Narrator's disappointment is palpable when, at a dinner party, he eventually meets the 'doux Chantre aux cheveux blancs' (I, 537) ['the gentle Bard with the snowy locks' (II, 139/164)] and is confronted with a youthful, short, red-nosed and goatee-bearded individual, not at all the disembodied sage he had imagined:

> J'étais mortellement triste, car ce qui venait d'être réduit en poudre, ce n'était pas seulement le langoureux vieillard dont il ne restait plus rien, c'était aussi la beauté d'une œuvre immense. (I, 537)

> [I was cruelly disappointed, for what had just vanished in the dust of the explosion was not only the languorous old man, of whom no vestige now remained, but also the beauty of an immense work.] (II, 139–40/165)

The Narrator is here – as so often he is – a victim of his own over-fertile imagination: by dint of building up a precise picture of yet-to-be-experienced situations he virtually ensures variance between imagination and fact, hence disappointment. An analogous example of this syndrome – it is in the same area of *A la recherche* – is his desire to go and see the actress la Berma perform: 'Hélas! cette première matinée fut une grande déception' (I, 437) ['Alas! That first matinée was to prove a bitter disappointment' (II, 17/20–1)]. In all such cases, the Narrator needs to adjust to unalterable reality. This duly happens with Bergotte, and subsequent references to the writer's art are more measured in their appreciation. Besides, with Bergotte's becoming a social acquaintance, the emphasis in the Narrator's life shifts away from concentration on what is purely literary.

This move is a fairly close reflection of the manner in which his existence, as it becomes more socially oriented, seems to be drifting further and further away from his youthful ideals of high art and a literary vocation. Have they disappeared forever? It sometimes seems so, but great moments of resurgence prove otherwise; and if these are few in number, their paucity is more than adequately compensated for by their power. In the case of Bergotte, his artistic apotheosis occurs, ironically, with his death, as he collapses at an exhibition, in intense contemplation of Vermeer's *View of Delft*. Even as he dies, he is learning important lessons from the painter: 'C'est ainsi que j'aurais dû écrire, disait-il. Mes derniers livres sont trop secs, il aurait fallu passer plusieurs couches de couleur, rendre ma phrase en elle-même précieuse, comme ce petit pan de mur jaune' (III, 692) ['"That's how I ought to have written," he said. "My last books are too dry, I ought to have gone over them with a few layers of colour, made my language precious in itself, like this little patch of yellow wall"' (v, 207/244)]. Bergotte physically dies, but not his art with him: in a series of metaphysical reflections the Narrator (here surely very close to Proust's own convictions) articulates the view that there exists (at least in connection with art) 'un monde entièrement différent de celui-ci, et dont nous sortons pour naître à cette terre, avant peut-être d'y retourner' (III, 693) ['a world entirely different from this one and which we leave in order to be born on this earth, before perhaps returning there' (v, 208/245–6)]. At any rate, Bergotte's literary work remains to be admired; and here, employing the purple-passage technique which the Narrator so admired in Bergotte's novels, he himself (and, of course, Proust as author) composes the ultimate in epitaphs:

> On l'enterra, mais toute la nuit funèbre, aux vitrines éclairées, ses livres, disposés trois par trois, veillaient comme des anges aux ailes éployées et semblaient pour celui qui n'était plus, le symbole de sa résurrection.　　(III, 693)

> [They buried him, but all through that night of mourning, in the lighted shop-windows, his books, arranged three by three, kept vigil like angels with out-spread wings and seemed, for him who was no more, the symbol of his resurrection.]　　(v, 209/246)

That is impossible to follow; but on the level of the Narrator's trajectory as Protagonist, it has to be followed – he is still nowhere near his goal, and the lessons learned from Bergotte have not yet borne fruit in any significant production of his own. What about other artistic lessons? Bergotte had marked the Narrator's childhood years; now the painter Elstir takes over where he left off, in eloquent pages bunched in the Balbec section of *A l'ombre des jeunes filles en fleurs*. The approach to Elstir is more detailed, more analytical, than was the case with Bergotte: as he grows older, the Narrator is clearly becoming more discriminating. Indeed, the occasion of his being at Balbec in the first place comes about as a result of an aesthetic project: his desire to see Balbec church, an edifice which he romantically imagines to be battered by sea-spray, and whose architectural style is, in Swann's words, 'almost Persian' (I, 378; I, 463/547). Predictably, emotion takes over, and transforms the church into an object far removed from reality. But not entirely; for we already know how appreciative the Narrator is of ecclesiastical architecture from the evocative and impassioned description of Combray church (I, 58–66; I, 68–78/80–91): importantly, its historic patina enables him to apprehend the fourth dimension of time. And churches are intimately connected to people: true, they are conceived by artists, but with a view to protracted habitation and interaction by successive generations of ordinary folk. Predictably, though, the Narrator's first encounter with Balbec church is a disappointment: in particular, its famous statuary, which should represent its 'liveliest' aspect, seems cold and dead to his gaze, and leaves him unmoved (II, 20; II, 273–4/323).

Providentially, it is Elstir who will set him right in these matters, but not straight away. The order in which the Narrator experiences the two major aspects which Elstir incarnates – painter and then critic – represents a sort of modulation from one activity to the other, the inevitability of which is henceforth to become a major feature of his own thinking – and eventually practice. First, then, we get to know Elstir as a painter, in particularly vibrant pages where the older Narrator brilliantly foregrounds his younger self's excitement. After the unpromising ugliness of Elstir's house, what he witnesses in the studio is tantamount to 'le laboratoire d'une sorte de nouvelle création du monde' (II, 190) ['the laboratory of a sort of new creation of the world' (II, 478/565)]. That word 'creation' is to be used time and again, with an insistence and with overtones of awe which set the artist apart as someone special. Indeed, the Narrator makes the very highest claims for Elstir, advancing the view that the latter's work

> consistait en une sorte de métamorphose des choses représentées, analogue à celle qu'en poésie on nomme métaphore et que si Dieu le Père avait créé les choses en les nommant, c'est en leur ôtant leur nom, ou en leur en donnant un autre qu'Elstir les recréait. (II, 191)

> [lay in a sort of metamorphosis of the objects represented, analogous to what in poetry we call metaphor, and that, if God the Father had created things by naming them, it was by taking away their names or giving them other names that Elstir created them anew.] (II, 479/566)

Note the critical vocabulary mixed in with the exalted comparison: this is not just an emotional over-the-top reaction. The notion of metaphor is an especially precise and strong one, and it runs right through the conspectus of Elstir's paintings offered for the Narrator's delectation. In *Le Port de Carquethuit*, just finished, metaphor represents the guiding principle of the whole painting: here, there is no fixed frontier, no absolute demarcation, between land and sea, but, given the way they interact, each is viewed in terms of the other, with ships' masts seeming to rise out of dry land, and buildings out of the sea. The Narrator's entranced and inquisitive eye roves all around the painting, noting the great range of variations Elstir plays on the land/sea metaphor. So, here distant churches rise from the water and produce, haloed by a rainbow, an effect which is 'irréel et mystique' (II, 192) ['ethereal, mystical' (II, 480/568)]; elsewhere, women fishing for shrimps seem to be placed in a grotto protected from the waves; the boat in which sightseers sally forth behaves like a carriage on land; so that, overall, 'la terre est déjà marine et la population amphibie' ['the land was already subaqueous and the population amphibian'] and everything is suffused by the omnipresent 'force de l'élément marin' (II, 193) ['strength of the marine element' (II, 481/568)]. None of this is accidental: Elstir has been playing on the spectator's expectations and constantly challenging them by this technique of metaphorical substitution. But, being an esteemed artistic creator, Elstir is not just some dry dogmatist: on the contrary, as the Narrator puts it in a sort of motto prefatory to the *Port de Carquethuit* meditation, 'les rares moments où l'on voit la nature telle qu'elle est, poétiquement, c'était de ceux-là qu'était faite l'œuvre d'Elstir' (II, 192) ['the rare moments in which we see nature as she is, poetically, were those from which Elstir's work was created' (II, 479–80/566–7)].

It is important for the Narrator to experience Elstir as a wonderful creative artist before hearing him express himself as a critic: quite simply, his credentials are displayed in emphatic style, giving him a substantial base from which to speak with authority. The case to which he addresses himself is Balbec church, in response to the Narrator's admission of disappointment. The words of enlightenment – a great monologue full of erudition, yet far from pedantic – guide the Narrator through what should have been his interpretative strategy on contemplating the statuary. The latter all fits together, possessing meaning which can be 'read' like a poem; in Elstir's eyes, it is 'la plus belle Bible historiée que le peuple ait jamais pu lire' (II, 196) ['the finest illustrated Bible that the people have ever had' (II, 485/573)]. The starting-point for the sculptures is, literally, the text of the Bible, which is translated into stone with the greatest exactitude, yet allowing the artist in the different medium to express a new delicacy and produce 'que de profondes pensées, quelle délicieuse poésie!' (II, 196) ['what profound thoughts, what delicious poetry!' (II, 485/573)]. And it is emphatically the hand of an individual artist at work; he may have lived many centuries ago, and be tackling much-treated subject-matter, but this does not make him any less of a genius:

> Le type qui a sculpté cette façade-là, croyez bien qu'il était aussi fort, qu'il avait des idées aussi profondes que les gens de maintenant que vous admirez le plus … Il y a certaines paroles de l'office de l'Assomption qui ont été traduites avec une subtilité qu'un Redon n'a pas égalée.   (II, 197)

> [The chap who carved that façade, take my word for it, was every bit as good, had just as profound ideas, as the men you admire most at the present day … There are certain passages from the Office of the Assumption which have been conveyed with a subtlety that not even a Redon could equal.]
>   (II, 486/574–5)

The offhand way in which Elstir uses the word 'type' ['chap'] to describe the medieval artist is not just an expression of parity between artisans, but is also telling in bringing the Narrator's (and our) perception of a creative artist distant in time right up to date, in an appreciation surpassing that of the highly regarded ultra-modern symbolist Odilon Redon. In this way, Elstir is able to provide the Narrator with an in-depth lesson of artistic life, one which couples, in a sort of indissoluble duet, the individuality of creative practice and the necessity of underpinning that practice with enlightened critical theory. Hence the Narrator's pronouncement that what he tasted in Elstir's studio were '[d]es joies intellectuelles' (II, 198) ['intellectual pleasures' (II, 487/576)] should be taken literally: an emotional enthusiasm, but one which is informed by reason.

This attitude is one which will liberally mark the Narrator's encounter with what is indubitably his most overwhelming aesthetic engagement: that with the music of Vinteuil. In Combray days, such an eventuality seemed highly improbable – Vinteuil was only an unremarkable music teacher there – but the accounts of Swann's hearing his violin sonata make us aware of what it is like not only to experience music of high quality, but also of how the feeling manifests itself in an individual's mind. At first, the music 'lui avait ouvert plus largement l'âme' (I, 205–6) ['had opened and expanded his soul' (I, 250/294)]; then, he becomes captivated by a recurrent little musical phrase, which he needs to hold onto because it seems to offer 'la possibilité d'une sorte de rajeunissement' (I, 207) ['the possibility of a sort of rejuvenation' (I, 252/296)]. But as we have seen, Swann goes on, not to celebrate the music as autonomous achievement, but to debase it by harnessing one of its most striking features (the little phrase) to his obsessive love for Odette. This is scarcely the sort of behaviour one would expect from someone who is supposed to be writing a book on Vermeer.

How will the Narrator fare when it comes to music? Given Swann's poor example, we might expect him to make some elementary mistakes; but it is not so, for the greater part of his musical experiences take place after the encounter with Elstir and the aesthetic lessons acquired on that occasion. But not totally: there is a section early on in *A l'ombre des jeunes filles en fleurs* (that is, before the Elstir experience) where we see the Narrator engaging in fairly sophisticated meditations about the unique effect which music produces. How, for example, one's priorities develop from hearing to hearing, with the initially perceived beauties making way for others, which now seem more profound. In the case of Vinteuil's *Sonata*, this shifting means for the Narrator that 'je ne la possédai jamais tout entière' ['I never possessed it in its entirety']; in this 'elle ressemblait à la vie' (I, 521) ['it was like life itself' (II, 119/141)], an important linkage between art and life. And this coupling takes on an additional, aesthetic dimension when it comes to consideration of the reception of great works, so often ahead of their time, when they lacked '[des] êtres capables de [les] aimer' ['persons capable of appreciating [them]']. The late Beethoven quartets are cited as examples of how 'ce qu'on appelle la postérité, c'est la postérité de l'œuvre' ['what is called posterity is the posterity of the work of art']; the artist must, in order for a work to achieve all it can, 'la lance[r], là où il y a assez de profondeur, en plein et loin-tain avenir' (I, 522) ['launch it, there where there is sufficient depth, boldly into the distant future' (II, 121/143)]. Words of wisdom remarkably early on in the Narrator's career.

This precocious maturity in musical matters, bolstered by the creative and critical example of Elstir, performs an invaluable preparatory function when it comes to the Narrator's own full-scale encounter with a matchless musical composition. The experience of hearing Vinteuil's posthumous *Septet* – surely the most immediate and exuberant evocation of music ever penned – finds him capable of engaging in the experience both emotionally and intel-lectually in an act of reception which goes beyond the individual moment and, in a supreme aesthetic gesture, points towards future creation. Not that the *Septet* makes for easy listening: at first, the Narrator feels he is in unknown territory, and parts of the music are strident, rhythmically discon-certing, even ugly. But all of this is more than offset by the massive impact of the 'chef-d'œuvre triomphal et complet qui m'était en ce moment révélé' (III, 756) ['the triumphal and consummate masterpiece now being revealed to me' (V, 284/335)]. In ever more brilliant language, Proust the writer conveys the spiritual excitement of his Narrator as the *Septet* advances, the little phrase of the *Sonata* making a reappearance, 'harnachée d'argent, toute ruisselante de sonorités brillantes' (III, 753–4) ['harnessed in silver, glittering with brilliant sonorities' (V, 281/332)]; out of nothingness, an 'espoir mys-térieux' ['mysterious hope'] arises, culminating in 'un appel ineffable . . . de l'éternel matin' (III, 754) ['the ineffable call . . . of eternal morning' (V, 282–3/333)]. 'Joie; fraîcheur; originalité; bonheur; trésor insoupçonné' ['joy; freshness; originality; happiness; unsuspected treasure']: the highly-charged words applied to the music provide as it were a rhythmical support to the intensity of the emotion, emotion which arises from the craft of a musician who is 'haletant, grisé, affolé, vertigineux' ['panting, intoxicated, unbridled, vertiginous'] in the act of creation, a veritable counterpart to Michelangelo's painting the ceiling of the Sistine Chapel (III, 759; V, 287/339). Proust does not, of course, attempt to imitate the sounds of music, rather the euphoria it produces, so that, to paraphrase T. S. Eliot, we are the music while the words last.

Vinteuil the dead composer is 'réincarné' ['reincarnate'], he 'vivait à jamais dans sa musique' ['the composer lived for all time in his music'] each of his works being 'une même prière, jaillie devant différents levers de soleil intérieurs' (III, 759) ['the same prayer, bursting forth like different inner sunrises' (V, 286–8/337–40)]. It is as if great artists – here Vinteuil stands for them all – come trailing clouds of glory from some other world; each is the citizen of a 'patrie inconnue, oubliée de lui-même, différente de celle d'où viendra, appareillant pour la terre, un autre grand artiste' (III, 761) ['an unknown country, which he himself has forgotten, and which is different from that whence another great artist, setting sail for the earth, will eventually emerge' (V, 290/342)]. In fervent virtuosity of increasingly metaphysical language, Proust and his Narrator (how can one separate them at this point?) are positively transported into the empyrean:

> Des ailes, un autre appareil respiratoire, et qui nous permissent de traverser l'immensité, ne nous serviraient à rien. Car si nous allions dans Mars et dans Vénus en gardant les mêmes sens, ils revêtiraient du même aspect que les choses de la Terre tout ce que nous pourrions voir. Le seul véritable voyage, le seul bain de Jouvence, ce ne serait pas d'aller vers de nouveaux paysages, mais d'avoir d'autres yeux, de voir l'univers avec les yeux d'un autre, de cent autres, de voir les cent univers que chacun d'eux voit, que chacun d'eux est; et cela nous le pouvons avec un Elstir, avec un Vinteuil, avec leurs pareils, nous volons vraiment d'étoiles en étoiles. (III, 762)

> [A pair of wings, a different respiratory system, which enabled us to travel through space, would in no way help us, for if we visited Mars or Venus while keeping the same senses, they would clothe everything we could see in the same aspect as the things of Earth. The only true voyage, the only bath in the Fountain of Youth, would be not to visit strange lands but to possess other eyes, to see the universe through the eyes of another, of a hundred others, to see the hundred universes that each of them sees, that each of them is; and this we can do with an Elstir, with a Vinteuil; with men like these we do really fly from star to star.] (V, 291/343)

A pause for breath and reflection is in order for all concerned: writer, narrator and reader alike. The experience of Vinteuil's *Septet* is clearly overwhelming; but what lies beyond, 'au sortir de ce paradis' (III, 763) ['on emerging from that paradise' (V, 292/344)]? The Narrator at first wonders whether the inherently unanalytical nature of music might have been a means of facilitating communication between 'souls', if language, with its analytical properties, had not been invented (*ibid.*). A pertinent speculation, because it prepares him for making a capital link between Vinteuil's music and the transcendental aspect of his own life. He has experienced an 'appel vers une joie supraterrestre' (III, 765) ['summons to a supraterrestrial joy' (V, 294/347)], and he will never forget it; but will this joy be realisable for him? It is exactly the sensation he enjoys in those rare moments of metaphysical insight such as the Martinville spires; they are 'comme les points de repère, les amorces, pour la construction d'une vie véritable' (*ibid.*; see also III, 876–7) ['as starting-points, foundation-stones for the construction of a true life' (*ibid.*; see also V, 427–8/504–5)]. The intersection of life and art could not be rendered more explicit, and it has all been made possible as a result of the creative mind of a seemingly insignificant Combray music teacher.

The Narrator's self-confidence in the artistic domain, at first so woefully lacking, is now almost complete. In a neatly judged *mise en abyme* effect, we witness a scene with Albertine where he acts out the same sort of pedagogic role as Elstir had performed in Balbec, one which recognises the necessity of applying analysis to the emotional impact which art conveys. In magisterial, yet unpedantic, tones, he pinpoints the most significant and revelatory features of various painters, writers and composers: Vinteuil, of course, but also non-fictional ones such as Thomas Hardy, Stendhal, Dostoevski, Vermeer. All display structural niceties of a particularly cohesive nature, their discrete works all being 'les fragments d'un même monde' (III, 879) ['fragments of an identical world' (V, 430/508)], vocabulary familiar from the *Septet* episode.

It is only a matter of time now before the Narrator embarks on the fulfilment of his literary vocation, so often put off. How will he effect the transition from inertia to action? We know now that he is fully aware of the need to take account of the theoretical and structural basis of art, without relying solely on the emotional impact – indeed, the latter is ineffectual without the former. So it is that, after the series of 'moments bienheureux' in *Le Temps retrouvé*, he realises that these sensations need to be interpreted and converted into an 'équivalent spirituel' ['spiritual equivalent']: 'Or, ce moyen qui me paraissait le seul, qu'était-ce autre chose que faire une œuvre d'art?' (IV, 457) ['And this method, which seemed to me the sole method, what was it but the creation of a work of art?' (VI, 232/273)]. A momentous realisation, and one which the Narrator is now fit not to flinch from. Instinctively, what he instigates immediately is a review of the critical and theoretical possibilities which the rhetorical question opens up: having had a multiplicity of aesthetic encounters over the years, he is now in the position of formulating his own aesthetic programme.

These pages of *Le Temps retrouvé* (IV, 457–99; VI, 232–86/273–336) have been criticised as being dry and unnovelistic. This is surely erroneous, for the plot of the novel is now the dynamics of the Narrator's own literary production, and aesthetic questions are part and parcel of the story-line. A very striking feature of this section – hardly ever mentioned by critics, if at all – is the almost total absence of reference to other writers, painters and composers: there is the odd passing allusion, but generally speaking this is a solo effort on the Narrator's part, all his own work. It is above all an aesthetics which is pragmatic, not doctrinaire, one which takes as its starting-point the Narrator's realisation (unsurprising after his meditations on Vinteuil's *Septet*) that

> nous ne sommes nullement libres devant l'œuvre d'art, que nous ne la faisons pas à notre gré, mais que, préexistant à nous, nous devons, à la fois parce qu'elle est nécessaire et cachée, et comme nous ferions pour une loi de la nature, la découvrir. (IV, 459)

> [in fashioning a work of art we are by no means free, that we do not choose how we shall make it but that it pre-exists us, and therefore we are obliged, since it is both necessary and hidden, to do what we should have to do if it were a law of nature – to discover it.] (VI, 235/276-7)

The ways of enacting this discovery are not obvious in themselves: the immediate task of the Narrator is to work out how, in his own case, this can best be done. Theory in itself is a hindrance: 'Une œuvre où il y a des théories est comme un objet sur lequel on laisse la marque du prix' (IV, 461) ['A work in which there are theories is like an object which still has its price-tag on it' (VI, 236/278)]; an aggressively realist, descriptive type of writing cannot simultaneously accommodate the individual's past and present *personae* (IV, 463-4; VI, 241/284); popular and patriotic literature debase reader and subject-matter alike (IV, 467; VI, 237-8/279-80); and documentary writing is hopelessly superficial (IV, 473; VI, 253/297-8).

The whole of the Narrator's artistic experiences are now concentrated on this one, crucial point of his existence. In a sudden flash, he grasps that 'tous ces matériaux de l'œuvre littéraire, c'était ma vie passée' (IV, 478) ['all these materials for a work of literature were simply my past life' (VI, 258/304)], a realisation that neatly dovetails with an assertion he had just made that '[le] livre essentiel, le seul livre vrai, un grand écrivain n'a pas, dans le sens courant, à l'inventer puisqu'il existe déjà en chacun de nous, mais à le traduire. Le devoir et la tâche d'un écrivain sont ceux d'un traducteur' (IV, 469) ['the essential, the only true book, though in the ordinary sense of the word it does not have to be "invented" by a great writer – for it exists already in each one of us – has to be translated by him. The function and the task of a writer are those of a translator' (VI, 247/291)]. The attitude of the artisan prevails over that of the theorist in a gesture of modesty – a frame of mind which touchingly informs the final pages of the novel. So, having declared that 'chaque lecteur est quand il lit le propre lecteur de soi-même' (IV, 489) ['every reader is, while he is reading, the reader of his own self' (VI, 273/322)], he prolongs the image by suggesting that readers of his future book would use it like one of those magnifying-glasses sold by the Combray optician: 'mon livre, grâce auquel je leur fournirais le moyen de lire en eux-mêmes' (IV, 610) ['it would be my book, but with its help I would furnish them with the means of reading what lay inside themselves' (VI, 432/508)]. And when it comes to the actual physical composition of the book, he would piece the individual sheets of paper together, 'je n'ose pas dire ambitieusement comme une cathédrale, mais tout simplement comme une robe' (*ibid.*) ['I dare not say ambitiously like a cathedral, but quite simply like a dress' (VI, 432/509)].

It is a disarming feeling – but a refreshingly agreeable one – that after so much fastidious and agonising investigation of the arts things should be 'reduced' to this humble level. Yet it demonstrates how completely the Narrator has learned the lesson that art and life intertwine inseparably, and in exercising his mastery in this area, he requires no further support from other artists' examples. It is in the humdrum details of existence that the seeds of greatness lie: he will take them as his starting-point and transform them into the permanency of art. 'La vraie vie, la vie enfin découverte et éclaircie, la seule vie par conséquent pleinement vécue, c'est la littérature' (IV, 474) ['Real life, life at last laid bare and illuminated – the only life in consequence which can be said to be really lived – is literature' (VI, 253/298)]. With this uncompromising credo freshly formulated, the Narrator can now leap into the future and become a creator. We as readers can readily share in his excitement as he embarks on his task: we know it will be a masterpiece, because we have just read Proust's.

NOTES

1 The fact is mentioned in all the biographies; see, for example, Jean-Yves Tadié, *Marcel Proust* (Paris: Gallimard, 1996), p.754.

2 On Mayol, see Tadié, *Marcel Proust*, p.598. On the street-criers, III, 624–5, 633–4, 643–4.

3 See Marcel Proust, *Pleasures and Regrets*, transl. Louise Varese with a Preface by D.J. Enright (London: Grafton Books, 1988), pp.138–9.

4 See Marcel Proust, *Against Sainte-Beuve and Other Essays*, transl. with an Introduction by John Sturrock (Harmondsworth: Penguin, 1988), pp.122–31.

13

DAVID R. ELLISON

Proust and posterity

As we turn the page from the twentieth to the twenty-first century, the literary reputation of Marcel Proust is clearly on the rise. Not only does he continue to be considered a primary figure in European Modernism occupying the same rarefied aesthetic atmosphere as James Joyce, Franz Kafka and Thomas Mann, but increasingly, within the field of French Studies, he is being singled out as *the* twentieth-century writer, or even, *the* French writer of all time. Thus Jean-Yves Tadié, the author of the most comprehensive biographical study on Proust to date and also the general editor of the 1987–9 Pléiade edition of *A la recherche du temps perdu*, does not hesitate to assert:

> [*A la recherche du temps perdu*] recapitulates the entire literary tradition, from the Bible to Flaubert and Tolstoy, and all literary genres. Proust's novel also espouses the romantic and symbolist dream, shared by Mallarmé and Wagner, of a synthesis of all the arts, painting, music and architecture. Thus are born works which escape the constraints of their time period, their country, their author, and whose glory continues to grow. It has often been said that, if England has Shakespeare, Germany Goethe, Italy Dante, France had no one writer to equal them. The number of critical works devoted to the author of the *Recherche* suggests that France now has, and will have tomorrow, Marcel Proust. (I, x-xi; my translation.)

Although many readers of Proust, including the author of this essay, share Tadié's enthusiasm and conviction, I think it also necessary to pose some direct and sober-minded questions about the posterity or 'afterlife' of Proust's novel. At a minimum, these questions would include: 1. Who has been reading Proust, and with what degree of acuity? What is the relation between Proust's fame or notoriety and the content of his literary production? 2. In what ways have his novel and also his earlier writings influenced modern and contemporary works of criticism, theory, and creative writing? I shall examine these two large questions succinctly (each of them would merit, in fact, a book-length response), always keeping in mind the proble-

matic connectedness and/or separation between the 'inside' of Proust's novelistic universe and the 'outside' of the reputation it has engendered.

To read Proust today, long after his death, is to encounter him enveloped in
celebrity, weighed down by reams of critical commentary, domesticated by
the wealth of facts and hermeneutical grids with which we can now arm ourselves to attack the complexities of his imaginary world. Proust has become
so well known that it may be difficult for us modern-day readers to imagine
just how revolutionary his prose style appeared to the majority of the reading
public during the period of 1913 to 1927.

Proust did not have an easy time getting the first volume of his novel, *Du
côté de chez Swann*, published, in part because, like Wagner's *Tetralogy*, it
sinned against the accepted order of magnitude for a work of art: the sentences were too long, the thoughts too convoluted, the general thematic aims
not apparent enough in their wide extension. In his amusing and intelligent
little book entitled *How Proust Can Change Your Life*,[1] Alain de Botton
reminds us of the immediate reaction of one Alfred Humblot, director of the
Ollendorf publishing house, who, in explaining to Louis de Robert his
refusal to publish Proust's work, had the following illuminating justification
for his decision: 'My dear friend, I may be dense, but I fail to see why a chap
needs thirty pages to describe how he tosses and turns in bed before falling
asleep' (Botton, p.33).

What poor Humblot did not understand, but what informed readers today
often know before they begin reading *A la recherche du temps perdu* thanks
to the literary grapevine (is it really possible today to encounter Proust's
work stripped completely of its aura of accumulated commentary?) is that
these opening pages are nothing less than a symphonic Overture which contains, in highly concentrated form, the thematic material for the rest of the
three thousand-page opus. The first pages of *Du côté de chez Swann* are all
about the threshold between sleep and wakefulness, non-being and being, a
liminary situation which, of course, cannot be reduced to a chap falling
asleep in the realistic or restrictive sense of that term. What is interesting,
however, is that the problem of the novel's length and of the syntactical com-
plications of its sentences, which made it so difficult for Proust to be published, is now precisely what constitutes the author's cultural value in our
postmodern/postcolonial/computerised 'post-writing' age. It would probably not be an exaggeration to say that Proust's fame rests upon the twin
pillars of a rather insipid pastry (the 'petite madeleine') and very long sentences. Proust, in other words, has become an icon, and the foundation
of his status as icon resides in the area of his work that offered the most

resistance to his early readers. The passing of time, in the case of the reception of Proust's novel, has had as its primary effect the transmutation of readerly frustration (Humblot was angry at Proust, not happy to be upset in his reading habits) into consumerist fun. A cartoon from the 20 December 1982 issue of *The New Yorker* shows a woman dressed in a fur coat and cowboy boots making the following request to a bemused clerk in a bookstore: 'I want something to get even for that new translation of Proust he gave me last year.'[2] In 1982 or the year 2000 we as belated readers of Proust do not have to understand why this 'revenge' is necessary: the lady in cowboy boots is just as outraged as Humblot was, and probably fell asleep herself over Proust's Narrator's 'sleeping'. We as readers of *The New Yorker*, however, because we are cognoscenti, because we know all about Proustian length and meandering, can have a good laugh and are not ourselves frustrated or angry. We think we now possess the aesthetic distance *from* Proust's book that allows for a hearty and uncomplicated laugh, that allows us to escape the difficulty *within* Proust's work.

In writing about the 'kitschification' of the *Recherche* in her book *Postmodern Proust* (1992), however, Margaret Gray has shown how the compulsive attachment to particular scenes in popular culture's appropriation of Proust – notably *the* scene of involuntary memory organised around the petite madeleine – betrays as strong an anxiety as that felt by Monsieur Humblot and his bewildered compatriots in 1913. The madeleine baking pans one can buy now, not just in Illiers-Combray, but all over the world, pans which purportedly allow us to create 'the same' delicate cakes as those enjoyed by Proust himself (and which might, therefore, unlock for each of us our own gates of memory), are interpreted in the languages of semiotics and psychoanalysis by Gray in the following manner:

> Such obsessive cultural attention to the madeleine scene as a sort of symbol or signifier for the *Recherche* in its entirety suggests a displaced, excessive emphasis on the part rather than the larger meaning it points to: an interest whose object is the madeleine itself, rather than its symbolic function as the cornerstone of 'l'édifice immense du souvenir'. The gadgety 'madeleine' pan would suggest the extreme veneration of an empty signifier, a signifier now disconnected from its original signified.   (Gray, *Postmodern Proust*, p.166)

The kind of disconnection which Gray describes here is at the origin of the most humorous references to Proust in popular culture, notably those of the Monty Python group, who use the signifier 'Proust' to represent all that is high and great in the literary tradition – a tradition from which we are now, in the Pythonesque world-view, grotesquely separated and alienated.

sustained treatment of Proust in the Python annal. the 'All-England Summarise Proust Competition', r sed first in a swimsuit and then in an evening dress, elate the plotline of the novel's seven volumes.[3] The usual vacuity of beauty pageants – which employ cliché-question-and-answer sessions with the contestants presumably to 'clothe' with dignity the voyeuristic nature of the spectacle which is, in fact, concerned with what is under the clothing – to the intellectual depths of Proust's novel works very well as humour; but the humour, once again, betrays anxiety, or, in Gray's terms, 'the ambivalent energies of desire and dread his [Proust's] text excites' (*Postmodern Proust*, p.170). Readers of Proust desire to understand him, but his work's difficulty is forbidding: to summarise him in fifteen seconds is an excellent way to flee his fictional territory as rapidly as possible, to be untouched by the difficult (and often, comical) truths contained in his text. Making the length of the Proustian text into a joke is, in other words, a defence mechanism based on envelopment or containment whereby the would-be reader attempts to defuse the 'bombs' ready to explode into his or her face – these metaphorical 'bombs' being the uncomfortable lessons about human nature which Proust is ready to relate to us, but only if we are willing to submit to the discipline of an interpretive reading.

The kind of 'kitschification' of which Margaret Gray writes with panache and good sense is easy enough to dismiss as one more sign of the superficiality and fundamental silliness of our time. One can imagine the reaction of conservative cultural critics to the antics of the Marcel Proust Support Group of San Francisco, whose members hold 'an invite-only memorial wake for Proust in the John Wickett Museum of Exotica, where a Proust impersonator lies in state, moustachioed and tuxedoed in his coffin, then rises from the dead for an interview and perhaps some cream cheese with crushed strawberries'.[4] Yet, as Gray points out, Proust himself is the great specialist of kitschifying or fetishising, which he diagnosed as an intellectual disease festering within himself and most literary people, and which he called 'idolatry' in the preface to his translation of Ruskin's *The Bible of Amiens* (Gray, *Postmodern Proust*, pp.166–7). The important thing to keep in mind is that, for Proust, the excessive attention to exterior detail to the detriment of interior meaning, to the outside rather than the inside of a work of art, is not a mistake one can easily (or ever) correct: it is not the sign of some aberrant form of behaviour which can be recognised as such and eradicated. Rather, fetishising or idolising an author and his work is an inevitable movement of error inscribed within the act of reading itself, a deviousness or

.version by which, in attaching ourselves to the glittering surface
.xt, we in fact remove ourselves from the text, and stop reading. In s.
to fetichise a text is *not to read it* because the text is dangerous. It is becau
the reader as explorer of unknown worlds knows, by anticipation, tha.
Proust's novel, like the Song of the Sirens, is fraught with peril, that it could
'change his life', that he plugs his ears and erects massive consumer-
monuments to Proust around the silent emptiness that constitutes his own
non-reading. What would happen, however, if one were to open oneself to
the Sirens' Song within the *Recherche*? What *has* happened, in fact, to those
readers who have allowed themselves to be permeable to Proust's charming
but upsetting and disquieting narrative rhythms? It is to these imaginative
interpreters and their own texts, that I now turn.

Although Proust's own output as literary critic was considerable between the
turn of the century and 1922, his influence on the themes and methods of
critical and theoretical discourse in France did not become evident until the
1960s and 1970s, at the time of the 'linguistic turn' – i.e., the period in which
French Structuralism began to build upon the insights of Russian
Formalism.[5] Up through the 1950s in France, with some notable and brilliant exceptions (one thinks here, *inter alia*, of Gaëtan Picon and Georges
Poulet), the work of literary critics continued to be dominated by studies of
the *homme et œuvre* variety inspired by the method of Sainte-Beuve, in
which careful documentation of an author's family and social life, correspondence, travels, loves, and even finances, was used to explicate the
general significance of his or her writings. Critics who continued to use this
method well into the twentieth century had doubtless not read or not taken
seriously Proust's own essay entitled 'La Méthode de Sainte-Beuve' (c. 1908),
in which the future creator of the *Recherche* had stated quite explicitly:

> L'œuvre de Sainte-Beuve n'est pas une œuvre profonde. La fameuse méthode,
> qui en fait, selon Taine, selon M. Paul Bourget et tant d'autres, le maître iné-
> galable de la critique au XIXe, cette méthode qui consiste à ne pas séparer
> l'homme et l'œuvre . . . méconnaît ce qu'une fréquentation un peu profonde
> avec nous-même nous apprend: qu'un livre est le produit d'un autre moi que
> celui que nous manifestons dans nos habitudes, dans la société, dans nos vices.
> Ce moi-là, si nous voulons essayer de le comprendre, c'est au fond de nous-
> même, en essayant de le recréer en nous, que nous pouvons y parvenir.
>
> (*CSB*, pp.221–2)

[Sainte-Beuve's work is not a profound work. His famous method, which made
of him, in the eyes of Taine, Paul Bourget, and many others, the incontestable
master of literary criticism in the 19th century, this method which consists of

not separating the man from his work . . . ignores what even a slight acquaintance with our own thoughts can teach us: that a book is the product of another self from the one which we manifest in our habits, in society, in our vices. If we wish to understand that self, we must seek it out in the depths of our consciousness, and try to recreate it.] (My translation.)

Proust's resolute refusal to lose himself as literary critic in a consideration of the minutiae of a writer's experiential activity was accompanied by an interest in the minutest *textual* details of that writer's work. Perhaps the single most brilliant critical study penned by Proust is the 1920 essay entitled 'A propos du "style" de Flaubert' (*CSB*, pp.586–600) which was published as a rejoinder to an article by Albert Thibaudet and which, among other items, dealt with Flaubert's 'rhythmical' use of prepositions and adverbs and his idiosyncratic manipulations of the imperfect and past definite verb tenses. According to Proust, these stylistic innovations constituted a revolution in literature of the same magnitude as Kant's invention of the 'Categories' in his *Critique of Pure Reason* (1781). The critical article on Flaubert contains many of the thoughts Proust had elaborated in his own novel, notably in the theoretical conclusion of *Le Temps retrouvé*, in which the smallest and rarest aspects of an individual's artistic style are shown to generate the largest, most consequential effects of that artist's vision of the world. Proust's special interest in the temporal nuances of Flaubert's novelistic universe – notably the 'blanks' or empty spaces to be found between episodes in *L'Education sentimentale* – not only corresponded to his own techniques in the *Recherche*, but also prefigured the important technical studies that were to be undertaken, a half-century later, by the French Structuralists.

The imaginary debate with Sainte-Beuve which began as a critical work but gradually turned into *A la recherche du temps perdu* during the transitional period of 1908–10 stands as an interesting foreshadowing of the most notorious controversy of the Structuralist period: namely, the polemical exchanges between Roland Barthes and Raymond Picard concerning the life and works of the seventeenth-century playwright Racine. Picard's *La Carrière de Jean Racine* (1961) was a massive example of the *homme et œuvre* methodology, replete with a quasi-Balzacian obsessional attention to Racine's financial dealings, whereas Barthes's own *Sur Racine* (1963) employed the contemporary vocabulary of semiotics and psychoanalysis to analyse the writer's 'imaginary'. Picard attacked *Sur Racine* in a pamphlet entitled *Nouvelle critique ou nouvelle imposture* (1965), and Barthes responded with a treatise called *Critique et vérité* (1966).[6] This Racine controversy helped to draw the critical/theoretical battle-lines in France; and these battle-lines were drawn in the shadow of Proust. It was Proust/Barthes against Sainte-Beuve/Picard in one more repetition of the late-seventeenth-century *querelle des anciens et des modernes*, with the modern side embracing Proust's appeal to style (grammar and rhetoric) and narrative technique.

From the 1960s until the present moment many of the most distinguished works of literary criticism and theory written in France either have Proust's writings as their subject or employ Proustian methods of interpretive reading. The kind of attention Proust lavished on Ruskin's 'polyphonic' writing style in the essays with which he framed his translations of *The Bible of Amiens* and *Sesame and Lilies* makes one think, inevitably, of the *critique thématique* practised by Jean-Pierre Richard, not only in *L'Univers imaginaire de Mallarmé*, but also in his study of Proust entitled *Proust et le monde sensible*.[7] Gérard Genette's early essays 'Proust palimpseste' and 'Proust et le langage indirect' are models of interpretive criticism based upon the same kind of acute attentiveness to stylistic phenomena that characterised Proust's piece on Flaubert. And when, a few years later, Genette undertook his magisterial systematic exposition of 'narratology' entitled 'Discours du récit', he based his treatise upon the narrative techniques contained in *A la recherche du temps perdu*.[8] Students of narrative theory throughout the world, even those with no specialised knowledge of French literature, are now familiar with Proust's novel because Genette chose it as the textual basis for his theorising. Richard and Genette, along with Gilles Deleuze, the author of the influential *Proust et les signes*,[9] showed the *Recherche* to be a complex system of themes, temporal movements and semiotic disruptions calling for an active interpretation. Their studies not only set a high hermeneutical standard for subsequent readings of Proust, but also helped to define the period of 1960 to 1980 as a time in which the study of literature was becoming more precise, more technically advanced, more 'scientific'.

From the early 1970s until now, France's Centre National de la Recherche Scientifique (CNRS) has made its own collective contribution to the science of literary study, in the form of ambitious philological and editorial projects. One of these was the fundamental re-organisation and re-classification of Proust's manuscripts, which culminated, in 1987–9, in a new four-volume Pléiade edition of *A la recherche du temps perdu*. This edition is twice as long (seven thousand pages versus three thousand five hundred) as the 1954 Pléiade,[10] largely because it provides, with its scholarly apparatus, numerous early drafts of episodes which Proust decided not to include in the published version of his novel. The textual ideology underlying the decision to print preliminary stages of a narrative segment as well as its definitive form is that of 'genetic criticism' (*critique génétique*) as practised in France, which can be summarised thus: the 'becoming of the text' (*le devenir textuel*), the process by which a text is generated, is just as interesting, perhaps even more enlightening to the critical reader, than the final form that text assumes.

In writing about the evolution of Proust's use of place-names in early and later versions of the *Recherche*, Claudine Quémar did not hesitate to claim that the genetic method of criticism is a 'return upstream that amounts to a return to life; a return to sources that enlivens the text by tearing it away from the marmoreal immobility of the "definitive" state to which the author condemned his work in decreeing it one day (and who will ever be able to say why?) "finished"'.[11] Although Quémar's philological work is of the highest quality, one has to wonder whether the novelist's own decision to include or not include an episode is as arbitrary as she seems to think. Why put scare-quotes around the words 'definitive' and 'finished'? Is it not possible that the act of authorial boundary-tracing is precisely one of the most important acts performed by the literary creator, and that a definitive or final form might show, in its disciplined structure, more vigour and complexity than the negative term 'marmoreal immobility' suggests? These are questions to which there is no easy answer, especially not in the limited space of the present essay. Suffice it to say, however, that not all Proust scholars have embraced the new Pléiade edition without intellectual qualms. Readers of Proust who would like to read recent *pro* and *contra* positions on the advisability of the inclusion of Proust's early fragments (*avant-textes*) within the 1987–9 Pléiade *Recherche* should read in tandem Jean-Yves Tadié's Introduction générale to volume one of the series and Roger Shattuck's polemical response to that Introduction (and to the methodological presuppositions of genetic criticism) in his *New York Review of Books* article entitled 'The Threat to Proust'.[12] Whatever position each of us readers decides to take on this issue, it is clear that the corpus of Proust's texts is at the centre of contemporary critical scrutiny in France, that the fragmentation and dispersion of those textual segments situated around rather than in the novel will continue to be the focus of theoretical debate for years to come.[13]

It might seem, from the barebones sketch I have been providing, that Proust's text, in becoming a battleground for ideological and theoretical disputation, risks becoming obscured *as individual text*, risks losing its own specific character or 'signature'. This is, fortunately, not the case. Three of the most important works on Proust of the last decade make admirable use of rhetorical, psychoanalytical and narratological modes of analysis coupled with a solid knowledge of the recent advances in Proustian genetic philology; but, in remaining always attuned to Proust's distinctive voice, they offer us readers a genuine personal interpretation. I am thinking of Antoine Compagnon's *Proust entre deux siècles*, Julia Kristeva's *Le Temps sensible: Proust et l'expérience littéraire*, and Malcolm Bowie's *Proust Among the*

Stars. Each of these works has a distinctive thematic emphasis and each differs from the others in style, but they share what I would call an ease in erudition that I find new in Proust studies. The insights derived from Freud and Lacan, from linguistics and semiotics, the concrete examples furnished by manuscripts, flow together with the critics' knowledge of Proust in a natural way and create what Proust himself liked to call, in reference to Ruskin, a *caisse de résonance* (*La Bible d'Amiens*, p.9), an echo-chamber in which the *Recherche* gains depth and relevance through its intertextual links with the European literary tradition as a whole. Compagon, Kristeva and Bowie know Proust was, throughout his career, a voracious reader: they read him *as a reader of texts* and, in so doing, invite us contemporary readers to participate in the same hermeneutical activity. Each of these critics sees the act of literary criticism not as the demonstration of a theory or the solving of an intellectual puzzle, but rather, in appropriately Proustian terms, as an 'Open Sesame' to a plurality of interpretive possibilities.

Proust's posterity is as evident in the field of creative fiction as it is in the area of literary criticism and theory. His direct and indirect influence over fictional writing in the second two-thirds of the twentieth century is probably as massive as that of Joyce or Kafka, but the forms this influence takes are so variegated and diverse as to render futile any effort to catalogue them. When we think, in the most general terms, of Proust, we think inevitably of a certain number of large themes: psychological interiority; the depiction of the social mores of Third Republic France; humour and comedy; time and memory; sexuality, especially homosexuality; a novelistic structure that is both closed upon itself and open-ended; the redemptive roles of literature, art and music. But at such a high level of generality, can these themes or aspects of Proust's work be called *specifically* Proustian? The first *roman psychologique*, *La Princesse de Clèves*, was written by Madame de Lafayette in 1678, not by Proust from 1910 until 1922; hosts of talented and mediocre writers wrote about Third Republic Society; humour and comedy have been with us from the dawn of literature; time and memory are repeatedly invoked by Homer and Virgil, but also form the fabric of Scheherazade's death-defying tales in *The Arabian Nights*; Balzac's homosexual pedagogue Vautrin, a witty and diabolical presence in several novels of *La Comédie humaine*, precedes and announces Proust's Charlus; writing at the same time as Proust but in a radically different style, Kafka also produced novels that were both finished and fragmented; and art as redemption is a theme Proust did not invent, but found in the works of Ruskin.

The point I am making is that the adjective 'Proustian', when applied to works of the literary imagination that supposedly bear the mark of Proust's influence, is usually far too general to be useful. The fact that a number of novels from Latin America, such as José Donoso's *The Obscene Bird of Night*, Gabriel García Márquez's *One Hundred Years of Solitude*, or Nélida Piñon's *The Republic of Dreams*, are situated in the labyrinth of human memory, makes them only vaguely, not essentially or primordially, 'Proustian'. Yet I do believe that it is possible to trace, within a discrete group of French-language writings, a more precise Proustian influence, one that is based upon the combination of the final two elements I mentioned above: namely, the depiction of the work of art as *the promise of a possible future redemption in its simultaneously open and closed form*. Three exemplary works I see as following in Proust's wake in this more precise sense span more than four decades of recent literary history and are important texts in their own right. They are: Jean-Paul Sartre's *La Nausée* (1938); Michel Butor's *La Modification* (1957); and Samuel Beckett's *Compagnie* (1980).[14] Despite the considerable differences in theme, mood and narrative technique that differentiate each of these fictions from the others, they all prolong, beyond the cut-off date of 1922, a genuine Proustian reflection on the aesthetically *and* existentially transformative power of fictional writing.

Readers of *La Nausée* will remember that the novel's protagonist, Antoine Roquentin, experiences a form of emotional respite or release from his bouts with existential anxiety ('nausea') when he hears, on a phonograph recording, the jazz tune *Some of These Days You'll Miss Me Honey*. Whereas the visual imagery used by the narrator to characterise the experience of 'nausea' is always that of fluidity, obscurity and undefined contours, when he first hears the jazz tune, he depicts it as hard, clear, bounded, geometrically precise. In temporal or narrative terms, whereas the brute experience of existing is a blind forward movement with no predictable endpoint, the musical phrase that fascinates Roquentin has an inevitability to its progression, an aesthetic teleology that prompts him to write of its formal perfection. Now it happens that the jazz tune is a transparent re-writing of Vinteuil's 'petite phrase' in *Du côté de chez Swann*; and when Sartre describes it as 'cette bulle de clarté bourdonnante de musique' ['this bubble of clarity humming with music'] (N, p.43), he is citing Proust, who had written of the final appearance of Vinteuil's motif in these more elaborate terms:

> Aussi Swann ne perdait-il rien du temps si court où elle [la petite phrase] se prorogeait. Elle était encore là comme une bulle irisée qui se soutient. Tel un arc-en-ciel, dont l'éclat faiblit, s'abaisse, puis se relève et, avant de s'éteindre, s'exalte un moment comme il n'avait pas encore fait: aux deux couleurs qu'elle avait jusque-là laissé paraître, elle ajouta d'autres cordes diaprées, toutes celles du prisme, et les fit chanter. (I, 346)

[And so Swann lost nothing of the precious time for which it [the little phrase] lingered. It was still there, like an iridescent bubble that floats for a while unbroken. As a rainbow whose brightness is fading seems to subside, then soars again and, before it is extinguished, shines forth with greater splendour than it has ever shown; so to the two colours which the little phrase had hitherto allowed to appear it added others now, chords shot with every hue in the prism, and made them sing.] (I, 424/500–1)

Sartre's homage to Proust extends far beyond this brief wink of a lifted phrase. The jazz tune, like Vinteuil's 'petite phrase', is nothing less than a promise of the possibility of redemption through writing. At the end of *La Nausée*, Roquentin turns away from the fortuitous and unpatterned rhythms of his previous life toward the creation of his own novel. It is in this novel, in the work required by its painstaking elaboration, that Roquentin hopes to find meaning in his existence, just as the narrator of the *Recherche*, at the very end of *Le Temps retrouvé*, decides to write a book which would envelop and contain, in the rigour of its aesthetic form, the previously impenetrable significance of his formative years. In his delicate balancing-act between existence and the world of artistic essences, between nausea and music, Sartre relied on Proust as his primary intertextual source for the depiction of aesthetic transcendence.

One finds a similar explicit homage to Proust's theme of the book and its aesthetic/existential value in Michel Butor's *nouveau roman* entitled *La Modification*. In this narratively complex and mythologically evocative experimental novel, Butor makes use of the most banal of literary plot conventions – a love-triangle in which the protagonist, Léon Delmont, is caught between his married life in Paris and a mistress in Rome – to examine, with a truly Proustian sense of rigour and detail, the 'modification' that takes place in Delmont's mind as he turns from the futility of his professional occupation as seller/distributor of typewriters to the sense of existential authenticity he associates with the future writing of a novel. Like Roquentin and like Proust's Narrator, Delmont is poised, at the end of the narrative we readers have just completed (here, the fictional text entitled *La Modification*), to write his own novel. The kind of circular structure characteristic of the *Recherche* and of *La Nausée* is thus repeated in the formal design of Butor's text. What is particularly interesting in the gradual psychological dissection Delmont performs upon himself is the way in which he discovers, by degrees, that his supposed love for his Roman mistress, Cécile, is in fact a love of the city of Rome with which he had associated Cécile. In other words, he had not loved 'Cécile in Rome', but 'Rome in Cécile', just as Swann finally understood that he had loved not Odette so much as

Vinteuil's 'petite phrase' in its association with Odette. The aura of demystification that pervades *La Modification* is thus a repetition of that same aura as it emanates from the inexorable negative progression of 'Un Amour de Swann'. Butor's text is a palimpsest of Proust's in much the same way as Joyce's *Ulysses* is a re-inscription of *The Odyssey*.

Although Butor's polyphonic novel is less didactic than Sartre's rather straightforward philosophical allegory, and although Delmont as fictional character is certainly more fully drawn and less of a caricature than Roquentin, in both novels there is an unmistakably similar seriousness, even earnestness, in the claims being made for artistic works and for the protagonists' novel-to-come. Roquentin thinks that it might be possible for the writer and the singer of the jazz tune to be 'saved' and 'washed clean of the sin of existence' (*N*, p.249) by their creative acts. Delmont speaks of his future novel as possessing the quality of 'necessity', and is convinced that the writing of this work will constitute a truth-saying capable of effacing the 'lies' which had insinuated themselves into his purported love for Cécile (*M*, pp.282–6). A future aesthetic triumph, in both cases, will allow the novels' protagonists to negate existential anguish and atone for inauthentic behaviour. Such an imagined triumph is, of course, exactly what Proust's Narrator projects in the lengthy theoretical discourse that provides the conclusion of *Le Temps retrouvé*.

As contemporary literary works have become increasingly fragmented in their formal designs and uncertain in their ethical underpinnings, faith in the redemptive power of art has faded considerably in recent years; but this faith remains as a kind of shadow or ghostly aura. This is the case in Samuel Beckett's *Compagnie*, a dense and difficult work which contains unmistakable echoes of Proust's novel. Beckett's concentrated and elliptical *récit*, like many of his late works, is so spare in its narrative development as to be highly enigmatic. What one can say, with some degree of certainty, is that the narrative describes a human figure lying in the dark telling stories (some of these being the lived experiences of Samuel Beckett) to himself. The act of telling, however, is not described as a conscious or voluntary act, but rather as the self's receiving of his voice from the outside or exterior world. The first lines of the story read: 'Une voix parvient à quelqu'un dans le noir. Imaginer' ['A voice comes to one in the dark. Imagine'] (*Ce*, p.7; *Cy*, p.7). The figure reclining in darkness throughout the narrative is, in fact, alone; but his storytelling, to use Baudelairian language, serves to 'people his solitude', to provide the company, or *compagnie*, without which there can be no human community. Beckett has reduced the social act of storytelling – in his words, 'fabulation' – to its minimal state: to one consciousness fabulating to itself. Unless that consciousness had split itself, there would be only solitude and no narrative. The split within the self, therefore, is the very origin of narrative. Narrative is generated from a primary and primordial self-reflexive disjunction whereby the self can view itself from the outside, whereby the self being told becomes a strange object, a curious thing, for the self doing the telling. Although Beckett's short-winded syntax is at the antipodes of Proust, and although the fictional universe of Murphy, Molloy, and our unnamed reclining figure would seem, at first glance, to bear little resemblance to that of Swann, Odette and Charlus, the one obvious and important similarity is, precisely, the unnamed reclining figure – who, in Proust's novel, appears on the very first page, in bed, between wakefulness and sleep, between his actual solitude and the incipient moment of narration. The strangeness of the situation in which the self splits into narrator and narrated is not peculiar to Beckett's wry humour or devious imagination, but inhabits Proust's novel, from the very beginning. Readers of the *Recherche* will not have forgotten that Proust's Narrator, in falling asleep while holding a book, relates a very interesting proto-Beckettian dislocation and fall into the abyss of impersonality:

> Je voulais poser le volume que je croyais avoir encore dans les mains et souffler ma lumière; je n'avais pas cessé en dormant de faire des réflexions sur ce que je venais de lire, mais ces réflexions avaient pris un tour un peu particulier; il me semblait que j'étais moi-même ce dont parlait l'ouvrage: une église, un quatuor, la rivalité de François Ier et de Charles Quint. (1, 3)

> [I would make as if to put away the book which I imagined was still in my hands, and to blow out the light; I had gone on thinking, while I was asleep, about what I had just been reading, but these thoughts had taken a rather peculiar turn; it seemed to me that I myself was the immediate subject of my book: a church, a quartet, the rivalry between François 1 and Charles v.] (1, 1/1)

As is the case in Beckett's *Compagnie*, the narrated self, in separating from the narrating self, becomes lost in the dizzying maze of fiction, of what Beckett, in his later works, will consistently call 'figmentation'. The reclining narrating figures in both *Compagnie* and the *Recherche* are both 'the immediate subject[s]' of their respective books. But to become the subject of one's book, one must first be subjected to the painful split whereby one becomes a church, a quartet, or, even more marvellously, a pure abstract relation – the *rivalry between* two sixteenth-century monarchs. The imaginary territory of Proust is no less strange, no less disorienting and vertiginous, than that of Beckett.

Aside from the obvious stylistic disparities I have mentioned in passing, the primary difference between the two writers resides in the tone with which each of them describes the initial split of self from self that sets off the narrative machine. If the reader takes the aesthetic affirmations of *Le Temps retrouvé* seriously, he or she will end by sharing the Narrator's conviction that the narrated self can be saved (in Sartre's terms, 'washed clean') by the narrating self, that the narrating self is capable of subsuming within the threads of his narrative all the wayward, misdirected thoughts and experiences of the narrated self. If this should be the case, the narrating self is never truly alone: he is, to use Gilles Deleuze's striking analogy, the spider at the centre of a vast resonating web of significance.[15] The solitude of the individual writer gives way to the solidarity the writer shares with the 'figments' of his imagination (and with his readership). This kind of aesthetic optimism produces, in the final lines of the *Recherche*, an imagery of dilation and expansion:

> Aussi, si elle [la force] m'était laissée assez longtemps pour accomplir mon œuvre, ne manquerais-je pas d'abord d'y décrire les hommes, cela dût-il les faire ressembler à des êtres monstrueux, comme occupant une place si considérable, à côté de celle si restreinte qui leur est réservée dans l'espace, une place au contraire prolongée sans mesure puisqu'ils touchent simultanément, comme des géants plongés dans les années à des époques, vécues par eux si distantes, entre lesquelles tant de jours sont venus se placer – dans le Temps.   (IV, 625)

> [So, if I were given long enough to accomplish my work, I should not fail, even if the effect were to make them resemble monsters, to describe men as occupying so considerable a place, compared with the restricted place which is reserved for them in space, a place on the contrary prolonged past measure, for simultaneously, like giants plunged into the years, they touch the distant epochs through which they have lived, between which so many days have come to range themselves – in Time.]   (VI, 451/531–2)

The conclusion of Beckett's *Compagnie* has a very different rhetorical resonance, and is grounded not in 'monstrous' or 'gigantic' expansion, not in the overcoming of solitude through aesthetic triumph, but rather in a retractive and shrinking movement-towards-the-end whose endpoint is voicelessness:

> Toi maintenant sur le dos dans le noir ne te remettras plus sur ton séant pour serrer les jambes dans tes bras et baisser la tête jusqu'à ne plus pouvoir. Mais le visage renversé pour de bon peineras en vain sur ta fable. Jusqu'à ce qu'enfin tu entendes comme quoi les mots touchent à leur fin. Avec chaque mot inane plus près du dernier. Et avec eux la fable. La fable d'un autre avec toi dans le noir. La fable de toi fabulant d'un autre avec toi dans le noir. Et comme quoi mieux vaut tout compte fait peine perdue et toi tel que toujours.
>
> Seul. (*Ce*, pp.87–8)

> [You now on your back in the dark shall not rise again to clasp your legs in your arms and bow down your head till it can bow down no further. But with

face upturned for good labour in vain at your fable. Till finally you hear how words are coming to an end. With every inane word a little nearer to the last. And how the fable too. The fable of one with you in the dark. The fable of one fabling of one with you in the dark. And how better in the end labour lost and silence. And you as you always were. Alone.]   (*Cy*, pp.88–9)

What Beckett understands and describes beautifully in his pared-down prose is that the act of fabulation is both impossible and necessary, futile and unavoidable. As long as there is a human consciousness capable of splitting itself into narrator and narrated, there will be stories, stories that unwind themselves until death and final silence. Labour is perhaps always 'labour lost', but life would be inconceivable without labour – in this case, that of fiction-making. There is perhaps no redemption in the act of writing for Beckett, but there is certainly an ethical dimension in the saving of 'figments' from oblivion. This ethical dimension inscribed within human memory, whereby that which might have been lost is, at least momentarily, preserved from the erosion of Time, is the area in which Proust and Beckett, despite their considerable differences, come together as imaginative writers. Perhaps the best homage one can make to a great novelist is to write otherwise from him, even to invert or pervert his master-images. Yet I think it is also possible to say that Beckett is, in fact, only uttering what Proust himself said, *sotto voce*, in the ringing conclusion of *Le Temps retrouvé*. The final phrase – 'dans le Temps' – is to be taken, I think, not as an ablative, but as an accusative: we humans do not live in Time in a fixed or static way, but are plunged into Time from the moment our consciousness awakens to itself. And in that moment, as both Proust and Beckett knew equally well, begins the literary word, its fabulation, its very long posterity.

NOTES

1 Alain de Botton, *How Proust Can Change Your Life* (New York: Pantheon, 1997).
2 I take this example from the excellent final chapter of Margaret E. Gray's *Postmodern Proust* (Philadelphia: University of Pennsylvania Press, 1992) entitled 'Proust, Narrative, and Ambivalence in Contemporary Culture'.
3 I am again indebted to Alain de Botton for this reference. See his description of the 'Summarise Proust Competition' on pp.34 and 35 of *How Proust Can Change Your Life*.
4 I quote from Caleb Crain's description of the Marcel Proust Support Group in his article 'The Year of Writing About Proust', *Lingua Franca*, May/June 1999, p.6.
5 Perhaps the most influential critic who helped to illuminate the theoretical affinities between Russian Formalism and incipient French Structuralism was Tzvetan Todorov. See the volume *Théorie de la littérature* (Paris: Seuil, 1965), which contains a number of seminal Formalist texts, all of which were chosen and translated by Todorov.

6 The complete references to these texts are: Raymond Picard, *La Carrière de Jean Racine*, rev. ed. (Paris: Gallimard, 1961), and *Nouvelle critique, ou nouvelle imposture* (Paris: J.-J. Pauvert, 1965); and Roland Barthes, *Sur Racine* (Paris: Seuil, 1963), and *Critique et vérité* (Paris: Seuil, 1966).

7 Jean-Pierre Richard, *L'Univers imaginaire de Mallarmé* (Paris: Seuil, 1961); and *Proust et le monde sensible* (Paris: Seuil, 1974).

8 Gérard Genette, 'Proust palimpseste', *Figures* (Paris: Seuil, 1966); 'Proust et le langage indirect', *Figures II* (Paris: Seuil, 1969); 'Discours du récit', *Figures III* (Paris: Seuil, 1972), pp.65–273. 'Discours du récit' is available in English translation as *Narrative Discourse: An Essay in Method*, trans. Jane E. Lewin (Ithaca: Cornell University Press, 1980). In response to the many comments and counter-theories generated in the international critical community by 'Discours du récit', Genette published *Nouveau discours du récit* (Paris: Seuil, 1983), which was once again translated by Jane E. Lewin, as *Narrative Discourse Revisited* (Ithaca: Cornell University Press, 1988).

9 Gilles Deleuze, *Proust et les signes*, 5th edn. (Paris: Presses Universitaires de France, 1979). The first edition of Deleuze's book was published in 1964. He later added two more sections to it in subsequent years: the book in its completed form was available as of 1973. Deleuze thus 'lived with Proust' for a very productive decade.

10 See *A la recherche du temps perdu*, 3 vols., ed. Pierre Clarac and André Ferré (Paris: Gallimard-Pléiade, 1954).

11 Claudine Quémar, 'Rêveries onomastiques proustiennes à la lumière des avant-textes', *Essais de critique génétique* (Paris: Flammarion, 1979), p.71; my translation.

12 Roger Shattuck, 'The Threat to Proust', *The New York Review of Books*, 18 March 1999, pp.10–12.

13 For those readers unfamiliar with genetic criticism, a good place to start is Almuth Grésillon's introductory volume entitled *Eléments de critique génétique: lire les manuscrits modernes* (Paris: Presses Universitaires de France, 1994). Grésillon has also written specifically on Proust. See: 'Proust ou l'écriture vagabonde: A propos de la genèse de la "Matinée" dans *La Prisonnière*', in *Marcel Proust: Ecrire sans fin* (Paris: CNRS Editions, 1996), pp.99–124; and also the volume *Proust à la lettre: les intermittences de l'écriture* (Tusson: Du Lérot, 1990), which Grésillon wrote in collaboration with Jean-Louis Lebrave and Catherine Viollet.

14 When quoting from these texts in my essay, I shall be referring to the following editions: Jean-Paul Sartre, *La Nausée* (Paris: Gallimard-Folio, 1996), hereafter abbreviated as *N*; Michel Butor, *La Modification* (Paris: Minuit 'Double', 1987), hereafter abbreviated as *M*; and Samuel Beckett, *Compagnie* (Paris: Minuit, 1980). The English-language version of *Compagnie* is *Company* (London: John Calder, 1980). In my references to Beckett, I shall abbreviate *Compagnie* as *Ce*, and *Company* as *Cy*. Translations of Sartre and Butor are mine.

15 See the final chapter of *Proust et les signes* entitled 'Présence et fonction de la folie: l'Araignée' (pp. 205–19).

MALCOLM BOWIE

POSTLUDE
Proust and the art of brevity

The editor of the present volume reminded us in his Introduction of the anxieties that are associated with the sheer length and bulk of *A la recherche du temps perdu*, and a number of contributors have returned to this theme, sometimes anxiously, but more often in a mood of celebration. Proust's novel has always been famous for being long, and it is currently getting longer as more and more sketches, drafts and cancelled passages become available to the international community of his readers. Yet brevity too is a Proustian watchword, and it is to this aspect of his literary art that I should like to devote these concluding pages. Proust's writing can often be brisk, pithy, pointed, laconic, concise, poetically compacted, and it would be unfortunate if these qualities came to be obscured by his long-range plotting, his wide-angle view of French society or the headlong inventiveness of his 'grand style'.

However, rather than immerse myself at once in the detail of Proust's text and in the Venetian episode that I shall shortly be quarrying for one of my main examples, I shall take a preliminary glance at a pictorial detail from the brush of a great Venetian painter who does not figure in Proust's pantheon. The painter is Canaletto (1697–1768), and the work in question a view of the Grand Canal from the Campo S. Vio. This scene was painted before 1723, and is now in the Thyssen-Bornemisza collection in Madrid.

Canaletto returned to this particular corner of Venice on a number of occasions and it is easy to guess why he was so fond of it. It offered the painter of views a spectacular tension between the diagonal thrust of the Grand Canal and a panorama of buildings and waterborne activity. This was a spot where the spectator's eye could take its plunge into the dimension of depth while being half-detained by an animated foreground crowded with vignettes of Venetian social life. The gateway through which the eye passes on its journey to S. Maria della Salute and the campanile of S. Marco is crested on the farther shore by those tulip-shaped chimneys of which Proust's

Figure 1. Canaletto, *View of the Canal Grande from S. Vio*. (© Museo Thyssen-Bornemisza)

Figure 2. Detail: Canaletto, *View of the Canal Grande from S. Vio.*

narrator is so fond (see II, 860, IV, 225, 229; III, 661/784, V, 742/876, 746/881) and, on the nearer shore, by a chimney-sweep poised precariously at the top of his ladder. Nothing in Venice thrusts further into the louring sky than the handle of the sweep's brush. This is my detail. The majesty of the scene is crowned not by a solid architectural feature but by a teetering workman, and this homunculus, far from being a casual invention, is elaborately connected to the rest of the scene. His ladder and his brush-handle echo the masts, rigging and gondola oars arrayed beneath him. They are part of the spindly geometry that Canaletto has superimposed upon his procession of proudly volumetric palaces. The sweep's gesture repeats that of the water-workers beneath him. He is a gondolier of the rooftops. What is more, his presence has practical consequences for the maid or house-keeper who appears on the balcony beneath him. Whereas in a later version of the scene the equivalent figure simply contemplates the bustle in the square below, here the woman is beating with a pole of her own and clearly coping with a recent invasion of soot.

Canaletto's sweep, isolated from the rest of the composition yet integrated into it, has about him qualities of swagger and exhibitionism that it will be useful to remember in reflecting on the status of the textual detail in the unfolding of Proust's very long novel. So many of the tasks facing Proustian scholarship and criticism are matters of *longue durée* requiring *longue haleine* of academic practitioners that it is easy to become impatient with features of Proust's writing that seem to inhere in mere sentences or sentence-parts. It is understandable that much of the finest critical discussion of Proust's textual details should dwell upon them in order to fill out a general scheme of one kind or another: the smallest separable parts of the book do of course contribute to its overall narrative momentum, and to its long-sustained pattern of internal echoes and refrains, and to the coherence of its moral, psychological, philosophical or aesthetic speculations. Microcosm and macrocosm are mutually enlivening. Moreover if big books are going to lie comfortably in the memory between readings they need to be allowed to leave a big schematic imprint upon us. Part of the reader's business as he or she proceeds through the text is to tame the singularity of individual sentences, lest the real time of reading begin to congeal, but another part of that business is to read slowly enough to notice and to savour Proust's exquisite small-scale contrivances. Proust's *art bref* is simply not available to readers who are in too much of a hurry. Adhering as far as possible to the principles of this art, I shall look at the detail of the novel from three viewpoints only: that of the phrase, that of the sentence and that of the self-contained narrative episode.

Proust's self-isolating phrases are of many different kinds. There are improbable adjectival strings, oxymorons, latecoming turns of the ironic screw, and short compacted similes thrown off while other longer things – including longer similes – are going on about them. 'The true reader of Proust is constantly jarred by small shocks', wrote Walter Benjamin in his essay 'The Image of Proust' (1929).[1] Minimal comparisons can be dense and overdetermined, and administer their small shocks by stealth:

La lumière, *inventant comme de nouveaux solides*, poussait la coque du bateau qu'elle frappait, en retrait de celle qui était dans l'ombre, et disposait comme les degrés d'un escalier de cristal sur la surface matériellement plane, mais brisée par l'éclairage de la mer au matin. (II, 195)

[The light, fashioning as it were new solids, thrust back the hull of the boat on which it fell behind the other hull that was still in shadow, and arranged as it were the steps of a crystal staircase on what was in reality the flat surface, broken only by the play of light and shade, of the morning sea.] (II, 484/571)

Sans doute, dans le Swann qu'ils s'étaient constitué, mes parents avaient omis par ignorance de faire entrer une foule de particularités de sa vie mondaine qui étaient cause que d'autres personnes, quand elles étaient en sa présence, voyaient les élégances régner dans son visage et s'arrêter à son nez busqué *comme à leur frontière naturelle.* (I, 19)

[And so, no doubt, from the Swann they had constructed for themselves my family had left out, in their ignorance, a whole host of details of his life in the world of fashion, details which caused other people, when they met him, to see all the graces enthroned in his face and stopping at the line of his aquiline nose as at a natural frontier.] (I, 20/24)

Transformational processes to which the novel devotes a great deal of intricate attention are suddenly, in each of these passages, condensed into a phrase. Fluids are transformed into improbable solids in the first case, the work of culture into strange new forms of natural growth in the second. The first, taken from the extended account of the Narrator's visit to Elstir's studio in *A l'ombre des jeunes filles en fleurs*, catches up one alteration of matter into another that imperfectly replicates it: light becomes solidified, capable of exerting a palpable pressure upon the hull of a boat, but this happens not inside a directly observable external world but as a feature of paint applied to canvas. This is Elstir's coagulated light, the product of paint drying, of new solids created from fluid pigments. What happens in nature happens in a man-made interior too. Process is packed into process. Similarly, in the evocation of Swann's social personality at the start of the novel, the constructed and interpreted signs of Swann's elegance flow back into the outline of his nose: a social construction is bounded by a frontier that is as 'natural' as a river or as a mountain range. Proust's brief simile recreates the interface between nature and human society. It performs in reverse the transformation that the *mondains* perform upon Swann: where they transport the tissues of Swann's face to a world of envious and admiring social seeing, the Narrator, with an ironic nod towards society, returns that face to nature. One process is given twice over, and the crossover point between its two versions is to be found in a single phrase.

Where a comparison has already introduced a pattern of sense-data into a predominantly abstract discussion, a single phrase will in many cases bring the entire sentence to a pinpoint of sensuous intensity:

Dissipe-t-elle, au contraire, d'un mot adroit, de tendres caresses, les soupçons qui le torturaient bien qu'il s'y prétendît indifférent, sans doute l'amant n'éprouve pas cet accroissement désespéré de l'amour où le hausse la jalousie, mais cessant brusquement de souffrir, heureux, attendri, détendu comme on l'est après un orage quand la pluie est tombée et qu'à peine sent-on encore sous les grands marronniers s'égoutter à longs intervalles *les gouttes suspendues que déjà le soleil reparu colore*, il ne sait comment exprimer sa reconnaissance à celle qui l'a guéri. (III, 697)

[If, on the contrary, she dispels with a tactful word, with loving caresses, the suspicions that have been torturing him for all his show of indifference, no doubt the lover does not feel that despairing increase of love to which jealousy drives him, but ceasing there and then to suffer, happy, mollified, relaxed as one is after a storm when the rain has stopped and one hears only at long intervals under the tall chestnut-trees the splash of the suspended raindrops which already the reappearing sun has dyed with colour, he does not know how to express his gratitude to her who has cured him.] (v, 213/251–2)

This sentence is part of the phenomenology of jealous feeling that occupies so much of *La Prisonnière*. Its culminating phrase is at once an exact description of a natural event – the diffraction of sunlight inside water droplets – and an exact projection on to that event of an altered emotional state, or a mood-swing as we might say in our current psychological vernacular: the droplets are tears transmuted, made polychrome, by a pining lover as he regains his trust in his partner's truthfulness.

What is particularly striking in these passages is the independent expressive power of obviously dependent sentence-parts. This effect may be enhanced either semantically, as in the following example, where a single expression deliciously hybridises the language of the Book of Genesis with that of the modern lonelyhearts column:

La brume, dès le réveil, avait fait de moi, au lieu de l'être centrifuge qu'on est par les beaux jours, un homme replié, désireux du coin du feu et du lit partagé, *Adam frileux en quête d'une Ève sédentaire*, dans ce monde différent. (II, 641)

[The mist, from the moment of my awakening, had made of me, instead of the centrifugal being which one is on fine days, a man turned in on himself, longing for the chimney corner and the shared bed, a shivering Adam in quest of a sedentary Eve, in this different world.] (III, 398/472)

or phonologically:

Les Courvoisier n'étaient pas davantage capables de s'élever jusqu'à l'esprit d'innovation que la duchesse de Guermantes introduisait dans la vie mondaine et qui, en l'adaptant selon un sûr instinct aux nécessités du moment, en faisait quelque chose d'artistique, là où *l'application purement raisonnée de règles rigides* eût donné d'aussi mauvais résultats qu'à quelqu'un qui, voulant réussir en amour ou dans la politique, reproduirait à la lettre dans sa propre vie les exploits de Bussy d'Amboise. (II, 759)

[The Courvoisiers were equally incapable of rising to the spirit of innovation which the Duchesse de Guermantes introduced into the life of society and which, by adapting it with an unerring instinct to the necessities of the moment, made it into something artistic, where the purely rational application of cut and dried rules would have produced results as unfortunate as would greet a man who, anxious to succeed in love or in politics, reproduced to the letter in his own life the exploits of Bussy d'Amboise.]   (III, 541/641)

Here the mental and social inflexibility of the Courvoisiers as distinct from the Guermantes sings out in an alliterative display piece. Their rigidity explodes upon the scene and rumbles on in a sequence of after-echoes. On occasion both kinds of highlighting may be applied at once, as in the last sentence of the Venetian episode in *Albertine disparue*:

Une bonne partie de ce que nous croyons, et jusque dans les conclusions dernières c'est ainsi, avec un entêtement et une bonne foi égales, vient *d'une première méprise sur les prémisses*.   (IV, 235)

[A large part of what we believe to be true (and this applies even to our final conclusions) with an obstinacy equalled only by our good faith, springs from an original mistake in our premises.]   (V, 754/890)

This phrase acquires its unmistakable summative force from the joint action of assonance, alliteration and playful etymologising, all unleashed at the end of a long theoretical excursus on the immanence of misreading in human affairs. At this highly exposed moment in the unfolding of Proust's plot, the language of theory goes into semantic and acoustic overdrive.

This brings us very close to my second viewpoint, that of the complete sentence, for although the words of this cadence from *Albertine disparue* have their independent expressivity they also bear the main burden of the entire proposition of which they are part. Throughout Proust's novel parts have the power to come unstuck from wholes and to acquire, by way of their unwonted semantic intensity, unofficial wholeness of their own. When it comes to single sentences proper, and to those that seem to want to pull away from their paragraphs, it is worth paying special attention to propositions that are by Proust's own standards relatively short, for while 'classic' Proustian sentences often have this air of undeserved autonomy about them, they also often contain, within their associative textures and within their subordinate materials, main carriers of the narrative: the story goes underground but remains trackable as a story.

My short single sentences are drawn from one episode in *Le Côté de Guermantes* and concern the Narrator in his familiar role of window-watcher and weather-vane. The first contains another characteristic hesitation between the works of nature and those of mankind:

Les rideaux de tulle de la fenêtre, vaporeux et friables, comme ils n'auraient pas été par un beau temps, avaient ce même mélange de douceur et de cassant qu'ont les ailes de libellules et les verres de Venise.   (II, 643)

[The tulle window-curtains, vaporous and friable as they would not have been on a fine day, had that same blend of softness and brittleness that dragon-flies' wings have, and Venetian glass.]   (III, 400/474)

This sentence has about it that multiplicity of internal relations, of symmetries foregrounded or deflected, that we expect to find, teeming within an individual stanza or couplet, in certain kinds of verse. Sound repetition inside the co-ordinated expressions 'les ailes de libellules' and 'les verres de Venise' individualises each of them in turn, but each of them also takes us back by a zigzagging path to the opening of the sentence, by internal rhyme in the first case – *tulle* → *libellules* – and by alliteration in the second: *vaporeux* → *verre* → *Venise*. Yet superimposed on this phonological reflection of phrase in phrase is another set of parallelisms, or of sense-rhymes as we might call them – between curtains, dragonflies and glassware on the one hand, and between the contrastive pairs *vaporeux/friables* and *douceur/cassant* on the other. These relations are clearly laid out by Proust's syntax, but it is exactly this clarity that exposes to full view the qualities of paradox and provocation that these relations possess. Dragonfly wings are suddenly re-imaginable as the products of human artistry, and Venetian glass as an animal or plant species native to the shores of the lagoon. Curtains no longer belong solely to the world of haberdashery and domestic design but are meteorological events taking place indoors: they have been precipitated by the elements rather than fabricated by human art. Placed at a central crossroads in the sentence, and overseeing this exchange of qualities, is the ambiguous nominalised participle *cassant*. While respecifying the quality *friable*, the word adds another dimension to it: that which breaks easily can easily break things other than itself. The shattering of glass produces threatening splinters. Even harmless dragonflies can suddenly become dangerous to the skin-surface of the human body.

The increase of internal relations that gives this sentence its stanzaic force can be observed on a slightly larger scale in my second example:

Lasse, résignée, occupée pour plusieurs heures encore à sa tâche immémoriale, la grise journée filait sa passementerie de nacre et je m'attristais de penser que j'allais rester seul en tête à tête avec elle qui ne me connaissait pas plus qu'une ouvrière qui, installée près de la fenêtre pour voir plus clair en faisant sa besogne, ne s'occupe nullement de la personne présente dans la chambre.

(II, 646)

[Weary, resigned, occupied for several hours still with its immemorial task, the grey day stitched its shimmering needlework of light and shade, and it saddened me to think that I was to be left alone with a thing that knew me no more than would a seamstress who, installed by the window so as to see better while she finishes her work, pays no attention to the person present with her in the room.] (III, 404/479)

Although there are a number of prominently placed assonances, alliterations and sense-rhymes here, the individuation of the sentence, and its power of cohesion, come from another source. It tells a self-contained story about the production and subsequent decay of metaphor. This fragment is of course richly connected to the rest of the novel. The sequestered uncommunicating couple, the working woman and the idling man, and the meteorological determinism that weighs down upon meetings and failed meetings between lovers are all familiar motifs: the Narrator's mother and grandmother, and Françoise, who is nearby, have all been involved in scenes like this, and Dutch interiors on this model of quiet co-presence between human agents have a significant role in the book. What the sentence does, however, is rein these allusions and filiations into a narrative that is complete in itself. Metaphor is announced confidently at the start of the sentence – the grey day is a needlewoman plodding away at her embroideries of mist and gloom – but then replaced by a simile ('qui ne me connaissait pas plus qu'une ouvrière . . .'). This repeats the first image while half-literalising it, and in turn gives way to an ordinary scene, depicting two isolated figures in a room, of a type which provides this whole episode with its dramatic core. Loosen your grip for a moment upon a metaphor, the Narrator suggests, and you will be mercilessly reabsorbed into the everyday world. A single sentence stages the whole process of making metaphors and losing them; and in so doing it lays claim to its own singularity, its own coherence and its own temporal rhythm. It is both a link in a greater concatenated plot and a plot in itself. It is both an element in the novel's overall design and an outlier or erratic block occupying the outer margins of that design.

The third and last of these viewpoints is that of the Proustian episode. 'Episodes' in the sense I have in mind are short sections of the novel that have this same erratic quality, and that are textured in such a way as to resemble prose poems built upon a cat's cradle of internal relations. The episode I have chosen, and whose culminating sentence has already been quoted, is that of the Narrator's delayed and then accelerated departure from Venice towards the end of *Albertine disparue*. This ten-page section of the novel is connected, as we should expect, to the remainder of the text in straightforward ways: the contest of wills that it stages between the Narrator and his mother is a high point in the novel's drama of family passion; the Narrator's continuing attempts to disentangle himself from Albertine, and from the jealous memories which were her legacy to him, reach their own high point of intensity and pathos; and his impending discovery of Saint-Loup's 'true' sexual disposition is foreshadowed. Yet the passage turns inwards upon itself, and upon Venice, in ways that make it readable not just 'for' the plot, but against it. Of all the threads from which the motivic interlace of this remarkable passage is woven none is stranger or more insistent than the Narrator's repeated refusal to settle the competing claims made upon him by the Italian and French languages:

> Comprimées les unes contre les autres, ces *calli* divisaient en tous sens, de leurs rainures, le morceau de Venise découpé entre un *canal* et la lagune, comme s'il avait *cristallisé* suivant ces formes innombrables, ténues et minutieuses. Tout à coup, au bout d'une de ces petites rues, il semble que dans la matière *cristallisée* se soit produite une distension. (IV, 229)

> [Packed tightly together, these *calli* divided in all directions with their furrows a chunk of Venice carved out between a canal and the lagoon, as if it had crystallised in accordance with these innumerable, tenuous and minute patterns. Suddenly, at the end of one of these alleys, it seemed as though a distension had occurred in the crystallised matter.] (V, 747/881–2)

The passage from *calli* through *canal* to *cristallisé* leads from one language to the other by way of a central term that is common to both, and culminates in an apparent triumph for French: with the exception of a single phoneme, *cristallisé* devours its predecessors whole and anagrammatises them. Later in this paragraph, the same linguistic itinerary is followed again, but with a new inflection lying in wait at the point of arrival:

> À ce moment quelque mauvais génie qui avait pris l'apparence d'une nouvelle *calle* me faisait rebrousser chemin malgré moi, et je me trouvais brusquement ramené au Grand *Canal*. Et comme il n'y a pas entre le souvenir d'un rêve et le souvenir d'une réalité de grandes différences, je finissais par me demander si ce n'était pas pendant mon sommeil que s'était produit, dans un sombre morceau de *cristallisation* vénitienne, cet étrange flottement qui offrait une vaste place entourée de palais romantiques à la méditation prolongée du clair de lune. (IV, 230)

> [At that moment, some evil genie which had assumed the form of a new *calle* made me unwittingly retrace my steps, and I found myself suddenly brought back to the Grand Canal. And as there is no great difference between the memory of a dream and the memory of a reality, I finally wondered whether it was not during my sleep that there had occurred, in a dark patch of Venetian crystallisation, that strange mirage which offered a vast *piazza* surrounded by romantic palaces to the meditative eye of the moon.] (V, 747–8/882–3)

The word *cristallisation* is in one sense quintessentially French, and contains its own reminiscence of Stendhal's *De l'amour* (1822), but in another sense it harks back to the productions of Italian craft. Murano is nearby, and Venetian crystal has become the very emblem of the distorting mental prism through which the Narrator's enchanted townscape is seen. Venice is continuing to exert its charm as a love-object, and revealing ever-new perfections in exactly the way that Stendhal describes in his celebrated account of amatory 'crystallisation' at the start of *De l'amour*. How can the Narrator report to the railway station and bid the city farewell when every local stone and speech-sound murmurs 'stay'?

The Narrator's hesitation between languages and between cultures, far from subsiding at this point, is reinforced by his extended tragi-comical improvisations on the title and the content of *O Sole mio*, that ubiquitous distillation of Italian popular song:

> Et quand fut venue l'heure où, suivie de toutes mes affaires, elle partit pour la gare, je me fis porter une consommation sur la terrasse, devant le canal, et m'y installai, regardant se coucher le *sol*eil tandis que sur une barque arrêtée en face de l'hôtel un musicien chantait *Sole mio*. Le *sol*eil continuait de descendre. Ma mère ne devait pas être maintenant bien loin de la gare. Bientôt elle serait partie, je serais *seul* à Venise, *seul* avec la tristesse de la savoir peinée par moi, et sans sa présence pour me con*sol*er. L'heure du train s'avançait. Ma *sol*itude irrévocable était si prochaine qu'elle me semblait déjà commencée et totale.
>
> (IV, 231)

> [And when the hour came at which, accompanied by all my belongings, she set off for the station, I ordered a drink to be brought out to me on the terrace overlooking the canal, and settled down there to watch the sunset, while from a boat that had stopped in front of the hotel a musician sang *O sole mio*. The sun continued to sink. My mother must be nearing the station. Soon she would be gone, and I should be alone in Venice, alone with the misery of knowing that I had distressed her, and without her presence to comfort me. The hour of the train's departure was approaching. My irrevocable solitude was so near at hand that it seemed to me to have begun already and to be complete.]
>
> (V, 748–9/883–4)

The Narrator's shortened version of the song's title is translated in part, for the real sun is going down as the sun-song is performed, and its first syllable then sets off on a lengthy associative journey. The cluster *Sole mio, seul, consoler, solitude* is soon to be followed by *seul, isolée, Sole mio* and then by a passage in which a resolution for the Narrator's indecision is repeatedly called for but not supplied:

Enfin, aucun des motifs connus d'avance par moi, de cette vulgaire romance ne pouvait me fournir la *résol*ution dont j'avais besoin; bien plus chacune de ces phrases quand elle passait à son tour devenait un obstacle à prendre efficacement cette *résol*ution ou plutôt elle m'obligeait à la *résol*ution contraire de ne pas partir, car elle me faisait passer l'heure. Par là cette occupation sans plaisir en elle-même d'écouter *Sole* mio se chargeait d'une tristesse profonde, presque désespérée. Je sentais bien qu'en réalité, c'était la *résol*ution de ne pas partir que je prenais par le fait que je restais là sans bouger.   (IV, 232–3)

[After all, none of the already familiar phrases of this sentimental ditty was capable of furnishing me with the resolution I needed; what was more, each of these phrases, when it came and went in its turn, became an obstacle in the way of my putting that resolution into effect, or rather it forced me towards the contrary resolution not to leave Venice, for it made me too late for the train. Wherefore this occupation, devoid of any pleasure in itself, of listening to O *sole mio* was charged with a profound, almost despairing melancholy. I was well aware that in reality it was the resolution not to go that I was making by remaining there without stirring.]   (V, 751/886)

Never has the potency of cheap music been celebrated with such an expenditure of repeated syllables, nor, since Ruskin at least, have the charms of Venice found a more resourceful prose writer to recreate them in words.

Proust's prose performs the Venetian manifold for us in this episode, interweaving visual images and sound patterns, and reproducing the connected *calli* and *campi* of the city in an ingenious network of syntactic pathways. So rich are passages of this kind, and so shameless in their self-removal from the requirements of the novel's plot, that I am tempted to call for a new analytic method which might do them justice. This would be a science of the episode, or an 'episodics', charged with bringing to the full attention of Proustian scholarship what many of Proust's lay readers already know: that his novel comes apart into ravishing fragments that are themselves wholes.

Before offering my concluding remarks, however, I should like to consider one further passage, which is at once a mere detail and part of the continuous Keatsian 'undersong' of the novel as a whole. Towards the end of *Le Temps retrouvé*, the Narrator remembers a visit from Albertine that had been recounted long before, in *Sodome et Gomorrhe* (III, 135–6; IV, 159/186):

Je me le rappelais aussi bien que la duchesse, moi à qui *Albertine* était maintenant aussi indifférente qu'elle l'eût été à Mme de Guermantes, si Mme de Guermantes eût su que la jeune fille à cause de qui je n'avais pas pu entrer chez eux était *Albertine*. C'est que longtemps après que les pauvres morts sont sortis de nos cœurs, leur poussière indifférente continue à être mêlée, à servir d'*alliage*, aux circonstances du passé. Et, sans plus les aimer, il arrive qu'en évoquant une chambre, une *allée*, un chemin, où ils furent à une certaine heure, nous sommes obligés, pour que la place qu'ils occupaient soit remplie, de faire *allusion* à eux, même sans les regretter, même sans les nommer, même sans permettre qu'on les identifie. (IV, 589)

[I recalled the fact just as clearly as the Duchess, I to whom Albertine was now as unimportant as she would have been to Mme de Guermantes had Mme de Guermantes known that the girl because of whom I had had to refuse their invitation was Albertine. Yes, I recalled the fact, for, long after our poor dead friends have lost their place in our hearts, their unvalued dust continues to be mingled, like some base alloy, with the circumstances of the past. And though we no longer love them, it may happen that in speaking of a room, or a walk in a public park, or a country road where they were present with us on a certain occasion, we are obliged, so that the place which they occupied may not be left empty, to make allusion to them, without, however, regretting them, without even naming them or permitting others to identify them.] (VI, 403–4/475)

Albertine has died and turned to dust, yet the Narrator's memory of her haunts all his other acts of remembrance. Her name flits through the text at this point. Just as Emily Brontë's characters Heathcliff and Hareton are reincarnated in the heath and the harebells upon which *Wuthering Heights* closes, Albertine is reborn in this sublime passage as an *allée*, an *alliage* and an *allusion*.[2] How fitting it is that the novel's central creature of flight (*être de fuite*: III, 599; V, 96/113) should have become a perpetual going, this composite companion an amalgam, and this unreliable linguistic performer a fluid figure of speech. In the tissue of Proust's text, Albertine is endlessly cancelled and reborn. She is the unexorcisable ghost in the textual machine. While a passage of this kind is fully intelligible and affecting only for those readers who have experienced the *longue durée* of the novel's preceding pages, it is none the less a complex entity possessing its own intrinsic patterns of meaning. The American critic Yvor Winters used to say that a great poet was anyone who had written at least one great poem. It would make a similar kind of sense to say that a great novelist was anyone who had written a part-paragraph as fine as the one just quoted.

As Canaletto grew older, and his style more stately, he came to dispense with details of the kind I began by describing. His *vedute* continued to have their miniaturised human actors, but none of them was as insolently exposed as that early chimney-sweep standing aloft over the Campo S. Vio. The story of the Proustian detail is very different, or perhaps it is simply the same story in reverse, for Proust came to set far greater store by textual curiosities in *A la recherche du temps perdu* than he had in his earlier writings, and gave them a prominent role throughout the novel's great length. When it comes to teetering above a crowded scene, Proust's very last paragraph has its celebrated stilt-walkers, a curiosity if there ever was one, paraded out in their awkward particularity. It is almost as if the large philosophical perspectives that the novel opens up in such abundance cannot be trusted to make sense without the anchorage and authentication that such local inventions afford. To produce this effect, however, these inventions must have their element of improbability, precariousness and risk. There must be danger in the detail. Being a novelist in the Proustian mould calls for a willingness to go out on a limb, run up ladders, stagger on stilts, and thereby seek release from the excessive security of a grand narrative scheme.

What lessons are to be drawn from Proust's art of brevity by those who devote long labour to his very long book? Perhaps the simplest such lessons are that any sustained critical argument needs to find ways of taking account of Proust's fierce local intensities, and that scholarly projects requiring patient toil in the Proust archives should always have room inside them for the surprise and astonishment that his writing can provoke. Beyond these unexceptionable home truths, however, another element of Proust's achievement in *A la recherche du temps perdu* is waiting to be rediscovered, and this has to do with the rhythm of concentration and dispersal in which Proust's details are caught. The phrases, sentences and episodes that have been rapidly reviewed in these pages all occupy tension-points in the texture of the novel. They direct the Proust reader towards a far horizon of narrative closure while detaining him or her in an incident-filled foreground. They are micro-dramas taking place in a grandly unfolding festal pageant. They are double agents working for connection and disconnection at the same time. Such details demand to be read rather than bypassed at speed or shunted off to the margins of consciousness, and when they are read they introduce an extraordinary air of rhythmic variety and syncopation into the reader's experience of the book. As soon as these rhythms are fully acknowledged, *brevitas* can take the place it deserves in the rhetoric of Proust's fiction.

NOTES

1 *Illuminations*, edited and introduced by Hannah Arendt, trans. Harry Zohn (London: Fontana, 1973), p.210.
2 The subtlest account I know of Proust's 'prose-rhymes' is to be found in Adam Piette's *Remembering and the Sound of Words: Mallarmé, Proust, Joyce, Beckett* (Oxford: Clarendon Press, 1996).

SELECT BIBLIOGRAPHY

The amount of critical studies devoted to Proust is now so huge that only a fraction can be presented here. There are many more works which would have been worthy of inclusion if there had been space: the following are those which the contributors to this volume have personally found most useful.

A la recherche du temps perdu

In French:
Proust, Marcel, *A la recherche du temps perdu*, ed. Jean-Yves Tadié. 4 vols. (Paris: Gallimard [Pléiade], 1987–9).
The most recommendable paperback editions are those published by Folio (ed. J.-Y. Tadié) and by Garnier-Flammarion (ed. Jean Milly). They both provide full critical apparatus.

In English:
Proust, Marcel, *In Search of Lost Time*. 6 vols. (London: Vintage, 1992).
Proust, Marcel, *In Search of Lost Time*. 6 vols. (New York: The Modern Library, 1993).
(The text of these two editions is identical, but the pagination varies.)

Extended editions of early versions

Alden, Douglas, *Marcel Proust's Grasset Proofs* (Chapel Hill: University of North Carolina Press, 1978).
Bales, Richard, ed., *Bricquebec* (Oxford University Press, 1989).
Bonnet, Henri et Bernard Brun, eds., *Matinée chez la princesse de Guermantes* (Paris: Gallimard, 1982).

Other important works by Proust

Le Carnet de 1908, ed. Philip Kolb (Paris: Gallimard, 1976).
Contre Sainte-Beuve, précédé de Pastiches et Mélanges et suivi de Essais et articles (Paris: Gallimard [Pléiade], 1971).
Contre Sainte-Beuve, suivi de Nouveaux mélanges, ed. Bernard de Fallois (Paris: Gallimard, 1954).

Ecrits de jeunesse (Paris: Institut Marcel Proust International, 1991).
L'Indifférent, ed. Philip Kolb (Paris: Gallimard, 1978).
Jean Santeuil, précédé de Les Plaisirs et les jours (Paris: Gallimard [Pléiade], 1971).
Textes retrouvés, ed. Philip Kolb (Paris: Gallimard, 1971).
Translations of Ruskin:
La Bible d'Amiens (Paris: Mercure de France, 1904).
Sésame et les lys (Paris: Mercure de France, 1906).

Available in English translation:
Against Sainte-Beuve and Other Essays, trans. and ed. J. Sturrock (Harmondsworth: Penguin, 1988); see also *On Art and Literature*, trans. S.T. Warner (New York: Carroll and Graf, 1997).
Jean Santeuil, trans. G. Hopkins (New York: Simon and Schuster, 1956; Harmondsworth: Penguin, 1985).
On Reading Ruskin, trans. and ed. Jean Autret *et al.* (New Haven: Yale University Press, 1987).
Pleasures and Regrets, trans. L. Varese (New York: Crown, 1948).

Correspondence

In French:
Correspondance de Marcel Proust, ed. Philip Kolb. 21 vols. (Paris: Plon, 1970–93).
[See also Yoshikawa, Kazuyoshi *et al.*, eds., *Index général de la Correspondance de Marcel Proust* (Presses de l'Université de Kyoto, 1998).]

In English:
Selected Letters. 4 vols. (London: Collins, then HarperCollins, 1983–2000).

Biography

Carter, William C., *Marcel Proust: A Life* (New Haven and London: Yale University Press, 2000).
Diesbach, Ghislain de, *Proust* (Paris: Perrin, 1991).
Maurois, André, *A la recherche de Marcel Proust* (Paris, Hachette, 1949). Available in English as *The Quest for Proust* (Harmondsworth: Penguin, 1962) and as *Proust: Portrait of a Genius* (New York: Harper and Brothers, 1950).
Painter, George D., *Marcel Proust*. 2 vols. (London: Chatto and Windus, 1959, 1965; often reprinted).
Tadié, Jean-Yves, *Marcel Proust* (Paris: Gallimard, 1996). Available in English as *Marcel Proust: A Biography* (London: Viking, 2000).
White, Edmund, *Proust* (London: Weidenfeld and Nicolson, 1999).

Journals

Bulletin d'informations proustiennes.
Bulletin de la Société des amis de Marcel Proust et des amis de Combray.

Critical Works

Album Proust (Paris: Gallimard [Pléiade], 1965).

Alden, Douglas W., *Marcel Proust and his French Critics* (Los Angeles: Lymanhouse, 1940).

'Origins of the Unconscious and Subconscious in Proust', *Modern Language Quarterly*, IV (1943), 343–57.

Autret, Jean, *L'Influence de Ruskin sur la vie, les idées et l'œuvre de Marcel Proust* (Geneva: Droz, 1955).

Bales, Richard, *Proust: 'A la recherche du temps perdu'* (London: Grant and Cutler, 1995).

Proust and the Middle Ages (Geneva: Droz, 1975).

Bardèche, Maurice, *Marcel Proust romancier*, 2 vols. (Paris: Les Sept Couleurs, 1971).

Baudry, Jean-Louis, *Proust, Freud et l'autre* (Paris: Les Editions de Minuit, 1984).

Beckett, Samuel, *Proust* (London: Cedar and Boyars, 1965). Other editions available.

Benjamin, Walter, 'The Image of Proust', in *Illuminations* (London: Collins/Fontana, 1973), pp.207–13.

Bersani, Leo, *Marcel Proust: the Fictions of Life and Art* (New York and London: Oxford University Press, 1965).

Bonnet, Henri, *Marcel Proust de 1907 à 1914*, 2 vols. (Paris: Nizet, 1971, 1976).

'Le "Rapport" de Jacques Madeleine', *Le Figaro littéraire*, 8 December 1966, p.15.

Botton, Alain de, *How Proust Can Change Your Life* (New York: Pantheon, 1997).

Bouillaguet, Annick, *L'Imitation Cryptée: Proust lecteur de Balzac et de Flaubert* (Paris: Champion, 2000).

Marcel Proust: bilan critique (Paris: Nathan, 1994).

Bowie, Malcolm, *Freud, Proust and Lacan* (Cambridge University Press, 1987).

Proust among the Stars (London: HarperCollins, 1998).

Brady, Patrick, 'Problematic Individuation in *A la recherche du temps perdu*', *L'Esprit créateur*, XXII, no.2 (1982), 19–24.

Brée, Germaine, *Du temps perdu au temps retrouvé* (Paris: Les Belles Lettres, 1969).

Trans. C.J. Richards and A.D. Truitt, *Marcel Proust and Deliverance from Time* (New Brunswick: Rutgers University Press, 1969).

Brun, Bernard, '*Le Temps retrouvé* dans les avant-textes de *Combray*', *Bulletin d'informations proustiennes*, 12 (1981), 7–23.

Brunel, Patrick, *Le Rire de Proust* (Paris: Champion, 1997).

Brunet, Etienne, *Le Vocabulaire de Proust*, 3 vols. (Geneva: Slatkine; Paris: Champion, 1983).

Bucknall, Barbara, *The Religion of Art in Proust* (Urbana: University of Illinois Press, 1969).

Butor, Michel, 'Les Œuvres d'art imaginaires chez Proust', in *Répertoire II* (Paris: Minuit, 1964).

Canavaggia, J., *Proust et la politique* (Paris: Nizet, 1986).

Carter, William C., *The Proustian Quest* (New York University Press, 1992).

Ed., *The UAB Marcel Proust Symposium* (Birmingham, AL: Summa Publications, 1989).

Chantal, René de, *Marcel Proust critique littéraire*, 2 vols. (Presses de l'Université de Montréal, 1967).

Cocking, J.M., *Proust: Collected Essays on the Writer and his Art* (Cambridge University Press, 1982).

Collier, Peter, *Proust and Venice* (Cambridge University Press, 1989).

Compagnon, Antoine, *Proust entre deux siècles* (Paris: Seuil, 1989).

Crain, Caleb, 'The Year of Writing about Proust', *Lingua Franca*, May/June 1999, p.6.

Curtius, Ernst Robert, trans. Armand Pierhal, *Marcel Proust* (Paris: La Revue nouvelle, 1928 [1925]).

Deleuze, Gilles, *Proust et les signes* (Paris: PUF, 1964, 1970 (augmented edition)).

De Man, Paul, 'Reading (Proust)', in *Allegories of Reading* (New Haven and London: Yale University Press, 1979), pp.57–78.

Descombes, Vincent, *Proust: philosophie du roman* (Paris: Minuit, 1987). Available in English as *Proust: Philosophy of the Novel*, trans. Catherine Chance Macksey (Stanford University Press, 1992).

Ellison, David R., *The Reading of Proust* (Oxford: Blackwell, 1984).

Ferré, André, *Les Années de collège de Marcel Proust* (Paris: Gallimard, 1959).

Géographie de Marcel Proust (Paris: Sagittaire, 1939).

Finn, Michael R., *Proust, the Body and Literary Form* (Cambridge University Press, 1999).

Fraisse, Luc, *Le Processus de la création chez Marcel Proust: le fragment expérimental* (Paris: Corti, 1988).

L'Œuvre cathédrale (Paris: Corti, 1990).

Gaubert, Serge, *Marcel Proust et la différence* (Presses de l'Université de Lyon, 1980).

Genette, Gérard, *Figures III* (Paris: Seuil, 1972). Available in English as *Narrative Discourse: An Essay in Method*, trans. Jane E. Lewin (Ithaca: Cornell University Press, 1980).

Nouveau discours du récit (Paris: Seuil, 1983). Available in English as *Narrative Discourse Revisited*, trans. Jane E. Lewin (Ithaca: Cornell University Press, 1990).

'Proust palimpseste', in *Figures I* (Paris: Seuil, 1966), pp.39–67.

Graham, Victor, *The Imagery of Proust* (Oxford: Blackwell, 1966).

Gray, Margaret E., *Postmodern Proust* (Philadelphia: University of Pennsylvania Press, 1992).

Grésillon, Almuth, 'Proust ou l'écriture vagabonde: A propos de la genèse de la "Matinée" dans *La Prisonnière*', in *Marcel Proust: Ecrire sans fin* (Paris: CNRS Editions, 1996), pp.99–124.

Hassine, Juliette, *Marranisme et hébraïsme dans l'œuvre de Proust* (Paris: Minard, 1994).

Hayes, Jarrod, 'Proust in the Tearoom', *PMLA*, 110 (1995), 992–1005.

Henry, Anne, *Marcel Proust: théories pour une esthétique* (Paris: Klincksieck, 1981).

Proust romancier: le tombeau égyptien (Paris: Flammarion, 1983).

Hindus, Milton, *The Proustian Vision* (New York: Columbia University Press, 1954).

Hodson, Leighton, *Marcel Proust: the Critical Heritage* (London and New York: Routledge, 1989).

Houston, John Porter, *The Shape and Style of Proust's Novel* (Detroit: Wayne State University Press, 1982).

Hughes, Edward J., *Marcel Proust: a Study in the Quality of Awareness* (Cambridge University Press, 1983).

Jordan, Jack Louis, *Marcel Proust's 'A la recherche du temps perdu': a Search for Certainty* (Birmingham, AL: Summa Publications, 1993).

Kasell, Walter, *Marcel Proust and the Strategy of Reading* (Amsterdam: John Benjamins, 1980).

Kilmartin, Terence, *A Guide to Proust* (Harmondsworth: Penguin, 1985 [1983]).

Kolb, Philip, 'Historique du premier roman de Proust', *Saggi e ricerche di letteratura francese*, IV (1963), 217–77.

Kristeva, Julia, *Le Temps sensible: Proust et l'expérience littéraire* (Paris: Gallimard, 1994).

Ladenson, Elisabeth, *Proust's Lesbianism* (Ithaca: Cornell University Press, 1999).

Mayer, Denise, 'Le Jardin de Marcel Proust', *Cahiers Marcel Proust* 12 (*Etudes proustiennes* 5) (Paris: Gallimard, 1984), 9–51.

Megay, Joyce, *Bergson et Proust: Essai de mise au point de la question de l'influence de Bergson sur Proust* (Paris: Vrin, 1976).

Mendelson, David, *Le Verre et les objets de verre dans l'univers imaginaire de Marcel Proust* (Paris: Corti, 1968).

Milly, Jean, *La Phrase de Proust* (Paris: Larousse, 1975; reprinted Geneva: Slatkine, 1983).

'Problèmes génétiques et éditoriaux à propos d'*Albertine disparue*', in *Ecrire sans fin*, ed. Rainer Warning and Jean Milly (Paris: CNRS Editions, 1996), pp.51–77. *Proust et le style* (Paris: Minard, 1970).

Minogue, Valerie, *Proust: 'Du côté de chez Swann'* (London: Edward Arnold, 1973).

Moss, Howard, *The Magic Lantern of Marcel Proust* (London: Faber and Faber, 1963).

Muller, Marcel, *Les Voix narratives dans 'A la recherche du temps perdu'* (Geneva: Droz, 1965).

Nabokov, Vladimir, 'The Walk by Swann's Place', *Lectures on Literature* (New York and London: Harcourt, Brace, Jovanovich, 1980), pp.206–49.

Nattiez, J.-J., *Proust musicien* (Paris: Christian Bourgois, 1984). Available in English as *Proust as Musician* (Cambridge University Press, 1989).

Nordlinger-Riefstahl, Marie, 'Proust and Ruskin', in *Marcel Proust: An Exhibition of Manuscripts, Books, Pictures and Photographs* (Manchester: Whitworth Art Gallery, 1956), pp.5–6.

Péchenard, Christian, *Proust à Cabourg* (Paris: Quai Voltaire, 1992).

Picon, Gaëtan, *Lecture de Proust* (Paris: Gallimard, 1995 [1963]).

Pierre-Quint, Léon, *Marcel Proust: sa vie, son œuvre* (Paris, Editions du Sagittaire, 1946 [1925]).

Piette, Adam, *Remembering and the Sound of Words: Mallarmé, Proust, Joyce, Beckett* (Oxford: Clarendon Press, 1996).

Poulet, Georges, *L'Espace proustien* (Paris: Gallimard, 1963). Available in English as *Proustian Space* (Baltimore: Johns Hopkins University Press, 1977).

Pugh, Anthony R., *The Birth of 'A la recherche du temps perdu'* (Lexington, Kentucky: French Forum, 1987).

Quémar, Claudine, 'Autour de trois avant-textes de l'"Ouverture" de la *Recherche*: Nouvelles approches des problèmes du *Contre Sainte-Beuve*', *Bulletin d'informations proustiennes*, 3 (1976), 7–39.

'Rêveries onomastiques proustiennes à la lumière des avant-textes', in Almuth

Grésillon, ed., *Essais de critique génétique* (Paris: Flammarion, 1979), pp.69–102.

Revel, Jean-François, *Sur Proust: remarques sur 'A la recherche du temps perdu'* (Paris: Denoël/Gonthier, 1960/70).

Richard, Jean-Pierre, *Proust et le monde sensible* (Paris: Seuil, 1974).

Rivers, J.E., *Proust and the Art of Love: the Aesthetics of Sexuality in the Life, Times and Art of Marcel Proust* (New York: Columbia University Press, 1981).

Rivière, Jacques, *Quelques progrès dans l'étude du cœur humain* (Paris: Librairie de France, 1926).

Rogers, Brian G., *Le Dessous des cartes: Proust et Barbey d'Aurevilly* (Paris: Champion, 2000).

'Deux sources littéraires d'*A la recherche du temps perdu*: l'évolution d'un personnage', *Cahiers Marcel Proust* 12 (Paris: Gallimard, 1984), 53–68.

Proust's Narrative Techniques (Geneva: Droz, 1965). Revised version forthcoming.

Rorty, Richard, 'Self-creation and Affiliation: Proust, Nietzsche and Heidegger', in *Contingency, Irony, and Solidarity* (Cambridge University Press, 1989), pp.96–121.

Rousset, Jean, *Forme et signification* (Paris: Corti, 1962).

Schmid, Marion, *Processes of Literary Creation: Flaubert and Proust* (Oxford: Legenda, 1998).

Shattuck, Roger, *A Field Guide to Proust* (New York: Norton; London: Penguin The Allen Lane Press, 2000).

Proust (London: Fontana, 1974).

Proust's Binoculars (London: Chatto and Windus, 1964).

'The Threat to Proust', *The New York Review of Books*, 18 March 1999, pp.10–12.

Slater, Maya, *Humour in the Works of Proust* (Oxford University Press, 1979).

Sprinker, Michael, *History and Ideology in Proust: 'A la recherche du temps perdu' and the Third French Republic* (Cambridge University Press, 1994; London: Verso, 1998).

Steel, Gareth H., *Chronology and Time in 'A la recherche du temps perdu'* (Geneva: Droz, 1979).

Stern, Sheila, *Marcel Proust: 'Swann's Way'* (Cambridge University Press, 1989).

Straus, Walter, *Proust and Literature: the Novelist as Critic* (Cambridge, Mass.: Harvard University Press, 1957).

Tadié, Jean-Yves, ed., *Marcel Proust: l'écriture et les arts* (Paris: Gallimard/Bibliothèque nationale de France/Réunion des musées nationaux, 1999).

Proust et le roman (Paris: Gallimard, 1971; reprinted 1986).

Proust, le dossier (Paris: Belfond, 1983).

Terdiman, Richard, *The Dialectics of Isolation: Self and Society in the French Novel from the Realists to Proust* (New Haven: Yale University Press, 1976).

Winton, Alison [Alison Finch], *Proust's Additions: the Making of 'A la recherche du temps perdu'* (Cambridge University Press, 1977).

Wolitz, Seth, *The Proustian Community* (New York University Press, 1971).

Yoshida, Jo, 'Proust contre Ruskin: la genèse de deux voyages dans la *Recherche* d'après des brouillons inédits', dissertation, Université de Paris IV, 1978. 2 vols.

Other Works Cited

Aron, J.-P., ed., *Misérable et glorieuse: la femme du XIXe siècle* (n.p.: Fayard, 1980).

Balzac, Honoré de, 'Author's Introduction', in *The Works of Honoré de Balzac*, trans. E. Marriage and E. Dowson (Philadelphia: Avil Publishing Co., 1901), vol. 1.

'Avant-propos', *La Comédie humaine* (Paris: Gallimard, 1976), I, 7–20.

La Cousine Bette (Paris: Librairie Générale Française, 1963).

La Fille aux yeux d'or, in *La Comédie humaine* (Paris: Gallimard, 1976), V, 1039–112.

The Girl with Golden Eyes, in *The Works of Honoré de Balzac*, trans. E. Marriage and E. Dowson (Philadelphia: Avil Publishing Co., 1901), vol. 23.

Barthes, Roland, *Critique et vérité* (Paris: Seuil, 1966).

Sur Racine (Paris: Seuil, 1963).

Beckett, Samuel, *Compagnie* (Paris: Minuit, 1980).

Company (London: John Calder, 1980).

Beizer, J., *Ventriloquized Bodies: Narratives of Hysteria in Nineteenth-Century France* (Ithaca: Cornell University Press, 1994).

Bennet, A., ed., *Reading Reading* (University of Tampere, 1993).

Bergson, Henri, 'Laughter', in *Comedy*, ed. Wylie Sypher (Baltimore, Johns Hopkins University Press, 1980), pp. 61–190.

Le Rire: essai sur la signification du comique (Paris: Presses Universitaires de France, 1940).

Blum, Léon, *Souvenirs sur l'Affaire* (Paris: Gallimard, 1993 [1935]).

Boigne, Comtesse de, ed. Jean-Claude Berchet, *Mémoires de la comtesse de Boigne née d'Osmond* (2 vols. Paris: Le Temps retrouvé/Mercure de France, 1999).

Bourdieu, Pierre, trans. Richard Nice, *Distinction: a Social Critique of the Value of Judgement* (London: Routledge, 1994).

Butor, Michel, *La Modification* (Paris: Minuit, 1987).

Cahm, Eric, *The Dreyfus Affair in French Society and Politics* (London and New York: Longman, 1996).

Cronin, Vincent, *Paris on the Eve: 1900–1914* (London: Collins, 1989).

Davies, Norman, *Europe: A History* (London: Pimlico, 1997).

Durand, Gilbert, *Les Structures anthropologiques de l'imaginaire: Introduction à l'archétypologie générale* (Paris: Bordas, 1969).

Feibleman, James, *In Praise of Comedy: A Study in its Theory and Practice* (New York: Russell and Russell, 1962).

Freud, Sigmund, trans. J. Strachey and A. Freud, *Standard Edition of the Complete Psychological Works of Sigmund Freud* (London: The Hogarth Press, 1953–74), vol. V.

Girard, René, *Mensonge romantique et vérité romanesque* (Paris: Grasset, 1961). Available in English as *Deceit, Desire, and the Novel: Self and Other in Literary Structure* (Baltimore: Johns Hopkins University Press, 1976).

Grésillon, Almuth, *Eléments de critique génétique: lire les manuscrits modernes* (Paris: Presses Universitaires de France, 1994).

Hunt, L., ed., *Eroticism and the Body Politic* (Baltimore: Johns Hopkins University Press, 1991).

Irving, Washington, 'Rip Van Winkle', in *Selected Prose* (New York: Holt, Rinehart and Winston, 1961), pp. 90–107. Other editions available.

James, Henry, 'The Art of Fiction', in *The Art of Fiction and Other Essays* (New York: Oxford University Press, 1948), pp.3–23. Other editions available.

Jung, Carl and Wolfgang Pauli, trans. R.F.C. Hull, *The Interpretation of Nature and the Psyche* (London: Routledge and Kegan Paul, 1955).

Kelly, D., *Fictional Genders: Role and Representation in Nineteenth-Century French Narrative* (Lincoln: University of Nebraska Press, 1989).

Lafayette, Mme de, *La Princesse de Clèves* (Paris: Dent, n.d.). Many editions available.

Laplanche, J. and J.-B. Pontalis, trans. D. Nicholson-Smith, *The Language of Psycho-Analysis* (New York: Norton, 1973).

La Rochefoucauld, *Réflexions ou sentences et maximes morales, suivi de Réflexions diverses* (Paris: Librairie Générale Française, 1965).

Nehamas, Alexander, *Nietzsche: Life as Literature* (Cambridge, MA: Harvard University Press, 1985).

Picard, Raymond, *La Carrière de Jean Racine* (Paris: Gallimard, 1961).

Nouvelle critique, ou nouvelle imposture (Paris: J.-J. Pauvert, 1965).

Richard, Jean-Pierre, *L'Univers imaginaire de Mallarmé* (Paris: Seuil, 1961).

Ruskin, John, ed. E.T. Cook and A. Wedderburn, *The Works of John Ruskin* (London: George Allen, 1903–12).

Sartre, Jean-Paul, *La Nausée* (Paris: Folio, 1996).

Schehr, Lawrence R., *The Shock of Men: Homosexual Hermeneutics in French Writing* (Stanford University Press, 1995).

Spitzer, Leo, *Etudes de style* (Paris: NRF, 1970).

Stambolian, G. and E. Marks, eds., *Homosexualities and French Literature* (Ithaca: Cornell University Press, 1979).

Stevenson, Robert Louis, 'A Humble Remonstrance', in *The Essays of Robert Louis Stevenson* (London: Macdonald, 1950), pp.365–75. Other editions available.

Todorov, Tzvetan, ed., *Théorie de la littérature* (Paris: Seuil, 1965).

Waller, M., *The Male Malady: Fictions of Impotence in the French Romantic Novel* (New Brunswick: Rutgers University Press, 1993).

Winock, Michel, trans. M. Todd, *Nationalism, Anti-Semitism, and Fascism in France* (Stanford University Press, 1998).

Zélicourt, Gaston, *Le Monde de la 'Comédie humaine': clefs pour l'œuvre romanesque de Balzac* (Paris: Seghers, 1979).

INDEX

An asterisk indicates a fictional Proustian character or place. Critics are indexed only where they form a substantive part of the argument.